Shaping Public Theology

Shaping Public Theology

*Selections from the Writings
of Max L. Stackhouse*

Edited by

Scott R. Paeth, E. Harold Breitenberg Jr., & Hak Joon Lee

WILLIAM B. EERDMANS PUBLISHING COMPANY
GRAND RAPIDS, MICHIGAN / CAMBRIDGE, U.K.

© 2014 Scott R. Paeth, E. Harold Breitenberg Jr., and Hak Joon Lee
All rights reserved

Published 2014 by
Wm. B. Eerdmans Publishing Co.
2140 Oak Industrial Drive N.E., Grand Rapids, Michigan 49505 /
P.O. Box 163, Cambridge CB3 9PU U.K.

Printed in the United States of America

20 19 18 17 16 15 14   7 6 5 4 3 2 1

Library of Congress Cataloging-in-Publication Data

Stackhouse, Max L.
　　[Works. Selections]
　　Shaping public theology : selections from the writings of Max L. Stackhouse /
　　　　edited by Scott R. Paeth, E. Harold Breitenberg Jr., & Hak Joon Lee.
　　　　pages　　　cm
　　Includes bibliographical references and index.
　　ISBN 978-0-8028-6881-7 (pbk. : alk. paper)
　　1. Public theology.　　I. Paeth, Scott.　　II. Breitenberg, E. Harold, 1955-
　　　　III. Lee, Hak Joon, 1958-　　IV. Title.
　　BT83.63.S73 2014
　　230 — dc23
　　　　　　　　　　　　　　　　　　2013042261

www.eerdmans.com

Contents

FOREWORD, *by Douglas F. Ottati*	vii
PREFACE	ix
Introduction	xi

Part One: Interpreting the Tradition of Public Theology

Toward a Theology for the New Social Gospel	3
Rauschenbusch Today: The Legacy of a Loving Prophet	21
Christianity in New Formation: Reflections of a White Christian on the Death of Martin Luther King Jr.	28
What Tillich Meant to Me	47
Alasdair MacIntyre: An Overview and Evaluation	54
A Premature Postmodern (Ernst Troeltsch)	71
Edwards for Us	78
Liberalism Dispatched vs. Liberalism Engaged	82

Part Two: Developing a Method for Public Theology

The Tasks of Theological Ethics	93
The Religious Basis of Cultural Activity	104

Contents

Public Theology and Ethical Judgment	116
Ethics: Social and Christian	133
Reflections on "Universal Absolutes"	154
The Fifth Social Gospel and the Global Mission of the Church	168
Civil Religion, Political Theology, and Public Theology: What's the Difference?	186
Covenantal Justice in a Global Era	204

Part Three: Constructing a Global Public Theology

A Post-Communist Manifesto: Public Theology after the Collapse of Socialism	221
The Moral Roots of the Corporation	230
Spheres of Management: Social, Ethical, and Theological Reflections	243
Globalization, Faith, and Theological Education	259
A Christian Perspective on Human Rights	271
Living the Tensions: Christians and Divorce	283
The Pastor as Public Theologian	286

Part Four: Looking Back, Looking Forward

Conclusion: The Lasting Significance of Max Stackhouse	305
A Response in Appreciation, by Max Stackhouse	317
Max Stackhouse: A Bibliography	321
ACKNOWLEDGMENTS	345
INDEX	347

Foreword

When I first read Max Stackhouse what struck me was the combination of extraordinary breadth, persistent realism, and prophetic conviction. When we first met (and as he encouraged the formation of a Covenantal Ethics Group in the Society of Christian Ethics), I was struck by his seemingly boundless energy. Years later, these first impressions remain.

Max is a prolific writer whose positions on important matters have changed and developed over time, but he consistently makes use of studies by sociologists, economists, political scientists, theologians, and ethicists. His books, articles, and edited volumes interpret practices in family, business, government, the arts, and religion in cultures from North America to Asia, Africa, and Europe. Max is an ethicist at home comparing the Bible and the Pali canon in Theravada Buddhism; he is, in short, a genuinely interdisciplinary and global thinker.

Max's exceptional breadth points to his realism, or to his sustained attention to basic institutions and social patterns in human life. Thus, when he wrote about theological education, Max didn't counsel seminaries and divinity schools to circle the wagons; he stressed the importance of training ministers to read and interpret concrete contexts. For Max, theological ethics is never merely a matter of identifying ideas and imagining ideals. It is always also the business of estimating and engaging the possibilities and limits of actual persons and communities in the real world. Hence the premium that he places on making use of all available tools to analyze social circumstances and realities.

The engine that drives the interdisciplinary breadth and the sustained analyses of circumstances and realities is a passionate practical aim. Max's prophetic conviction is that, for a covenantal Protestant Christianity, atten-

Foreword

tion to social structures and the quest for reconciliation, reformation, and justice never end. This is why he not only interprets but also evaluates institutional forms, and why he not only analyses policy options but also advocates those he thinks best.

Breadth, realism, and prophetic conviction — these qualities make Max an original and dynamic thinker who advances the promise of social Christianity. Indeed, year after year, and book after book, he has proven a worthy (though never uncritical) successor to the Ernst Troeltsch of *The Social Teaching of the Christian Churches,* to Walter Rauschenbusch's social gospel, Reinhold Niebuhr's Christian realism, and James Luther Adams's liberal Protestant humanism. The editors of the present volume call Max "a public theologian *par excellence*," and their apt description, which names the combination of breadth, realism, and practical conviction, requires that we add only one thing. In Max's judgment theology is more than a confessional enterprise, and theological ethicists are called to give publicly available warrants for the stances they take and the judgments they make.

These, then, are some of the reasons why the book you now hold in your hands is a timely invitation to study and to savor one of the most engaging theological voices of our time. Read it, and I think you will also agree that Max L. Stackhouse put his extraordinary energies to remarkably good use.

Douglas F. Ottati

Preface

The editors of this volume are pleased to make available this collection of works by Max L. Stackhouse, one of the most important, prolific, and influential Christian theological ethicists of the last half-century. The materials were selected from his vast corpus and stretch across five decades: from the 1960s to the 2000s. Deciding which works to include was both a pleasure and a challenge, due in part to the sheer number of Stackhouse's publications. Those included here illustrate much of the breadth of his work and represent some of the depth of his scholarship. Together they demonstrate various ways in which Stackhouse has shaped the field of public theology in a distinctive way. They also serve as an introduction to his extended and expansive comprehensive public theology project. Also included is a bibliography of Stackhouse's work that is as complete and up-to-date as we could produce.

A book such as this has been needed for some time, and we are happy we could collaborate in its production. Along with many others, we have gained insight from Stackhouse's many lectures and presentations, learned from his numerous writings, and benefited from various interactions with him. He has been singularly influential to our educations and professions. Scott Paeth and Hak Joon Lee studied with Stackhouse at Princeton Theological Seminary, while Hal Breitenberg's doctoral dissertation focused on his public theology. Over the years we have profited greatly from our many conversations, emails, and telephone calls with Max, who has always been more than generous with his time, energies, and support. Our shared interests in his public theology and the many different areas it addresses helped bring us together and gave impetus to this collaboration. Moreover, his passion for theological ethics, joy in life, and continual efforts to faithfully live out his Christian vocation — and

Preface

encouragement of others in their own callings — remain inspirations for us. This volume was a collaborative effort on the part of our three co-editors, each of whom contributed considerable time and resources in bringing it to its completion. While we were all involved in the project as a whole, in terms of the final product, we would like to note that the introduction is jointly the work of Scott Paeth and Hal Breitenberg, while the concluding essay was written by Hak Joon Lee.

We extend our warm thanks to those who, at various times and in different ways, knowingly or not, encouraged us in this endeavor, including Stephen Healey, Charles Sweezey, Deirdre Hainsworth, Doug Ottati, and of course our families. In particular, we thank Brian White for his considerable help with proofreading, formatting, and footnotes. We extend our sincere thanks to Oh Sung Kwon, whose help in completing the index for this volume was invaluable. We are also grateful to Jon Pott at Eerdmans Publishing Company for his willingness to take on this project and for his longtime interest in and support for Max's work. Additionally, we are grateful for the editorial work of Jenny Hoffman at Eerdmans, who aided us in the construction and completion of what was at times a very complicated project. Finally, we thank Max, without whose assistance, advice, encouragement, and friendship we could not have brought this project to fruition.

We trust this volume will enhance readers' understanding of public theology and of Stackhouse's many notable and influential contributions to it. We hope the publications presented here accurately summarize and portray the gist and substance of his approach to public theology. Finally, we share in the desire that the book will convey a sense of Stackhouse's comprehensive project for a global church and society and its potential for the future. Any deficiencies in the collection or errors that have been introduced are our own.

SCOTT R. PAETH
E. HAROLD "HAL" BREITENBERG JR.
HAK JOON LEE

Introduction

Max L. Stackhouse is one of the most prolific and influential American theological ethicists of the last half-century. As the author or editor of more than twenty books and hundreds of articles during his five-decade tenure as a theologian and ethicist, he has engaged in many of the most pressing moral debates within the Christian church and the larger society. His influence has been recognized, both domestically and internationally, by a diverse array of theologians, ethicists, and others who have seen in his work the development of many of the most important ideas within the emerging field of public theology. In this volume, we bring together for the first time many of Stackhouse's most important shorter writings, ranging from some of his earliest reflections from the mid-1960s to his more recent contributions.

Stackhouse's work has been central to the development, dissemination, and popularization of the idea of public theology, as noted by many.[1] As one of the major theoreticians of the concept, one of public theology's most productive practitioners, and its most persistent advocate, he has helped form its meaning and application within the Christian church, academia, and the larger public. Whether or not all who have engaged with him have agreed with him, they have found him to be an indispensable conversation partner and formidable disputant. His contributions range from commentary on the

---

1. For example, "Stackhouse's work, through the years, and especially his and his many contributors' work on the God and Globalization series, has deeply imprinted and very constructively contributed to the thinking and practice of public theology in the contemporary context. In particular, he has deliberately modeled the importance of interdisciplinarity in theological ethics and has very astutely observed pluralism in the various intersecting spheres of globalizing life." Michael S. Hogue, "After the Secular: Toward a Pragmatic Public Theology," *Journal of the American Academy of Religion* 78, no. 2 (2010): 363-64.

Introduction

civil rights movement and the death of Martin Luther King Jr., to controversies surrounding the doctrines of liberation theology, to the question of how Christian ethics should be done in a post-socialist world of globalization. Major works such as *Ethics and the Urban Ethos, Creeds, Society, and Human Rights,* and *God and Globalization* have met with wide acclaim. Along the way, he has contributed to conversations about Christian conceptions of the family, the importance of democracy and human rights to the maintenance of a just society, relationships between religion and economics, and the continuing relevance of the theologies of Ernst Troeltsch and Walter Rauschenbusch. There are few American theologians of the past fifty years whose contributions have been as broadly influential as those of Max Stackhouse. He is a public theologian *par excellence*.

Max Stackhouse: Intellectual and Biographical Sketch

Max Stackhouse was born in 1935, the son and grandson of a Methodist preachers. Growing up in Indiana in the run-up to World War II, he was raised in an atmosphere of both religious piety and inquiry. His father ministered to congregations throughout the state before settling into a large church in Fort Wayne. During his senior year in high school, his father was diagnosed with spinal cancer and died at the age of forty-four.

Stackhouse attended college at DePauw University, where he played football, sang, and majored in "pre-theology," with the aim of continuing the family tradition and becoming a minister. While there, he joined the philosophy club, where he immersed himself in the Western philosophical tradition from the ancient Greeks to Hegel and Marx. His experiences as a student during the 1950s, in the midst of the McCarthy era, shaped him profoundly. As he began questioning the Methodist theology of his childhood, he also began to embrace a more radical stream of political thought, becoming a socialist and a pacifist, as well as an agnostic. He wrote a column for the campus newspaper that he called "The Ax by Max," but was unclear on where he should go next in life.

Following the advice of a professor, he applied for and received a scholarship to study in the Netherlands. During that year abroad he studied economics, learned to speak Dutch, and became acquainted with post–World War II Europe. It was also during his Dutch sojourn that he became conversant with the thought of two figures who would feature prominently in his later thought: Paul Tillich and Abraham Kuyper. Following Tillich's trail, he

Introduction

enrolled in Harvard Divinity School upon his return to the United States. There he studied with Tillich, Erik Erikson, and Talcott Parsons, but he was particularly drawn to the social ethicist James Luther Adams.

At Harvard, the core elements of Stackhouse's identity as a theologian and ethicist began to take shape, as he borrowed ideas from his mentors. From Erikson he took the insight that biography informed the development of personal faith, while Parsons taught him that social change took place through the complex interactions with social systems. Reinhold Niebuhr challenged his pacifism and social idealism, while at the same time he drew inspiration from Martin Luther King Jr.'s commitment to the use of nonviolence in the civil rights struggle.

James Luther Adams became Stackhouse's primary mentor during his time at Harvard, exposing him to the rich tradition of Protestant social ethics, from the Puritans to the social gospel movement. Adams's belief in the importance of religion to the creation of a morally robust public life, and his emphasis on the place of covenanted institutions in the construction of a sound social fabric, became key elements of Stackhouse's own subsequent work.

After teaching for a year at Harvard, Stackhouse was appointed as a professor of ethics at Andover Newton Theological School, where he was to spend the next several decades. Andover Newton's joint doctoral program, run in conjunction with Boston College, gave him the opportunity to become more deeply acquainted with Catholic theology, and his discussions with colleagues such as Gabriel Fackre on the Protestant side and David Hollenbach on the Catholic side gave Stackhouse insights into both the importance of an ecumenical approach to Christian theology and the possibilities and limitations of the Catholic tradition. It was during this period that Stackhouse wrote many of his most important early works, such as *The Ethics of Necropolis* (1971) and *Ethics and the Urban Ethos* (1973).

In 1973, Stackhouse took a year-long sabbatical to teach at the United Theological College in Bangalore, India. This experience opened up the idea of Christianity as a genuinely global reality to him. The twin facts of religious diversity and extreme poverty alerted him to the challenges that faced Christianity outside of the relatively sheltered enclaves of the first world. His time in India also sparked an abiding love of the country — its culture, religions, and people — which motivated a great deal of his subsequent research. His interest in and involvement with India continued after his return to the United States, and led to the development of collegial relationships with Indian scholars such as J. T. K. Daniel, K. C. Abraham, and Thomas Thangaraj, which continued for many years.

Introduction

Subsequent world travels, particularly his time teaching in what was then the German Democratic Republic, convinced Stackhouse of many of the fatal flaws in the brand of socialism endorsed by many American leftists. The combination of economic and political authoritarianism represented in the "Communist Bloc" countries was ineffectual as a vehicle both for human rights and economic justice. This recognition drove him away from some of his colleagues on the political left, and led him to resign from the Religion Section of the Democratic Socialists Organizing Committee.

His experiences in India and East Germany contributed to a shift in Stackhouse's approach to theological and ethical questions, as reflected in *Creeds, Society, and Human Rights* (1984) and *Public Theology and Political Economy* (1987), a well as his involvement in the massive anthology *On Moral Business* (1995). Central to his concerns during this period were the need to rethink the prevailing conceptions of the relationship of morality, social justice, and economics in light of the failures of really existing socialism, in order to ensure a robust yet socially just economy and a basic respect for human rights in every society, and the central role that religious faith, teaching, and practice had in the creation of social institutions.

In 1994, Stackhouse moved from Andover Newton to Princeton Theological Seminary. There he deepened his appreciation for the work of Abraham Kuyper that he first developed as a student in the Netherlands and began to engage in a set of conversations about the place of theology in the People's Republic of China.

During this period he began work on his major four-volume project titled *God and Globalization*. The first volume, *Religion and the Powers of the Common Life*, was published in 2000. The second volume, *The Spirit and the Modern Authorities*, came out in 2001, and *Christ and the Dominions of Civilization* was published in 2002. Each of these volumes was comprised of a series of essays by theologians, ethicists, and others, and edited by Stackhouse, whose substantial introductions to each book framed the major themes of the texts. The fourth and final volume, *Globalization and Grace*, was published in 2007. Using the overarching structure of the apostle Paul's invocation of the "powers and principalities," Stackhouse examined the ways in which various institutional structures and social forms developing within the emerging global economy could be informed and challenged by theological insights of the Christian faith. In the final volume, which was written solely by Stackhouse, he drew together themes that had been both implicit and explicit in his work from the beginning in order to develop an architecture for a genuinely public theology that has the capacity to aid in answering Christian concerns

Introduction

for the creation of a just peace, not only within small ideologically and theologically enclosed communities, but for a global society.

Core Themes and Ideas

There are several core themes and ideas that tie Max Stackhouse's theological project together, and these themes are evident in one way or another in the essays included in this volume. These themes unify Stackhouse's approach to public theology on a deep conceptual level and are most often in play, either implicitly or explicitly, in the positions he stakes out on both broad ideological and philosophical issues and on particular moral or public policy questions. While it is possible to engage with these core principles without necessarily coming to the same conclusions as Stackhouse, his work makes a compelling case that one cannot engage in a genuinely public theology without offering an account of the place these themes play in the theological analysis of public life.

The first, and in many ways most fundamental, theological theme in Stackhouse's work is covenant. Stackhouse's approach to the concept of covenant is grounded in the Reformed, and particularly Puritan, covenant theological tradition. The idea of covenant provides a basis for understanding human interrelationships in society under God, defining both the moral possibilities and limitations that are encoded within the structure of human communal life.

It is this framework that provides the structure for Stackhouse's commitment to a conception of human rights as a core social value. The covenantal relationships that bind us together within society create the obligation that we have to treat one another with basic human dignity and stand as the guarantor of the array of rights we categorize under the headings of "life, liberty, and the pursuit of happiness." To exist in covenant is to be entitled to the expectation of just and humane treatment, and places the obligation upon the larger social setting to which we belong to ensure that such treatment is ensured by the basic laws of society and applied via the legislative and political structures through which the society operates.

A second theme that runs throughout Stackhouse's work is the importance of social pluralism. Forms of society that rely on a strongly unified set of institutions and a top-down authority structure are, as Stackhouse stresses at many points in his work, both less efficient and more apt to abuse than those that consist of different but overlapping sectors or spheres of society

Introduction

and rely on a diffuse set of institutions and mechanisms of authority. It is here that Abraham Kuyper's influence on Stackhouse is most apparent, and Stackhouse's debt to Kuyper's conception of "sphere sovereignty" is clear in his insistence that social justice is made possible through the maintenance of distinct realms of social life and the institutions particular to them, such as families, businesses, governments, and schools. These spheres of common life are not interchangeable, and cannot take the place of one another without violating their essential characteristics and respective institutions that make them each what they are. While their forms are not necessarily wholly immutable, they are also not infinitely malleable. A society that recognizes various basic, significant, and enduring areas of human social life, along with their proper boundaries and institutional forms, can better serve the common good.

At the same time, Stackhouse is quite clear that the Christian community has a crucial role to play in the creation and maintenance of social justice within society. The church cannot and should not become the state, and the state cannot and should not absorb the church; Christian social responsibility requires that Christians bring their moral insight, informed by their faith, teaching, and practice, to bear on questions of the public good. This represents another crucial theme in Stackhouse's work, and gives content to what he means by "public theology."[2] Theology is public precisely because it is grounded in the Christian imperative to speak about questions of social justice, political responsibility, civic virtue, and the proper ends of government

---

2. Stackhouse developed, expanded, and refined his conception of public theology over many years and in numerous publications. For example, he drew upon and expanded the public theology for which he called in "An Ecumenist's Plea for a Public Theology" into the one that informs *Public Theology and Political Economy*. Moreover, several definitions and descriptions of public theology appear in various contexts in many of his books, articles, and essays and some differences exist between them. A number of definitions are quite short and come in the midst of broader arguments. For example, "Still, in the wedding of these motifs [from Hebraic and Greek thought], in the formation of a new alliance between revelation and reason, Christianity had established by the time of Athanasius (and still more firmly by the time of Ambrose and Augustine) a 'public theology,' a creed held to be philosophically viable and capable of giving moral shape to complex civilization." *Creeds, Society, and Human Rights: A Study in Three Cultures* (Grand Rapids: Eerdmans, 1984; reissued, Nashville: Parthenon Press, 1996), p. 39. Stackhouse summarized his conception of public theology in three dictionary and encyclopedia entries: "Theology, Public," in *Dictionary of the Ecumenical Movement*, ed. Nicholas Lossky et al., 2nd ed. (Geneva: WCC Publications, 2002), pp. 1131-33, "Public Theology," in *The Encyclopedia of Christianity*, vol. 4, ed. Erwin Fahlbusch et al., trans. Geoffrey W. Bromiley (Grand Rapids and Leiden: Eerdmans and Brill, 2008), pp. 443-47, and "Public Theology and Ethics," in *Dictionary of Scripture and Ethics*, ed. Jacqueline E. Lapsley, Rebekah Miles, and Allen Verhey (Grand Rapids: Baker Academic, 2011), pp. 646-49.

in a way that is genuinely reflective of the Christian faith yet also applicable to the questions that motivate a religiously and socially pluralistic society.

This dimension of Stackhouse's thought is grounded not only in Kuyper's conception of social pluralism; it is equally strongly rooted in the American social gospel tradition of Walter Rauschenbusch, Shailer Matthews, and Washington Gladden. As Kuyper gave Stackhouse the social model into which to pour a conception of the common good, the social gospel gave him the prophetic imperative to seek passionately for social justice in the midst of unjust circumstances. One can see this passion for justice and critique of "the powers and principalities" reflected in early works such as *The Ethics of Necropolis* and *Ethics and the Urban Ethos* as well as in his contributions to *God and Globalization*. Throughout his career as a theologian and ethicist his social analysis has been rooted in many of the same concerns that stood at the heart of the social gospel.

A fourth theme in Stackhouse's work emerges from the recognition that the passion for social justice has to be connected to the need for both pragmatic, real-world solutions and a recognition of the limits placed on any ambition for social projects by the realities of human pride, sin, and finitude. This sense of realism, informed particularly by Reinhold Niebuhr, allows Stackhouse to ground his understandings of Christian social responsibility and the imperative toward social justice in the knowledge that justice-making is always a question of the relative less-and-more of compromise in the context of competing social interests.

It was this brand of Christian realism that led him away from those more doctrinaire forms of socialism to which he had been committed earlier in his career in light of his firsthand observations of life under "really existing socialism." As he saw it, the idealism of American socialists who would not acknowledge that life in communist countries was not on the whole actually better than life in the industrialized West represented a failure to acknowledge that sin was a universal human problem, and that no political system, least of all one that relied on an authoritarian power structure and state monopoly on the means of production, was able ultimately to overcome it.

This realism was also at the heart of many of Stackhouse's critiques of both the reflexive liberalism of many mainline Protestant denominations and the sectarian impulse represented by the kinds of "neo-anabaptist" theologies of Stanley Hauerwas and John Howard Yoder. In the first case, he criticized the mainline denominations' refusal to engage in the complexities of detailed social analysis, or to recognize the importance of social and political compromise around questions of social justice. Their idealism, he argued, often led them to seek ideals that were unrealizable and unsustainable. In the second

Introduction

case, the forms of sectarianism represented by those who believed that Christianity should separate itself in some substantive way from the concrete social and political context in which it dwells and has always dwelt represented a different form of unrealistic idealism, which believed that Christian life was to be lived in a pure sense, even at the cost of the failure to respond to the needs of the larger social context and moment, an approach warranted by God's creation of, will for, and incarnation in this world.

Finally, a fifth theme in Stackhouse's work is one that has particularly motivated the latest stage of his career, namely the importance of a religious and ethical analysis of the phenomenon of globalization. As national boundaries become less and less significant to the movement of people, capital, and information, the need to understand the dynamics that underlie the emergence of a genuinely global society becomes imperative.

As business becomes unmoored from its responsibilities to the laws and mores of particular nation-states, as certain cultural forms (movies, music, television) become instantly mobile in the wake of the "digital revolution" and its aftermath, and as the peoples of the world and the multiple publics they inhabit become increasingly interconnected, the question of what kinds of moral constraints can be placed on the use and misuse of not only products but also persons becomes increasingly important. If government, the economy, and culture exist to serve human needs, rather than the other way around, what is needed is the creation of an ethical infrastructure that grounds participation in the global society, one that takes account of the often radical pluralism of globalized life, but sees in the human condition a common set of moral categories and a common plight, and seeks to respond to that plight in a way that can ensure a genuinely human life can be lived sustainably in a global setting.

There is, Stackhouse argues, an implicit theology embedded within all social and cultural forms. The struggle of a global public theology is to draw out those implicit theologies in order to provide a basis for comparing them and constructing a set of moral and religious categories that can ground a global civil society, one in which a myriad of institutions work cooperatively for the sake of constructing a truly global conception of the common good.

Introduction

Key Components and Distinctive Features

In addition to these core themes and ideas, several other components are key to Stackhouse's public theology and contribute to its importance and distinctiveness. Moreover, public theology is itself critical to understanding his works as a whole and to better grasping his larger effort.

The first publication in which Stackhouse referred to public theology, "The Church and Political Life: A Loss of Confidence," appeared in 1981. Although the term *public theology* did not originate with Stackhouse, he soon embraced it, modified it, and extended it.[3] He has championed it ever since. As a rubric, public theology expressed much of what Stackhouse understood Christian theology and ethics to be about; as a label it encompassed the vast majority of what he had done and sought to do as a theological ethicist. Throughout his many publications and by his participation in numerous conferences, consultations, and programs, Stackhouse advocated on behalf of public theology while at the same time he carried out his own public theological efforts in public theology. Over the years, public theology increasingly became the overriding and organizing concept for his work.[4] Indeed, the best way to conceive of Stackhouse's works *in toto* is to view them as a comprehensive public theology project.

In significant ways, Stackhouse's public theology is both similar to and different than that of others. However, certain key components of Stackhouse's project contribute to its significance and distinctiveness. Along with many others, in his public theology Stackhouse interprets many of the various issues and interactions of society, especially those he understands to be

---

3. Martin Marty introduced the terms *public theology* and *public theologian* in 1974. See "Two Kinds of Two Kinds of Civil Religion," in *American Civil Religion*, ed. Russell E. Richey and Donald G. Jones (New York: Harper & Row, 1974), pp. 139-57, and "Reinhold Niebuhr: Public Theology and the American Experience," *The Journal of Religion* 54, no. 4 (October 1974): 332-59. Marty's references to public theologians and public theology are on pages 148 and 333-34, respectively.

4. Evidence of this can be seen by comparing Stackhouse's two introductions to Rauschenbusch's *The Righteousness of the Kingdom* (Nashville: Abingdon, 1968; Lewiston, NY: Edwin Mellen, 1999). The first Introduction was written before the concept of *public theology* had been introduced. In the latter Introduction, Stackhouse makes several references to *public theology*, e.g., "Thus, the study of the social gospel as well as its allies and modifiers, precisely as they anticipated and pointed toward a Public Theology[,] might provide us with an alternative postmodernism, one that renders moral guidance to society" (p. xi). The way Stackhouse conceived of Rauschenbusch did not change but the manner in which Stackhouse described him, in terms of *public theology*, did.

Introduction

constitutive of it. Additionally, he offers evaluations of and guidance for persons, groups, areas of society, and institutions. Moreover, Stackhouse maintains that interpretation, evaluation, and guidance are essential features of public theology and central tasks for it.[5] These should also be carried out in ways that can be understood by, and potentially be persuasive to, those inside the church as well as those outside the Christian tradition.[6] While many others who participate in public theology offer interpretations of the various interactions and institutions of society, not all who do so think public theology can be intelligible to those outside the tradition from which it originates and speaks. Fewer still share Stackhouse's view that public theology should have an evaluative function or seek to be persuasive to the broader society, and some explicitly reject these as goals for public theology. These aspects of Stackhouse's project are closely related to his understanding of theology and the complex relationships he sees between theology, religion, and ethics. For Stackhouse, theology is the discipline best suited for evaluating religion.[7] At

---

5. "This form of discourse seeks to offer an interpretation of the common life and to provide the moral and spiritual vision to guide it, and it claims that theology is indispensable to both tasks." Stackhouse, "Theology, Public," in *Dictionary of the Ecumenical Movement*, p. 1131; "A Public Theology recognizes that some dimensions of faith are properly 'private'; they involve dimensions of the soul's intercourse with God. . . . But Public Theology also attempts to identify those universal criteria and the warrants for them by which various confessional traditions can be evaluated whenever they presume to guide public behavior, influence public policy, or shape public discourse on social and ethical matters. In addition, Public Theology holds that humans can reliably know something about God, that careful attention to the structures and dynamics of the decisive touchstones of spiritual and moral authority (Scripture, Traditions, Reason, and Experience) can allow adjudication between religious confessions about God, that not all religions are of equal weight in terms of their capacity to contribute to public discourse, and that a valid theological stance will morally require responsibility in and for the common life." "Religious Freedom and Human Rights," in *Our Freedoms: Rights and Responsibilities*, ed. W. Lawson Taitte, introduction by Andrew R. Cecil (Austin: University of Texas Press, 1985), p. 104.

6. "We may discuss the issues in ways that can speak to and with people who are not already persuaded that 'our' religion is convincing. This is one reason we inevitably need what I and others call a public theology, a warranted discourse about these judgments that is able both to persuade those who may not agree on social, philosophical, or religious grounds and to offer plausible, defensible guidelines for personal and social decisions." *Covenant and Commitments: Faith, Family, and Economic Life* (Louisville: Westminster John Knox, 1997), p. 7.

7. "Religion needs theology to avoid obscurantism, fanaticism, and privileged claims. Indeed, it needs 'public theology.' If religion is to be heeded in any public discussion, it must make its case on the basis of its truth and justice as knowledge of these is accessible by 'common grace' and 'general revelation.' If religion speaks to the society on confessional grounds

Introduction

the same time, he argues that ethics should assess both theology and religion,[8] while ethics is itself to be evaluated by other disciplines, especially theology.[9]

Related to this, Stackhouse's conception of ethics is also a key component and distinctive feature of his public theology. According to him, ethics focuses on the good, the right, and the fitting and as such it takes three forms: deontology, teleology, and ethology or the study of the ethos. He sees all three as important and integral to theological ethics. None should be singled out as the true or appropriate form of Christian ethics, in part because in the midst of life "[w]e more or less triangulate toward the best judgments we can make."[10] These three forms correlate with the three tasks Stackhouse sees for theological ethics. Stackhouse repeatedly calls attention to this particular understanding of ethics and its three forms in numerous publications that span most of his career.[11] Together they also play an important role in his

---

alone, it runs the risk of being simply another interest group. . . . Theology in this sense is what tells us which religion is worth having. It is dependent upon a graceful intellectual amplitude that allows us to debate the ultimate issues, in public discourse, with those who do not already agree with us." Stackhouse, "Liberalism Revisited: From Social Gospel to Public Theology [with Responses]," in *Being Christian Today: An American Conversation*, ed. Richard John Neuhaus and George Weigel (Washington, DC: Ethics and Public Policy Center, 1992), p. 42.

8. "The fact that people argue about religion, and think that arguments count — that utter unreasonableness or obvious injustice discredits one religious position in the face of another — indicates that religions can be evaluated by theology and ethics in public discourse." Stackhouse, "Beneath and Beyond the State: Social, Global, and Religious Changes That Shape Welfare Reform," in *Welfare in America: Christian Perspectives on a Policy in Crisis*, ed. Stanley W. Carlson-Thies and James W. Skillen (Grand Rapids: Eerdmans, 1996), p. 26 n. 11.

9. "In concert with most classical traditions and in contrast to many modern trends that divorced or even opposed the two disciplines, we hold that theology and ethics are mutually supportive, even necessary to each other. Still, we must acknowledge the validity of the modern insight that the two are analytically distinct in a way that allows them to correct one another. Thus, we may use ethics to assess the assumptions and implications of every theologically approved practice and dogmatic claim. We may demand further that valid ethical criteria find ultimate sanction in what is truly universal and enduring, and not only in what is religiously and temporarily 'mine' or 'ours' at the moment. This is one of the characteristics of 'public theology,' which works with, but also beyond, confessional and dogmatic theology." Stackhouse, "General Introduction," *God and Globalization*, vol. 1, *Religion and the Powers of the Common Life*, ed. Max L. Stackhouse with Peter J. Paris (Harrisburg, PA: Trinity Press International, 2000), p. 7.

10. Stackhouse, *Covenant and Commitments*, p. 7.

11. For example, see *Ethics and the Urban Ethos: An Essay in Social Theory and Theological Reconstruction* (Boston: Beacon Press, 1972), pp. 66-67; *Apologia: Contextualization, Globalization, and Mission in Theological Education* (Grand Rapids: Eerdmans, 1988), pp. 202-8; *On Moral Business: Classical and Contemporary Resources for Ethics in Economic Life*,

Introduction

public theology. While deontology and teleology are often identified as two of the main forms of or approaches to ethics, ethology is not. Indeed, the significance Stackhouse places on ethos and the study of it is unique among contemporary Christian theological ethicists. For him, the importance of the ethos and study of it is due in large part to the inherent, significant, and lasting influence Stackhouse sees in the various main sectors and spheres of society and institutions particular to them. Although he sees religion as "the chief bearer of ethical values,"[12] Stackhouse maintains that such values are also borne by, learned in, and fostered by other areas of society and their institutions, such as families, governments, businesses, schools, and hospitals. Because of this, these other areas and institutions of the common life are rightly studied and should be given appropriate attention by those concerned with ethics, especially persons and groups engaged in Christian theological ethics. And essential to this is giving sustained and critical attention to and study of the ethos as it exists in the multiple overlapping sectors and spheres of the common life.

Noticeable by its absence in Stackhouse's discussion of ethics and its three forms is virtue. Although many scholars refer to virtue as one of the three primary forms of ethics, Stackhouse does not. In this regard he swims against one of the main streams in Christian theological ethics of the last several decades. The main reason Stackhouse gives so little attention to virtue, both as a major type of ethics and as the kind of ethics the church should embrace, is because of the multiple areas of life in which persons — religious or not — come by their virtues. Virtues are not the exclusive domain of the church or other religious bodies, and Christians too learn their virtues from multiple sectors of society and their institutions. For Stackhouse this should be evident. It is also not a bad thing and is, he thinks, part of the ways God can be and is active in the world, a perspective grounded in Stackhouse's Christology. In addition, he sees virtue as a kind of teleology, thus not itself one of the major forms of ethics.[13]

Another key component of Stackhouse's public theology and distinctive of it is its comprehensive nature. As noted above, his works in general are best understood as comprising a comprehensive public theology project. There

---

ed. Max L. Stackhouse, Dennis P. McCann, and Shirley J. Roels, with Preston N. Williams (Grand Rapids: Eerdmans, 1995), pp. 19-31; and *God and Globalization*, vol. 1, pp. 9-24.

12. Stackhouse, "Beneath and Beyond the State," p. 25.

13. In conversations between Max Stackhouse and Hal Breitenberg on this point, Stackhouse said he regards both virtue and sanctification as part of teleology. As he sees it, virtue must be understood from the standpoint of sanctification; it requires conversion.

Introduction

are three dimensions to this claim. First, Stackhouse combines and integrates the three main forms of and approaches to public theology, as evidenced in the literature devoted to it: historical, interpretive, and descriptive accounts of persons and groups as exemplary public theologians or their work as instances of public theology; discussions of the method appropriate to or necessary for public theology; and constructive and normative public theology proposals.[14] Although most who write about public theology generally focus on only one of these areas, and while some writers address two, Stackhouse is among the very few who regularly approaches public theology from all three perspectives. Moreover, he consistently combines them in his works. As both a major voice in discussions of method for public theology and a leading figure in constructive public theology proposals, throughout his publications Stackhouse also frequently incorporates and interweaves interpretations of leading theologians, past and present, as public theologians and their work as examples of public theology. As he sees it, from its earliest days to the present, when the church has been most true to its calling it has carried out a public theology as part of its core mission — and both reclaiming that tradition and continuing it in the future is an important and necessary task for the church today. In terms of a method appropriate to public theology, Stackhouse has argued on behalf of certain warrants, or touchstones of authority, for public theology: Scripture, tradition, reason, and experience,[15] which can best be brought to bear on issues, institutions, and interactions of the common life through a set of themes — creation, liberation, vocation, covenant, moral law, sin, freedom, ecclesiology, Trinity, and Christology — that can be selectively combined and employed, as appropriate for a given subject.[16] Stackhouse also connects the importance of the ethos with the various sectors and spheres of society, arguing that each comprises its own "public" and that we live our lives in multiple and overlapping publics, including religious, political, academic, economic, and legal publics.[17]

Second, Stackhouse's public theology is comprehensive in that he ad-

---

14. For a discussion of these three kinds of public theology, see E. Harold Breitenberg Jr., "To Tell the Truth: Will the Real Public Theology Please Stand Up?" *Journal of the Society of Christian Ethics* 23, no. 2 (Fall/Winter 2003): 55-96.

15. Stackhouse, *Public Theology and Political Economy: Christian Stewardship in Modern Society* (Grand Rapids: Eerdmans, 1987), chapter 1.

16. Stackhouse, *Public Theology and Political Economy*, pp. 17-37. An early list that includes many of these themes, prior to Stackhouse's adoption of the term *public theology*, appears in "Ethics: Social and Christian."

17. For example, see Stackhouse, "Human Rights and Public Theology: The Basic Val-

xxiii

Introduction

dresses a wide range of issues and topics dealing with church and society and in so doing tries to apprehend, interpret, evaluate, and guide a broad spectrum of persons, events, issues, interactions, beliefs, practices, and institutions. His public theology is comprehensive in terms of the breadth of subjects he has addressed that are of concern to those engaged in various ways with public theology, the number of contemporary and enduring issues to which he has given attention, and the complexity of the method he has developed, proposed, and used for public theology. A third comprehensive aspect of Stackhouse's public theology is that the bulk of his efforts together comprise a single, albeit protracted and expansive, public theology project. In addition to whatever they may be individually, the attention he gives to human rights, vocation, covenant, sectors and spheres, institutions, ethos, globalization, contextualization, pluralization, economy, corporations, democracy, theological education, urbanization, professions, polity, military, technology, missions, ecclesiology, and other topics; his continuing efforts to develop a detailed, complex, and nuanced public theology method; and his interpretations of various persons, groups, and features of the Christian tradition all contribute, in their own way, to his overarching public theology project.

Taken as a whole, Stackhouse's public theology might be seen as offering the outlines of a systematic theological ethics. It also stands as a new social gospel for the world, a world marked by religious pluralism and multiple publics, that is increasingly interconnected in numerous and varied ways.

For all of the ground that Stackhouse has covered in his long career, there is no lack of material yet to be explored. What Stackhouse's approach to public theology has done is to bring together strains of thought in Christian theology and ethics that wed the interpretive, methodological, and constructive strands of Christian public morality together into one body of work. In doing that, he has provided a model for doing public theology in a global context that sets the standard for how such theology can continue to be done going forward. The essays gathered together in this volume offer a set of lenses into how public theology *has* been done by Max Stackhouse, and, we hope, can provide a pathway for how public theology *may be* done in the future.

---

idation of Human Rights," in *Religion and Human Rights: Competing Claims?* ed. Carrie Gustafson and Peter Juviler (Armonk, NY, and London: M. E. Sharpe, 1999), p. 20.

Introduction

Shaping Public Theology

The articles that comprise the current volume are intended to reflect the diversity of Stackhouse's contributions to the field of public theology, both as a form of reflection on the means by which theology has offered commentary on the multiple spheres of public life, and as a constructive enterprise that establishes the place of public theology in the realm of contemporary Christian theology.

We have divided the selections into three parts: Part One establishes the place of public theology in the larger Christian theological tradition, especially in conversation with some of the key figures of modern theology. The first essay, "Toward a Theology for the New Social Gospel," relates the pressing issues of the mid-1960s, the time at which Stackhouse was writing, to the social gospel approach of Walter Rauschenbusch. Stackhouse identifies three debates in contemporary theology to which the social gospel may provide a response — the "death of God" theology, various approaches to "contextualist" versus "principlist" theology, and the perennial "Christ and culture" conversation.

Each of these three debates continues in one form or another in the Christian theology of the early twenty-first century. The death of God theology has recently seen a resurgence in various forms of "postmodern" theologies or forms of "Christian atheism," such as that endorsed by Slovenian philosopher Slavoj Žižek. Meanwhile questions of context versus principle continue to be central to arguments over the applicability of Christian thought to myriad moral and social issues, from questions of genetics, to the nature of the family, to issues of economics and justice. Similarly, questions of Christ and culture have not faded from controversy within the church, as the issue of how Christ might be seen as "transforming" culture continues to be of importance to all Christians who believe in the relevance of the Christian message to contemporary society. In the end, Stackhouse argues, the tradition of the social gospel can help to illuminate these issues, but at the same time, must ensure that it remains itself connected to its historical and theological roots.

The second essay in this collection, "Rauschenbusch Today: The Legacy of a Loving Prophet," attempts to do precisely that by offering a profile of one of the key figures of the social gospel movement, an analysis of his thought, and a defense of his continuing importance. Framing his defense in the form of an extended review of a biography of Rauschenbusch, Stackhouse uses this platform to offer a critique of those who would dismiss the social

Introduction

gospel movement as either an underdeveloped form of liberation theology or a passé remnant of the Progressive Era. "Those who would leave the legacy of the social gospel behind," he writes, "must be sure they have something better to put in its place. Many worse options, and few better ones, stand in the wings of history."

The third essay in the collection, "Christianity in New Formation: Reflections of a White Christian on the Death of Martin Luther King Jr.," is a reflection on the status of Christian theology in the wake of King's assassination. Stackhouse views King's murder as a revelatory event, one that discloses both the limitations and new possibilities inherent in the theological and moral movements that either failed to embrace the vision of justice and peace that King upheld or else took up King's challenge and sought to refashion Christianity in light of the imperative to justice represented by the civil rights movement. He calls upon white theologians, himself among them, to repent for having not fully recognized King's prophetic call; but more than that, he calls on them to embrace the righteous and deeply religious anger called for by King's assassination, and use it as a vehicle to continue King's struggle to achieve genuine racial and social justice in the United States. King's death, he argues, presents the possibility for both personal and social transformation, for those who are willing to allow themselves to move beyond mourning toward the creation of new forms of Christianity to deal with the crisis of the present time.

The rest of the articles in this section deal with prominent figures in the development of public theology as a distinctive approach to Christian social engagement, both as architects and as critics. In "What Paul Tillich Meant to Me," Stackhouse explains the debt that he owes to Tillich's theology, and the role that Tillich's approach played in the development of his own public theology. Tillich, Stackhouse argues, "made the quest for an apologetic, cosmopolitan Christian social ethic imaginable."

On the other hand, in "Alasdair MacIntyre: An Overview and Evaluation," Stackhouse takes up the challenge posed by one of the fiercest critics of the idea of universal moral categories, and showing that, taken as a whole, MacIntyre's project, while provocative and often insightful, does not offer the kind of resources necessary to make any form of genuinely public moral discourse possible, and may not even be clear on what the nature of the underlying problem might be.

The next two, shorter, essays, offer appreciations of two figures that were important to Stackhouse's own theological development. The first, "A Premature Postmodern," addresses the way in which Ernst Troeltsch's sociology of religion affected Stackhouse's understanding of the way in which social problems should be interpreted and addressed within the church, while the second, "Edwards for Us," offers an analysis of the continuing importance of the theology of the Puritan theologian, pastor, and philosopher Jonathan Edwards. "Edwards knew the holiness of beauty, and the beauty of holiness," he writes, encouraging his readers to look beyond the stereotypes of Puritan theology in general, and Edwards in particular. Stackhouse himself took Edwards's appreciation of natural beauty very much to heart, going so far as to move to Edwards's old stomping grounds in Stockbridge, Massachusetts, from which he took much of his inspiration, and attending the church that was once Edwards's pulpit.

The final essay in this section takes on a figure whose approach to theology and public life is in many ways the polar opposite of Stackhouse's — Stanley Hauerwas. In "Liberalism Dispatched vs. Liberalism Engaged," Stackhouse offers an extended critique of Hauerwas's project. Written as a review of Hauerwas's *Dispatches from the Front*, it presents Stackhouse's most succinct and pointed critique of Hauerwas's project, demonstrating that in Hauerwas's critique of the "incoherence" of culture in liberal societies, "He blinds himself to the deepest levels of coherence."

By failing to recognize that there is a concrete and inescapable set of social implications to any theological project, and that therefore there is always a public dimension to any theology, even one that attempts to isolate itself from accountability to larger forms of public discourse, Hauerwas fails to provide any reason to prefer any particular account of human life and activity to any other, including that of a church made up of "resident aliens."

In Part Two of this volume, we gather together a set of essays that illuminate Stackhouse's contributions to the distinctive methodology of public theology. The first, "The Tasks of Theological Ethics," lays out the basic elements of his approach to Christian social ethics. The first task of theological ethics, he argues, is to interpret the social context in which Christian ethics does its work in light of the deep wells of theological and spiritual tradition from which it emerges. Secondly, theological ethics is concerned with identifying the normative standards of action to which Christian behavior should conform. The third, prescriptive, task, he argues, is to attempt to articulate the basis for the creation of a more morally and spiritual adequate ethos, which corresponds to the spiritual depths of the Christian tradition and normative conditions of Christian behavior.

The next essay, titled "The Religious Basis of Cultural Activity," explores the way in which religion can provide a resource to inform other dimensions of cultural life, particularly the arts. Reflecting on the degree to which the arts have been divorced from Christian theology and spirituality in the modern era, Stackhouse argues that, properly understood, theology has important contributions to make to the arts, even when the particular artistic expressions are not themselves explicitly religious. Theology has the capacity, he argues, to rescue the arts from purely subjective aestheticism and to connect them to a larger concern with the moral and spiritual reality of which they are a part.

The next essay, "Public Theology and Ethical Judgment," offers a description of Stackhouse's understanding of what is meant by the term "public theology" and how it connects to the larger project of Christian theology and ethics. Describing the multiple "publics" to which public theology addresses itself — the religious, academic, political, and economic — Stackhouse argues that each is involved with the moral categories of "intelligibility, moral integrity, and respect for others." Public theology offers insight that may enable these various publics to understand their own moral foundations more adequately, while at the same time raising new and pressing questions for those within the Christian theological tradition about how adequately those traditions are prepared to deal with a changing social landscape.

The next essay, "Ethics: Social and Christian," offers a further analysis of the methodology of Christian ethics, specifically in its consideration of the way in which Christian thought deals with the questions of deontology, teleology, and ethology, or "the right, the good, and the fitting." The categories define the core questions that any Christian ethic must confront — what action conforms to the divine principles that govern human life and behavior, what actions will have the most beneficial results for human well-being, and what actions are most appropriate to the time and place in which we act. The answers to these questions will not always necessarily be in harmony with one another, yet they are always to be understood in relationship to one another, and the answers to each will provide us with a roadmap of the moral possibilities we confront. Beyond this, he argues, it is crucial for ethics that it be rooted in some form of social theory capable of offering a fruitful analysis of the ethical situation with which Christianity is confronted, including issues of power and responsibility.

The next essay, "Reflections on Universal Absolutes," confronts the question of whether Christian morality is rooted in natural law or other universal principles. Taking up an argument by Michael Perry, Stackhouse argues that while human rights must be rooted in a form of universal moral principles, they are best understood, not in a decontextualized or abstract way, but rather precisely in the midst of the contextual situation in which they are formulated. They are, Stackhouse argues, "regulative for the common good," and "essentially instrumental to persons and personal morality."

The next essay, "The Fifth Social Gospel and the Global Mission of the Church," extends Stackhouse's determination to address the public implications of theological ethics to the (at the time it was written) emerging question of globalization. Returning to his roots in the social gospel of Walter Rauschenbusch, Stackhouse argues that the new global situation requires a reassessment of received theological traditions in order to gauge their adequacy to the changing setting of theological reflection. In order to develop a social gospel that is capable of grappling with the demands of globalization, he argues, it must be "de-provincialized from its Americanist roots" in order to engage in a constructive project in an interreligious setting.

In the next essay, "Civil Religion, Political Theology, and Public Theology: What's the Difference?" Stackhouse differentiates the project of public theology from these two other, associated, approaches. In contrast to these other terms, he argues, public theology is not embedded in the civic, ethnic, cultural, or political structures that they confront. While public theology is concerned with questions of civil organization, cultural identity, and political order, it stands at a critical distance from all of these dimensions of human society, and approaches each of these publics with the aim of probing both their inherent possibilities and limitations in light of the reality of God's action in and intentions for the world.

This section ends with the essay "Covenantal Justice in a Global Era." In this essay, Stackhouse examines the relationship between the concepts of justice and covenant, arguing that, while complete justice is elusive within society, the promise of final justice is rooted in the covenantal dimension of God's relationship with the world. In an increasingly globalized society, this demands both the protection of individual rights and the acknowledgment of the communal dimension of all human association. This necessitates institutional forms that are capable of allowing both social structure and the capacity for individual self-expression. It also requires respect for human rights and the creation of structures of democratic governance for the sake of ensuring that governments are accountable to morally and politically binding standards of justice.

As globalization reshapes social and institutional forms across the board, forcing us to reevaluate how justice is sought and administered, the question of how both political and economic justice can be ensured becomes an increasingly important question, to which there is not yet a clear answer. By rooting the demand for justice in the covenantal relationship between hu-

Introduction

man beings and God, the churches have the capacity to imagine new possibilities for the creation of justice within a global society.

Part Three develops the idea of public theology's constructive role within a global society more fully. The first essay, "A Post-Communist Manifesto: Public Theology After the Collapse of Communism," situates the conversation in the midst of the struggle to reimagine questions of global responsibility in a post–Cold War world. Whereas for the better part of fifty years, questions of global importance had taken place within the bipolar world of great power conflicts, the problems of a genuinely global society were much more diffuse. In this essay, Stackhouse and his co-author Dennis McCann establish the question of how theology should be constructed in light of the passing of communism as a real political option for social engagement and reform. "A theology adequate to the cosmopolitan challenges," they argue, "must develop a social ethic for the emerging world in which democracy, human rights, and a mixed economy are acknowledged as universal necessities. It must address a world linked by technology, trade, and a host of new interdependencies."

Making sense of the cosmopolitan challenges of the global, post-communist world requires grappling with the fundamental institutional forms that make up common social life. In the essays that follow, we provide a set of representative samples of Stackhouse's reflections on some of those institutional forms.

First, we turn to the sphere of the economy. Globalization is defined by its economic forms as much as anything else, and Stackhouse's reflections on the role of the corporation in global society, and its importance for the creation of a stable yet responsive business environment are among his most significant contributions. In "The Moral Roots of the Corporation," he examines the ethical foundations from which the modern idea of the corporation arose, and demonstrates that corporations, in their intent if not always in their execution, are an expression of a theological sensibility and a spiritual heritage that needs to be recaptured for the sake of a morally adequate understanding of a properly functioning economy.

In a similar vein, "Spheres of Management: Social, Ethical, and Theological Reflections" offers an analysis of the way in which management as a practice is central to the creation of well-functioning and ethical forms of institutional life. In political life, economic life, in the various spheres of association to which we belong, and in our lives as members of the ecological systems of which we are a part, what we understand to be the proper management of those organizations requires serious reflection. The churches, he

Introduction

argues, have a crucial role in providing a platform for such reflections, particularly with regard to the role of moral management in the realm of modern corporate business.

Next, we turn to the question of theological education in a globalizing society. In "Globalization, Faith, and Theological Education," Stackhouse makes the case that theological education, in order to make sense of and form pastors to confront the changing global landscape, must take account of the spiritual "powers and principalities" of the common life in global society, and make the case for the creation of forms of life rooted in covenantal and federalist organizational philosophies that acknowledge the ultimate sovereignty of a God who rules over the other spiritual powers of the common life, and who gives them their proper forms and ends.

"A Christian Perspective on Human Rights" offers an analysis of the growing importance of human rights discourse in a global setting. While the language of human rights may have emerged from the philosophical background of the Western Enlightenment, informed by Christian concepts of human dignity and integrity, it has been, in the decades following the end of World War II and the establishment of the UN Human Rights Charter, widely adopted as a set of universally applicable principles. In this piece, Stackhouse traces this development, noting the continuing arguments about the possibility of a universal morality. He writes that "human rights foster specific kinds of pluralism first of all because theologically based moral judgments are, in principle, demanding of a universalistic reference point, but are simultaneously pluralistic in their internal structure." These principles are ultimately, he argues, part of the constitutive nature of the human conscience, and thus transcend individual cultural and religious categories, but can be recognized as valid irrespective of such divisions.

Moving from the global to the intimately local, the next essay deals with an issue of perennial importance to Stackhouse: The nature of the family. If the family is the basic structure of human society, how it is understood and what is done to protect its integrity are crucial subjects for ethical reflection. In "Living the Tensions: Christians and Divorce," Stackhouse offers his analysis of the way that Christians should deal with the reality of divorce, which has become an increasingly dominant reality in modern family life. He pleads for faithful compassion for those who experience the pain of divorce, arguing that Christians "must neither lower the standards set by their faith to suit the convenience of the times, nor let themselves be trapped by legalistic applications of the ideal." Rather, we must live in the tension between the ideal situation where marriage is a lifelong relationship of love between two

Introduction

partners, and the reality that, far too often, such lifetime relationships cannot be sustained.

The final essay in this collection examines the role of the pastor in the construction of a global public theology. In "The Pastor as Public Theologian," he posits Christian ministry as a vocation through which it is possible to mediate between the larger world of public responsibilities and societal obligations and the more personal world of spirituality and communal intimacy. The church is the "concrete embodiment of relative intersections between the vertical, the historical, the horizontal, and the communal dimensions of existence," and thus pastors are those who have the responsibility to interpret the responsibilities that emerge out of dwelling at those intersections, and making concrete how those responsibilities may be fulfilled. As public theologians, then, pastors have an apologetic task, making Christian faith comprehensible in a world in which it can seem increasingly strange, and making the Christian claims about truth and justice imperative demands to be met by both the church and the world.

This volume ends with two new essays. The first is an evaluation of the lasting significance of Stackhouse's work. In this essay, the editors offer what we take to be the central contributions made by Max Stackhouse to theological discourse in the twentieth and twenty-first centuries. It is our belief that Stackhouse has offered a way of doing theology in public that is a lasting resource for the Christian community, and offers a method of constructive ethics that can yield great insights with regard to Christian ethical action in the world.

The final essay in this volume is a brief retrospective by Max Stackhouse, in which he offers commentary on the changes he has undergone in the decades of his teaching and writing, and some final thoughts on what remains to be done.

A Note on the Text

The selection of texts for this volume was a particular challenge. Given Stackhouse's prolific output stretching across six decades, there was an immense amount of material to sift through in an effort to compile a representative sample of his most important contributions to the field of public theology. We could easily have filled a book twice this length. In the end, our choices were made on the basis of several factors: the importance of the texts, the perspective they offer into Stackhouse's thinking, the way in which they illu-

Introduction

minate key motifs we observed in his work, and the continuing relevance of their central arguments. Even articles that were very much "of the moment," and were often rooted in ideas that sustained them beyond the particular circumstances of their writing, exhibit characteristic or noteworthy aspects of his public theology, or both.

One complicating factor was presented by the multiple interlocking facets of Stackhouse's way of doing public theology, all of which he developed over many years and to which he gave repeated and substantial attention, coupled with the large number of topics he addressed over several decades. Thus in seeking to offer a representative sample of his work, we sought to ensure that there was minimal overlap in the main arguments and ideas among the articles.

Additionally, copyright considerations constrained some of our choices. There were many articles that we would have liked to use, but were not able to gain permission to reprint. On the other hand, we were pleased at the willingness of many of the journals and other publications for which Max Stackhouse had written over the years to work with us in securing copyright permissions, and we are very grateful to those publishers for their aid in completing this project.

In most cases, the editors did very little actual editing of these articles when it came to content. One exception is "The Tasks of Theological Ethics," which was originally published under a different title and appears here in substantially redacted form. In addition, we standardized the format of citations; because of the wide array of journals for which Stackhouse published, the requirements for citations varied from article to article. Beyond that, other than occasionally changing a word, inserting a clarifying punctuation mark, or (rarely) correcting an error that appeared in the text as originally published, not much else was required. Aside from those changes, the articles in this collection appear as they were originally published.

It has been our privilege and pleasure to work on this project, and we hope that the final published volume allows the reader a view into the development of Max Stackhouse's thought and its key themes and motifs. It is our belief that the ideas represented in this volume, and the larger corpus of work to which they belong, have a central place in the field of public theology, and our hope is that the publication of this volume will draw attention to their continuing importance.

PART ONE

Interpreting the Tradition of Public Theology

Toward a Theology for the New Social Gospel

In 1916 Walter Rauschenbusch penned the initial words of what was to become his most famous writing: "We have a social gospel. We need a systematic theology large enough to match it and vital enough to back it."[1] One half-century later, we who see Christian involvement in civil rights, poverty programs, housing projects, community organizations, and international affairs as legitimate and central, we who see the definition, criticism, vindication, and transformation of the *ethos* as the central task of Christian theological ethics, and we who have a hope for a more humane society have also a social gospel and need a theology capable of sustaining and broadening it. Our social gospel is not a recapitulation of the old one, although it could not have developed without its parent, and although we claim that the earlier movement has too frequently been slandered and, just as frequently, suffered the more ignominious death by dismissal. Yet, it is true, the old social gospel did fail, for it claimed more than it possessed; it spoke of God without sufficiently saying what it meant; it developed a theology of history laden with idealistic conceptions; and it was never able to deal with the charge of "culture Christianity," although it was a protest against other "culture Christianities." The newer social gospel has been duly chastised by subsequent theological movements; it does not make the claims of its predecessor. We do not claim to *have* a message of redemption and sanctification that needs only to be implemented in the social order to be fulfilled. Instead, we have the "good news" that we think we know where the gospel is located in a day when many think it irretrievably lost. And we think we know what some concrete implications

---

1. Walter Rauschenbusch, *A Theology for the Social Gospel* (New York and Nashville: Abingdon, 1917), p. 1.

Interpreting the Tradition of Public Theology

of the gospel are, even if we don't *have* it. It is by involvement in, reflection upon, and transformation of the social, political, and economic dilemmas of contemporary history that one comes closest to the whence and whither of human existence, for the Lord of history has been incarnated into that history's possibilities, the values that govern life have been plowed into the furrows of time, and the fundamental convictions of men about the ultimate with which man has to do, positive or negative, have been built into the institutions they have constructed.

We who are proponents of a new social gospel, like Rauschenbusch, need a theology capable of sustaining our inklings, at least until we find out what is valid and invalid in them. We need a conceptual framework upon which to work out our emergent sensitivities and by which we can defend these sensitivities against the premature attacks of the perennial spiritualizers, reductionists, privatizers, and ideological dogmatists of Christianity. We assume, let it be noted, in part what Rauschenbusch assumed: that theologies are constructed as critical, polemical, and expressive tools to build a frame around some segment of experience that is thereby designated as central and becomes the organizing principle for other dimensions of life. A social gospel theology, for example, points toward a reality that is actually at another level of experience than the theology itself — the historical level. We also assume that theologies may be judged valid or invalid in part because of their ethical power in history; that theology is of instrumental, not consummatory, value. Theology, thus, is a necessary but not a self-validating enterprise — one that involves the construction of fundamental conceptual models to allow the identification, interpretation, and actualization of that most significant reality with which all men have to do. In the present situation, however, we have no ready-made models for that toward which the new social gospel wants to point. We can neither transplant the old social gospel (although a renewed and thorough reading may be helpful), nor adapt any present theology ready-made. Rather, we, like every theological generation perhaps, need a more subtle combination of recovery, reconstruction, exorcism, and elaboration. And to do this we must engage in an assessment of the theological resources at hand and make some suggestions as to the potential shape of a new theology for our new social gospel.

Three Debates

The contemporary debates in theology and theological ethics that have gained the most widespread attention are only partly helpful in providing tools for the construction of a new theology for the social gospel.

The "Death of God" movement is an unavoidable case in point. It may be, as Harvey Cox suggests, that the Death of God proponents and the defenders of God need each other "like Punch and Judy." It is certainly true that the slapstick scrimmaging between those who shout "God is dead, for I don't experience him" and those who shout "He lives, for I experience him" are of that order, but they offer nothing of substance to the debate, since their arguments are equally vapid.

But the "Death of God" movement is not to be dismissed so easily, in spite of the ways it is sometimes represented or refuted. The spokesmen for the position are raising fundamental issues. One of the most crucial is the question of the continuity of faith. What kind of continuity do we have with previous believers? Do we believe the same things? Hardly, else theology would have frozen into the recapitulation of implicit faith. The "Protestant Principle" allows no such possibility. Theology must, and indeed frequently does, continue to reformulate explicit faith with candid integrity. But that is part of the problem, for each generation and each geographical area has its distinctive, explicit theological style. How then can there be continuity of faith? Two related possibilities have been widely suggested.

The first sees theology as an outworking of the interior logic of the language of theology. Ironically, the position that is usually engaged polemically in a refutation of developmental theories of history assumes development in theology. Thus, Christianity is seen as a special variety of intellectual history, and it is at the level of the outworking of doctrine or dogma that essential Christianity is grasped. Further, theologizing, the constructive task of the church in each generation, is seen as the projection and filling out of the logic of past ideas through the present toward the future. In this case, Christian intellectual symbol manipulation is seen as the activity that primarily bears the "essentially" Christian continuity of faith. This mode of thinking has not only been part of theology in the twentieth century, but also of much philosophy. In both cases, there has been a frequent and noticeable tendency to shift from engagement with historical problems to a concentration on the ideational level of culture. Significant segments of both Continental theology and British philosophy have tended to engage in the outworking of the internal logic of a given symbol system rather than struggling with concrete historical and ethical issues, in spite of a few noble stands *against* history that had important historical consequences.

Now, we can explain why they made this shift: we can speak of a loss of moral nerve (in spite of a courageous theological or philosophical audacity) in the face of morally incalculable events, the need to assume an absolute position not relative to historical contingencies of the time for which adequate analytical tools were not available, or we can speak of the need to find a security for the two disciplines at a time when they were threatened by ideological inundation. But such explanations do not show that the efforts are right or wrong. The contemporary secular theologians, interestingly and deeply influenced by these previous movements, are, it seems, illustrating the frustrations to which their forebears led and are calling for a recovered openness to culture and history as well as asking, indeed praying in an excruciating way, for a new sense of continuity with the Christ and "meaningful language systems" they want to continue to confess.

The second possibility sees not the process of theologizing, but the object of theology as that which alone bears the continuity of Christianity. The eternal is placed over against the temporal in a way that makes any temporal continuity, even theologizing, religion, and ethics, a pretension. This option describes only a succeeding series of discrete moments in human experience, each of which is empty except for the *a priori* character of "the Word," understood as either divine judgment-affirmation, or the divine inducing of existential decision. Our only continuity with Paul, Augustine, Thomas, and all the others is that of analogy. As they were existentially related to the Word, so are we. As they pointed authentically to the eternal in their day, so we can point to the eternal in ours. Or as they spoke "the Word," a contentless, eternal, decision-inducing, superhistorical function, so must we. We are among the faithful when we speak such a word now. History is not finally informative about either "the Word" or about the ultimate decisions evoked.

The "Death of God" movement in its various forms seems to me to be the result of the above tendencies and a powerful indictment of both options. While it may be that the former option is the easiest to teach and hence will continue to have considerable reputation in the academic centers, and while it may be that the latter is the easiest to preach and hence will ever have its chief defenders among the priesthood who need to invoke sanctity and evoke commitment, the Death of God theologians are forcing us to ask again as to our continuity with our fathers. It is, I think, no accident that one of the initial and primary discussions of the whole problem is William Hamilton's *The New Essence of Christianity,* for there is indeed a quest for a new statement

Toward a Theology for the New Social Gospel

of that core that is continuous with today's past. William Hamilton speaks to the question as posed by the first of the two options by rehearsing the intellectual history of previous "essences of Christianity." From Feuerbach's effort to transform theology into anthropology, to Harnack's attempt to separate the husk from the simple and powerful kernel of the teachings of Jesus, to Schweitzer and Troeltsch and Nygren, Hamilton shows that "neither philosophy nor historical method . . . can give us any theological residuum that we can adopt from the past, without change."[2] Hence, "all our theology, even our essences of Christianity, must be done afresh in every generation."[3]

It is ironic that, in showing the relativity of those whom he interprets as having tried to establish an intellectual-historical interpretation of Christianity, he adopts their dilemma. For, as they were seeking for an essential *idea* that needed to be worked out intellectually or conceptually, Hamilton also wants to preserve a theological or ideational "residuum." He does not ask whether Christianity and the essence of Christianity is "idea" at all, but only whether it is a particular God-idea. He wants to see it as Christ-idea, or rather, a set of Christological fragments that suggest an idea-style.

Hamilton is not worried so much about faith understood as trust. Indeed, he says, "faith is, for many of us . . . purely eschatological. It is a kind of trust that one day he will no longer be absent from us. . . . Faith is hope."[4] The problem is faith as the outworking of essential ideas in theologized belief and conceptualization. As the theological revolution of the early twentieth century is usually seen as a response to the poverty of its parents, so might we see the Hamilton branch of "Death of God theology" as the response to the poverty of the first theological alternative.

And Altizer prevents the adoption of the second option. He points out that, in the face of crumbling Christendom, Christianity has tried to establish an unassailable position. "Faith is then declared to be either *a priori* or autonomous. Transcending a historical ground it is open to no human experience whatsoever. . . . Wholly isolated from our history, the word of faith is now silent."[5] And later, he makes the point in an even stronger fashion:

---

2. William Hamilton, *New Essence of Christianity* (New York: Association Press, 1961), p. 19.

3. Hamilton, *New Essence of Christianity*, p. 19.

4. Hamilton, *New Essence of Christianity*, p. 64.

5. Thomas J. J. Altizer, "Creative Negation in Theology," *Christian Century* 82, no. 27 (July 27, 1965): 864. His formulations here, however, seem directly to contradict the major themes of "Nirvana and the Kingdom of God," *New Theology No. 1*, ed. M. E. Marty and D. G. Peerman (New York: Macmillan, 1964), pp. 150ff.

Interpreting the Tradition of Public Theology

> A proclamation of the Incarnate Word can never be simply a negation of history, even if the history which it confronts is a radically profane moment of time. A final no-saying to history is a renunciation of the incarnation, a refusal of the word which has actually become incarnate....[6]

There are, of course, a good number of other themes that continually crop up in the essays and books of the "Death of God" theologians, but again and again they return to the question of historical continuity posed by the late nineteenth century and shouted down, not answered, by the twentieth. Indeed, much of the dilemma is that they are attempting to ask a question in a post-Barthian and post-Bultmannian era when whatever tools theology once had to answer it have been swept aside.

The "Death of God" theologians thus represent a dead end of those branches of Christianity that see "essential Christianity" as borne exclusively either by the process of theologizing or by a superhistorical object of faith wholly other than anything experienced or known in human history. Yet, they sense, evidently, part of the way out of their dilemma, for they ask as to the historical character of Christ and attempt to suggest styles of Christian obedience. Further, they suggest that we begin a deeschatologizing of history and propose a historicizing of faith and eschatology. That is, rather than seeing each historical moment as a discrete absolute of finality, as Barth does in making eschatology the eternal that stands over time and breaks it at each juncture, or as Bultmann does in making each decision moment the eternal now, historical moments become part of a pattern of expectation toward future possibility in which we have some, if cautious, trust.

A second debate that is only partly helpful is the running exchange between the "contextualists" and the "principlists" in theological ethics. Although James Gustafson[7] has shown that the terms "contextualist" and "principlist" each apply to sets of figures whose theological-ethical stances are so different as to make the terms quite imprecise, one can say in general (and only in general) that the disagreement lies between those who, on the one side, see the task of ethics as one that tries to spell out the fundamental guiding rules for moral life in a way that makes them pertinent to new situations and those who, on the other, see rules as a cumbersome legalism to restrict the freedom and honesty of the loving self as it tries to work out a mature and

---

6. Altizer, "Creative Negation in Theology," pp. 865-66.

7. James Gustafson, "Context versus Principles," *Harvard Theological Review* 58, no. 2 (April 1965): 171ff.

appropriate response to the inevitable uniqueness of every moral situation. The principlists tend to rely upon the "new law of Christ," "the command of Love," the moral function of reason, and/or the rich traditions of natural law theory. The contextualists tend to rely on the perennial Protestant critique of legalism, the radical historical tradition that recognizes the individuality of each event, the inner resources of a dispositional ethical theory, and much of the pragmatic tradition.

The debate between these two perspectives has sometimes been tedious, and even cantankerous. Yet, in spite of efforts to get beyond the dispute, it lives on. James Gustafson in the article referred to above, not only shows that there are four levels of moral discourse (following H. D. Aiken's "Levels of Moral Discourse") and that the principlists speak more flexibly to the context than their detractors admit, while contextualists use hidden principles, but also claims that any systematic ethic must deal with all the four levels of the moral situation. He is, I think, right, and many ethicists on the basis of the article have laid the debate aside.

And the debate might well be over for the radical principlists and the radical contextualists, for the moral experience of man entails more than either historically unaffected norm or totally unguided situation. The absolutists of the authoritarian, though thoroughly "principled," variety are indeed not much help; but no responsible moralist would claim that a principlist must needs be one who applies a principle in exactly the same way in all cases, irrespective of circumstances. Nor are the existentialist contextualists much help, for surely some kinds of factors besides the authenticity of the self in each momentary context come into the play of moral decision-making. Indeed, those few moralists who are on the extremes are only recapitulating, in even less edifying terms, the problems of continuity and discontinuity that the secular theologians point to. Yet, the debate persists.[8]

Is it possible that something is at stake that has not been seen? To say that ethics must, and for the most part does, touch all bases does not seem to mitigate the dispute; for much rests on accents. Perhaps the question is at what level of human historical experience we are to find that which is most real, most capable of providing Christian moral power. To answer that it is at all levels does not seem helpful. Indeed, one may suggest that this dispute takes the question that the "Death of God" theologians are raising one

---

8. Cf., for example, Paul Ramsey, "Deeds and Rules," *Scottish Journal of Theology Occasional Papers*, no. 11 and Joseph Fletcher and Herbert McCabe, "The New Morality," *Commonweal* 83, no. 14 (January 14, 1966): 427-40.

step further. For the principle-contextual protagonists, as ethicists, are all convinced that one of the principal features of "essential" Christianity is its historical character and its ability to suggest "styles" of Christian obedience. Their dispute, then, is not whether historical reality in contrast to ideation or a nonhistorical object is that which sustains continuity of Christianity. The best theological ethicists of both stripes are interested in man in history for the sake of Christ and the glory of God. But they ask whether creative continuity is to be found by successive definition and redefinition of ethical legal formulations (for the principlist), or by "responsive" personal engagement in the moral situation and pragmatic calculation of consequences (for the contextualist).

At stake in this dispute, we might suggest, are complex issues. One is a primal perception as to whether the "problem" with history is that it continually threatens to break into chaos and must be ever and again ordered constructively toward righteousness, or whether the "problem" of history is that it has been over-institutionalized and ordered so that new freedoms and creativities cannot break forth. In short, is the creative continuity of history to be found in breaking free from false bondage, or providing frames for organized purpose? A second dimension of the dispute is whether induction or deduction is the proper ethical logic. But we are here accenting a third issue, although a fundamental one. While the "Death of God" theologians are pointing to the emptiness of nonhistorical interpretations of Christianity, the principlists and contextualists are asking, among other things, as to the level of human historical experience that bears the preconditions and consequences of viable historical Christianity.

Paul Ramsey places this question squarely when he points out that most "contextualists" seem to find that Love sees "only decisions to be made and acts to be done, never any order or at least no moral order in the world surrounding personal claims."[9]

Yet, he continues, the contextualists when pressed also admit that the construction and maintenance of a series of moral nets are necessary in society. "Christians are bound to construct a net, to repair the net, but also to criticize and transform it in the direction that love requires. . . . This is one form of rule-agapism."[10]

The question, then, that we wish to extract from the contextualist-

---

9. Ramsey, "Deeds and Rules," p. 26.

10. Ramsey, "Deeds and Rules," p. 27 (quoted from Bishop Robinson's *Christian Morals Today*).

principlist debate is: Can one establish a particular level within history as the central bearer of the Christian "essence" in history?

The third set of discussions that seems to occupy much of the semi-popular, semi-scholarly discussions of contemporary Christianity is the masochistic self-lashing of the church by those who have learned some sociology. In this movement, perhaps a little past its peak of influence in the seminaries, but not yet in the churches, the historical manifestations of Christianity are assumed to be "essential," and the structural factors are more important in the analysis than the "contextual" response. At least, so it would seem in terms of the methodological assumptions of the sociology of religion. However, after adopting modes of analysis that show the church to be a part of the structural and historical setting in which it occurs, the church and the moral nets it represents are scolded for being "culture Christianity." And, usually quoting H. R. Niebuhr,[11] it is assumed that everybody knows that Christ should only transform culture.

The problems, however, remain. How is Christ present to transform? Is he mediated from a superhistorical locus? Is that the realm of religious *a priori*? If he is not mediated but direct, where is he? Are we speaking of a metaphysical spirit? Is Christ a universal *logos*? Then how do historical phenomena that are manifestations of that *logos* become separated from their roots? But these are strange and awkward ways to speak and to think today. Is, then, Christ only Jesus, the man? In what way is that first-century historical person related to contemporary life?

The quasi-sociological critics want, it seems, to see Christ as being borne from the first century to the present by sociologically traceable structural effects, but they draw back for fear of the "Christ of culture" charge. They chastise the church, on the one hand, for its lack of cultural relevance and for not being on the vanguard of every cultural change (as if God only works in history through the conscious intentions of the Board of Deacons), while, on the other hand, they "prophetically" indict the church for not withdrawing sufficiently from the world to establish its peculiar (and hence more real?) faith and identity.

Yet these critics raise a third question that follows on the two previous ones: Can a historical view of Christian continuity ever become more than a sanctification of what is going on in the culture at large?

---

11. H. R. Niebuhr, *Christ and Culture* (New York: Harper, 1951).

Interpreting the Tradition of Public Theology

Why Important: An Aside

The three sets of discussions that we have just reviewed may call ultimately for a throwing up of the hands in despair. Indeed, the frequent reaction of many academic theologians is precisely a contemptuous rebuff. But I do not believe that we can do so, so easily. One of the distinguishing marks of most theology, in contrast to, say, some movements in philosophy, is that theology is called upon to speak from academic heights to an institution that is not primarily academic. This can often lead to a drive for a cheap "relevance" without long-range substance, but it also preserves theology from systematic irrelevance. The questions raised by these discussions are, in a sense, widespread in the churches today and could be dealt with if for no other reason than that.

But we might further point out that much of the debate on these three fronts takes on its importance precisely because it is being carried out in a semi-academic and semi-popular way. Whereas theologians of previous generations had two poles to their work, the pulpit and the theological tradition, each informing the other, the level of contemporary preaching has fallen into a state of relative deprivation (for it is, after all, a rather obsolete form of communication) and the level of academic research has become more specialized. Hence, an intervening level of discourse, always present but not always as important, has come to the fore in a new way. This semi-scholarly tractarianism, related both to academic and to the kerygmatic, apologetic, and critical tasks of the vital preacher, has captured sizable sections of the paperback book market, church-related journals, and, more recently, even the slick commercial magazines. Now, this is not altogether new, for one can see strong precursors in the social gospel movement, the Christian Socialist movement on the Continent, and the historic production of tracts by the sects; but its importance shows every sign of pending and dramatic crescendo. Further, the consensus shaped by this new, slick tractarianism is widely reforming the social and theological sensitivities of Christian pastors. We might therefore suggest that professional theologians no longer have their point of contact with the churches *directly* but only *mediately* through a growing body of middle-level literature (and through middle-level organizations such as conferences, seminars, institutes, and denominational or ecumenical associations where this literature is discussed).

Further, the problems that concern these men are, in fact, crucial for professional theologians as men, whether it is their primary vocational concern or not. It is no small thing that all these movements are dealing in one way or another with the problem of history and that all the persons involved in these various debates, it would appear from their writing, have an intense commitment to efforts for justice, freedom, and renewal that has shaped their theological efforts. They are, I would suggest, pointing toward the new social gospel in significant ways, partly because of their social engagement. The fact that the theological frameworks they employ leave us woefully dissatisfied should not obscure their contributions nor the importance of their level of discourse.

What Is Required?

But what, precisely, are the questions, and how can they be phrased in manageable ways? And, most important, how can we begin to deal with them? I say "begin," for it is beyond the scope of this paper and the competence of this writer to finish the task. But due to an irritable impatience with those who tell us what needs to be done without trying to do it, a constructive, if provisional and skeletal, series of options and choices will be made.

The question about a new essence of Christianity, with hints about its Christological and hence its historical character, is almost the right question. There is a dramatic need for Christian thinkers to attain some clarity about that which is peculiar to Christianity, to specify where in the world Christ is. But posing the question in terms of a "new essence" and a "Death of God" vocabulary is not helpful, for the connotations of "essence" are laden with idealistic metaphysics and a tradition that continually draws a distinction between interior and exterior, with anything exterior and formal being unauthentic. The "Death of God" language, further, misdirects the writers and the readers, for it leads them to speak of a kind of emptiness at the level of nonhistorically conditioned experience rather than toward the partial fullness that they want to speak of at the historical level. Their readers, whether enthusiastic antireligionists, confirmed theists, enterprising journalists, or whatever, therefore continually press the questions concerning that about which they cannot speak rather than that about which they can speak. What they want to do (or, at least, their strongest theological move) is to construct a theology that delineates history as the primary locus of revelation and signification.

Yet the "new essence" language is better than the "Death of God" language. A new theology for the new social gospel may well be deeply informed by the "quest for the essence of Christianity," old and new, for it is precisely a quest for some kind of historically borne continuity with Christ.

Interpreting the Tradition of Public Theology

The essence of Christianity has been placed, displaced, and replaced at several levels of historical experience, as has been shown by Hans Frei's brilliant essay on the theological background of H. R. Niebuhr.[12] The "essence" has been variously conceived as a unifying consciousness that stands behind all particular acts and teaching; a unique and uncaused event, the continuing interpretation and reinterpretation of which forms a chain of continuity; a novel set of interrelated symbols or images that have an interior logic that can be inexhaustibly developed in each historical epoch; a kernel of historically taught truths separable from their cultural husks; or the ideal rules governing the process of historical development itself, cut off from any metaphysical ground. In nearly all cases, the definition of "essence" was deeply influenced by residual idealism.

An effort partially to recapture and partially to reconstruct, for the new social gospel, the centrality of the historical sensitivities that obtain in both the old and the new quests for the essence of Christianity, requires first of all a departure from the notion of essence. But it does not thereby abandon the effort to find an answer to the question of how Christ is historically mediated to the present. Indeed, a new theology for the social gospel, viewing theology as a heuristic framework or model that delineates that which bears the continuity in a way that focuses on creative change, must be primarily a theology of history calling for a new reformation.

Nor must we allow our efforts to be confused by the traditionalist interpretation of the relationship of theology and history. It is not sufficient to make a distinction between "reform" and "reformation," between reform of the moral and institutional life and reformation of doctrine and theology, seeing one as a secular and the other as a sacred task. The new theology must not allow its center to be reduced to moral energy *or* new symbol manipulation. We cannot allow Luther's formulation to stand on this point: "Doctrine and life are to be distinguished. Life is as bad among us as among the papists." "But if doctrine is not reformed, the reform of morals will be in vain, for superstition and fictitious holiness cannot be recognized except by the Word and by faith."[13] While it may well be that we are no better than our Catholic brethren, as we now call them, he has missed the point. The aggressive sectarian tradition that is the root of the social gospel movement,

---

12. Hans W. Frei, "Niebuhr's Theological Background," in *Faith and Ethics*, ed. Paul Ramsey (New York: Harper, 1957).

13. Quoted by G. H. Williams, "Friends of God and Prophets," *Harvard Divinity Bulletin* (October 1965): 14, in a discussion of H. Oberman's "Das tridentinische Rechtfertigungsdekret im Licht spätmittelalterlicher Theologie," *Zeitschrift für Theologie und Kirche* 61 (1964).

old and new, is frequently confused with populist, humanist, often apocalyptic reform movements in which the reform comes first and for its own sake. But the aggressive sectarian tradition, which the sentiment quoted above helped suppress on the Continent, but which cropped up again in the British Calvinist traditions, moves by quite a different logic. For it says, as do its modern theological counterparts concerned with history and life and the new social gospel, that a right, if partial, theology directs one to the proper locus of meaning and demands an empirical and consequential reform precisely at the historical level so that the promise of seeing in full may become a more immediate reality. Further, reform is not constructed out of man's own resources, but is an integral part of the response to and of grace that is historically mediated. Thus reformation is not mere reform and certainly not mere reformulation, but a thorough reformation of theology and history. And that integral relation of the two demands a theology of history, a historical theology of history.

The phrase, historical theology of history, demands explanation. It implies a theology, a set of related, formal categories, that points to history and that is itself subject to historical correction. Let us look at each of these terms in more detail.

Theology, as here understood, is a discipline that attempts to set a frame around the center of meaning and righteousness. It requires, thus, some conception of "reality," "Being," or "God." But in view of modern man's inability to know or experience anything much of a superhistorical person, it may be that we shall have to utilize one or another of those "natural theologies" that attempt to state the formal conceptual and/or functional requirements for speaking of historical experience. There are, it seems, formal categories that are *a priori* required for the interpretation of life and meaning. Not only do mathematical and logical relations seem to have this character, but every people in every culture has a concept of "ought" or "requiredness," and a sense of what is "real" or "final." Even if these formal categories are, as some claim, very deeply rooted *conventions,* and not *a priori* forms at all, the fact that every people requires these conventions points toward a formal boundary that does not seem to be affected by historical events.

A theology for a new social gospel, however, would have to claim that these boundaries are discovered by historical experience and that, further, they serve not as the shape and plot of life, but as a stage whereon the real drama takes place. The same stage is sometimes a ship, sometimes a drawing-room, and sometimes a forest; the historical outworking of conflict and resolution, interacting plots and characterization impute the meaning. Theology must provide proper lighting for the stage, to press the metaphor, not to illumine the stage itself, but to allow the drama to be seen.

History consists of the remembered and interpreted patterns of events that define the present and give rise to expectation. Various dimensions of the patterns are organized into systems. Thus our focus is upon a dynamic and creative set of interacting "systems," each of which undergoes interior structural change and is involved in a continual series of constellational changes. Among the major "systems" are some that we can delineate: language systems, legal-political systems, educational systems, mores and folk-ways (that amorphous context of pragmatic expectations that pervade every *ethos*), economic-technical systems, and psycho-biological systems.

We come, then, to the question posed in part by the principlist-contextualist debate, namely, which level of historical experience is to be accented?

A truly "historical" theology of history for the new social gospel would not be caught designating one "system," or level of experience, as crucial and calling that "the essential one." But, as we have pointed out previously, neither is it sufficient to say they are all important all of the time, for the question of accents is crucial. Rather, we must suggest a shifting point of reference. At some periods of history, it is historically shaped language that bears the burden of recovering, preserving, redefining, and transforming that which was brought to life in history by Jesus Christ. At other moments, the economic-technical systems bear the crucial values, or the legal-political ones, and sometimes a combination of several, and so forth. It is possible, for example, to say that the shifting of levels by Barth, vis-à-vis the nineteenth century, from an understanding of history that had become highly subjective and interior to a recovery and renovation of an objective language system, was a way of keeping alive the historical influence from Jesus Christ at a time when other levels of experience or "systems" were faltering or actively consumed by an orgy of self-destruction.[14] But that is not to claim that we should stay there, or that one kind of language is the only authentic bearer of Christianity. To say that leads to a linguistic Amishness. Rather, the kind of analysis

---

14. But even the success of this singular language system was partially assured by the military aspects of the political-legal systems of Switzerland and the allies. Hence one must postulate the relationship between particular language and political-legal systems in this period of crisis that is not sufficiently accounted for by the proponents of the Barthian language system. Cf. Reinhold Niebuhr's scathing indictment of Barth and Barthians on this point. "Karl Barth and Democracy," *Essays in Applied Christianity* (New York: Meridian, 1959), pp. 163ff.

that leads us to such a suggestion about Barth leads us also to the conclusion that we can never claim that we should always stay in one language system. Not only does the aggressive sectarian position, out of which an historical theology of history grows, force us to other levels, but it drives us to suggest that an exclusive claim by any one "system" or level leads to idolatry. Indeed, the proponents of the new social gospel are now suggesting that it is another level of experience besides a historically conditioned system of "God talk" that now bears the crucial set of influences and to which we must attend if the gospel that we know in part is to be known more fully.

Now, of course, one might ask how are we to know where, among the "systems," one is to find that shifting cipher that gives life to the empty stage? Or how, within a theology of history that points to the dynamic interaction of creative "systems," are we to discern which "system" or set of "systems" is crucial at the moment?

The question calls in part for an empirical answer. By technical analysis of historical data some indications can be found.[15] But the answer can also only be understood through a concept historically related to some sectarian interpretations of "Spirit."

A theology for a new social gospel can only deal with spirit as a historical phenomenon. It does not know what would be referred to if by "spirit" is meant a metaphysical substance. Metaphysical substances do not provide discerning power. They are, if anything, what is supposedly discerned. Nor is it necessary to retreat to subjective interiority. A careful theology for the new social gospel does not want to choose between misplaced objectivity and unreliable subjectivity. It turns instead to the structured *esprit de corps* of those covenanting together to discern the signs of the times. It sees participation in the organized body of the committed as crucial. The primary, although by no means exclusive, institutional form of interacting systems that attempts to be that body is the church.

We are led thereby to the question posed by the quasi-sociologists of religion. What is, and what is to be, the role of the church in modern society as it attempts to find and define that which it knows to be enlivening and transforming in history? An absolutely fundamental ingredient of the new theology for our new social gospel, thus, is ecclesiology. The church that is alive is one that reenacts the unity — linguistic, legal-political, educational,

---

15. Robert Boguslaw, *The New Utopians* (Englewood, NJ: Prentice Hall, 1965), makes some very suggestive remarks to this point in a quite different context. Cf. also my article "Ethics and Technical Data," *Journal for the Scientific Study of Religion* 5 (1966).

Interpreting the Tradition of Public Theology

moral, economic, and psychological — of the implications of Jesus Christ. It attempts continually to sustain appropriateness of the several systems for each other and for the prospective shape of history as we look to future possibility. Indeed, the church is a metahistorical model of history living in history that attempts to preserve the integrity and transform the sustaining power of all the systems, within itself and for society at large. Marx was right when he said that the criticism and transformation of society begin with the critique of religion. And, we might add, organized religion at that. Thus, the theology for the new social gospel must concentrate on ecclesiological polity and action, the ways in which the systems can be and should be arranged and the things the church can do, so that the effects flowing from Jesus Christ are not stultified and the holy *esprit de corps* is not suppressed. It is the conviction of this writer that the best models for this reconstruction of a historical theology of history, focusing on ecclesiology, may be found in the "polity" sectarian churches, i.e., those defined by their principle of organization — Presbyterian, Congregational, Baptist, etc. However, the debates about conciliarism, collegiality, and "people of God" at Vatican II seem also very suggestive.

But more, the church can be, and sometimes prophetically is, the anticipation of the potential transfigured integrity of the interacting "systems" of the future. The conception, borne by the church, of the eschatological Kingdom and the vision, borne also by institutions indirectly influenced by the effects of Christ, of a universal society constitutionally bearing the conditions that would allow "seeing in full" in its economic, social, and political life have ever been important ingredients of theology, but require particular attention in view of much contemporary obscuring of the issues.

Two issues are raised by the preceding suggestions. First, there must be a fresh reading of church history itself, for much church history sees the activity and polity of the church as only secondary. Gabriel Fackre struck precisely the right notes in an address given at the first annual meeting of the United Church of Christ ministers who teach in theological seminaries:

> Much present reading views the period of the world's tutelage as a time of priestly imprisonment. The church smothered human creativity, and now when the world comes of age its tyranny is thrown off. While this interpretation does, in fact, describe the priestcraft that resisted the Galileos, it does not do justice to the better sallies of the church onto secular terrain — scouting parties that did not go out to imprison but to release captives, not to wound but to heal and humanize. The hospital, welfare, educational, crusading, justice-seeking and peace-making ministries

were in large part efforts of the church to stumble onto the Jericho roads following the secular Christ. Why? In order to "fill in the gaps" — to be the Dutch boy at the dike — yes, let us use the awful words, to be a kind of "Deus ex machina," filling a human need for which the secular community had neither the will nor the way. From the care of the prisoner, hungry and aged and the attack on the exposure of female children in the ancient world up to monitoring the Jackson, Mississippi, TV station's segregated programming, the church has pioneered the human task. In its halting, awkward way, the church, at its best, has moved onto secular turf to fill needs, to bind up wounds. It has been a tutor of the world, a schoolmaster — and to call this tutelage imprisonment, and to demean it, is really quite ludicrous.[16]

But, secondly, there is always the haunting issue of "Christ and Culture." The quasi-sociologists frequently drew back from their own suggestions for fear of the charge that they are suggesting a "Christ of Culture." And do we not thereby succumb to a belief in the inability of Christ to transform culture? The new theology must suggest that the dichotomy is a false one (and based, incidentally, on suspect reading of Ritschl, the Christian Socialist movement, and the old Social Gospel). It is not a question of Christ in, *or* Christ transforming, culture, but a question of the gospel which we do not know precisely, being borne by cultural systems in history and transforming them toward a new, enlivened, just, future possibility — pointing ultimately to an eschatological judgment and vindication of history, a final seeing face to face. The eschaton is the only final point of transcendence for man. Until then, he must operate within the boundaries of, and with the meaningful content of, history, although the opening of the present toward the future provides an opportunity for novelty.

If there is to be an adequate new theology for the new social gospel, then, some of its main outlines are clear. A theology for a new social gospel must not, as some of its predecessors frequently did, cut itself off from resources beyond its immediate environment. The work of philosophical theology at the boundaries of experience remains significant and not mere empty speculation. The attempt to explore and define the nature of historical and conceptual *a priori,* the universal phenomenon of "ought" language in every human culture, and the fundamental boundaries of nature or creation, these

---

16. Delivered in June 1965. Part of the address may be found in *The Ministers Quarterly* 21, no. 4 (Winter 1965-66): 25ff.

Interpreting the Tradition of Public Theology

all remain highly germane, even if the new social gospel claims that what populates these forms with special meanings and brings them to life is the peculiar set of historical conditions that obtain from Jesus Christ, defined, reenacted, pointed to, and anticipated by the church.

However, in pointing out potential allies, it is possible to suggest that particular fundamental accents must become central today. An adequate theology for the new social gospel must involve a theology of history; it must allow a shifting point of reference in the interaction of historical systems; it must entail a new concentration on ecclesiology and polity; and it must demand an eschatological point of reference. Whether such a theology can be fully constructed in the near future remains a question, but the situation remains as Rauschenbusch defined it. "We have a social gospel. We need a systematic theology large enough to match it and vital enough to back it."

Rauschenbusch Today: The Legacy of a Loving Prophet

Modern American Protestantism has not, for the most part, focused on the lives of the saints. The psychic energy of contemporary pastors, theologians, and church leaders has more often centered on the kerygmatic Word as it encounters "the problem of history," on struggles against the idolatries of fascism and Stalinism abroad and racism, classism, and sexism at home, or on the development of the professional skills of ministry.

But what has been ignored at the front door has entered by the side. Both psychohistory and narrative theology have evoked a rebirth of what our grandparents called "testimony" — the stories of personal pilgrimage. People do need models; we like to tell our own tales; and we like to get the scoop on everyone else.

Some of this is little more than pious gossip, and is pernicious. When it becomes the primary focus of attention, faith is endangered: we slide easily into the conviction that theology is basically a reflection of a quest for identity, or is poetry projected onto the cosmos rather than a fundamental claim about what is true or just or holy — just what the greatest skeptics about religion have claimed for several centuries.

The best preachers and teachers do not talk too much about the self and do not concentrate on personal experience alone. They know that psychobabble can easily become a substitute for good news, and that temptations to avoid theological insight and social responsibility in favor of self-preoccupation are all too frequent.

Nevertheless, the current burst of interest in biography may be a corrective for lopsidedness in other directions. For Christians, the divine revelation, the historic redefinition of meaning, the cosmopolitan insight — all those things that are deeper and wider than the self and that can reshape the self — have, finally, also to come to fruition in the life of persons. Even the long-expected idea of the messianic kingdom had to have a particular personal locus to be fully compelling. A testament with all the discursive writings of Paul, John, and the pastorals but without the Gospels would be incomplete.

Biographical interest can be seen in the continuing fascination with the lives of modern martyrs such as Dietrich Bonhoeffer and Martin Luther King Jr., and in the way some feminist and Third World thinkers use stories to evoke fresh modes of reflection. Consider, for example, how often Alice Walker's *The Color Purple* is used in seminary teaching, or how C. S. Song, Kosuke Koyama, and Lamin Sanneh draw on personal cross-cultural encounters to bring new perceptions to scriptural and theological themes. The pervasiveness of this emphasis can now be seen even in Christian social ethics, the field born out of the social gospel movement and one that in the name of prophetic spirit and social analysis has been critical of Protestantism's tendency to focus on personal piety.

A refreshing effort to reflect on the intimate connection of prophecy, piety, and social insight is Paul Minus's biography of the father of the social gospel, *Walter Rauschenbusch: American Reformer*. As much as any other single figure, Rauschenbusch brought nineteenth-century pietism into the twentieth-century world of cities, factories, immigrants, clashing classes and subcultures, and problems of housing, transportation, and employment. For many, the path that led from the historic patterns of Protestant pietism to ecumenically engaged, socially involved, and intellectually critical evangelicalism, and away from constrictive fundamentalism, forked at Rauschenbusch.

No one can read him deeply, or read about him, without thinking that they know him personally. Everyone is inclined to call him, as did his friends, "Rauschy." Yet, like John the Baptist, he always points beyond himself to something greater. Perhaps that is why many of those indebted to him do not take him as their final master.

The outline of his story is simply rehearsed. His father was a German Lutheran pastor who immigrated to this country and converted to the Baptist faith and the democratic polity as a young man. Born in 1861, Walter Rauschenbusch imbibed from his family a profound personal piety, a love of learning, a sympathy for the oppressed, and a sense of mission. His studies both in the United States and in Germany cultivated his many gifts and reinforced his sense of having been called to a great task for God. They also gave him an abiding love of both German and American cultures.

He became a pastor in a German Baptist church in a raw section of New York City. In the course of a very successful ministry — informed by piety (he wrote wonderful prayers), pastoral experience (he cared for his flock), and learning (he regularly wrote reviews and articles for journals) — he became increasingly critical of the economic system of the late nineteenth century. That system seemed to undercut the democratic gains that were being made in law, politics, education, and family life; it tended rather toward a new feudalism, dominated by robber barons and served by a new class of industrial peasants.

The prophetic emphases in his thought developed roughly during the same time he discovered his love for Pauline Rother, who later became his wife, the mother of his children, and a beloved companion in hard work and tender play. Previously unpublished quotations from letters between the two reveal how intense their spiritual and physical intimacy was, and how they discovered qualities of marriage that were not present in their parents.

Such matters are significant in part because they reveal to a contemporary generation that a prophetic spirit and a passion for social justice need not be born out of suspicion, alienation, or victimization. They can be, and they have been, born of an amplitude of love, in which case righteous anger can be directed against manipulators of distrust and hate, and not against those who are not "like us."

With a number of fellow pastors who became lifelong friends, Rauschenbusch studied, read, talked, debated, and plumbed the new social theories of the day, especially those of the non-Marxist socialists whom John C. Cort has recently traced in *Christian Socialism*. The pastors wove these theories together with biblical themes to form "Christian Sociology," a hermeneutic of social history that allowed them to see the power of God's kingdom being actualized through the democratization of the economic system (see James T. Johnson, editor, *The Bible in American Law, Politics and Rhetoric*). They pledged themselves to new efforts to make the spirit of Christianity the core of social renewal at a time when agricultural-village life was breaking down and urban-cosmopolitan patterns were not yet fully formed.

When Rauschenbusch became ill and lost some of his hearing, he accepted an invitation to become a professor on the German faculty, and later the English faculty, of what became Colgate Rochester Divinity School. From that position he became one of the most famous speakers on Christianity and social problems of his day, as well as a beloved teacher and honored author of several books. Until his death in 1918, in the midst of what was for him a tragic war between Germany and America, he helped develop one of the most important theological-ethical positions of modern Protestantism.

Minus's study of all this is craftsman-like. Simply as a piece of scholarship, it surpasses the mostly hagiographic portrayal written by Rauschenbusch's student and assistant, D. R. Sharpe, nearly half a century ago. Minus's book shows a mastery of materials not publicly available to Sharpe — including, for example, those identified in my edition of Rauschenbusch's *The Righteousness of the Kingdom;* those made available by Klaus Jaehn in *Rauschenbusch: The Formative Years;* and those recently collected by Winthrop Hudson in *Walter Rauschenbusch: Selected Writings.*

Minus's work and its subject matter are sure to be compared with Richard Fox's recent biography of Reinhold Niebuhr, the neo-orthodox proponent of Christian realism, and with the autobiography of James Luther Adams, a "liberal" with certain affinities to contemporary liberation thought, now under preparation with the help of Linda Barns. These three figures are arguably among the most influential Protestant social ethicists of twentieth-century America, and in any case offer a representative spectrum of opinion.

Minus clearly has a different agenda from Fox's. In *Reinhold Niebuhr: A Biography,* Fox is interested in which of his teachers, Robert McAfee Brown or Michael Novak, is closer to their teacher's (Niebuhr's) legacy, and in how Niebuhr's Christian realism might influence the future of civilization. Sadly, Fox seems to lose interest in the issue along the way, perhaps because Novak seems to have the best case and Fox does not want him to. He ends up not liking Niebuhr very much and not quite caring about the fate of Christian realism. Nevertheless, his work confirms that Niebuhr stands on Rauschenbusch's shoulders and surpasses him. Rauschy's *Theology for the Social Gospel* is simply no match for Reinie's *Nature and Destiny of Man.*

Minus's concern is for recovering and recasting a creative link between populist theology and active social witness. He ends up liking Rauschenbusch very much, so much that he has to guard against hyperbole. Still, he appears to be less concerned than Rauschenbusch was with the more expansive questions of how faith and doctrine shape civilizations and how doctrines might shape human destiny. The wider scope of history and the role of ecclesiology in it are not in his immediate horizon. This Methodist biographer is, in this respect, more Baptist than his subject.

Nevertheless, we can see that Rauschenbusch had a better sense of how grassroots social institutions work than did Niebuhr. Furthermore, like the two-volume Adams autobiography, Rauschenbusch's biography is studded with stories of people from every level of society. Workers and seminarians always came to hear both men speak; but they were also friends of those who did not work with their hands — like John D. Rockefeller, in Rauschenbusch's case.

Rauschenbusch remained more self-consciously rooted in Scripture than did Adams, however, and he maintained closer ties to church circles than to academic ones. While the two share a pronounced sense of the importance of the Holy Spirit, just below the surface of Rauschenbusch's thought is a Trinitarian framework and a preference for an organic society over a voluntaristic one. In comparing Rauschenbusch to Adams, the differences between a religious liberalism (Adams left the Baptists to become a Unitarian Universalist) and a progressive evangelicalism become clear; indeed, we can see how conservative Rauschenbusch really was.

A bigger difference remains in the telling of the individual story. In the Minus biography, characters do not always come alive; points are sometimes only summarized in a quotable aphorism. Of course, Adams is a constitutional raconteur. He teaches by parable, which he seems to be able to connect to systematic thought — whether it be in the philosophical-theological traditions of Whitehead and Tillich or the sociohistorical traditions of Troeltsch and Weber. Those who use Minus's book to teach the next generation how Rauschenbusch brought many in a previous generation, most of a denomination, and much of ecumenical Protestantism to embrace "Social Christianity" may want to translate his material into that kind of revealing art which simultaneously embraces evocative parable and systematic clarification. The deeper promise of Minus's effort would then be fulfilled.

What does Rauschenbusch's social gospel mean for today and tomorrow? Is it the American form of liberation theology, belatedly discovered by Latin American Catholics, Third World Protestants, and others who had not previously been led beyond their distinctive forms of pietism by historicism and sociology? Or is it a blip on the screen of history, born of the Progressive Era among minorities in a strange land, institutionalized in the New Deal, and now left in the dust by the neoconservative revolution?

If by "liberation" people mean that Christian thought and life are to be socially engaged, committed to those forms of systemic change necessary for the greater actualization of social justice, and open to the dynamic movements of the Spirit among the people, then there is little doubt: the social gospel is America's indigenous form of liberation theology. It forms base communities, it overcomes resignation with greatness of soul, it ministers to those with greatest need, it empowers the voiceless. Indeed, the more one reads of Rauschenbusch, the more one sees of the social gospel in Martin Luther King Jr., and even Dorothy Day.

But if by liberation theology one means other things, then differences emerge. If one means, for instance, an epistemological privilege of the oppressed, in the sense that the poor, the suffering, and the dispossessed have some intuitive knowledge of God, righteousness, and social reality not available to others; if one means that victims know best how to overcome their condition and build new institutions; and if one means that knowledge based on "experience" makes academic excellence unnecessary, then liberation thought and the social gospel diverge.

The reason for working among the dispossessed, and the reason for training teachers, preachers, and missionaries to do so, while insisting on the highest standards, and the reason for fighting to get disadvantaged people access to educational and leadership resources is to equip them with epistemological possibilities not already available to them.

A similar distinction would have to be made if one means by liberation what Dorothee Sölle, for instance, means when she writes that "Political Theology is a theological hermeneutic which, in distinction from a theology that interprets reality from an ontological or existentialist point of view, holds open an horizon of interpretation in which politics is understood as the comprehensive and decisive sphere in which Christian truth should become praxis" (*Political Theology*, p. 59). The legacy of the social gospel *might* challenge the notion that theology has the capacity to transcend ontological and existential questions; but it would *certainly* repudiate the social presuppositions of Sölle's statement. Her view, it would say, reflects a heritage rooted in religious establishment, even if today it wants to establish a radical theology instead of a conservative one.

Rauschenbusch, like most in the social gospel movement, believed in the free church. He thought that Christ not only taught us how society works if we read the scriptures deeply enough, but that Christ demanded of his followers a social theory of politics, not a political theory of society. That is, Rauschenbusch would have denied that politics, or for that matter a political economy that put production and distribution in the hands of the state, could be "the comprehensive and decisive sphere for Christian truth or praxis" without bringing tyranny with it.

Indeed, he would say that both theology and sociology require us to recognize that the church is the more decisive, and society the more comprehensive, category of the common life. Society is also more shaped by the church than modern thinkers — including a number of church leaders, when they think about such questions — acknowledge. Thus, church and society are the chief areas of Christian concern; politics and political economics are, and must be, their servants, else they will follow Mammon entirely, trailing along, often generations behind, only appearing to be innovators. That is why the church can and must speak about "social salvation," and do so wisely. On this point, Adams and Niebuhr would join with Rauschenbusch.

What most separates contemporary theology and ethics from Rauschenbusch is his emphasis on the kingdom of God. He was one of the last great American leaders to take the kingdom of God as his governing symbol. H. Richard Niebuhr taught us in *The Kingdom of God in America* that the triune themes of the sovereignty of God over the whole world, the reign of Christ in the heart, and the expectation of a coming kingdom in and beyond time were all embedded in the term "kingdom of God," and that these themes were decisive in the way Christian theology and ethics provided — with differing accents in different periods — a spiritual and moral rudder for American civilization, from its founding through the industrial era.

Such themes have faded. Few speak of the kingdom of God that way today. If, for the sake of biography and narrative, or for reasons of liberation or political solidarity, we leave this symbol behind, we must ask what the organizing principles of our public theology will be in the twenty-first century. What will become the inner guidance system for this superpower in a postindustrial era?

Those who leave the legacy of the social gospel behind must be sure they have something better to put in its place. Many worse options, and few better ones, stand in the wings of history.

Christianity in New Formation: Reflections of a White Christian on the Death of Dr. Martin Luther King Jr.

The pastor from Montgomery, the doctor of the church, the prophet of peace with justice, the lover of the unlovely, is dead. As his life was dramatized on one side by care for a tired Rosa Parks and on the other by concern for garbage collectors, the tragedy of his death has been accented by assassinations of political advocates for those who had no advocate. But unlike the loss of the Kennedys, the death of a servant to those who served is a tragedy not only for the black man, not only for poor people, not only for the oppressed of all races, not only for a party, and not only for the nation; his death is a tragedy that strikes to the very foundations of Western culture. His death lays bare the incapacity of the major forms of religious, ideological, and ethical loyalty that are at the very center of modern social, personal, political, and cultural life to endure direct challenges to moral and economic distinctions based on race and class and caste.

We have seen that there is no stride toward freedom without agitation; no progress without struggle; no advance without confrontation; no concession without demand. Yet the society of freedom has destroyed the agitator, the civilization of progress has capped the struggle, the "advanced peoples" have avoided confrontation, and the culture of compromise has denied the demand. Modern culture has been laid open before our eyes. It is a time of revelation!

Exegesis of an Event

It is a time of revelation in that the utter ugliness of a brutal act forces us to a deeper understanding of man, his God, his society, and his relations with man. The assassination of no other man in the world would disrupt the continuity of our conception of these matters, stop the souls and grip the hearts of men like the death of this man. The assassination of no other man, even of political heroes like the Kennedys or Medger Evers, would automatically invite comparisons with the one, who, after the plagues, and the Passover, led the people out of slavery to free Israel; and with the one who, after the march to the city while the people shouted "Hosanna!" faced the crucifixion to free also the gentile for the new Israel. What has been occurring in the civil rights movement in this country, with its links to people of other lands, is more than a struggle for rights and privileges. Man and society are laid bare in a new way and the present divine intolerance of covert inhumanity is as significant as the divine intolerance of overt slavery of previous ages. No one may any more suggest in jest or rage that such things are the work of bleeding-hearts and do-gooders and rabble-rousers. These are now questions of how and where God reveals himself to man in this time. And these are now questions as to how man responds to divine revelation occurring, as it always has, not in earthquakes and lightning, nor psychic messages, but in the midst of human lives, in fundamental demands for justice, righteousness, love, and compassion. We are in the time of a new religious formation with radical social reform as its empirical concretion. King knew that what causes fundamental shifts in society and political economics is finally the question of legitimacy. The fact of oppression and alienation does not cause revolution. Whoever has tried to organize the oppressed and the alienated and whoever has read the history of oppression knows that. But who provides an ultimate legitimation for organizational and integrating action, a moral purpose, a genuine sense of righteousness, he engenders the possibility of serious social, economic, and political shift.

It is a time of revelation in that the depths of the religious tradition are neither abandoned nor distorted, but reclaimed in a fresh way. Traditional interpretations of the "principalities and powers" are replaced by intellectually and existentially compelling analysis of the overwhelming weight of "astronomical intimidation" upon the few who almost see the vision of freedom and justice. The radical, fantastic, apocalyptic language of the New Testament is not dismissed as first-century ravings, nor spiritualized to another realm, but recognized as the disturbingly revolutionary rhetoric of poor people. Resurrection city is established as an appropriate existential interpretation of the post-crucifixion event, an exegesis that proves the zombie theories of the conservatives and the demythologized phenomenological theories of the modern scribes vacuous and dry as dust. Atonement is understood as imply-

Interpreting the Tradition of Public Theology

ing preference for the oppressed as a moral and practical way of establishing some degree of justice for centuries of injustice. The social exegesis of the tradition, in short, allows us not only to see dimensions of what the major religious traditions of the West mean, but also what they meant.

It is a time of revelation, for multiple sources of meaning are caught up in a vision of what it means to be religious in the twentieth century. Reaching beyond the confines of the West, Dr. King wedded the strengths of the Judeo-Christian tradition with the contemporary flower of Eastern philosophy through Gandhi in a way that both broadens our perspectives and forbids our getting lost in mysticism. Using motifs of social Christianity from the black church and black culture, from the "social gospel" and the "realists," from the "neo-orthodox" and the "liberals," he selectively synthesized a new social gospel around the catalytic force of his deep southern piety. He was the first major spokesman to link Vietnam to domestic racism and violence as a fundamental religious and moral problem. He became the only man in America who preached to the throngs in Washington and made the nation confront what it means to feed the multitudes. He became the only man of our age who wrote a letter from a Birmingham jail in a reply to "Pauline" Christians that is comparable to one of the letters of Paul. He became the only voice that could mobilize ten thousand bishops, rabbis, priests, ministers, and nonbelievers to lay their lives on the line for righteousness' sake at a moment's notice and without demagoguery. He divided and united in new ways.

It is a time of revelation in that an ethic of militant demand for love and justice is surging through the decisive groups of society, dominated by and made militant by a hope. Martin Luther King, as much as anyone, engendered that hope, cultivated that love, and nurtured that justice. He articulated a vision of a brotherly world. His life bore a promise, a declaration toward the future, an announcement of a coming reality that does not yet exist. His hope awakened the sleeping hope of millions — and especially with those who had least stake in the present, the black, the poor, the students, and the clergy. Their hopes avoided the magnificent monstrosities of Sisyphus and of Prometheus, of the Underground Man and Faust, and instead fastened on the vision of a humanized society of love and justice. He occasioned a moment of hope for many which in turn lit the fuse and broke the log jam, although he refused to become the explosion or the turbulent flood of freed human timber. He exposed divisions of injustice and indifference so deeply hidden and subtly masked that no one knew their depths.

Commentary

Contemporary white theologians and churchmen, for all our efforts to catch every nuance of novelty, did not fully see his significance. We were blinded by our racism and our economic advantages. We kept talking of prejudice and demonstrations, of discrimination and civil disorder, of Jim Crow and civil rights. And he was telling us about sin and salvation, about chaos and community, about justice and redemption. We spoke of urban strife. He told us that the Lord has a controversy with his people. We worried about those we pitied. He spoke of the soul of a nation in sin. We saw modern society in a situation of stress. He saw it to be founded on a metaphysical disease of racism and violence and economic self-interest. We saw problems to be solved. He saw systemic death to be overcome. Our diagnosis was much milder than his. We wrung our hands. He acted in faith.

In this land we have not seen the smokestacks of Dachau or the death camps of Siberia or the systematic assassination and terrorism of leadership by or of the revolutionary infrastructure. But we have seen our most creative, most dedicated, most imaginative representatives of that which is potentially good struck down by the savagery of daemonic spirits borne in the very structure of our institutions. Our failure to wrestle with these daemonic and savage spirits, our failure to subdue them, our failure to recognize how far they range, and our failure to acknowledge how deep they penetrate is evidence of our own possession by false spirits.

Thus more powerful than the guilt and the anguish that we must feel is the awareness of a new spirit being born in a just and righteous and deeply religious anger. It is an anger that this moment in history calls for, and that may provide the resources to exorcise our false spirit. It is an anger engendered by the unmasking of false gods in society and the false worship of the true God in the churches.

It is righteous and just and religious anger at a President and a Congress who consciously avoid reports of pending catastrophe.

It is a righteous and just and deeply religious anger at a culture that daily compounds its felony against the blacks and the poor at home and abroad. To deny this fact is an intellectual and moral dishonesty that cannot now be debated.

It is a righteous and just and deeply religious anger at a church and a ministry half full of passive, dependent people who perceive religion as the manicuring of their own psyche, who perceive trust as the forgoing of judgment, who perceive love as the absence of tension, who perceive honesty as true confessions.

Interpreting the Tradition of Public Theology

It is a righteous and just and deeply religious anger at those who claim that Martin Luther King got what he deserved because he always provoked violence; while they mean that, confronting in him the challenge to their own racism, they felt provoked and violent.

It is a righteous anger at those who claimed that they still judge people strictly according to ability and skills not according to race; but who derive psychic and physical sustenance from a society that systematically deprives great numbers of people of access to skills.

A righteous anger at the false prophets who warn "prophetically" of black racism or socialism like those who warned of Zionism and Bolshevism during the rise of Hitler.

A righteous anger at the cheap prophets who love the status of angry young men and live by the drift of slogans.

Yet the spirit of righteous anger that we feel is ambiguous. It is evoked by the assassination of a man who in the face of the greatest provocation still tried to love. The only justification for the spirit of righteous anger is the fact that once possessed by it we may begin to live and to perceive in a new way at several levels and thereby get beyond or at least use our anger.

The First Level of Response

The first step beyond simmering with immobilizing and self-destructive anger is the awareness that we must *do* something. But what shall we do? Shall we mourn? We must mourn. But mourn first for ourselves. We have been dead — we "believers" who claim to be called to discern God's will and did not see it until God grabbed us by the back of the neck and shouted "Look!" We have been dead — we who claim to be men of "good will" and did not see the evil that we did until God forced us in tragedy to open our eyes and see. We must mourn first for the death in which we have been living. Then shall we be free to mourn God's prophets.

What shall we do? Shall we send money? Yes, we are the rich camels who cannot get through the eye of a needle. Synagogues, churches, organizations, and conferences that can and do support the cause that is King's legacy need our help. But we must also move beyond the ordinary forms and channels of charity. We must send our money also to those groups and candidates that agitate and lobby for, promise and deliver, an increase of taxes and a reallocation of public funds to human priorities. Such impersonal forms of love are the demands of charity today.

Christianity in New Formation

What shall we do? Shall we demonstrate? Yes, when necessary. But not to display righteousness. Nor shall we demonstrate at every moment or on every issue. But there are times when we can do no other than stand with those who are called out to transform life toward justice and love. There are times when we must walk with those who have caught the vision of the promised land. There are seasons when we must strategically testify with those who have seen the depths of good and evil in our souls and in our institutions. There are situations when we must support those who cry in the wilderness for the recognition of the promise and pathos of life. There are strategic moments when only a dramatic action can focus the attention of a nation, a people, a culture, or a religion on its own needs. In those times and in those seasons, we must witness with our bodies as well as our words.

What shall we do? Shall we act? Yes, we cannot afford not to. But we cannot act out of context. We must act in concert. Can we ourselves find a black man a home? Yes, and that is good. But we must also join Fair Housing. For it finds a thousand homes and lobbies for ten thousand more. Can we find a poor man a job? Yes, and that is good. But also join those groups that demand guaranteed income or those that put the pressure on labor and management for altered employment policies and wage scales. Can you help a minority person get to college? Yes, and that is good. But also join the Inter-racial Council, the Social Action Committee, the Outreach Commission, Citizens for Better Public Schools. For they are demanding a system that prepares hundreds to participate in producing creative lives. Can you give a hungry woman bread and her children milk? Yes, and that is good. But also support Mothers for Adequate Welfare who raise questions of human rights to human dignity without paternalism. We must act in personal and responsive ways. But we must also work for structures of justice in a responsive and responsible society. Therefore, we must find a group. Find the SCLC; find the Resistance; find the ADA; find ACLU; find SNCC; find the NAACP; find, and if they are not in existence, found political parties and voluntary associations where justice is proleptically present. Find and found these to lead, and to be led; to heal, and to be healed; and thus in our help are we helped. Find or found some center that organizes our grief and our righteous anger and purges them of bitterness. Find some network of trust that builds the infrastructure of new relationships. Become a part of a set of communications, actions, links, by which we get beyond our momentary grief and by which we are sustained beyond the whims of our emotion. The covenants are being formed. The coalitions are operating. They are the outward and visible symbols of an inward and spiritual grace. And if we would act, we must join them. There is no other way that is not trivial.

Interpreting the Tradition of Public Theology

The Second-Level Response

But a deeper second level of response is needed for the religious reconstruction in both its intellectual and emotive dimensions that provides a framework to sustain the new direction. And, in the person, cause, and legacy of Dr. King is a new Christianity, linked on one side with a new Judaism and on the other with a new humanism that transcends Christianity of the capitalist West, the Judaism of ethnic nationalism, the ritualized humanism of Marxist countries. It is not a sect or a denomination, a cult or a church, a party or a doctrine. It is a new spirit taking shape as a movement, linking a new conception of a just order and a new focus for personal identity. This new spirit was anticipated in the abolitionists and the Andover theologians, in the social gospel and in the religious socialists. There are touches of it in the Chicago liberals and strong lodes in the New York realists, as well as in many Jewish and secular humanist groups. And, most important, it has been constitutive in the black church, often under the mantle of conservative theological leanings. What is new is that these anticipations have now moved to the center of theological focus, forcing new sets of categories that cut across old ideological divisions and new emotive sensitivities to persons and groups, words and styles.

Historical breaks and cultural shifts in society or religion are seldom dramatic or certain. Troeltsch and Tillich knew a generation ago that it was the end of the Protestant era. And those who participated in the new formation know that they are no longer Protestants in the ordinary meaning of that term. They now see much of neo-orthodoxy and existentialist theology as well as sentimental liberalism as both part of the death throes of Protestantism and the prologue to the new era. For to a large degree Protestantism, left and right, is pathological and incapable of recognizing its own pathology. Have we not seen fascism and racism rise again and again in Protestant countries on all continents? Other religions and peoples are not exempt from these pathologies; but Protestantism has built into it a self-critical principle that demands its own dismissal if it is found to be no longer valid. Nor is Catholicism exempt from these pathologies; for it has, far too long, assumed a defensive and reactionary posture as a bastion against the modern world. It has propped itself up by leaning against Protestantism and other modernisms. Now, when the prop falls, the bastion also collapses. The collective rubble is mixed up on the ground, seeking a foundation and architecture.

But we have been confused in the twentieth century and could not recognize the emerging marks of new formation. Our racism tempted us,

Christianity in New Formation

our self-interest seduced us, and our conceptions of faith gave birth to new paganisms. Christian faith has been so badly represented that if it were necessary to believe it, as frequently held, men of integrity would have no choice but to speak of the death of God, the end of Christendom and secular Christianity, for the sake of justice, righteousness, love, and peace. Hence our theologians have been confused.

God has not died. The Christocentric Christianity Protestantism has died.

Metaphysics has not died, although Plato has. Modern man is consumed by a metaphysical disease that has prevented us from coming to grips with the realities of the world beyond our own skin or class.

Christendom has not died; only its nationalistic and ethnocentric clothing has been torn to shreds.

It is not, as widely suggested, even the post-Constantinian period. That is a specific Protestant (and post–Vatican II Catholic) way of laying the blame on the Catholic tradition for all religious ills in a personalistic protest against social Christianity. It is the notion that by restitution of some pure pre-Constantinian spirituality we can reform the church. It is one of the most reactionary of radical views.

What has died, in short, in the birth of the new formation and in the contemporary theological preoccupation with death, is our Christocentric Protestantism and its correlates: cultural Catholicism, ethnic Judaism, and class humanism.

These are what is dead. We smell the stench in the Christianity or humanism preached in many pulpits. We feel the social disease that has a theological foundation. And we die the more we misidentify the deceased or claim nothing has died.

The pathology of Protestantism from which the new formation now departs is manifold: First, it is built on a principle of protest against humanity, for it theologically sees an infinite qualitative distinction between God and man. With a zero-sum concept of potential goodness, Protestantism is fundamentally negative in its evaluation of the possibilities of man, especially in rational, political, and erotic activities. It protests human enterprise. Such an orientation is intended to avoid idolatry and pretention; but it protests also, therefore, the human structures of civilization and sees their ultimate destiny as more one of judgment than fulfillment. The synergistic progressive Christianity of the new formation sees in man and in man's institutions the possibility, through transformation, of fulfillment as well as the necessity of judgment.

Interpreting the Tradition of Public Theology

Second, Protestantism has ever justified its reformation by an appeal to the themes of, and often a latent desire for, restitution. It has thus been in essence backward looking and oriented toward recovery. Such reactionary motifs appear not only in the biblicism and bibliolatry of Protestant piety, but also in the Protestant hagiography of Luther, Calvin, and Wesley and the incapacity of Protestantism since Münzer to see the importance of revolutionary movements that speak of transformation of values which are the promise of the future.

Third, Protestantism is based on a Christocentric rather than a Christological theology. Christocentric motifs have become so established in a metaphysic of absolute individuality that it does not seem capable of extricating itself from personalistic concerns even long enough to build institutions to protect persons against rape by an industrial, atomized, impersonal society. It has successfully disjoined the person from his social political responsibilities and abandoned the community to pragmatic struggles for power. It produces intramural Christological debates that lead in a variety of ways to "sweet Jesus" idolatry, to individualized crisis decision-making, to liberal doctrines of individual character formation, to hidden correlations between God and self, to concepts of the election of the self out of the community, to the deification of the ego in religions of self-fulfillment, to psychiatric existentialism as the new dogma, or to personal idealism as one of the characteristic modern philosophies of the church. Such doctrines have at times freed the self from conventions of social practice to leap ahead to citizenship in the kingdom of God. But except in the black churches and certain radical semi-Calvinistic and Anabaptist groups, they have not bound the self to responsibility for and to the neighbor or the kingdom of God.

Fourth, when there is a social dimension, Protestant theorists for generations have seen the institutions of the ancient Teutonic tribes as the authentic model of community and koinonia, thereby sanctifying white tribalism by the baptism of biblical text and tradition. White racism did not have its origins among illiterate Klansmen and rednecks. The ravings of political lunatics and fanaticized assassins can be traced to the very "respectable" and subtle distinctions of "scholars" in cloister, college, seminary, and pulpit from whence they have become embedded in the very structure of the culture.

And, finally, Protestantism is warped by a premature eschatology. It preaches an ethic of interpersonal love and reconciliation, goals of all Christian ethics, as immediate means to solve recalcitrant structural problems. It thereby fails to recognize that justice and mutuality of power are the impersonal forms of love necessary for significant human interaction.

The Protestantism represented by these motifs is the dominant contemporary religion of the West, and is found in large doses in Catholicism, Judaism, and humanism. It is functionally, if not doctrinally, racist and elitist. Indeed, it has been a fundamental impetus to the development of modernity. But it has now proven itself incapable of organizing, guiding, and sustaining our personal, family, and intellectual lives, our human relationships, our society, or our culture into deep and responsible channels.

Many students of this generation knew something was out of joint. They sensed the dynamics of the situation and saw the religious, intellectual, and emotive vacuum. They grasped part of it but often were so superficial that they continually confused their own subjective de-provincialization with an objective revolution. Thus they frequently were dismissed as irrelevant or wrong. They were wrong in a way. Revolutionary jargon is cheap on the college campus today, yet it is not a time of revolution in the ordinary sense. The romantic visions of a coup d'état against the establishment or of escalating the riots into armed rebellions as a first step to full overthrow of the establishment is ridiculous. Such attempts, given the structure of our semi-democratic order, are both unnecessary and necessarily abortive. They are the opiate of the alienated. But if they mean by the word *revolution* a radical reform of society, coupled with a new conceptual reformulation and undergirded by a fundamental definition of what is ultimately valuable and powerful, that is a reality. That is the new formation. And that is more profound.

Implications

What, then, is the character of this new formation into which post-Protestants are precipitated by the death of Martin Luther King that has shaken us to our roots?

Is personal experience important in this new religion? Yes, absolutely crucial. But only when it is linked to the objective reality of forging a new social fabric that holds personal values and interpersonal relationships as central ingredients.

Is piety important? Yes, and we will no longer be embarrassed by it and no longer slander it. But neither will we wallow in it. It is useful to express and celebrate, in spontaneous or ordered reverence, the truth that has to be said, often.

Are emotions and feelings important? Yes, powerful and fundamental to our lives. Who can deny it? But emotions and feelings are not the point.

Interpreting the Tradition of Public Theology

They betray as often as they assure, unless they are directed at some critical and strategic level to transform life for the weak brother and not for the self. And they distort and delude as often as they intuit, unless they are kept faithful by the rigors of evidence and reason.

Is it a new social gospel? Yes, not because it tries in a new way to apply the gospel to social problems, but because it tries to articulate the good news of ultimate meaning in a Christian social philosophy to succeed the organic hierarchy and the individuated plurality that typified Catholicism and Protestantism respectively.

Is the new formation a product of the social economic and political changes of our times? Yes, but it is more than these forces analytically described. The new formation is the finding of a center of meaning and an ultimate legitimation at the center of these interacting forces. It involves a personal and social conversion to the fact that these forces are derived from that which is ultimately powerful and ultimately worthy in the universe. It is the acknowledgment that these forces are of God and not against God. And until that theological point, by whatever name, is made, the legacy of religion is resistance, reaction, and delay while bitterness, premature violence, and contempt are the temptation of those called out to the new movement. Today's social, economic, and political revolution toward racial and economic justice is, in its depth, nothing else but the shape of divine will, its judgment and mercy, its wrath and its promise. Whoever is called to this is part of the church, which has often left the churches.

And what of those who do not see it thus? Are they not of another faith? If they see this movement as of the devil, they either falsely worship the same God or they in fact worship another God, one disconnected from that which moves men's souls and determines the destinies of nations and empires. The new formation was neither in King's hands nor in that of his heirs primarily a plunge into secularity in an attempt to purge modernity of religion. Rather, it is a finding of new depths that demand new and radical construction of a more human commonwealth. The God of the new formation is one who evokes a capacity to stand in the midst of relativity, of change, of movement, of insecurity, and of dissensus. It is intolerant only of the incapacity to tolerate the dynamism of a living God.

In this new formation, what is to be our relationship with those called Protestants? What is the relationship between those of us who, out of a Protestant heritage, now feel called to a new formation and those who do not? What is our relationship to the churches and to those persons who are still Reformers, Christocentric, and Protestant? Did Judaism die when Christianity was born? No. Judaism reformed itself and remained in God's eternal covenant. During centuries of persecution, Jews remained faithful and often at the forefront of prophetic movements. Did Catholicism die when Protestantism was born? And did God forsake the Catholics then? By no means, and his people are flooding to the "underground church" as it breaks into the open — a manifestation of the latent possibility for the new formation within Catholic styles of life. Did Anglicanism die when first Separatism, and then Wesleyanism emerged in Britain and on the frontiers of America? It did not. And the Lord did not forsake his people. And did the need for religion and depth of meaning die under the impact of the intentional secularization of Eastern Europe and the accidental secularism of the Western industrial megalopolis? No, only the magical self-interest of elite classes wrapped in sanctity collapsed and the people have been led to spiritual drift.

Will modern Protestantism die? No, it will live on in the hearts and loyalties and institutions of men, and it may even reform itself after it gets over the shock of not being at the center of religious reality, as did the great traditions before it. Yet, without recognition of disjunction, the reform of the old may never occur. Nor need we now fight the Thirty or Hundred Years' War over it. Instead we must try to construct around three centers: symbols, organization, and a righteous cause.

People live by clusters of images and symbols. Images filter experience and allow us to appropriate that experience. Images give perspective and either distort or clarify. And symbols organize our images in meaningful patterns. People justify their interests by symbols. People mask their motives by symbols. People invest their money, itself a symbol of value, in that which symbolizes what they value highest. People die for symbols.

But what symbols will you choose? That is the key to the future. For the days of prophecy, from the moral passion of the abolitionists through the "social gospel" of Walter Rauschenbusch and the early days of the labor movement to the prophetic climax in the nonviolent direct action of Martin Luther King, are over. The legacy of that prophecy can degenerate into crude apocalyptic and thereby dissipate its energy; or it can weld itself into a new covenant.

The symbols these prophets used point toward a new covenant, for they told it like it is. They said things that grasp and articulate, capture and evoke, plumb and point to, free and command, the loyalties of man. True symbols gather up the several levels of existence, the psychological, political, economic, and conceptual, into a new unity of purpose. Truth is found in those symbols that touch the centers of death and life, hope and despair, meaning and purpose, emptiness and fullness, confrontation and reconciliation. And in the death of Dr. King, these matters have been touched in a particular way; the symbols connect persons with institutions, experience with the intellect, subject with the object, the private need with the objective condition, hope with actual possibility. Such symbols are religious; they point to God, the ultimate integrating center of worth and power.

The symbols that the new formation uses must thus be true. But they must also be connected. Herein does Christianity of the new formation differ from philosophy, education, and even from Protestant preoccupation with "the Word." For genuine religious symbols are not only true, or only true "for me in my depths"; they also must evoke participation in new processes of group formation. Organization is a center for the new formation. The locus of the new formation is not the lectern, nor the pulpit, nor the altar. It is the committee room. People are called by religious symbols, not only to truth and wisdom and prayer, but into a movement of world-historical scope and consequence. Symbols change nothing by being spoken. Only when engaged in or expressive of the mechanisms and specifics of social, economic, cultural, and personal systems do symbols become effective in any respect. Symbols of truth are today sufficiently disengaged that "the Word" spoken outside of a social, economic, and personal matrix drifts into nothing. It cannot be heard even by listeners. As King recognized, "the Word," properly understood, derives part of its power from an integral relationship to a process of new community formation. It is the organizing moral, emotive, and intellectual link between speaking and acting, between agitation, conversion, and organization, founded on what is ultimately powerful and worthy of loyalty.

The symbols of the new formation are true and connected. They are also governed by justice, love, and hope. Every age has accented its own theological virtues. Paul praised faith, hope, and love; the medieval church celebrated charity, obedience, and purity; the Reformation radicalized faith and linked it with obedience and work. The modern secular world endorses efficiency, progress, and order. In continuity with Martin Luther King, as was mentioned above, the new formation is fundamentally motivated by an active hope for a loving and just society. Justice implies restructuring of society to ensure equity of resources, opportunity, and power. Love entails a capacity to relate to indifferent and hateful people and situations openly and without indifference or hate. And, in a day of rising expectations, hope is the motivating promise of real possibilities that are not yet realities.

The New Formation and the Church

And *where* is this new formation happening? Sometimes in the ordinary structures of the church. But often the ordinary structures serve as merely the base from which operations begin. The new formation is, for the most part, taking place just above and just below the present patterns of parish and denomination. It is happening in the ecumenical or interfaith action and study groups just *below* the parish or the denomination. And it happens just *above* the parish or the denomination in the new councils, in the new associations, in the new ecumenical movements that are developing there. It is above and below the present centers that the new formation is taking institutional shape at the local level or at the national level. Our organizations, our church institutions, are fat in the middle. What is now happening is that below and above those centers, parish or denominational, there is a new concentration of spiritual activity, sometimes dwelling in, sometimes living off, and sometimes working against the fat in the middle. If a local church cannot move, then the council of churches, or some spinoff groups, even "secular" groups, may raise the fundamental question of ultimate human loyalty that cuts across the churches. If a denomination cannot participate in the new formation, the "united" churches, or the council of denominations, or some churches in it may. The SCLC and the National Council of Churches, the National Council of Christians and Jews, and Clergy and Laymen United are nationwide prototypes of the locus of the church today. In these cases, the church has spilled over the boundaries of the churches.

Does this mean that we too are to leave the churches? By no means. There is money, time, talent, machinery, space, and the residues of unused commitment that must be appropriated and restructured. The churches are filled with both needers and doers, those who on the one hand are spiritually, psychologically, sociologically, or intellectually incapacitated, and those who on the other hand have been given the foundations of common grace. This division intersects with the question of whether the real focus of the church's concern is within itself or beyond itself, in the world. We cannot leave the churches, but the true functions of the church of the new formation cannot be confined to or essentially defined as preaching of the Word and performing the sacraments. Instead, a fourfold formula must be used: Where there are those with interior needs, there must be a cure of souls. Where there are those with exterior needs, there must be advocacy for those who have no advocate. Where there are doers inside the church, there must be the upbuilding of the organization in service, especially above and below the present centers of activity. And where there are doers focused outside the church, there must be transformation of the sociopolitical order by the creation of a social fabric of trust and righteousness. All are the proper functions of the church, and where these are done, there is the church of the new formation.

Does all this mean that we merely become participants in the contemporary critical theology that exposes the nakedness of ordinary Protestant, Catholic, and Jewish piety? No, we have no more time for that. Though we are still part of the critical period, we must begin to think in a post-critical fashion. We are, today, expert critics. We offer critiques of pure and practical reason as the essence of wisdom. We can tear apart another person's defenses. We can rip his best ideas to shreds. We can find the chinks in the armor of society and expose its vulnerability. We can cynicize and satirize at all levels of thought. We critically analyze the scriptures. Our whole education is critically oriented. Nor must we ever abandon this critical capacity, for to do so would cause us to lapse into magic and mindless piety. The religion of the new formation is on the other side of criticism and confrontation. Hegel and Kant, Nietzsche and Feuerbach, Marx and Freud, Darwin and Durkheim, Wittgenstein and Whitehead, Sartre and Heidegger are, in varying degrees, right. Not to pass through them intellectually or emotionally is evidence of insensitivity or dishonesty in the modern world. But on the other side of them is still the demand to say something about truth and life and meaning. Out of the rubble of Protestant culture are being selected those stones that can be tested for their ability to stand the stress of the new formation. The stone rejected is the cornerstone. We must now enter a post-critical period and begin to construct. We must begin to put back together. We must begin to take the pieces that we have sorted out and reorganize them around a new center.

To pastors, to teachers, to laymen, the new formation demands that they first look at the matters that evoke the passions of the people when they are quite certain. What is that which moves them? What is it that brings inarticulate people to their feet? What is it that evokes the passions of the cool? What is it that evokes justifying rationality from those who do not ordinarily reason and bother to justify? What is it that people discuss with their closest friends when they get beyond their personal cares? What, in short, is the movement of the spirits? Look and see and discern the signs of the times and see where they may be leading us. It is among these spirits that we must seek and discern.

And how shall we seek? What will be our key? Are we sociologists? No. Are we psychologists? No. Are we political scientists? No. To pretend to be so makes us the laughingstock of the professionals. But what are we? We are preachers and teachers and laymen, who preach and teach and try to live by the best understanding of what is, in reality, the ultimate power and center of worth in the universe. It is that by which we discern the movement of the spirits in this world. Do we then preach on matters that affect society? Do we preach on matters that pertain to the psyche? Do we preach and teach on those things that directly affect politics? Without question, and to fail so to do is to deny the humanity implicit in our ultimate concern. For we have a kind of power, by virtue of our calling, to exorcise the false powers that distort humanity. It is the power to discern prophecy in an age when we must demand a shift from the priesthood of all believers to the prophethood of all believers. For we have the power to create and use and organize and relate those understandings by symbols, organization, and a passion for justice, love, and hope to the immediacy of life.

The death of a black pastor who bore the conscience of the West has forced us to see that what was on the edges before is now in the middle. What was peripheral is now in the center. What was an implication is now an assumption. What was presented as a deduction from the gospel is now, for this time, the definition of the gospel. It means a new definition of our calling, a new conception of the church, and a new understanding of the God we worship. It means that we abandon the white tribal God with all the attributes of affluent society whom we have learned to love and, indeed, whom we have created. It means that we begin to ask anew about the God that we in fact worship, whatever our mental prayer wheels. It means that we turn to worship the God of all men, the God of truth and justice and righteousness. It means that the political, social, and economic pathologies of our day are not political, social, and economic pathologies with no roots; but they are rooted in theological pathologies. As every culture has at its core a set of ultimate presuppositions of what is true, worthy, and powerful, so does modern culture. The core of our culture has been wrong. But the movement that Martin Luther King represented was not only against, it was for. The modern, this-worldly communion of saints is called to a new formation in the name of God.

There is danger in this view. The quest for righteousness ever walks the border of self-righteousness. The audacity of calling a movement prophetic, its foundation divine, and a man saintly, may turn to fanaticism. And radicalism that tries to cut to the root of human loyalty may ruthlessly uproot the fundamental character of man. But one can test the spirits by asking whether or not the view engenders compassion for those who are the victims of injustice, openness even to those who are rigid, and participation in the formation of new social fabrics of trust and righteousness.

Interpreting the Tradition of Public Theology

King and the New Formation in Wider Perspective

The selection of the life and death of King as one of the crucial paradigmatic events of modern revelation and the shift from unintended but very real racial and economic elitism of Protestantism and its correlates to a new formation must be seen in wider perspective. Why should other centers of the quest for reform not be taken as normative? Why not choose the development of secularized neo-mysticism as celebrated by Dr. Leary and his fellow gurus, East and West? Why not identify the student upheavals as the first fruits of a new order, as has Herbert Marcuse? Why not recognize the cultic celebration of Black by Carmichael, Brown, Malcolm X, or even Frantz Fanon as a fundamental new formation among an oppressed people? One could also see the religious revolutionism of Mao as decisive for the destiny of man. All of these are evidence of the exhaustion of Christianity as ordinarily understood. And each represents an attempt to find a thought and action nexus that reveals the interior logic of the transformations of the twentieth and twenty-first centuries.

The least significant of the modern religious movements is hippy mysticism, the radicalization of spiritualized Protestant pietism. Our civil policy must protect the hippies from official and unofficial harassment. But theologically they must come under the same scrutiny as any quasi-religious movement. The egocentric, idealistic mysticism of a middle-class love ethic and nostalgia for nature, which has in suburbia also often dropped out of serious confrontation with the issues of urban society, has been taken to its psychic and cosmic limits. It is protest by reduction to absurdity. It reduces tension by processes of psychological and chemical negation, often using sound and sight and sex as a means to assault the senses and undermine intellectual and institutional life. What considerable creativity there is in the movement is found in the fact that it intentionally forces the recapturing of dedifferentiated and holistic existence; but when developed into a social philosophy or style of life, it becomes a mere appendage to modern urban life, not a challenge to its injustice. Further, it ultimately destroys selfhood and its capacity for primordial experience of ultimate cosmic presence the movement intended to produce. It is a spiritualistic revolt within Protestant society, not a revolution of it.

Much more serious are the varieties of revolutionary development that are close parallels to and sometimes the mask or form of the new formation. These do not destroy all categories, group processes, and patterned forms of sensation and expression that intervene between the self and reality. They replace them. But they replace them in different ways.

The student generation, feeling the existential poverty of both traditional religiosity and the contemporary philosophies of existentialism and positivism, are lusting for a new ideology that opens the door to meaningful action. In this group there are fantastic resources of personnel, capacity, energy, and leadership. And the university is a chief center for recruitment and coming to human and social consciousness (traditionally called evangelism and conversion). But, in the long run, the new formation cannot be built on this base. Student constituencies are too transient; there is no long-term power base, and the sensitivities of student generations evaporate too quickly. Students are too preoccupied with ideological analysis unconnected to institutional structures and power relations even (or, often today, precisely) where they are ideological about institutional and power structures. When coeds and accountants' sons speak glibly of revolution, there is an overwhelming sense of illusion. And the student protest is incapable of overcoming, in its present form, the new elitism of esoteric language and leadership in its own protest. It is the highest, closest, and perhaps most transitional form of secularized Protestantism; but it is not yet integral to the new formation.

The new religion of Black is another domestic variety of revolutionism that bears fundamental redefinitions of what is ultimately worthy. It is a necessary answer to psychological needs for newfound identity and beauty that also, by counter-assertion, helps undermine the dogmatic white gods of modern culture. Indeed, if it is a question of choice, black gods are superior; for they represent the emerging struggle for justice on the side of oppressed peoples rather than retention of position by the privileged. But, in the long run, as King recognized, no tribal loyalties or racial deities are capable of sustaining the fundamental cultural symbols or the political coalitions of those called out to form a new humanity large enough for modern society. Black gods are only necessary weapons to destroy white gods that have been used as weapons of suppression. And gods that are mere tools are no gods.

The experiment of permanent revolutionism of Mao is the most serious secularized contemporary religion, for it is by far the largest in concept and constituency. It is at once the most analogous and the most distant parallel to the new formation. It is the nearest revolutionary analogue and ally in that Mao has become a symbol for the creation of an economic democracy, the attempt to overcome the weight of bureaucratized existence by continual humanizing revolution, and the symbolic restructuring of "a new law of the gospels." The importance of the "thoughts of chairman Mao" upon which "People's China" meditates day and night is found in a fundamental transvaluation of values that are connected and governed by justice and love. As yet,

Interpreting the Tradition of Public Theology

however, Maoism has not found how to create economic democracy without sacrificing political democracy. But neither has anyone else. And Maoism has not been able to develop permanent revolution without fundamentalist apocalypticism and the perennial expectation of a far-too-literal Armageddon. Nevertheless, both the demand for economic democracy and the militant opposition to "imperialistic" forces are, like Black Power, necessary psychological, political, military, economic, and sociological correctives to white Protestant power.

But the new formation of which Dr. King is paradigmatic must keep one eye on a larger vision: a broader human community than any nation, a deeper future than tomorrow's conflict, a higher conceptuality than necessary tactics and counter-positions. For King asked not only the questions of particular human groups; he asked what it meant to be a part of the community of man. He demanded not only concrete plans for today and tomorrow; he asked about the ends of existence. He not only became a brilliant tactician in direct confrontation; he sought reconciliation beyond difference and without compromise. He asked the ultimate questions of the social revolutions of the twentieth century and found grounds for thought and action in the intersection of transcendent purpose and immanent event.

Are we sure of this indication and discernment of prophecy? We have no certainty. It is only possible to speak in tribute to a great Christian martyr and out of risk and hope. But the possibility of the resurrection after the assassination of a Christological figure who saw from the mountaintop a vision of the promised land is worth the risk. Whether it will be fulfilled depends on the providence of God and upon the responsiveness of his people to a new witness and willingness to be drawn into the vortex of God's activity. If what is here said is not true, the vision and the energy, the organization and the will, will dissipate. If what has been discerned is true prophecy, it will consolidate our goals and energy and link them with the common faith of those before and after who have also participated in the quest for justice and truth, love and peace in the name of God.

What Tillich Meant to Me

By the time I started to study with Paul Tillich, I had been told for several years that *pietas* and *intellectus* could not join. In fact, I had tried to convince everyone, including myself, of this. My experience confirmed it. My father, a generous, liberal, loving pastor who fought both fundamentalism and rationalism in his attempt to hold faith and reason together, died of cancer shortly before I started college. That was absurd. It reduced my mother, a schoolteacher and a pillar of integrity and good sense, to pious blubbering. Family friends, mostly clergy families, visited regularly and spoke soothing nonsense. They could not explain the justice or injustice of life. I have always believed since then that pastoralia is often a studied way of obscuring the big questions. In any case, the evidence was clear: one could be either a believer or intellectually honest. One could not be both.

My undergraduate years at DePauw University reinforced this view. The best professors were ex-believers, still fighting in the classroom the phantoms of their former faith. Though they were not always persuasive, they were passionate teachers. Their conviction that one's beliefs mattered contrasted with the attitude of many of the sharper students, who were contemptuous of religion if not merely bored by it. My best friends were pre-med and pre-law students, and in our liveliest bull sessions we discussed what is today called sociobiology, politics (it was the McCarthy days), or religion. Though some very good students and natural leaders were in pre-theological studies, one never sensed that basic questions of meaning or justice drove their lives.

Such questions did fuel the philosophy of religion department, but a great conflict was under way in those years. The generation of elder personalists, pacifists, and Fabian socialists, students of Bowne and Brightman at Boston University, was nearing retirement. New professors from Yale and

Chicago — political Niebuhrians — were joining the faculty. The battles of the Titans confirmed my fear that faith and reason pressed in contrary directions. Nor could one simply observe the battle. The destiny of souls and of civilizations hung on the choice.

Two serious options faced those who wanted to go to graduate school. Believers were encouraged to go to Yale, where Wittgenstein, hermeneutics, and Barth were on the rise; scholars to Chicago, where Otto, sociology, and Whitehead were ascending. No friend who took either part of this advice, by the way, is in a theological field today.

But the tension between fideism and scientism didn't make sense to me; somehow, the whole cake had to be cut a different way. Either choice plunged us into a metaphysical, moral, epistemological, and religious relativism. When I later learned of the deconstructive postmodernists, dada in art, Nietzsche in philosophy, and emotivism in ethics, I experienced the shock of familiarity.

I spent a summer in the 1950s working on the railroad by day and reading Sartre and Marx by night. My small group of friends and I felt positively subversive. The next fall, I began writing a column for the school paper, "The Ax by Max." As the campus advocate of existentialist socialism, I used mostly the blunt end of the ax. I knew that there was some adolescent posturing in this, and I partly overcame it by helping found a somewhat gentler literary magazine.

That year I read a very impressive essay by Tillich, whom one professor presented as the most important new thinker. I was convinced. Hearing that Tillich was going to teach at Harvard, I applied there, telling them I wanted to work with Tillich. I was admitted. But a professor who approved of my politics and wanted to wean me away from such foggy idealism arranged for me to get a scholarship to a Dutch institute that trained people going into politics, international affairs, and diplomacy. He wanted me to learn more about what I was always talking about — and to become more diplomatic.

So I went to Holland. In this program everyone had to choose a special topic for independent research in addition to the usual courses in political economics, international trade, European military history, and that new science imported from America, "management." I selected Heidegger, and began to plow through esoteric German — which became only partly confused with the barroom Dutch I picked up in Amsterdam on the weekends. Halfway through my project, I became convinced that Heidegger had no grasp of either the basic problem of injustice (since he had no vision of normative order) or of the social issues that had attracted me to Marx. I suspected that Heidegger would lead philosophy eventually to ethical and social irrelevance —

something that Sartre discovered when he agreed to sign the Algerian Manifesto two years later. On Heidegger's or Sartre's grounds, there could be no call for such an abstract thing as "justice," certainly not in the name of "all that is holy."

About that time, the institute accepted several refugees from the Hungarian uprising of 1956. I was asked to tutor them in English, since many textbooks were American. In those tutorials, my Hungarian students, Marxists themselves, began to question my alleged socialism. They exposed to me the fact that I was, like most Marxists they had known at home, merely against something — something conveniently labeled conventional, bourgeois, capitalist, unhistorical, or idealistic thinking — but that neither I nor the communists had yet fully confronted the implications of trying to organize personal or social life on a Marxist basis. It can't be done, they said. That is why the way was open to Lenin and Stalin. Marxism was a powerful tool of destruction, but it had no resources for reconstruction. It was the turning of the Marxist critique against itself that had given them courage to face the tanks. Now that was existential! That was socialistic! That was religious in a nontheistic sense! It sounds almost *au courant* to recall this today.

I discussed these things with my research supervisor, who advised me to study with Paul Tillich in America. He told me Tillich had one of the most creative minds in the world dealing with the interaction of existentialism, Marxism, Heideggerian thought, and Christianity. This was my second nudge toward Tillich. I reactivated my application to Harvard, making sure they now understood that I came as an atheist. It was a major admission. When I told my girlfriend about this she said she didn't think she could marry me. How could she trust an atheist just back from Amsterdam? Besides, what kind of future is there for an atheist going to divinity school? At Harvard, of course, that was not a problem. They presumed that I was a Unitarian and assigned me to James Luther Adams. He became a father figure in several ways, healing my grief. But regarding the intellectual and faith issues, he guided me once more to Tillich.

To study with Tillich, I soon learned, did not mean small seminars or tutorials. It meant that one arrived early to get one of the five hundred seats. However, I had one advantage: having just returned from Europe, I had some sense of how Germanic people spoke English words. Unlike my peers, I could understand his pronunciation. That made me popular among the novices, for I could at least take fairly reliable notes.

In a larger sense, it was not misleading to try to encounter Tillich through the problem of language. It was one of his most important projects, as thinkers as divergent as Adams and Sallie McFague have stressed, to find a new vocabulary, a new mode of symbolic expression, a new metaphorical language to deal with the most fundamental questions. I was not surprised to read Hanna Tillich's recollection that it was Hitler's vocabulary and expressions that turned them against him before they had come to a full political awareness of what he was saying or a full theological assessment of its implications.

Tillich attended to words. He knew, with John, that the *logos* was at the beginning. But he wanted the word also incarnate, in the midst of vitality. He thus deliberately expressed himself in existential and nontraditional ways, as is well known. In his lectures he also used the vocabularies of psychology, cultural and philosophical history, sociology, anthropology, art, and politics. Yet the terms did not function the way they did in courses on these topics. One could almost hear the words' religious dimension — one could discern the Germanic construction in the English vocabulary and grammar.

At least, that is the way I heard him. But my new friends were hearing other things. Being from rather conservative Christian backgrounds — Southern Baptist, German Lutheran, Mennonite, Nazarene, and rigorously orthodox Presbyterian — they were suspicious of my fascination with Sartre, Marx, Heidegger, and Unitarianism. Besides, I smoked and drank beer like a Dutchman, and could not remember ever believing in miracles or virgin births or the literalist interpretation of scripture. But I shared their alliance against Barth, who sounded to them too much like what they were fleeing. To me he sounded like a brilliant celebrant of the split between faith and reason. That, I thought, was the crisis of the church, academia, and society.

What my companions heard in Tillich was what we might today call "liberation." Tillich was their path from pietistic or heteronymous Christian doctrine to a revealing encounter with Greek and German philosophy, with exotic realms of *cosmos, mythos, kairos,* and even *eros* — not to mention *Angst, Kunst, Socialismus,* and *das Unbedingt*. From the biblicistic worlds of their youth my friends found their way into the wider and deeper ranges of *Kultur*. He was, for the bright who were ready to hear, a classic *gymnasium* and German university education wrapped in pithy paragraphs.

My friends were often preoccupied with how the "unconditioned," as Tillich spoke of "it" (although all my friends knew he meant God), could "erupt" and reveal "itself" in the midst of life — beyond the church, outside of religion, without anything resembling worship and in terms one could not read in the Bible or hear from the pulpit. Tillich gave a kind of moral and spiritual permission to raise the question of Christ and culture, and not only

What Tillich Meant to Me

to live in Christ, against culture, although some returned to that stance later. He gave others the courage to face the Abyss, which they knew was there but which they dared not peer into, lest they fall into that bottomless pit. Some did, and lost faith. He enticed others to face the historicity and conditioned character of belief. Whether they knew it or not, he was making Nietzsche tolerable. For he had seen that no existing form, no empirical reality, no manifestation of personality or society is unambiguous in time, and that we, to be authentic, have to admit doubt and relativity into our consciousness — and then marshal the courage to be on the other side of doubt about being and worth. Tillich seemed to have faced the pit and the doubt and survived to tell of it. Indeed, he sometimes suggested that these were also the occasions for, if not quite the source of, creativity. Of course, some Tillichians seemed to enjoy wallowing on the brink of the Abyss and doubt, hoping for creativity yet never doing anything creative.

I never quite believed this part of Tillich's message — or what I believed about it was its obverse. What most fascinated me was that he could talk about these things. He could speak of emptiness and change and, by turning them over and inside out, find that the whirl had a structure and the void had a heart. That demonstrated to me that it was possible to develop categories that could comprehend and embrace these realities without being swallowed by them. It was enough to make one a Neoplatonist if not yet a believer.

Unlike my friends, I had already left the faith. I had decided that culture, in the forms of philosophy and social analysis, was, for all its problems, more reliable than Christ. I was persuaded that the bottomless pit was exactly how things were, although I didn't think it was just that it should be so. Thus, I believed it noble to fight the purposelessness of fate. I was further convinced that the historicity of everything was obvious and that we were doomed to an arbitrary voluntarism in which the only choices were risk and life or caution and death. Hence, I was much taken also by Tillich's teacher, Ernst Troeltsch, as well as by Tillich's friend and translator, James Luther Adams, both of whom also wrestled with questions that have fascinated me for a third of a century.

Also striking to me about Tillich was that he saw these things as ambiguous. He taught that these views of life, as well as religious doctrines, scientific theories, and works of art, obscured as well as revealed that of which they were an eruption from the depths of being. These matters were much debated among the students I knew. Many fastened on the fact that things religious *obscured* as well as revealed the Unconditioned, and they began to see the lack of difference between the things of faith and the things of reason. But some of us latched onto the fact that religion *revealed* as well as obscured the Ultimate, and began to find reasons to think of God again. From their positions in a heteronymous world, some found a pathway to autonomy. Those of us already psychologically in an autonomous world saw a path toward theonomy open before our eyes. In the terms of the method of correlation, those who had been trapped in essence found themselves catapulted by Tillich into existence, while we who thought existence was all found hints of the possibility of knowing something essential. Slowly but increasingly over the years, I became preoccupied with the prospects of knowing something of an onto-theological reality by which issues of truth and justice in church and civilization might be addressed.

Some found it possible to test their faith by reason; we found it possible to find faith because the deepest truth of faith is not contrary to reason — it may be reason in ecstasy. Some found it possible to examine their religion in the terms of critical philosophy; we found it possible to see and evaluate transcendent religious dimensions of presumably secular thought. Many found it possible to leave the church and enter the academy with a good conscience; I personally found it possible — indeed, personally necessary — to enter that branch of the academy that stands within the church and to attempt to reconstruct what Troeltsch called a Christian social philosophy, and what today some of us call a public theology.

Tillich is not responsible for how I have applied his thought. While admitting my full responsibility I must add that Tillich did not speak in a vacuum. He has not influenced me — or, I suspect, anyone else — strictly on the basis of the power of his own thought. Nor is the extent to which his thought influenced us proportional to the intensity of the dialogues or disputes he had with others. Young scholars experienced Tillich at a time when we were building an intellectual nest out of his and others' intellectual influences.

In my own case, it was not only Tillich plus Troeltsch with his sometime roommate Max Weber and Adams with his colleague George H. Williams who were influential, but also Walter Rauschenbusch's use of the social analysis of his day to restate biblical themes; Reinhold Niebuhr's refutation in *The Nature and Destiny of Man* of Marx's, Kant's, Nietzsche's, and Freud's understanding of human nature; Talcott Parsons's systematic study of the role of religious values in *The Structure of Social Action;* George Ernest Wright's exposition of the Prophets; and Masatoshi Nagatomi's gentle introduction to Asian modes of thought. Martin Luther King Jr. also influenced us with his insistent activism that appealed to a higher moral law. These and others created the matrix of discussion within which Tillich was received; each student, of course, heard him within the context of his or her own personal story.

This also means that we did not accept Tillich on every point. For instance, I have never shared his views of technology, which I think reflect the kind of Romanticism evident also in Heidegger. Parsons is surely more correct. Second, he remained too much a situationalist in his ethics. He could never bring himself to embrace deontological modes of moral reasoning that speak of normative duties. He seemed to be too much the Lutheran antinomian, too fearful that Kant's categorical imperatives were merely bourgeois, and too protective (for less than theological reasons) of Dionysian excess without fret about Apollonian constraint or long-range consequences. He could have learned from Wright about the prophetic tradition on this point.

Third, like nearly every great theologian of that generation, Tillich was too unambiguous in his embrace of Marxism. Here I tread on the one canon of orthodoxy that has remained sacrosanct among those who have relinquished nearly every other canon. My critique of the wholehearted acceptance of quasi-Marxist presuppositions among colleagues at Harvard Divinity School during the Vietnam War alienated me from a number of my Tillichian, pacifist, and liberationist friends. But the later Niebuhr probably had a better reading of Marx, and his mature sense of Marxism's limited utility and its grave dangers may be easier to see now than either I or my friends saw then.

Finally, Tillich's greatest weakness was his relative inability to discern in classic religious symbols the fresh complexity of meaning that he found (with ease, insight, and fluidity) in symbols from ancient Greek and modern secular culture. Apparently he credited this to the symbols' inadequacy or the pretension of the religious groups that used them. He thus left too much to the Swiss theologians of his day who claimed to have cornered the meanings of classical biblical and dogmatic traditions. On this point Tillich probably erred. Today, an unwillingness by liberal and progressive thinkers to use and wrestle directly with classic Christian symbols may well lead to a neo-pagan refusal to assume the responsibilities entailed by those symbols, or even be an abdication in the face of the philistines. In these areas, we must turn to others.

Regardless of these shortcomings, I still feel a deep gratitude to Tillich. He made it possible for me to become a Christian as no other figure before or since has (although I can today find similar inspiration from Hans Küng and David Tracy among the Catholics, and Alvin Plantinga and Nicholas Wolterstorff among Reformed Christians). More, he made the quest for an apologetic, cosmopolitan Christian social ethic imaginable. He helped me join *pietas* and *intellectus* as a basis for *veritas* and *justitia* in a way I once doubted was possible.

Alasdair MacIntyre: An Overview and Evaluation

Nothing has marked twentieth-century intellectual and social life so much as the protest against liberalism. Liberalism, of course, has had many definitions, but that is partly because it has many enemies. Nevertheless, it seems to have survived a peculiarly short century which, they say, did not begin until 1914; and it seems again to be on the horizon as we are being prematurely thrust into a new global era. In between we have seen the rise and fall of the hypermodernism of Marxism-Leninism with its drive to a militant liberation, the postmodernism of Nietzsche and Heidegger with their impulses to romanticized barbarism, and the anti-modernism of traditionalism with its disdainful condescensions toward democracy, human rights, technology, and pluralism. All have proclaimed liberalism empty or dead. Alasdair MacIntyre shares with our century this judgment; his writings are a series of epitaphs for liberalism.

He is not altogether persuasive. His harsh estimates of anyone who holds that context-transcending principles of any kind are real, knowable, and reliable means that he is unlikely to get a favorable response from any who believe that such principles are indispensable to serious philosophy, profound religion, or the moral life.

Further, his accounts of Protestantism, of epistemology as it developed since the Enlightenment, and of the intellectual foundations of pluralist social theories are, at best, cramped. He is so convinced that they are empty delusions that he treats them as much as caricature as portrait. Consequently, serious critiques of MacIntyre, such as those by Richard J. Mouw of Fuller Seminary (1990), Franklin I. Gamwell of the University of Chicago (1990), and Jeffrey Stout of Princeton (1987), although they would disagree with each other, are compelling on these particular points. Nevertheless, they too know that they wrestle with a major mind and, through it, with some of the reigning confusions of the age.

His Histories

MacIntyre's work can be summarized and evaluated in terms of history and in terms of structure. The historical emphasis must come first, not only because he is such a wonderful storyteller, nor only because his work supports "narrativist" thought, but because he declares his commitment on the first page of his first "big" book, *A Short History of Ethics: Moral Philosophy from the Homeric Age to the Twentieth Century*:

> Moral Philosophy is often written as though the history of the subject were only of secondary and incidental importance. This attitude seems to be the outcome of a belief that moral concepts can be examined and understood apart from their history. Some philosophers have even written as if moral concepts were a timeless, limited, unchanging, determinate species of concept.... In fact, of course, moral concepts change as social life changes. (1)

From this early work to his Gifford Lectures of 1988 (published 1990) he tells basically the same story, from the same point of view, although chapters and themes and "little books" expand or contract or embellish as he unfolds his tale and although we shall note one major shift of perspective later on.

The basic pattern is elaborated with new accents in *After Virtue* (1981), which contains his most pessimistic reading of modernity, and it is refined in *Whose Justice? Which Rationality?* (1988), which, oddly, has been read as a convincing argument that we can do little better than make a blind leap of faith between conflicting points of view, and as a turning point toward a new natural theology. These, along with several shorter writings, are basically about the wisdom of the classical views of virtue, *telos,* and social coherence in close-knit communities in contrast to the foolishness of modernity with its accent on individualism, pluralism, cosmopolitanism, and abstract science.

He tells this story for a purpose: He believes that we must get off the "treadmill of Hume, Kant, Mill and Moore . . ." (1966, preface). The date is not insignificant, for he is explicitly interested in providing an alternative to the perspective of Henry Sidgwick whose *Outlines of the History of Ethics* appeared one century before. That volume and its companion, *The Methods of Ethics* (1878), summarized the history of moral philosophy from a point of view indebted precisely to Hume, Kant, and Mill, evoked the work of G. E. Moore, in some ways standardized categories of analysis, and became the basic texts by which generations of moral philosophers (at least in the British tradition) entered the lore of their discipline. At stake are the terms of debate for what Canada's George Grant calls "English-speaking justice."

In MacIntyre's view the early Greeks had an awareness that morality is related to the concrete practices by which people sustained life in community. Further, they believed that natural human inclinations incline people to the good, and that proper nurture of these impulses and desires produces great-souled persons living for the common good. This is reflected already in the pre-philosophical narratives where fact and value are not differentiated. The "alleged logical gulf between fact and appraisal is not so much one that . . . [was] bridged in Homer. It has never been dug. Nor is it clear that there is any ground in which to dig" (1966, 7). The "good," or rather the conceptual ancestor of what we call good, *agathos,* is what a person is and does when that person lives well and does well in an integrated society bound together by the same traditions. Moral terms require an immediate "social anchorage."

Only later do we begin to see the breakdown of a sense of morality as the social order begins to fall apart. Then, efforts to treat what is "good" become more and more abstracted from social behavior, communal practice, and common memory. New problems appear, such as the relativism of the Sophists, the quest for something more reliable by Socrates, and the increasing abstraction of Plato. If not arrested, we find the rise of a dualism of one kind or another, with moral and spiritual reality set over and against common practice and human desires — as is especially manifest in Plato's doctrine of the "Forms" (and all subsequent "formalism") that made goodness independent of and sometimes contrary to this-worldly happiness.

Here, in brief, is the plot that is to unfold repeatedly in MacIntyre's narratives: in situations of social solidarity morality has an integral function that corresponds to what being human is all about — performing well what we desire to do in a functional communal role that is understood by all through participation in a common tradition. However, society sometimes breaks down under the impact of speculative, individualizing, and cosmopolitan pressures. Then all sorts of abstractions begin to creep in, removing us from our desires and from those commonly understood practices at which we are, more or less, good. The fall into abstraction, however, can be overcome by the concrete exercise of *phronesis* (or *prudentia*), which reestablishes socially embedded virtue and commonly understood behavior. In ancient Greece the one who understood this more clearly than anyone else was Aristotle. Aristotle duly repudiated the "Forms" in the effort to return attention to the actual contexts and behavioral practices by which virtues could be developed and social character maintained. What he said in that context becomes the decisive clue for MacIntyre's prescription for philosophy, ethics, and the modern situation generally. "Aristotle . . . challenges not merely the Kantians and the puritans to come, but also the Platonists" (1966, 60). MacIntyre's narrative, we soon recognize, is a morality tale told in double dialogue — with the texts and with the present. One could title it "Aristotle: From Homer to Derrida."

As he proceeds he challenges also the Stoics, who developed views of universal natural law, and the Christians, who not only borrowed from the Stoics but accented more than anyone else the notion that every person is somehow equal before God and claimed that in God happiness coincided with virtue, at least in another world. But such ideas as we find them in Jesus and Paul are, MacIntyre says, of pertinence only to a Messianic kingdom when history is brought to a conclusion. They thus have to do with a realm other than historical, earthly life, as Augustine recognized when he established, by drawing on Plato, a dichotomy between "the world of the natural desires and the realm of divine order" (1966, 117). "We cannot, therefore, expect to find in what they say a basis for life in a continuing society" (1966, 115). It is not until Aquinas, working under the influence of and with full knowledge of these themes, that we find a new grasp and, indeed, an improvement of Aristotle:

> Aquinas, in fact, shows us how the conceptual links between virtue and happiness forged by Aristotle are a permanent acquisition for those who want to exhibit these links without admiring . . . [the Greek view of humanity] or without accepting the framework of the fourth-century *polis*. Aquinas's theological ethics is such as to preserve the nontheological meaning of the word *good*. "Good is that to which desire tends." . . . The natural man, without revelation, can know what is good, and the point of moral rules is to achieve goods, that is, to achieve what satisfies desire. (1966, 118f.)

As MacIntyre traces the history of moral theory in the West, first Occam and, subsequently, Luther and Machiavelli broke down this new synthesis and generated a voluntarist proto-nihilism. Before long, Scottish Protestants, French philosophers, and German theoreticians were leading the West to the Enlightenment with its devotion to abstraction above all — the greatest fall, the root fault of modernity. The Enlightenment wants to speak of persons

Interpreting the Tradition of Public Theology

as if they were not embodied in flesh, driven by desires, members of communities, and enmeshed in tradition; and to do this they postulated an abstract reason. The essential point of the Enlightenment, says MacIntyre, is that since we have now come to recognize that all these forces make "men behave irrationally . . . the recipe for social improvement is that henceforth men should behave rationally" (1966, 183).

There are some wonderful passages as MacIntyre lays out his suspicions about early-modern and modern thought. His story about Hobbes's lie as to why he gave alms to a poor man and his recognition that the lie reveals that "[h]uman nature and human motives are not and cannot be what he says they are" is priceless (1966, 135f.). His treatment of the implications of Spinoza's argument to the effect that "[r]eligion needs not so much to be refuted as to be decoded" (1966, 141) is devastating to many subsequent authors who accent the "hermeneutics of suspicion." And his claim that "by Hegel's time all the fundamental positions have been taken up" is dramatic. "After Hegel (and Marx)," he writes, "they appear in new guises and with new variations, but their reappearance is a testimony to the impossibility of fundamental innovation" (1966, 199). Yet, the claim anticipates what he was to write in subsequent books.

The two most important works between *A Short History of Ethics* and his Gifford Lectures are the widely regarded volumes, *After Virtue* (1981) and *Whose Justice? Which Rationality?* (1988), already mentioned. In these he extends his attack on modern thought. One major target is Emotivism, "the doctrine that all evaluative judgments and more specifically all moral judgments are *nothing but* expressions of preference, expressions of attitude or feeling, insofar as they are moral or evaluative in character" (1981, 11). MacIntyre thinks that the heirs of Hume may be admired for exposing the fraud of Locke's "natural law," but they also anticipate moral sentimentality. (See also *Hume's Ethical Writings*, 1965.) Another target is Rationalism, the notion that "reason itself supplies morality with a basis . . . such that we have adequate grounds for rejecting emotivist . . . accounts" (1981, 20).

But he reserves his heaviest artillery for Kant, in part because Kant more than any other moral philosopher since Plato challenges Aristotle's presumption that morality is to be defined in terms of *telos* and context as woven together in social practice. Instead, Kant argues that every reasonable person knows that there are some things that are right and others that are wrong and that these things can be known abstractly — that is, without full knowledge of either particular desires or specific contexts. Further, they may be invoked to constrain desires or transform social contexts or identify cross-culturally binding principles of human obligation (see, e.g., Green, 1978), since desires, contents, and cultures can be wrong.

MacIntyre is convinced not only that Kant (and the Enlightenment generally) fails to make a viable case for such principles (1981, ch. 4) but that the effort had to fail (1981, ch. 5), "since the whole point of ethics is to enable man to pass from his present state to his true end" (1981, 52). Of course, this critique simply reasserts a teleological test, which any attempt to define the issues of morality in deontological terms would automatically fail. He further draws out the consequences, as he sees them; modern society talks much of "self-evident principles," of "moral law," or of "rights," but has no way to justify their existence or define them or to judge between conflicting claims about them. The basic reason there is so much disagreement about these matters, he believes, is that none of these things exist.

In *Whose Justice? Which Rationality?* MacIntyre is concerned to retell the story so that no one will misunderstand the fact that there are rival traditions and thus that no one can speak abstractly of what is universally moral. At the same time, he recognizes a possibility that those within each tradition can learn a second language and, in some measure, comparatively evaluate both their own and the newly learned tradition. Such a possibility invites new levels of reflection about some generic epistemic capacity that MacIntyre does not seem to have fully faced.

A deep ambiguity in MacIntyre's thought appears in this double argument: What is the status of moral philosophy if we are locked into our cultural and historical situations or if morality only counts if it is rooted in the living contexts and practices of our lives? How could we allow Aristotle or Thomas or anyone else not an immediate part of our contexts to challenge modern social practices and values? This ambiguity is of long duration and is rooted in nineteenth- and twentieth-century theories about the relationship of substructure to superstructure. In his early *Secularization and Moral Change* MacIntyre gives a substructural reductionist account of the source and nature of moral and religious ideas that would seem to render all intellectual work questionable:

> I have argued for two propositions in the course of these lectures; the first was that the explanation both of the secularization of English society and of the limits to that secularization are to be found in the changes in the value-system of the community, brought about by the Industrial Revolution and by the consequent class division of English society; the second was the corollary that the view that moral and social change is

consequent upon the decline of religion is false, and the view therefore that such change could be arrested or could have been arrested by halting the decline of religion is also false. I have argued instead that the causes of moral and social change have lain in the same urbanization and industrialization that produce secularization. In so far as there is a causal relationship between morals and religion it has been changes in the moral climate and in the forms of social life that have rendered Christianity apparently irrelevant or incredible, rather than unbelief in Christianity which has produced moral change. (1967, 58)

Even in *After Virtue* he explicitly states that "a moral philosophy . . . characteristically presupposes a sociology" (1981, 22). These and numerous other passages seem to suggest that morality is essentially the ordered values and traditions of a society — mores, folkways, and conventions of adaptation. Indeed, he is contemptuous of the way some philosophers treat "taboos," without giving them due respect. He is suspicious of standards — religious, ethical, philosophical — independent of cultural-linguistic ethos by which a critique of a society or its morality could be made. Yet, in another early writing, *Marxism*, he appears to embrace a superstructural "idealism" approvingly:

> It is the Idea, it is thought, which is, in Hegel's phrase, the demiurge of reality. To change reality you must change thought. To change the reality of society you must change the thought of society, and equally to preserve and safeguard society . . . , you must preserve and safeguard its thought. Thus the battle between political and social conservatives and reformers is essentially a battle of ideas, in which . . . the philosophers will take the foremost place. (1953, 30-31)

MacIntyre's narrative in *Whose Justice? Which Rationality?*, in other words, articulates and exemplifies an enduring confusion in MacIntyre and much contemporary reflection about the nature and character of thought of any kind — one that appeared in his work with Dorothy Emmet on *Sociological Theory and Philosophical Analysis* (1970), one that is built into the tension between Hegel and Marx, and one that reappears frequently in contemporary debates about education. Is what we think primarily a reflection, expression, or projection of our socioeconomic status, psycho-sexual orientation, or ethno-political interests? Or is there some basis on which we might develop a view of justice, or of rationality, or, for that matter, of humanity or "Truth" that transcends particular traditions and allows us to evaluate some cultures, societies, philosophies, or religions or practices as dehumanizing?

MacIntyre's program must resist this last option, for it would involve a capitulation to forms of abstraction that he does not approve. Hence, he takes great pains in *Whose Justice? Which Rationality?* to attack — with a severity that sometimes overrides his desire for an open inquiry — those who try to make the case that the word "human" has universalistic moral implications whatever the particularities of circumstance or the ends pursued. Plato's theory of "Forms," for example, is treated only as a hypothetical theory of enquiry that has and could have no substantial meaning except that which Aristotle later formulates (1988, 75 *et passim*). And Cicero's arguments about *lex naturalis* (against the Greeks' *physis nomos*) have to be treated as "really" reflecting an imperialist patriotism (1988, 75f.), not as a quest for an ecumenical view of human morality. He gives similar twists to later Protestants and Humanists who seek a post-Aristotelian and non-tradition-dominated basis for science, morality, social order, and religious understanding. And yet we find references to Thomas's revision of Aristotle that he seems to approve and that would seem to point in directions he rejects. This part of his thought is, apparently, not yet finished.

The Structure

The more one reads of MacIntyre, the less of a narrativist he appears to be. Aristotle, of course, had argued in the *Poetics* that every story has a pattern and we best grasp the meaning of the story when we grasp the pattern. Gradually, the structure behind MacIntyre's narratives becomes more explicit. It reflects the fact that three things are always involved in making ethical judgments: principles or rules of right and wrong; a vision of the good end and thus the need to cultivate those virtues and practices that enhance good ends and avoid evil and vice; and a way of reading the concrete contexts of life wherein the issues of right and wrong, good and evil find embodiment. Each of these dimensions of ethical thought — often studied through the three main subdisciplines of ethics, deontology, teleology, and ethology respectively, as they are sometimes called — has multiple variables within it, and the issues of how each variable should be weighed within one of the three major "modes of moral discourse," of how one "mode" should be weighed in comparison to the other modes, make for much of the disputatiousness of ethics both in scholarship and daily life.

Interpreting the Tradition of Public Theology

MacIntyre's distinctive emphasis is clear and consistent: he seeks to recover and reestablish a eudaimonistic view of teleological ethics. "[T]he point of moral rules," he writes, "is to achieve goods, that is, to achieve what satisfies desire" (1966, 118f.). At the same time, he is convinced that morality is constituted by social convention. As he states in *Secularization and Moral Change*, wherever people lose "social agreement as to the right ways to live together, [they cease] ... to be able to make sense of any claims to moral authority" (1967, 54). In other words, he links a historicist ethological account of the context of human action with a classicist view of teleology. He believes that pluralist democracy with its market economics and human rights obscures these connections.

It is not that he is opposed to principles *per se*; it is that principles, in his view, are more instrumental than regulative. They are less to be heeded because they have some universal validity than they are to be heeded if and when they conduce to some fulfillment of desire or moral possibility of community otherwise not at hand. In other words, they have to be linked to and justified by their relation to some specific end that can be actualized in concrete practice.

An example of this is his intriguing little book *The Unconscious* (1958a). MacIntyre writes with a sharp pen against views he doubts. And it turns out that he does not think much of a number of Freud's (or Jung's or others') theories of the "unconscious." One thus expects the flaying of the subject, such as one gets in a later book, *Marcuse* (1970c). Yet his treatment of Freud is relatively benign — precisely because Freud linked his theory to a practice that attempted to improve the lives of people by building on the natural desires they have.

However, MacIntyre is vigorously opposed to utilitarian (and pragmatic — "the American strain of the same virus") ways of dealing with principles, which are what he thinks is found in capitalism and philosophically in far too much contemporary moral philosophy. Utilitarianism is a thin and sad teleology, in his view. It, like deontology, tends toward formalism. If Locke and Kant lead to empty and pompous abstraction, Bentham and Mill lead to empty, morally pretentious calculations of cost and benefit.

There are substantive changes in his ethology. Earlier in his writings a rather pervasive Marxism shaped his reading of the social and historical contexts of life and his sense of what we might desire and hope for. It is a rather Hegelian reading of Marx, not quite a Leninist one; but it is very pronounced. This is not, of course, altogether strange. Both Aristotle and the Left Hegelians were convinced that life is driven by a deep and natural teleology. Aristotle, after all, was the only required classical philosopher in the departments of Marxist philosophy in Eastern Europe over the past seventy years.

Alasdair MacIntyre

Further, one finds a blending of Aristotelian and (Hegelian-) Marxist concepts among Latin Liberation thinkers, even when they claim they are against the hegemony of "dead Greeks and dead Germans." It might even be said that as Aristotle resisted the "Forms" of Plato and demanded an engagement with the organic structures of material life, so Marx (as a "Left Hegelian") tried to overcome the *a priori* categories of Kant and demanded an engagement with the sociohistorical structures of material existence. Both Aristotle and Marx have been seen as allies by Christian thinkers in ethics.

For many years, this triple dependence, on Aristotle, Marx, and radical Christian theology, grinds the glasses through which MacIntyre reads the ethos and grounds his hope, as we can see in his *Marxism,* written for the Student Christian Movement:

> We began with a parable of Jesus. We have traced the pattern of the new humanity that is to be created from the poverty of man's estrangement from its origin in the Gospel through its intellectualization in Hegel and Feuerbach to the compassion of Marx. We have seen how the divorce of the Church from the modern world discredited prophetic vision and forced Marxism to seek a scientific mode for its prophecy. We have seen how the religious virtues and the religious vices alike found their home with the Marxists, and the lesson here is surely that it is only those who have seen these virtues and vices in their true contemporary form, that is Marxist form, who know the greatness that the gospel preaches. . . . (1953, 108)

There is a deep pessimism about society in this; but there is also a metaphysical optimism: the intellectual, religious, moral, and social forces are gathering for a reconstructive transformation.

But in subsequent writings references to Bultmann, Tillich, and Bonhoeffer disappear, although a reference to St. Benedict here, an appreciative comment on St. Thomas there, remain. These latter appear, however, as alternatives to the perils of modernity, not as part of the promise of the present. And, significantly, both Hegel and Marx are gradually abandoned. Hegel is mentioned only briefly in each of his last three books — as if the collection of essays on Hegel's philosophy that MacIntyre edited in 1972 disposed of him. And just before that, MacIntyre writes that ". . . to be faithful to Marxism we have to cease to be Marxists; and whoever now remains a Marxist has thereby discarded Marxism. . . . Young Hegelianism . . . turns out alas to be senile" (1970c, 61). Marx does not even appear in the index of his last two books.

Interpreting the Tradition of Public Theology

This is a great loss for MacIntyre, not replaced by any of the post-Marxian theories of society, as we can see in the final pages of *After Virtue:*

> When Marxism does not become Weberian social democracy or crude tyranny, it tends to become Nietzschean fantasy. . . . A Marxist who [today refused fantasies] . . . would be forced into a pessimism quite alien to the Marxist tradition, and in becoming a pessimist he would in an important way have ceased to be a Marxist. For he would now see no tolerable alternative set of political and economic structures which could be brought into place to replace the structures of advanced capitalism. This conclusion agrees of course with my own. For I too not only take it that Marxism is exhausted as a political tradition . . . , but I believe that this exhaustion is shared by every other political tradition within our culture. (1981, 244)

Increasingly, what takes the place of Hegel and Marx is a growing sense of a great divide: modernity is read in terms of the coming of the "World Night" of Nietzsche or as the time of a great return to St. Thomas, such as Leo XIII called for in *Aeterni Patris*.

Warnings about nihilism begin to play a greater and greater role in his comments on contemporary conditions. Passages from his last several books, on this point, parallel Allan Bloom's *The Closing of the American Mind* in remarkable ways. MacIntyre conveys a sense that modern civilization is crumbling before our eyes; all has become "perspectivist" — the claim that every point of view is equally valid and thus that no view of anything is or could be superior to any other view. If this is so, it is the termination of science, art, religion, and thought generally.

The suspicion that Nietzsche had in fact grasped the vacuity of modernity is modulated only in *Whose Justice? Which Rationality?* (1988) by a "soft socialist" analysis derived from a Durkheimian view of modern "normlessness":

> Nietzsche is of course not the only intellectual ancestor of modern perspectivism and perhaps not at all of modern relativism. Durkheim, however, provided a clue to the ancestry of both when he described in the late nineteenth century how the breakdown of traditional forms of social relationship increased the incidence of *anomie*, of normlessness. *Anomie*, as Durkheim characterized it, was a form of deprivation, of a loss of membership in those social institutions and modes in which norms, including the norms of tradition-constituted rationality, are embodied. (368)

But for the most part *Whose Justice? Which Rationality?* presumes a Hobbesian world — there is no normative order of justice, no general or common reason unless it is one imposed by some authority or adopted by a specific community. In this respect it is his most anti-intellectual book. These grim views are also accompanied by increasingly overt nods in theological directions, a fact that commends the volume to some believers who say that faith has nothing to learn from modernity. This poses a very interesting set of problems in the interpretation of MacIntyre: Has he substituted a theocratic view for his earlier socialist one?

Earlier he had resisted theism, as we see in *Difficulties in Christian Belief* (1958b), *Marxism and Christianity* (1968), *The Religious Significance of Atheism* (1969), and *Metaphysical Beliefs* (1970a). He thought that theology (especially in its fideist forms of Kierkegaard and Barth) simply restated old philosophical conundrums in obscurantist terms and that so-called modern "radical" theologies only recapitulated the arguments of the great "masters of suspicion":

> Nothing has been more startling than to note how much contemporary Christian theology is concerned with trying to perform Feuerbach's work all over again. For if Christianity . . . is able to present itself as having a relevant content and function, it is forced to present itself as having a secular content and function. (1968, 142)

In consequence, it becomes indistinguishable from contemporary philosophy in that it simply leads us again to one or another version of Nietzsche, as Heidegger recognized, and as subsequent deconstruction (e.g., Derrida) and radical pragmatism (e.g., Rorty) seem to certify.

However, while the "anti-modern" arguments of MacIntyre would seem to ally him with current "postmodernism" (and he is sometimes read that way), he in fact moves in a different direction. The reason for his cryptic references to St. Benedict, such as at the end of *After Virtue,* becomes clear: it is not possible to redeem modern civilization. One must form enclaves of commonality and retrieve neglected dimensions of tradition so that meaning and character can be cultivated outside or against both modernity and postmodern decadence. It is this anti-modernist, communitarian aspect of MacIntyre that has appealed to a variety of perspectives of the last decades, as one can see in sectarian confessionalists such as Stanley Hauerwas or communitarian social theorists such as Robert Bellah.

Signals of another accent, however, have been present in a number of works; it appears in full force in his Gifford Lectures, *Three Rival Versions of Moral Enquiry: Encyclopaedia, Genealogy and Tradition*. MacIntyre not only reveals an intellectual, social, and spiritual despair about society and the capacity of thought to find any viable way of relating divergent modes of moral discourse. He also overtly announces a Thomistic "Traditionalism" against liberal, Enlightenment "Encyclopedia" and radical, Romantic "Genealogy," with its hermeneutics of suspicion or deconstruction. As philosopher Joseph Prabhu, himself a student and interpreter of MacIntyre, has pointed out to me, it is a new dependence on Thomas that has given his thought a new "Pre-Modernist" vigor. It is from this perspective that he now mounts his anti-Whig, anti-Protestant, anti-Enlightenment, anti-Romantic polemic with a new confidence. This seems to reflect not only his personal religious conversion to Roman Catholic Christianity but his as-yet incomplete philosophical quest for a metanarrative with theistic rootage that can be shown to be metaphysically defensible.

In this, of course, he differs from Allan Bloom and offers his final Gifford lecture on education explicitly to differentiate himself from Bloom's proposals. It is not a question of getting "the good old classics" restored to the curriculum, he argues; the most serious major points of view are incommensurable and untranslatable. We can only hold firm in the midst of an expectant and dialogical dissensus that may refine Tradition as it gets polished and gradually adopted ever more widely by abrasive contact with other traditions.

An Evaluation

MacIntyre forces contemporary ethics to clarify itself, and he is surely correct that much of modern moral philosophy is so tediously boring and that people are more dependent on their traditions than they admit. Further, he is surely correct in thinking that there are indispensable resources in the great thinkers of the premodern era. Most of their wisdom has not been surpassed.

But it is a serious question as to whether he has clearly seen other issues that he treats. For one thing, the glasses through which he reads the contemporary situation have blinded many. Both Marx's and Nietzsche's attempts to grasp the fabric of modernity seem increasingly unreliable. Those philosophers, theologians, and social analysts who use these frames of reference to discuss modern natural and social science are, properly, increasingly embarrassed by the twentieth century. They do not accurately read how things are, what forces cause things to work or fall apart, and how bourgeois, democratic, middle-class, religious, and moral values operate in modern, complex societies. And it is not clear that Thomas is helpful in this way — unless one understands Thomas in ways that, for example, Jacques Maritain or John Courtney Murray have, and these are directions of interpretation that MacIntyre explicitly rejects.

Part of what has made these views obsolete is "Liberalism," a term that, in the context of MacIntyre's writings, means precisely that modern attempt to articulate the nature and character of universal moral principles that may come to expression in the context of one particular society but one that can bridge multiple traditions. Of course Plato and Cicero, Locke and Kant are not universalistic in all respects, nor are all those neglected by MacIntyre who tried between them to establish more clearly the philosophical and theological grounds for the idea of a common moral law for all humanity — Althusius, Suarez, Grotius, Pufendorf, for examples. But it only helps to offer an account of such notions, narrative or otherwise, if we acknowledge that they point toward a human commonality larger than the specific contexts where they appear. It does not help if our traditions, societies, and sense of virtue have become so conflictual that we cannot readily define a "common good," extend the range of what is "common" to include those previously excluded, or be sure that what some traditions hold to be "good" is actually so. This dimension of ethics has not and cannot do everything, but it has given impetus to the formation of constitutional democracies with human rights, to cosmopolitan human interactions, and to the critique of slavery, oppression, segregation, and *apartheid* even where they are common practice and viewed as virtuous.

Nor is it beside the point to mention in this connection that there is not a single reference to Moses, the Torah, the Old Testament, the Ten Commandments, or any prophetic standards of judgment in this entire corpus of works on ethics in the West (let alone any treatment of Solon, Justinian, Manu, Confucius, Muhammad, etc.)! It is as if the idea of a universal moral law, present in the mind of God, established over all creation, and written on the hearts of all people, had never been discussed, except as an absurd speculation. Still further, there is no reference to the fact that the development of ideas of human rights in the Puritan movement of Britain and America, subsequently on the Continent, and most recently in the United Nations and in the constitutions of some 157 countries of the world represents one of the most dramatic moral developments in human history. The idea that we ought not murder, lie, steal, rape, torture, or exploit, or honor those religions, philosophies, or authorities that do, no matter what the social practice and no matter what end we pursue, is not a peculiar, modern, Western foible. Mac-

Intyre's account of "encyclopedia," in short, is very suspect precisely because no treatment of ethics is complete without reference to this dimension of the moral life, even if this dimension is not and cannot supply the whole of an ethical life.

Even with regard to teleology we must ask whether he may have missed something. His account of Thomas seems to miss the degree to which the angelic doctor depends on elements of Augustine's teleology (see O'Donovan, 1986), and thus MacIntyre's account tends to remain in a very Pelagian (or Arminian) mode. The larger *telos* requires not merely the fulfillment of natural human desire, nor the actualization of the human practical behaviors in society, nor even the Aristotelian "contemplation of contemplation." Augustine sees a larger purpose beyond that seen by the Greeks, and Thomas does too. If MacIntyre is to claim this tradition as his own, it may yet entail more transformations than he wants.

Here we confront the deepest problem of MacIntyre and his work. He may be correct in what he criticizes and mistaken in what he proposes for exactly the same reason. He does not yet quite know what God has to do with ethics, yet his narrative and the structure of his arguments press him to God. It may well be, as Reinhold Niebuhr argued in his own Gifford Lectures, which also exposed the thin and distorting gruel often fed us by modern moral philosophy in the utilitarian/pragmatic, Kantian, Marxist, Nietzchean, and obscurantist traditions, that finally only God can hold things together and that most of human life — in our ethical judgments, personal character, and social institutions — involves only relatively decent compromises that nevertheless, through grace, inject a note of ultimate optimism into the midst of proximate pessimism and allow the quest for truth and justice to proceed. If so, moral philosophy in its understanding of its own history or structure, and in its deontology, its teleology, and its ethology, will have to be more dependent on theological ethics than this body of work exemplifies — as Thomas also knew.

REFERENCES

Bellah, Robert, et al.
1985   *Habits of the Heart.* University of California Press.

Bloom, Allan
1987   *The Closing of the American Mind.* Simon & Schuster.

Gamwell, Franklin I.

1990   *The Divine Good: Modern Moral Theory and the Necessity of God.* HarperCollins.

Green, Ron

1978   *Religious Reason: The Rational and Moral Basis of Religious Belief.* Oxford University Press.

Hauerwas, Stanley

1981   *A Community of Character.* University of Notre Dame Press.

MacIntyre, Alasdair

1953   *Marxism: An Interpretation.* SCM Press.
1958a   *The Unconscious: A Conceptual Study.* Routledge & Kegan Paul.
1958b   *Difficulties in Christian Belief.* SCM Press.
1961   *New Essays in Philosophical Theology.* Edited with A. N. Flew. SCM Press.
1965   *Hume's Ethical Writings.* Editor. Collier-Macmillan.
1966   *A Short History of Ethics.* Routledge & Kegan Paul.
1967   *Secularization and Moral Change.* Oxford University Press.
1968   *Marxism and Christianity.* Schocken.
1969   *The Religious Significance of Atheism.* Edited with P. Ricoeur. Columbia University Press.
1970a   *Metaphysical Beliefs: Three Essays.* With S. Toulmin and R. W. Hepburn. Schocken.
1970b   *Sociological Theory and Philosophical Analysis.* With Dorothy M. Emmet. Macmillan.
1970c   *Marcuse: An Exposition.* Viking.
1971   *Against the Self-Images of the Age.* Schocken.
1972   *Hegel: A Collection of Critical Essays.* Editor. Anchor.
1981   *After Virtue: A Study in Moral Philosophy.* University of Notre Dame Press.
1988   *Whose Justice? Which Rationality?* University of Notre Dame Press.
1990   *Three Rival Versions of Moral Philosophy.* University of Notre Dame Press.

Mouw, Richard J.

1990   *The God Who Commands: A Study in Divine Command Ethics.* University of Notre Dame Press.

Niebuhr, Reinhold
1939-41   *The Nature and Destiny of Man.* 2 vols. Charles Scribner's Sons.

O'Donovan, Oliver
1986   *Resurrection and Moral Order.* Eerdmans.

Stout, Jeffrey
1987   *Ethics After Babel.* Beacon Press.

A Premature Postmodern (Ernst Troeltsch)

Few would dispute, although some regret, the fact that the single most influential voice in twentieth-century Protestant thought as it bears on religion in the public square is Ernst Troeltsch (1865-1923). Only Reinhold Niebuhr and Dietrich Bonhoeffer can compare in generating key concepts and intellectual loyalties that have reproduced themselves for generations. Yet the reception of and resistance to Troeltsch's thought has left deep marks in the religious and social history of the century now past.

To be sure, Troeltsch was largely ignored by statist-oriented "political theology" as it derived on the right from Carl Schmitt and on the left from Ernst Bloch, although Troeltsch energetically jumped into the struggle to establish a republic in Weimar after World War I. Further, it was his friends and heirs (including, in many ways, Niebuhr) who stood against the rising tide of radical ideologies after his death, and who later most energetically mobilized the Protestant churches outside of Germany against the Nazis and later the Communists. Indeed, as Ronald Stone of Pittsburgh Theological Seminary has shown in a new book that contains the translations of broadcasts to the German people during World War II by Troeltsch's student Paul Tillich, the Protestant resistance movements against the Nazis were likely inspired as much by Troeltschian motifs as by the more widely celebrated Barmen Declaration, written by Karl Barth, and the writings of the martyr Bonhoeffer.

Troeltsch was also ignored, or treated as a "neoliberal," by the advocates of Liberation Theology as it played out in Latin America in the 1960s and 1970s, the belated fruit of the Catholic revisionist Maurice Blondel and the Marxist revisionist Antonio Gramsci. Indeed, when the World Council of Churches began to modulate its earlier Barthian accents to become a center of liberation advocacy, Troeltsch's influence further declined in those Protestant circles.

Interpreting the Tradition of Public Theology

Yet it was the students of Troeltsch, then already a full generation removed from him, who often worked ecumenically at local levels in the West, who advocated the embrace of the UN Declaration of Human Rights by the Protestant churches, and who marched with Martin Luther King for civil rights in America. In doing so, they often parted ways with other Protestants who were nationalistic or racist — as well as with those who were so alienated from Western culture in general and American culture in particular that they uncritically echoed every liberation voice that protested against them.

More recently, Troeltsch has come under fire from neo-sectarian pietists such as John Howard Yoder and Stanley Hauerwas, and treated with harsh contempt by those who have appointed themselves the guardians of "radical orthodoxy," such as John Milbank. But it is not at all clear that they understand Troeltsch. Besides, they tend to accuse anyone who seeks to address public issues theologically of selling out to "the principalities and powers." They note, for instance, that Troeltsch sometimes advocated the necessity of a "compromise" between the gospel and the world. But they fail to note that he clearly defined the "compromise" he intended as finding the synthetic possibility in a particular historical moment that was "co-promising" between basic theological insights and the social realities at hand.

The nonsectarian traditions of twentieth-century Protestantism, however — the parts that have not become cadres of liberation or advocates of pious communitarianism, and are thus likely to continue their public influence into the next century — have been shaped directly or indirectly by Troeltsch and his followers more than is acknowledged. He was cited often by the founders of the American social gospel and Christian labor movements early in the century as they generated what later became the New Deal. He was utilized heavily by H. Richard Niebuhr at midcentury in studies of religion, the church, and American life. He was made mandatory reading by several generations of leading Protestant teachers of Christian ethics — James Luther Adams, Walter Muelder, Paul Ramsey, Roger Shinn, Edward Long, James Gustafson, and Gibson Winter (and their many students) in the post–World War II period. He has been cited by intellectual historians and social theorists from Leo Strauss to David Martin and Peter Berger. And he has been taken up in divergent ways by such Catholic thinkers as David Tracy, Dennis McCann, Michael Novak, and, until his untimely death, Theodore Steeman. All, in one way or another, struggle with the issues of how to accept the historical nature of Christianity without succumbing to relativism, how to affirm the transcendent claims of Christianity without recourse to supernaturalist metaphysics, and how to more fully actualize

A Premature Postmodern (Ernst Troeltsch)

the commitment of Christianity to universal justice without imposing the values of one culture.

As a professor of theology at the University of Heidelberg, Troeltsch lived with his family in the other half of a duplex where his "religiously unmusical" (as his wife said of him), morally rigorous, and sociologically brilliant colleague, Max Weber, wrote his five volumes on the sociology of religion. They were friends also with the famous Jewish historian of law Georg Jellinek, who wrote a definitive work on the theological foundations of modern human rights law, and the conservative Dutch Calvinist Abraham Kuyper, who developed the theory of "sphere" pluralism that has increasingly been in conversation with Roman Catholic theories of "subsidiarity." They all had sympathy for aspects of natural law theory and discussed appreciatively the reinvigoration of the social encyclical tradition by Leo XIII.

These figures obviously did not agree on all things, but they did all recognize that the deep structures of existence and the long traditions of religion shape the present and the future more than most of modern scholarship has acknowledged. They also knew that the repudiation of that reality, as fact and as value, had been taken in radical and destructive directions by Marx and Nietzsche, the godfathers of postmodernism. They were, at the same time, also critical of traditional dogmatics, not only because it made unbelievable claims, but because it could not, in their view, withstand the historicist assaults that they saw on the intellectual horizon as the influence of Marx's militant secularism and of Nietzsche's nihilist romanticism flourished.

Troeltsch saw the problems of their historicism early and acutely. It had something to it, he saw, in that it recognized that much of our thought and life is deeply embedded in historically constructed and changeable patterns. But that recognition was not the whole truth, and he was convinced that historicism's partial truth could give us no moral guidance for life. Indeed, he held that certain "religious a priori" were intrinsic to human nature and had to be acknowledged in social theory. The critical issue was whether theology could acknowledge the depths of historicity and social theory the depths of religious consciousness.

In the decade before the turn of the twentieth century Troeltsch produced a number of articles that called for his contemporaries to face these matters directly; and in the first ten years of the new century he struggled mightily with this problem, writing *The Absoluteness of Christianity and the History of Religions* and *Political Ethics and Christianity,* plus a number of essays contrasting historical and dogmatic approaches to faith. (See *Religion*

Interpreting the Tradition of Public Theology

in History, collected and translated by J. L. Adams and W. Bense.)[1] Troeltsch's *Der Historismus und seine Probleme* ("Historicism and Its Problems"), never published in English, appeared later and identified most of the issues now known to us as postmodernism.

Troeltsch was convinced that the dogmatic theologians of his tradition were ignoring the situation, and that those who tried to face every problem by simply reclaiming "the spirit of love," as advocated by several postdogmatic reformers, were not intellectually serious. Neither group appreciated that theology and ethics, when they are alive, are always in dynamic conversation with the cultural, philosophical, existential, and social contexts in which they are found, just as every civilization, even an apparently secular one, needs an intellectually plausible religious center or it will collapse for want of an inner moral architecture.

The question was whether, in the new situation, a new synthesis was possible on Christian grounds, one analogous to that of Augustine with regard to biblical religion and Neoplatonic philosophy, or Thomas with Augustine and Aristotle, or Calvin with Luther and the legacy of Stoic thought. These great synthesizers abandoned neither tradition and faith, as had the Enlightenment, nor the dynamic contributions of philosophical and cultural insight, as did the dogmatists.

Troeltsch was not interested, therefore, only in a condemnation of his opponents. It was the prospect of a new synthesis that drove him. Such a proposal came into fuller view when he offered an address in 1906 to the Ninth Congress of German Historians, In his highly influential lecture, Troeltsch put forward the view that Protestantism was, in profound if little-recognized ways, the womb of "modernity" and that "modernity" could not be understood either as a purely scientific "coming of age" of reason, or as a full-scale secularistic rejection of the Christian past.

Of course, many theologians feared modernity and many Enlightenment philosophers relished the "defeat" of religion as so much myth and magic. Troeltsch disagreed with both. Some things in the Enlightenment were novel, but that did not mean that they were by definition incompatible with the faith. Indeed, many features of modernity were nothing other than strikingly fresh developments of classic, catholic motifs in conversation with a new cultural context that a reformed Christianity might well be able to take in new directions. This view comported well with the ways in which some church fathers had related the faith to the Greco-Roman world. It also echoed

---

1. Ernst Troeltsch, *Religion in History* (Minneapolis: Fortress, 1991).

A Premature Postmodern (Ernst Troeltsch)

previous efforts of some humanist Catholics (such as Erasmus), some Phillipist Lutherans (following Melanchthon in manifesting a renewed interest in Aristotle), and a number of free church reformers (such as the Puritans who sought to establish a Christian commonwealth in the American colonies using both Stoic republican and Reformed Christian motifs). Troeltsch also adopted insights from Schleiermacher, who sought to establish theology as a university discipline; from the post-Hegelian philosopher of history Dilthey; and from the American philosopher and student of religious experience William James. In time, Troeltsch expanded that lecture into a little book, translated as *Protestantism and Progress: The Significance of Protestantism for the Rise of the Modern World* (1912).[2]

Troeltsch's title identified the issue. Many Christians found their faith in deep conflict with modernity. Could some kind of "catholic neo-reformed Christianity" creatively link the rationality, empiricism, personalism, and historicism of the modern world to the classical traditions of the faith? Could, as Troeltsch sometimes put it, a Christian social philosophy and a Christian personalist psychology be developed? If not, the brilliant terrors of Marx and Nietzsche would likely shatter societies and souls. But if so, a fresh version of Christianity could be the springboard of a future beyond modernity. It is this that allows one to speak of Troeltsch as the father of a certain kind of postmodernism.

Of course, not everyone agreed that what he was seeking could or should be sought. The Lutherans in his native Germany and the pietistic evangelicals in America had little sympathy with the effort. They could not imagine a nonconfessional state shaped by a theological ethic, a tolerant pluralist culture rooted in a Christian conviction about freedom of conscience and association, or a civil society centered in a nonestablished church. (It was impossible for Troeltsch, as for almost any Protestant of his time, to imagine the pre–Vatican II Catholic Church as the source of renewal toward a new Christian synthesis.)

Troeltsch's greatest work, in size and significance, *The Social Teaching of the Christian Churches and Sects* (1911),[3] has been a centerpiece of graduate courses in Christian Ethics in Protestant circles since it was published. It is an extended overview of his subject, organized, in the first instance, according

---

2. Ernst Troeltsch, *Protestantism and Progress: The Significance of Protestantism for the Rise of the Modern World*, trans. W. Montgomery (New York: G. P. Putnam's Sons, 1912; repr. Philadelphia: Fortress, 1986).

3. Ernst Troeltsch, *The Social Teaching of the Christian Churches*, rev. ed., trans. Olive Wyon (Louisville: Westminster John Knox, 1992).

Interpreting the Tradition of Public Theology

to a series of "departments of life" — obviously a revised understanding of the "orders of creation" so deeply rooted in Lutheran thought. Thus, he takes up questions of politics and power, economics, work and class, science, learning and education, family and sexuality, and art and culture as these spheres had been addressed by the church. But although some biblical and doctrinal themes are perennial, Troeltsch did not think that one constant perspective has prevailed historically, a fact that leads to the second feature of the work's organization.

Troeltsch holds that the New Testament has a series of fundamental elements that give concrete substance to the "religious a priori" of human consciousness. These are combined in various ways by the biblical authors as they were in later developments of doctrine and morals. Theologians through the years also drew from philosophical and ethical resources in the cultural environment of the church. Thus Troeltsch traced the formations and reformations of Christian ethics as believers addressed the issues that the various "departments of life" posed for them in ever new ways.

Troeltsch recognized the pluralism of answers that had been developed over time, although he thought that certain great syntheses provided the most creative and enduring responses. He charted these perspectives, drawing comparisons and contrasts through five periods of development — the early church, the medieval synthesis, Lutheran Protestantism, the Calvinist Reformation, and the various sectarian and spiritual impulses that developed first into the monastic movement and later in the directions of "withdrawing sects," "aggressive sects," and "spiritual movements." His famous "church/sect" typology, now used by scholars and journalists when speaking of religious movements and their impact on public life, derived from this work.

Less widely noted is the fact that Troeltsch saw the twentieth century as a time of vague, free-floating "spirituality," of little importance for the great issues. Modern churches lacked social significance because, contrary to what had been the case in all the preceding ages, they lacked a high view of the church. Ecclesiology is, indeed, essential to Christian social philosophy, since the church is the place where persons are formed theologically and ethically to live responsibly in the wider society.

In one sense, Troeltsch's monumental work can be understood as a self-critical search for a corrective to the German Lutheran tradition, with its tendency to divide law and gospel too radically and to hand the exterior church over to the state while confining the inner church to the heart. Troeltsch thought that only two great syntheses have been generated in the long history of the Christian heritage — the medieval synthesis of the Roman

A Premature Postmodern (Ernst Troeltsch)

Catholic tradition, and the "modern" tradition that derived from Calvin as modified by the sectarian heritage and Enlightenment thought. Lutherans would, Troeltsch thought, sooner or later have to bend back toward Rome or ally with their Reformed cousins.

He considered the withdrawing and aggressive sects in considerable detail, seeing the root of one in the monastic impulses of the early and medieval church, and the root of the other in the episodic attempts to bring the kingdom of God by forced righteousness. The fruit of the first is the quietistic "peace churches"; the fruit of the second is Christian Socialism. Troeltsch was attracted to the sectarian desires for a "pure faith" and a "righteous society," but he concluded that only the great church-types of the Catholic and Reformed traditions could sustain both the church and the various spheres of the common life. He thought, however, that these too had become wooden, and he did not see clearly how they could be renewed, although that was his hope. Those who have followed Troeltsch are those who have not despaired of the effort.

We do not know whether the future will bring an extended or renewed interest in Troeltsch. We do know that in Germany new critical editions of his works are appearing under the leadership of Trutz Rendtorff, Friedrich W. Graf, and Klaus Tanner. Also, at Harvard Divinity School, Sarah Coakley has introduced new reflections on Troeltsch's Christology, while at Yale Thomas Ogletree is seeking to update Troeltsch's insights for our era, and graduate seminars are regularly held on Troeltsch at Princeton. Indeed, Troeltsch continues to be mined in many places for suggestions about how to handle the continuing dilemma of facing up to pluralism and historicity without falling into the pits of relativism or, in reaction to that temptation, retreating to premodern dogmatics. The problem, as ever, is for the church fully to engage the world without in the process sacrificing its theological integrity.

Edwards for Us

The Puritans were earnest folk. They had little patience with those who had no depth, no deep conviction, no profound concern with what God was doing in their lives. They wanted everyone to become a believer, of course — to assent to the reality of God and God's providence, justice, and compassion, and thus find a confidence for living in this precarious world. Those in drift could not do that; they were like a bug on a leaf in a river during a storm. They had no sense of where they were or where they were going.

Jonathan Edwards was, to put it mildly, religiously serious, and he was so from an early age. He is so interesting for contemporary theologians because he developed a balance of brilliant intellectual honesty, fidelity to the biblical traditions, and an openness to new insight brought by personal experience.

He reports that it was some verses in Paul's Letters to Timothy that helped him sort his faith out. Paul writes about how as a young man he himself had been something of a holy terror, but when he received God's mercy he learned of the "love that issues from a pure heart and a good conscience and sincere faith." He was so grateful that he could write: "To the King of ages, immortal, invisible, the only wise God, be honor and glory forever and ever." That text, Edwards said, changed his life.

Three themes are embedded in this story about Edwards's development

---

This article is adapted from a sermon Stackhouse gave at a conference in Massachusetts marking the tricentennial of Jonathan Edwards's birth. The conference was sponsored by the Berkshire Institute for Theology and the Arts and was hosted by the Stockbridge Congregation Church, where Edwards was once pastor.

that are pertinent to the work he did the rest of his life and to a serious faith. Those themes are free will, love, and glory.

When we are drifting through life, or being cynical, the question arises: Can we simply will to change our ways? When we feel far from God, can we just decide to reestablish a relationship? Of course, in daily life, we often have real choices — whether I should go out with this person, whether I should accept this job, whether I should use what money I have this way or that. But do we have the will to alter the basic course of our lives?

Many people, when they look back on the choices they have made, see that many "free" decisions were in fact in the cards before the decisions were made. Often we just have to sort out what is really going on in life. And that is the issue: How deeply embedded in the conditions of our lives is the freedom of our wills?

We need to honor and protect our political freedoms, and hold people morally and in some cases legally accountable for their decisions; but we ought not overestimate the will's powers. The will needs guidance and support from the mind and the heart, and, even more, from a power beyond ourselves. A.A. knows this, as do all the effective self-help groups. It is not all self-help! All the great religions also point to a power beyond our own will. And the believer comes to know that support and power can come to us, by God's grace.

Edwards knew how complicated this simple fact can be. One of his most famous works is *The Freedom of the Will*, in which he argues that the will is truly free when it is in accord with what God intends for us; otherwise it loses itself in drift or cynical arrogance. This approach puts the issue in a theological framework. Many today fear profound religious commitment as loss of autonomy, and others fear that it breeds terror. But that is not what Edwards thought profound religion is about. True religion, he thought, energizes the will. And he thought true religion always involves love and beauty.

No one is against love, I take it. But there is a good bit of confusion about what the Puritans thought about love. Essentially, love is the inner power that draws persons together and bonds them to each other and to the right and the good. It shows up in many forms. It appears in acts of charity when we give to those in need. It draws us to particular persons whom we recognize as a gift to us from God. Most important, it takes shape when we discern the love of God for us and respond in love of God. In all these forms, love gives shape to the moral life, in that we become bound into appropriate covenants of mutual obligation and fidelity under God. True love penetrates the heart and reorients the will.

Interpreting the Tradition of Public Theology

It is sometimes said that the Puritans were prudes about sexual love and had a repressive view of sexuality. This is simply not so. Some people, reacting against the prudery of the Victorian era and the moralistic legalism into which some churches had devolved, blamed the Puritans, and tried to liberate sexuality from all religious constraint. It is as if they set aside a zone of life and said, "No religious ethics allowed here." Some have tried this in other areas also. Well, they have been successful in many respects, but the liberation has gone in unanticipated directions. It has brought us record numbers of divorces, absentee dads, troubled kids, and the scourge of AIDS. Do we really want to liberate ourselves from all religious constraints?

Puritans had a dim view of extramarital relations, but that was because they had a very high view of sexuality in marriage. Love, like the will, needs boundaries and channels; it needs a trusting and trustworthy context. The scholar Edmund Leites has studied hundreds of Puritan sermons about love and sex (there are many), and he has documented how much they preached about the duties to desire and how they saw the marriage bed as the "other altar of love." (The communion altar, of course, is the first.) But they also knew that love, if it is to be sacred, needs a deep set of moral rudders. It needs to be modeled on the way God loves us. For nurturing awareness of the love of God, a vibrant community of faith is needed. For nurturing the love between persons, a faithful marriage is the context.

If and when love becomes unfocused or distorted, it takes moral and spiritual renewal to correct its course. It may sometimes even need legal limits. Mary Stewart Van Leeuwen, a feminist Christian scholar, has reported that, according to court records, one of the major causes of being put in the stocks in the Puritan era was violence toward one's family or otherwise irresponsible behavior with regard to one's family.

The Puritans believed that a marriage needs constant grace and repeated renewal. Without it, both religion and sex can become like the human will without God: they can fall into the powerlessness of drift or become hardened into cynicism. They can show up as halfway commitments, or be locked into purely opportunistic behaviors. Could it be that a little dose of Puritanism could be a corrective to the licentiousness of our times? Not too much, but a little? Is this area of life not a holy passion, in which the radiance of God's purposes and design of life can shine through? Edwards thought so, and he thought it was a beautiful thing.

This brings us to our last point — beauty. The text from Timothy that touched Edwards refers to the "honor and glory" of God, and these terms are related to beauty. It is interesting that the Hebrew of the Bible has no single word for "beauty." The word *kabôd* is often translated as "glory" or "radiance." Our hymns have used "splendor," but the word can also mean "weighty," in the sense of something being really important, and thus being worthy of "honor." And the Greek of the New Testament uses *kalos,* which also means "comely," "charming," or "attractive." Edwards knew his biblical languages, and thought that God's way of relating to the world and to our lives involved an aesthetic as well as a willing and a loving aspect.

Edwards believed that everyone could, at some level, understand this. We might say today that this is why, in one sense or another, everyone is "spiritual" even if not all are "religious." The natural person can recognize the glory of nature in spite of natural disasters, pests, and disease; the splendor of the cultivated arts, especially music, in spite of art's occasional pomp and pretense; and the radiance of virtuous persons in spite of the flaws we can find in the best of them. He could see these beautiful qualities in the Indians. These qualities are magnificent, and are to be honored wherever they occur in God's world.

Edwards lived in an agricultural era, and he knew that nature had to be tended to manifest its best. Humans had to be stewards of creation — and that meant cultivating its possibilities to make its potential splendor manifest. Nothing so captures Edwards's message as his sense of the beauty of God. It is the beauty of God, he said, "that will melt and humble the hearts of men . . . draw them to God, and effectually change them." Moreover:

> A sight of the awesome greatness of God may overpower our strength and be more than we can endure; but if the moral beauty of God be hid, the enmity of the heart will remain in its full strength, no love can be enkindled, [our will] will not be effectual . . . but will remain inflexible; whereas the first glimpse of the moral and spiritual glory of God shining into the heart produces all these affects, as it were with omnipotent power, which nothing can withstand.

Edwards knew the holiness of beauty, and the beauty of holiness. If you do not already know this, you may want to find out more about Edwards. It could even be that you will be grasped by what he saw. You could change your will, your loves, your sense of God. You could find the source, the norm, the power that allows our promises to be fulfilled and our covenants to be complete.

Liberalism Dispatched vs. Liberalism Engaged

Review of *Dispatches from the Front*, by Stanley Hauerwas

Stanley Hauerwas hates liberalism. He hates liberal theology, liberal ethics, liberal churches, liberal politics, liberal economics, and liberal democracy. He uses military terms like "dispatches," "front," and "engagements" to signal that he is part of a great battle against liberalism, waged on behalf of virtue, character, and pacifism. His weapons in this struggle are narrative theology and postmodern philosophy (plus some bluster). This book, like several of his others, is less a sustained argument than a series of occasional thoughts in this course of struggle.

Liberalism, to be sure, is an easy target, in part because it has so many definitions. One can fire wildly at it and be sure to hit some squadrons. Liberals have been the favorite target of communists, fascists, nationalists, Barthians, conservative Republicans, radical liberationists, feminists, and fundamentalists. At the same time, various process theologians, Tillichians, Niebuhrians, moderate Republicans, progressive Democrats, advocates of racial and sexual justice and of public theology may use the term with approval — but not all mean the same thing by it.

The theological liberalism that Hauerwas is most concerned about is largely identified with what George Lindbeck, one of his teachers, calls "experiential expressivism" — the view that theology is essentially an "expression" of what is subjectively "experienced." This is the view taken, for instance, by Ludwig Feuerbach, who treated religion as the projected experience of groups, and by William James, who focused on religion and individual psychology. Hauerwas attributes this approach to the Enlightenment's hostility to theology. But he goes on to include in liberalism the view that theology must respond to the intellectual and social challenges of our times, especially economic and political realities. In his judgment, liberals do little more than shower holy words on the changing biases of personal or social experience, and then turn around and show how these words are nothing more than the social constructs of some time or place or condition.

To say that all liberalism leads to that is to slander the role that some forms of liberal theology have played in discerning the distinction between authentic and inauthentic forms of religious expression. It also falsifies the relationship between faith and philosophy historically, ignores key aspects of Christian theology, and denies our ethical responsibilities to use our minds before God. In other words, Hauerwas's definition of "liberal" is at once too narrow and too broad.

Christianity has a liberal element at its core. Following Jesus, Christians have been willing to challenge tradition when it becomes legalistic, ethnic, or impervious to prophetic insight. Guided by Paul and John, and Philo and the authors of the Wisdom tradition, it has engaged philosophies and cultures from beyond its own roots. The Synoptic Gospels acknowledge that the Good News is presented in several voices from several perspectives that do not fully agree. In every age, Christianity addressed the epistemological and social challenges of its ever-expanding and ever-changing contexts — always part of the task of mission, evangelism, and apologetics.

In fact, it is impossible to understand the Renaissance, Enlightenment, or the liberalism that has brought us, among other things, modern science and technology, constitutional democracy, and the struggle for human rights without understanding that they rest on assumptions worked out by theology. At each point, the "liberal" impulse of Christianity has selectively used resources from beyond itself and was willing to modulate contextual aspects of the faith's own roots. Christianity, in other words, does not simply trust religion as a given. It demands critically interpreted and socially engaged theology in which philosophy and ethics and social analysis play decisive roles.

The fact that contemporary academia has ignored (or repudiated) the foundations on which these features of modernity rest suggests only that academia is in very serious difficulty and that a philosophically, ethically, and socially engaged theology is desperately needed for the intellectual life. This difficulty in academia is not a good reason to accept purely secular accounts of life and history, especially when they argue that increased secularism is the destiny of liberated humanity and that liberalism is the necessary antithesis of everything religious. Nor is it reason to hold that science, democracy, and contemporary economics are opposed to everything religious and ethical — especially not when it can be argued that these features of modern life arose in contexts informed by theology. Instead it is the responsibility of theology and ethics to show that true freedom, authentic human living, and intellectual life itself depend on universally valid, partly liberal faith assumptions.

Hauerwas the anti-liberal laments that he is not much liked by his professional colleagues, and he constantly takes potshots at the university. He is mistaken — on both points. Who could not enjoy this bumptious child of the Vietnam protest era, the one with the quick wit, the furnished mind, the clever phrase, the brazen tongue, and the disarming effrontery of the clown? Furthermore, his views are rooted in the historicist reaction against those forms of Enlightenment thought that embraced universalistic principles, a reaction that has recently become mainstream in the liberal arts departments of our universities.

I suspect that Hauerwas is most liked by those whose religious traditions have always been suspicious of classical, systematic theologies, high culture, and abstract thinking, and who feel the sting when the pieties of their youth are treated with disdain in the universities. Some people do not want to be forced to give an account of the faith that is within them, or do not know how to, or think that it is improper even to ask for such an account. They like Hauerwas's convenient philosophic conviction that since all claims are equally without foundation, religious claims are immune to rational criticism. They want *theos* without *logos*.

More of Hauerwas's followers seem alienated from, hostile to, and generally poorly equipped to interpret the social transformations of our era. They simply assert their beliefs against any who challenge them. Some are genuinely disenchanted with the ways in which the classical heritage of theology and ethics has been divorced from piety in some church circles, and they want to reclaim the authenticity they remember, which they think Hauerwas supports.

Some of us, however, remain convinced that some forms of liberal thought are not foreign to the faith but intrinsic to it. For instance, many of us believe that we are not bound to the cultural-linguistic traditions of the sociohistorical contexts from which we come. Not only can we critically reflect on the faith and morals handed down to us, but we can convert or transform what we inherit — and offer a reasonable account of why we do so.

Some of us who might be called liberal Christians believe that human life has, at its root, a very profound *logos*, rooted in *theos*, that makes it possible for Jews, Christians, Hindus, Muslims, and humanists to talk reasonably with one another and to live together in a society governed by a modicum of justice. Further, we can, in some measure, talk across boundaries and more or less discern what is valid and not valid in what others say. And we expect others to understand us and to challenge us when we do not make sense.

Such liberal views are rooted in the Bible and have been embraced by Augustine, Thomas, Luther, Calvin, Wesley, and Edwards — and, for that matter, by Locke, Kant, Weber, Troeltsch, Whitehead, and the Niebuhrs. This kind of liberal Christian believes that Christianity offers the best account of why it is that all humans can come to this table of conversation ("general revelation," *justitia originalis,* the gift of reason in the *imago dei,* all distorted but not erased by sin). And this kind of liberal Christian also believes that one of the key tasks of the church is to continually rediscover, extend, and thereby refine our understanding of this capacity so that it may help sort through the religious stories, principles, and actions that people use to see which are most adequate to God and for holy living.

Many readers appreciate the freshness and energy Hauerwas brings to neglected themes of "character" and "virtue," but in this area too he repudiates too much — nearly everything that has to do with social, political, and economic analysis. This does not mean that he does not have opinions on these matters; his essays bristle with social, political, and economic judgments. He claims that he is simply "telling the story of Jesus." But, to quote Bishop Tutu, "What Bible is he reading?"

Three characteristic problems pervade this collection of speeches and essays. One appears on the first page when Hauerwas writes that he does not want his students to learn "to make up their own minds," but wants them "to think just like me." Anticipating those who find such a view fanatical, he goes on: "I am, of course, a fanatic. I want, for example, to convince everyone who calls himself or herself a Christian that being Christian means that one must be nonviolent."

To be sure, this could be a ploy to destabilize those conditioned by modern education to think that they have to start everything anew. Still, it is not clear just what he means. Does he really want or does he incidentally model the power of a cult leader or an ideologist? Every believer has to "do his own believing," as Luther says. Each of us finally has to make up his or her own mind on the most important questions with the aid of evidence, logic, and the gift of grace. The teacher's (and preacher's) peculiar role is to present the evidence and the logic with as much integrity and love as can be mustered, and to allow the seeds that are planted to take on the coloration of the soils in which they are planted. Evidence and logic can be judged, but it is wrong to demand conformity of conscience. Nor is it enough to suggest that the church does the believing for us. Why join it? Why nurture our children in it? Why locate oneself in a tradition? Do we do so only on some preacher's say so?

On the matter of using force, Hauerwas does not want any of his disciples to develop either the principles or the capacity to discern sociohistorical situations that would lead to selective conscientious objection or selective conscientious participation in situations of conflict, a position that, it seems to me, an ethics teacher ought to encourage, and one that both the Bible and the Christian tradition advocates. Hauerwas views those who use violence as "them," while the church is composed of those who are opposed to "them." Does he mean that those who engage in wife-beating, child abuse, or abortion are to be excluded from the ministries of the church? He never states these implications of his position. He writes as if not only these people but all who have a vocation in law, politics, military, or police work are excluded from the community of faith because they must use instruments of coercion. So no prison guard or federal marshal can be a Christian? Pastors should not preach about Christian vocation to or for them?

Hauerwas writes that he refuses to believe that politics is about coercive power. But this refusal does not make it less so. Even if politics is not *only* about that, it is not politics if it does not involve the accumulation and exercise of power. Is all that outside the church, outside faithfulness?

I do not believe that pastors "must" exclude from the communion rail all who unrepentantly serve in these public professions. Nor do I believe that it is simply a "liberal accommodation" to "secular democratic" culture to suggest that the church is made up also of citizen-soldiers and magistrates. Indeed, I think that the Protestant churches have, more than any other single force, generated modern democratic polity out of their intrinsically protodemocratic, conciliar ecclesiology, and that in consequence faithful believers ought also to be responsible participants in civil society.

Hauerwas praises Barth for standing for Christ, but he does not treat Barth's decision to join the Swiss militia. He loves the idea of the Confessing Church in Germany in the 1930s but does not mention Bonhoeffer's refusal to sign the Confessing Church's Barmen Declaration since it took its stand on Christological principles that could be seen as excluding Jews, nor does he mention Bonhoeffer's decision to join the plot to kill Hitler. He wrestles episodically with Rauschenbusch, Niebuhr, and Ramsey, but he dismisses them all as too liberal and too Constantinian — their ethics is too closely aligned with or enmeshed in political and social power.

Hauerwas cannot imagine anything like global responsibilities for a truly catholic or ecumenical church. That would be too "abstract." Nor does

Liberalism Dispatched vs. Liberalism Engaged

he recognize that the newer forms of international trade, communication, law, and cultural exchange challenge the version of "postmodernism" that sees us all trapped in our social locations or cultural-linguistic frameworks. While Hauerwas and others talk about the inevitable limits of our particularism, new international commonalities are being unveiled on every side.

In "Theology as Soul-Craft" [the first section of the Introduction], Hauerwas contends that the world needs more virtues rooted in the practices of particular communities, and that we can craft the soul by the cultivation of virtue. He does not mention that the word "virtue" seldom appears in the New Testament, and that there is no corresponding Hebrew word for it. When the term does appear, it seems to mean either the excellence of God or excellence in the surrounding culture, with the suggestion that Christians adopt these "things of good repute." But that is not what Hauerwas has in mind. (The term "virtue" does appear in Qumran writings, and it's significant that these anti-societal sectarians turned out to be "sons of truth" only in their own eyes.)

Hauerwas combines a touching confidence in the cultivation of the virtues for the improvement of character with a conviction that "society" does not really exist, or at least that it is a mistake to see God's presence in it, or to regard the transformation and upbuilding of the structures of the common life as part of the vocation to which God calls us. For Hauerwas, God exists, persons exist, traditions and practices exist, and the church exists (mostly in Mennonite territory), but society as a system of interacting "orders" sustained by the vocations by which God calls us to serve our neighbors in the world does not.

When Paul went to Rome, he found a righteousness already written on the hearts of nonbelievers, thought even its government was instituted by God, and said that Romans rightly knew the God they could not name. When Augustine contemplated the crises of civilization and of human love, he saw that the City of God was not only in tension with but also present in the city of humanity, and that we had to understand each to grasp the other. When we think about modern society, we have to recognize that parts of it are rooted in theologies that regard the responsible intervention in nature and in social history as an obedient reordering of a sinful world rather than a secular compromise with that world.

Although he uses the word "concrete" a lot, Hauerwas is decidedly anti-institutional. He appeals to the idea of church constantly, but without telling us anything about its polity, discipline, creed, constitution, or liturgy. Which church does he mean? He discusses relationships between doctors and patients without mentioning that they meet in an office or hospital under conditions in which some have insurance and some do not; he treats marriage as a doubtful option; he is contemptuous of business, law, and the professions, ignoring the fact that most believers are for most of their waking hours engaged in a complex interweave of activities in these aspects of life and properly want their relationship with God to inform their lives in these areas. Nor does he recognize that these areas of life have been shaped by Christian influence over the centuries and can be reformed by it in the future.

Pastors concerned to help people see where, in the midst of the complex contexts of a global civilization, God's providence may be at work, will not be helped by this approach. Those deeply alienated from society, who view the West as little more than an imperialist, market economy driven by greed, and who thus see the church as calling people out of the world, may be excited by Hauerwas. But the question remains as to whether we are most faithful the more we oppose cultural, social, and civilizational life, or whether the God witnessed to by the Bible and present in Jesus Christ lives among the peoples of faith in all walks of life.

Hauerwas doubts the relationship of theology to such questions. He writes that the churches will allow "fellow Christians [to] doubt that God is Trinity, but they would excommunicate anyone who does not believe, as I do not believe, in 'human rights.'" On this point he has a long footnote about a book by Michael Himes and Kenneth Himes on the public significance of theology (*Fullness of Faith*, 1993). The authors argue that in the doctrine of the Trinity, which states the dignity and distinctness of each person rooted in the self-giving of God, we find an authentic statement of the deep logic of the biblical faith, stated in post-biblical terms. The doctrine of the Trinity serves as the decisive charter for Christian existence in complex societies and bears within it implications that enhance ideas of human rights. The authors challenge the secular political philosophers and the anti-modern dogmatists who see democracy and human rights as secular doctrines, for they show that these modern political developments draw from a deeper well.

Hauerwas is puzzled by all this. He cannot see any connections at all. He asks why these authors think these connections matter, and who cares. If he means that neither the human rights office of the State Department nor the Chinese government cares much whether human rights is rooted in the doctrine of the Trinity, he is probably right. But if he doubts that the church discovered something of universal importance in developing the doctrine, or that it has decisive implications for the fundamental ordering of the common life, he is surely wrong.

When Muslims deny Trinitarian thought in favor of an undifferentiated

Liberalism Dispatched vs. Liberalism Engaged

monotheism, it has manifest social consequences. When liberationists such as Leonardo Boff modify it toward a quaternity, when eco-feminists repudiate it in favor of an organic monism, or when contemporary "pluralists" challenge it in favor of a "new polytheism," as Alan Miller calls it, much is at stake in both the faith of the church and the life of humanity — if, of course, one thinks that belief shapes common life. When the bishops met in Nicaea and Constantinople to debate these issues, when both Catholic and Protestant scholars took them up with care, and when contemporary theologians from Barth and Pannenberg to John Paul II and the Faith and Order Commission debate these questions, they have known that they are very close to the connection between the inner life of God and the way God relates to and wants us to live together in the world.

In an "incoherent culture," as Hauerwas calls it, it is the break from, not the connection to, the common life that he wants. He does not see how the Christian theology of the Trinity or the ethic of human rights can be universally true. He does not trust cosmopolitan thought; he wants particular narratives. But in pursuing this concern he blinds himself to the deepest levels of coherence.

Early in the volume, Hauerwas announces the narrative that will be his focus. "The heart of this book is constituted by two essays built around the work of Anthony Trollope." Hauerwas is alert to the fact that these Victorian novels that focus on the manse and the manor are a "highly refined form of gossip," and admits that that is "what I am trying to do. . . ." Why Trollope? Hauerwas replies: "I use Trollope because I love to read Trollope."

We all have preference in these matters, and there may be good reasons to like Trollope. Some pastors live entirely in that world. But a more serious question lurks behind Hauerwas's arbitrary move. Why would anyone choose one narrative over another? Can any criteria ever be given, besides preference, for what one chooses to spend one's time with (and much ink on)?

The question has a lot to do with the issues posed to theology today. Why choose the biblical narrative and not the Qur'an or the *Mahabarata*? If we say, with Hauerwas, that it is because the Bible is ours, or because we prefer it, or that its meaning is self-evident to all who are truly faithful and that there is no other reason that could be given, then we confirm what critics of the Christian faith have thought for some time — Christian thought is groundless, has no justifications whatsoever, and is unwilling to talk seriously about itself and its presuppositions.

Many of us cannot follow Hauerwas's lead. We will not allow vague attacks on liberalism to undercut the legacy of open, critical, and systematic

Interpreting the Tradition of Public Theology

philosophical theology and theological ethics. We will turn to other ways of thinking for the ethics to guide our lives and the theology to guide our faith — ways that are more likely to connect rather than disconnect the soul and God, the heart and the mind, virtues and first principles, the life of the church and the fabric of society, the microcosms of our lives and the macrocosms of civilizations.

PART TWO

Developing a Method for Public Theology

The Tasks of Theological Ethics[1]

Christian Ethics is about how the God whom we know in Jesus Christ wants humanity to live in a world where many "principalities and powers, authorities and dominions" are at work in our hearts and in our societies. We are called by God to live in this world in accord with norms that are not simply "worldly," but are in accord with the laws and purposes of God, and with the love of Christ. These are in principle universal in character and pertinent to the particularities of life in the world as well as to the ultimate destiny of our lives and of the biophysical cosmos as a whole. Further, Christian Ethics as a field is, as I understand it, a specific form of religious ethics, one brought under philosophical-theological critical and comparative examination and linked thereby to the analysis of human nature and the dynamics of socio-historical life. It is, thus, inevitably interdisciplinary. It always involves theo-

---

1. This paper is adapted from themes developed in my "General Introduction" to *Religion and the Powers of the Common Life*, vol. 1 of *God and Globalization* (Harrisburg, PA: Trinity Press International, 2000). See also the "Introductions" to *The Spirit and Modern Authorities*, vol. 2 of *God and Globalization* (2001), and *Christ and the Dominions of Civilization*, vol. 3 of *God and Globalization* (2002), both also from Trinity Press International. Vol. 4, *Divine Covenants: Public Theology and the Emerging Global Society*, is under preparation. [Volume 4 was subsequently published under the title *Globalization and Grace: A Christian Public Theology for a Global Future*.]

This essay was originally published as "Christian Ethics, Practical Theology and Public Theology in a Global Era," in *Reconsidering the Boundaries Between Theological Disciplines*, ed. Michael Welker and Friedrich Schweitzer (Münster: LIT Verlag, 2005), pp. 99-111. It appears here in shortened form. Endnotes in portions of the original essay that were removed in the creation of this shorter piece were also deleted and the remaining endnote numbers updated accordingly. *The editors.*

retical and practical matters, and is held by many of its specialists to be a, if not the only, primary bridge between biblical, historical, and systematic theological reflection on one side and the practice of both ministry in the church and the various vocations we have in the several spheres of life on the other.

Christian Ethics presupposes, in this regard, that we humans can, through the testimonies of those touchstones of theology — scripture, tradition, reason, and experience — come to some publicly defensible models, all mutually corrective and open to continual discussion and debate, of how we ought to live, even if we do not always do so. The very idea of theology as a modifier of ethics in this definition has several presumptions built into it: That the term "God" refers to something about which we can reasonably speak, that this reality is concerned about life, especially human life in the world, and that this life is to be lived both under conditions of finite time and space and while taking constant account of that which transcends the temporal and spatial. Further, it is a distinctive claim of the Christian form of theology that the inevitable tension between the transcendent and immanent is overcome in principle and in promise in Jesus Christ, and that all who come to know God's principles and purposes are called to be instruments of that integrative possibility by working for an ethos that honors and actualizes those principles and purposes of God within the worldly spheres of life. That is, the principles and purposes are brought to bear, so far as possible, in the structures of civil society: the family and community, the economy and culture, the school and university, the clinic and hospital, the professions and political processes that shape the regime — in ways that can nurture, channel, or constrain the God-given energies and talents of humanity toward the service of others and the glory of God. In this regard Christian Ethics is inevitably also "practical theology."

Today we are aware that we always think about such matters while living in a specific context, and that it is the context that often presents issues to us that demand our theological, ethical, and practical attention. Indeed, we have had a generation of thinkers deeply influenced by a century of critical reflection on social history and the social sciences, who have sought to become more and more specific about the nature of the context from which we speak. Some, indeed, have come to argue that our theology and our ethics are nothing but the reflection of our particular social location. This has tended to correct the impression left by some interpreters of Christian doctrine that normative ideas leap like unencumbered electric charges from mind to mind. But both theoretical and practical considerations invite us to modulate both forms of reductionism. For one thing, it is difficult to ignore the fact that people are able to think about context-transcending realities such as ethical norms that are not present in this or that context, but think they should be and work in the context to implement them. Victims of racism or patriarchy, for example, appeal to principles of justice that are not obviously operative in their context. Their contextual situation may prompt a search for something that transcends their social condition; for their context, by itself, cannot supply the vision of a more just possibility, or even the conviction that according to the laws and purposes of God, the context that enforces their subordination is wrong. In some cultures and according to some religions, for example, the subordination of people by ethnicity or gender is understood to be part of the metaphysical-moral logic of the universe which cannot be altered and ought not be attempted.[2]

For another, the context in which we live is forcing us to think in more universalistic terms than recent contextual thought has allowed. Today, the world as a historical interaction of people and societies is undergoing a dynamic transformation that is called "globalization." While many think of this essentially as an economic phenomenon marked by the expansion of Western or even American capitalism, a deeper view recognizes that insofar as this is taking place it is a secondary effect of a far deeper and wider set of sociocultural and technological changes that have many implications for "our worlds" as the familiar institutions of civil society, for "the world" as biophysical planet, and for "worldly concerns" as a philosophical-theological focus on conditioned existence in contrast to one focused on unconditioned being. The extent of this change demands a reassessment of those traditions that have not only contributed to the dynamics now reshaping what we have, but invites our reconsideration of the more ultimate principles of justice that stand over and above the world in which we live. A reconsideration may influence our capacity to participate in, avoid victimization by, and constructively guide key aspects of what appears to be the creation of a new encompassing, complex world civilization.[3] . . .

---

2. The most challenging modern treatment of this view is found in Louis Dumont, *Homo Hierarchicus: The Caste System and Its Implications* (Chicago: University of Chicago Press, 1970, trans. from the French edition of 1966). This view is, today, being challenged by Christian, neo-Buddhist, and some Islamic thought which has prompted a striking reassertion of caste-oriented politics in India. See *God and Globalization,* vol. 3, especially the Introduction and chapter 5, "Hinduism and Globalization: A Christian Theological Approach," by Thomas Thangaraj.

3. In this connection, it is quite remarkable that noted contemporary practical theologians include both theological ethical and sociohistorical analyses of globalization in their current work. See Don S. Browning, *Marriage and Modernization: How Globalization Threat-*

Developing a Method for Public Theology

Moreover, a generation of Christian theologians and ethicists who basically accepted the liberation ideologies of the decolonializing period, with their heavy dependence on Marxist social analysis, continue to see globalization as nothing more than the obviously evil expansion of transnational corporations. It is as if the spread of constitutional democracy, the extension of human rights agreements, the rapid growth of international law, the growing awareness of ecological responsibilities, the formation of massive new middle classes in, for instance, India, China, Southeast Asia, Korea, Malaysia, Brazil, Argentina, Chile, etc., the expansion of communications capabilities, and the reduction of nationalism in new regional modes of cooperation were not parts of globalization.

This is not to deny the fact that some Western political policies, and, in particular, some American ones, have both advanced aspects of globalization and failed to make a credible case for what is going on. It is a scandal, for example, that both Europe and the United States advocate free trade as the way for poor countries to develop, yet subsidize various products, from agriculture to steel, that other parts of the world could produce cheaper, trade to the West, and more quickly come to participate in the benefits of a global economy. It is also damaging to the future of international relationships that the United States government did not make a cogent case for repudiating the Kyoto Accords regarding global warming or for invading Iraq. It could be that both actions were justifiable, but the administration did not utilize available ethical arguments that the protection of our common ecological future could be handled better by alternative means, or that the protection of the human rights of the Iraqi people required a regime change under criteria of "just war" and "humanitarian intervention," as was argued with regard to Kosovo. The fact that the actions taken were taken without due moral argument tends to leave us in a situation where economic and political aspects of globalization have a legacy where power at least appears to be unconstrained by moral insight or cross-cultural debate, in a way that makes arbitrary action ethically naked. This legacy may well be more difficult to overcome in the foreseeable future than the consequences of the actions themselves. Such actions both discredit global developments and encourage views blind to what globalization entails at other levels. . . .

In partial contrast to dogmatic theology, which seems always to take

---

ens Marriage and What to Do About It (Grand Rapids: Eerdmans, 2003); and Richard R. Osmer and Friedrich Schweitzer, *Religious Education between Modernization and Globalization* (Grand Rapids: Eerdmans, 2003).

its point of departure exclusively from the Bible and the classic creeds of the Christian church, and tries to make sense of these for contemporary believers, those forms of theology that are most decisive for Christian Ethics in regard to our globalizing era and to practical theology within it also include as points of authoritative reference, as mentioned earlier, reason and experience, including not only the findings of the social sciences but now also the comparative study of the various religions and metaphysical-moral philosophies around which civilizations form their defining structures of meaning. Insofar as this "public theology" is distinctively Christian, it must show how and why it makes sense to hold to the authority of the Bible and the classic creeds.

One critical issue in the effort to develop a public Christian Ethics is that it must make the warranted argument as to why and how adherence to the traditional centers of authority, scripture, and tradition allows us to ethically and spiritually understand how human civilizations work and how they can become more clearly guided by the highest principles and ultimate ends that God intends. The study of these aspects of the tasks of ethics becomes thus a critical ingredient in any serious practical theology. For one thing, this approach allows us to address questions that doubters and seekers have already in their minds. For another, common issues of justice, vision, and responsibility, of righteousness, hope, and compassion, and of truth, anticipation, and virtue are intrinsic to the theological task, for no one can authentically give loyalty or credence to a view of God or an ethic or a civilizational order based on them that does not evoke, ground, manifest, and sustain these qualities. In our emerging global civilization, therefore, theological ethical issues become practically unavoidable. Insofar as we can know these things, we must come to a judgment about the world and how God wants us to live in, respond to, and shape it. . . .

Because of these several, complex relationships and interactions it is necessary to clarify the primary tasks of any who engage in theological ethics. One indispensable task, as already suggested, is to interpret the social contexts of life at the deepest moral and spiritual levels possible. This task demands close attention to the work of historians, social scientists, and those who have become skilled professionals in a specific area of human activity. Theological ethicists are thus inevitably social ethicists. And while some become specialists in a specific discipline related to these areas of study, analysis, practice, or reflection, more become generalists, reading widely in the social and historical sciences, for they know that it is impossible today to do good work in theological ethics without drawing on the research and experience of these fields. The concern of theological ethics at this juncture is to discern accurately the operational norms and values built into the ethos of the areas in which these "experts" work.

An "ethos" is the subtle web of "values" and "norms" — obligations, virtues, convictions, mores, purposes, expectations, and legitimations that constitute the operating norms of a culture in relation to a social entity or set of social practices. The values and norms of an ethos may not be agreed upon by all. In fact, they may be sharply contested. At some point, though, they became the organizing scaffolding of common behavior and moral debate in an institution, movement, organization, or tradition, even if many people hold, as personal convictions, other values and norms.[4] Theological ethics seeks to discern what these operating values and norms are as they play out in various areas of behavior and belief, what the functioning or regulative structures and dynamics of an ethos are; in brief, what is going on morally and spiritually.

Moreover, ethicists want to know, at the deeper levels of motivation and commitment, what sustains the values and norms when and if they are thwarted, violated, or denied by various contrary forces, or when they demand sacrifices contrary to the ordinary complementary interests of those who hold them. To discern "what is going on" at this level, ethicists become theological in the descriptive or phenomenological sense. They seek, with the more profound social analysts and historians, for example, to articulate the vision of ultimate reality that is thought to stand behind the ethos to legitimate it and provide its compelling meaning. The theological ethicist will inquire into the explicit or implicit view of what is holy, sacred, or inviolable about various values or norms in the ethos of this or that practice, institution, sphere of society, culture, or civilization. Only some among the many modes of historical, social-scientific, cultural, or religious analysis available are helpful at this point. Some comprehend more aspects of complex human actions than others; some go more thoroughly into the basic conceptions of ultimate reality that legitimate the values and norms of the ethos; some offer a deeper portrait of the human condition. "Ethology" studies these contextual factors, but does so in a way that transcends most contextual analyses — not a few of which are cases and others of which are simply a situation, both within a

---

4. Gertrude Himmelfarb, *One Nation, Two Cultures* (New York: Vintage, 1999), does ethics a great service as an historian and cultural critic when she points out that the theologically based Puritan founders of the United States established an order that harbors a now dominant anti-theological counterculture, but still upholds a democratic civil society under law.

The Tasks of Theological Ethics

sociohistorical ethos that brought them into being and defined their problematic character.

Theological ethics involves a second task. This is the assessment of whether what is going on ought to go on. Are the operating values and norms that ethology discerns really valuable and normative? Are the habituated or professed virtues truly virtuous? Are the functioning principles and governing goals valid? To ask these questions is to suggest that all operating values and norms, all examples of ethos as they are carried by various institutions, cultures, societies, or civilizations, are not equal and that it is possible, even if difficult, to recognize the difference between authentic and inauthentic meanings, values, virtues, principles, goals, and ends as these operate in various organized bodies by various groups. Thus, the attempt to do theological ethics presumes that it is in some significant measure possible to evaluate and assess, comparatively and critically, both the values and norms of an ethos and the various views of what is holy, sacred, or inviolable as they legitimate this or that particular ethos, beyond the task of indicative or descriptive discernment.

The question can immediately be raised, however, as to what, or whose, standards we should use to engage in this evaluation. This is a matter to which much attention has been given in both philosophy and theology.[5] Some argue that the standards derive essentially from recognizable and constant principles of right and wrong, and others argue that the standards derive from the desired, probable, or actually resulting good or evil consequences of intended behavior, some of which are built into the human condition and some of which are peculiar to various stages of social and cultural development....

A public theology will not only note the presence and importance of these factors in certain traditions, however; it will seek to show that these more clearly grasp the actual dynamics of human existence than other known

---

5. The issue was acutely posed by Alasdair MacIntyre, especially in his *Whose Justice? Which Rationality?* (Notre Dame: University of Notre Dame Press, 1988), whose arguments paralleled a series of attacks on, especially, Protestant forms of theological ethics and Enlightenment morality. However, the Leninist and Nietzschean roots of his views were not at first clear to many, especially to pietistic Christians who found in his work a negation of the general values of "modernity," and a rationale as to why they could assert their premodernist and highly particular subcultural values without having to make a case for them in the public domain. His views have been effectively challenged, in my view, by, among others, William Schweiker, *Power, Value, and Conviction: Theological Ethics in a Postmodern Age* (Cleveland: Pilgrim Press, 1998).

Developing a Method for Public Theology

alternatives. In this, public theology has an apologetic, sometimes a polemical element.

To be sure, those who are not consciously in a relationship with God are often also able to recognize the differences of right and wrong because these differences are scripted into the very fabric of life, to know when they are seeking good rather than evil by the critical examination of their own and their society's projects, and to approve the relative forms of righteousness and the proximate possibilities of exemplary goodness in the complexities of sociohistorical life that are present in the actions and societies of those who do not believe as well as of those who do. Plato argued this long ago, and it has been echoed in multiple forms subsequently, that these possibilities are to be honored, protected, and cultivated. But it is difficult to deny that we humans, believers or not, are forever caught up in ethical trade-offs and compromises. If we are honest, we must confess our complicity in "ambiguity" even if we are allergic to the word "sin."

Believers also hold that humans are called and enabled by God to be defenders of the right and instruments of the good, and are in principle able to do this with less distortion precisely because they know themselves to be "sinners," faulty beings who know but do not adhere to the highest standards of right or pursue the best ends. For this reason also, the second task of ethics requires a theological basis, for at certain levels of attitude and behavior, theological ethics points out, humans cannot integrate the right and good in life or in theory without God.[6] The moral confidence of every humanism must be muted by realism, modesty, and contrition in view of a holy source of morality, beyond humanity. The issue is not whether believers are more righteous than nonbelievers, a very difficult case to make, but whether believers have a better account of why we all are as we are in moral and spiritual matters, and why we need not despair.[7]

The attempt to find a faith-transcending, critical, secular base for universal human values and norms beyond religion has been explored at various times in intellectual history — most notably in the West among the ancient Greco-Roman philosophers, again in the Renaissance, and once more in the Enlightenment. Moreover, in the last several centuries the West has become aware of very subtle religious philosophies that have developed in other

---

6. See, for example, Glenn Tinder, *The Political Meaning of Christianity* (Baton Rouge: Louisiana State University Press, 1990).

7. In spite of some criticisms posed by contemporary feminist scholars, this is one of the central and enduring issues posed by Reinhold Niebuhr's *The Nature and Destiny of Man*, 2 vols. (New York: Charles Scribner's Sons, 1939-41).

contexts, those of Hinduism, Buddhism, and Confucianism particularly. However, it is more and more clearly recognized that many of the celebrated "secular" foundations for thought about philosophy, politics, economics, and science are less secular in their derivation than their advocates claim.[8] Under close examination it has become clear that "onto-theological" assumptions always lurk beneath the surface — sometimes masking interests and patterns of domination precisely whenever they do not (or cannot) defend their own foundations or admit that their own deepest presumptions are theological in nature. They often became political crypto-theologies and ideologies, some rather benign, many temporarily useful, a few positively vicious. Contemporary "postmodern" thought has exposed many of the pretensions of these efforts, even if the nihilist element in their exposé is unable to allow discernment of the deepest values and norms of an ethos, to evaluate fairly their normative content, or to suggest how an ethos ought to be sustained, revised, or transformed. This leads us to another task of theological ethics.[9]

The third task of theological ethics is prescriptive. It offers practical guidance about how we might, insofar as it is possible, form a more valid ethos and develop those attitudes, institutions, habits, policies, and programs that are in accord with critically evaluated first principles and ultimate ends of life in a more ethically viable ethos, rightly legitimated by a valid theological view of ultimate reality. The allies of theological ethics at this point are less the social scientist, historian, and professional, and less the philosopher, scientist, or specialist in the study of religions than the religious leader, the missionary, and the reformer — the latter often including the activists and advocates among those from these other fields who want to use the resources of their fields to improve the world and who grasp from their religious heritage or ethical environment a glimpse of the ultimate issues beyond the way life is at present.

---

8. This is not the place for a full argument on this point, but key representatives of the current arguments can be cited. See, for example, in regard to philosophy and political theory, Joshua Mitchell *Not by Reason Alone: Religion, History, and Identity in Early Modern Political Thought* (Chicago: University of Chicago Press, 1993); in economic and social thought, Robert H. Nelson, *Economics as Religion* (University Park: Pennsylvania State University Press, 2001); in science and technology, David F. Noble, *The Religion of Technology* (New York: Alfred Knopf, 1997).

9. See, for example, Mark C. Taylor, *Erring: A Postmodern A/theology* (Chicago: University of Chicago Press, 1984); and John Milbank, *Theology & Social Theory: Beyond Secular Reason* (Oxford: Blackwell, 1990). But also see J. Wentzel van Huyssteen, *Essays in Postfoundationalist Theology* (Grand Rapids: Eerdmans, 1998).

Theological ethics always has, and must have, a place for this prophetic, priestly, and political dimension, which the biblical tradition identified as the three "anointed offices," which always have missiological, constructive, and reformist aspects, and which are inevitably close to practical theology. While, at its best, this third, prescriptive task of ethics resists wildly utopian adventures and apocalyptic visions, it seeks to constrain evil systems and to construct better ones; it offers the prospects of a deeper, wider, more valid view; it seeks to improve things for persons and societies; and it hopes to alter the destiny of souls and civilizations by offering a vision that reaches beyond things as they are without sacrificing the realistic awareness that they have to work in and with recalcitrant people in a broken and imperfect world. These are the ones who help bring others to conviction about a previously unknown or disbelieved point of view, who feel called to persuade others that a different quality of life can be organized on a more adequate moral foundation warranted by a more ultimate framework of legitimacy. These are they who work, most often, in and through the organizations, religious and voluntary, of civil society, building networks of conviction that, if successful, play themselves out in reshaped spheres of life and the establishment of new roles and identities that can be assumed by people in them.[10]

It is clear that various religious leaders, pastors, missionaries, and reformers have sometimes been imperialistic, using their offices or credentials to impose the particularist values and norms of their own ethos on others without first engaging in the careful discernment of other people's contextual ethos or critical evaluation of their own. But a case might well be made that religious leaders, missionaries, and reformers have more often been governed by a religious zeal to reform things because they have a discerning ethical framework that allows them to recognize what needs reform. A vision of holiness illuminates the depths of corruption. On this basis, they have more often sought to constrain the imperialistic impulses of those advocates of "self-evident" superiority than being a party to them. Still, it must be recognized that religion is potentially explosive. If it had no power to influence life, few would care about it. Those who engage this proactive, change-oriented task of ethics must see that what they offer is just to all, based on the most universal realities we can know, and, so far as possible, voluntarily accepted.

If a religious perspective is propagated without a clear sense of ethics, without a direct reference to what is universally just and promotes per-

---

10. See my "If Globalization Is True, What Shall We Do? Toward a Theology of Ministry," *Theological Education* 35, no. 2 (Spring 1999): 155-65.

sonal integrity, it is more likely to be explosive. And if it is simply imposed, it is unlikely to claim the loyalties of those it presumes to aid. People have to decide for the message of the religious leader, the missionary, the reformer. They have to agree that what is advocated is right and good under God and fitting to the real or potentially real contexts of life. Even more, they have to conclude, after due consideration, that the warrants for these moral claims are comprehensible and comprehending — valid for them personally and, in some significant way, for humanity. If the message of the religious leader, the missionary, and the reformer is not convincing, people will sooner or later cease to attend to it, decide against it, subvert it at every opportunity, turn to other authorities, ideologies, or faiths, and raise every practical and theoretical objection to it they can think of. For these reasons, too, theology is necessary to ethics, and the third task of theological ethics must work by persuasion or it will not work at all. Only those theologies that are able to live by the power of the word, by reasonable communication that is able to reach across barriers of culture, civilization, and context and call people to conviction, will be compelling.

There is growing evidence that a recovery and recasting of "covenantal" thought can be critical in showing how the ethological, deontological, and teleological aspects of moral living can become more integrated in various spheres of the common life, open our vision to a more just global civilization, and become the guiding core of our practical theologies. It implies that, in the final analysis, a God-based framework for discernment, evaluation, and transformation is indispensable if we are to comprehend the moral and spiritual variables at stake in current globalizing developments. It can help us identify which ones are potentially right and good as these relate to the fitting manifestations of the human conditions, argue critically and reasonably for them in public discourse, evoke a commitment to them from the people, and draw the people into communities of commitment to reform and channel the principalities and powers, authorities and dominions in ways that allow humanity to flourish and to witness to God's glory.[11]

---

11. In integrating these three tasks, theological ethics also relates "common grace" (or "natural law") to community-forming covenants of conviction and to integrative views of "vocational" service, as is argued in volume 4 of *God and Globalization*.

The Religious Basis of Cultural Activity

I. Signals of a Wider Problem

Recently I was a member of a team, along with an artist and an historian, to interview a series of young scholars for Kent Fellowships. Drawn from a wide range of fields, these men and women from several countries represented some of the most promising future leaders of Western intellectual and cultural life. The grants for which they were competing were to be awarded not only on the basis of competence and promise in their fields, but also on the basis of their commitment to relate basic values to their professional work, their capacity to work in interdisciplinary settings, and their assumption of responsibility for the general structures of civilization as they bear on the common life of humanity. In short, we were asked to make judgments as to who were most likely to be among the decisive bearers of culture in the coming generation.

It was an amazing group. Even the weaker candidates were interesting. Of course, each had a unique set of values, a particular passion, a distinctive style, and a specific quality of thought. All cared deeply for their studies and gave of themselves to them. Yet there were some disturbing common features that can be noted.

All had decided to give their lives to academics or the arts. They believed their work was important, and they loved their work. But they often gave evidence of a deep suspicion that their work would not have a formative effect on civilization or politics. The latter have to do with structures, hardened interests, and power constellations, which in fact run the show. Their work would somehow be divorced from and probably irrelevant to what really determines the shape of things. Perhaps this feeling was due to a decent modesty, but we interviewers suspected more. We suspected that this generation did not really believe that the realms of *theoria*, of image, symbol, or concept, and of culture generally, had within them the power to shape civilization, or the capacity to civilize power. To be sure, these candidates could show how previous intellectual and artistic patterns *correlated* to previous civilizations and political arrangements. But there was the underlying question as to whether political power and civilizational structures had not, in fact, *produced* the cultural patterns. Were cultural values, religions, artistic creations not themselves primarily an expression of the civilization and the political regime? And, if so, is not giving oneself to "culture" the dedication of one's life to a mere epiphenomenon?

This view does not imply that there are no grounds at all for *theoria* or *ars* or strong value commitments. Recurrently in our conversations with the candidates, a concern for the "religious" and "genuinely human" appeared. But when the candidates were pressed to tell what the "genuinely human" or the "religious" is, their responses took two forms: a protest against "dehumanization," and an affirmation of very personal experiences. "Religious" was indistinguishable from the "aesthetic." And the "genuinely human" seemed always to be expressed in terms of the calm or ecstasy of music, the joy and pain of being in love, the agony and invigoration of existential decision, the exhaustion and exhilaration of highly particular scientific or imaginative achievement. The "human" was treated as situational and anecdotal. There was little of the dramatic. That is, there was no character, no plot, no history, and less future. There was no basis or foundation for coherence. There was no wrestling with God or with ultimate evil. The implicit mild humanism in the responses was not a broad conception applicable to politics or civilizations, but confined to the private, the momentary, the personal.

The anguish that I sensed in these highly sensitive people approached the tragic. They could articulate no basis for doing what they had done or for understanding how they had done what they had done. They had transcended their family backgrounds, many aspects of American society, and ethically criticized the society on public issues. They showed familiarity with the nuances of political life. And they had chosen a life's vocation that would make them constant companions of the realm of concepts, images, and symbols, interpreters of the past and the present; but they did not, somehow they could not, believe in anything that actually transcended empirical reality.

In their private perspectives, they were moral absolutists. They held firmly to beliefs that some things about our "capitalist" civilization and our recent political directions were absolutely wrong. Yet, there was a pronounced reticence to say why they are wrong. They held a fundamental doubt that anything was normatively valid in ethics, that there was a verifiable theoretical touchstone of cultural interpretation, that there was anything real about the life of the mind. All that smacked of abstraction, of projection, of idealism, of speculation. Plato is dead, Thomas is dead, Kant is dead; indeed, God is dead as an objective reality serving as a basis for social judgment (even among those for whom personal religious beliefs were profoundly significant).

It is possible, of course, that out of the recesses of private feelings, born of personal needs and interests, powerful emotions can well forth and provide resistance to those forms of "peace" that are in fact systematized violence. Oppression posing as order, but in fact hiding organized chaos, can be experienced widely in idiosyncratic ways. All the delicate tissues of ordinary human meaning become fractured or suppressed. Out of such experience can issue screams of indignation. The poet, the painter, the religious prophet, and the revolutionary leader may, in these contexts, lift up the private, the particular, and the concrete so that they become paradigmatic symbols of resistance. The cry for liberation ascends. At other times the meaninglessness of all the "official reasons" for destruction may be protested. The bearers of culture may become critics, knowing and showing that those reasons are no reasons. They do not make sense. In either case, however, there is an implicit assumption that there is some genuine human meaning that can become articulate, a sense that something transcends the particularity of this or that personal experience, this or that specific reason. And to discuss the significance of such protest or resistance requires an awareness of the structural patterns against which they occur.

Protest and resistance by themselves, however, do not require that basic assumptions become articulate, and they have not been articulated. In protest and resistance there is the recognition of negation, and the negation of that negation. But the negation of negation does not supply affirmation. Affirmation requires a cultural vision of that which has not yet been actualized, and the assumption that the bearer of culture has a rootage in something real beyond what is or has been the case. The intellectual and the artist surely have to be able to suggest what is so good about justice and peace and meaning since they seem to appear so seldom. But such suggestions, even more pronouncedly than resistance or protest, require a common, and commonly believed, affirmation of what can and ought to be beyond both the empirical situation and the merely personal. A vision of genuine peace, justice, and meaning requires that the action of the bearer of culture be based on a view that the cultural vision transcends the empirical civilization. Even more, such a vision must be rooted in something that is believed to have potency to effect things. It is incredible as only a figment of private preference or group imagination.

And now we see the critical problem of these young people, indeed of many bearers of culture in academic, intellectual, and artistic circles. Nothing that they can conceive of can "really" be a basis for a new vision. Religion is human need writ large, as Feuerbach said; ideals are introjected neuroses, as Freud claimed; cultural images are the ideology of the ruling classes, as Marx indicated; morality is the convention of the mediocre according to Nietzsche; and philosophy is the testimony of personal authenticity according to Sartre. In reaction to various reified forms of Christian theology, moral absolutism, and idealistic philosophy, which assumed a fixed supernaturalism of deities or ideas, these pioneers of critical thought have produced a debunking attitude toward any claims that there is a basis of meaning or culture other than concrete historical experience. Religion, ideas, morality, and the arts are deprived of their power to inform a civilization or political power in a fundamental way. They are but epiphenomena of the concrete, the historical, the empirical. They have no power to guide, to inspire, to evoke response except perhaps to the unlettered. They have no worth except the capacity to control the yet unilluminated masses. To borrow Peter Berger's terms, the "Sacred Canopy" has collapsed; we are left with a "Homeless Mind."

Modern generations who experienced the Industrial Revolution, World War I, the Russian Revolution, the Depression, and World War II were already forced to think new thoughts, to develop new models for society, to suspect there are powers we know not of that drive the forces of human history, and doubt the efficacy of their own commitments to culture. Various forms of "realism," precisely the opposite of previous philosophical and religious realisms, had become the conventional wisdom of the age before this generation was born. But these earlier movements were, to use Paul Tillich's fortunate phrase, "belief-full realisms." That is, they were realisms that saw new cultural possibilities precisely *in* political and civilizational change.

In contrast to absolutized cultural visions of Gods, eternal Ideas, or natural, universal laws, which were linked to fixed traditional patterns of civilization, change itself was celebrated: social change as a self-authenticating process gave rise to social visions, to grand hopes, to utopian thinking, to the reconstruction of religious affirmations, to ethical demands for a new order in both culture and civilization. To be sure, some of these hopes and visions were pathological, and they quickly degenerated into self-destructive movements. But others gave artists, poets, journalists, dramatists, social scientists, philosophers, and theologians an impetus to imaginative work, an inspiration for expectant action. And in these "belief-full realisms" the vision was glimpsed of a universal, just peace, a human harmony achieved through and beyond the immediate pain of conflict and suffering, and resting on an emerging universal sense of meaning.

The grounding of this universal sense of meaning was widely debated. Yet all of its diverse expressions involved a genuine, if intrahistorical, interaction between one or another conception of "theory" and "practice," between idea and the biophysical universe, between being and existence, between the divine and the created, or between culture and civilization. The locus of meaning was in any case "historical." If a two-story universe had come tumbling down piece by piece, there was a residue of optimistic expectancy in the rubble. A dialectic of relative factors takes place in history. History produces cultures and civilizations and they interact on one another. But if this dialectic held, it would be necessary to ascribe a creative power to history itself. One could find the creative vision for peace, justice, and meaning in the very logic of human experience. The bearer of culture no longer was the surveyor of superordinate images to solve the factious conflicts of human civilization. Instead, the progressive and inevitable struggle of the logic of history would in the outworking of civilization itself bring a new age, a new stage, or a new being into existence.

The responsibility of the bearer of culture in such a world is to discern, by politically engaged analysis, where the genuinely creative powers within history lead. The bearer of culture stands, in this view, not above civilization struggles, bringing eternal truths to the realm of temporal strife, but on the "front edge," at the "tip of history's thrust," identifying and clarifying where it is going. The basis of meaning is found in the *process* of cultural and civilizational change. Human historical experience is not something that the intellectual or artist renders meaningful by lifting paradigmatic moments into consciousness, nor is it something to be escaped in a search for immutable truths that overarch it. In contrast, human historical experience is meaningful in itself. The intellectual and the artist anticipate the future to which this experience will take us all. History is full of meaning in its own dynamic thrust toward the future. It contains in its own directions, the promise of an eventual peace.

Such is the view of various providential, evolutionary, progressive, and revolutionary theories of history that allowed earlier generations to hold to a "belief-full realism." Their chief enemies were those who still held to a dualism of fact and value, meaning and happening, of thought and experience;

The Religious Basis of Cultural Activity

and their intramural debates, often the more vicious, were whether the cutting edge was more evolutionary or more revolutionary. The whole of humanity would in any case inevitably be led to democracy, to socialism, to equality, to justice, and thereby to peace and the fulfillment of meaning.

The young candidates we met wished mightily that this belief-full realism were so. But they, like so many more mature scholars, do not really believe it. They see this view too as part of the "sacred canopy" that has collapsed. The "hidden hand" of the capitalist market that was to lead to harmony and plenty; the "dialectic of history" that was to produce a new social order and a humanity beyond tyranny and exploitation; the "manifest destiny" of democracy; the "wave of the future" of the "Third World" are not really dead. They are living ghosts, legacies of the period of "belief-full realism." But to these people, the vigor of these ghosts is gone, and some of them need to be exorcized. The inevitability of progress in and through history cracked under the strain of twentieth-century experience.

Humanity does not have noticeably fewer illusions after Feuerbach, even if the older ones are exposed. Indeed, some theologians (such as Karl Barth) have turned Feuerbach on his head, agreeing that, indeed, theology is anthropology, but asserting that theology is prior to anthropology. The disciples of Marx have indeed changed the face of the world and established a relative economic democracy. But the capacity to generate or tolerate self-critical cultural expression, or to permit a political opposition the right to move the dialectic along toward the expected new humanity (and with its appearance the demise of the coercive state) remains minimal. The couch of Freud has for multitudes replaced the confessional, but the mental health of the people is not noticeably improved. The destruction of the conventions of morality after Nietzsche seemed less to bring the nobility of the new superman than racism and genocide. The dead end of the existentialist search for the authentic self, where "hell is other people," is surpassed only by the rediscovery of a new social and universal humanism, but the grounds for this rediscovery remain foggy.

It is possible, as many claim, that these are but transitional states of affairs. We must press through these transitional states to the more radical future. But the attempt to press through these trends by climbing out further onto the cutting edge of history produces a dizziness. As social history seems to move at an increasing pace, the bearer of culture standing at the tip to discern meaning in its direction becomes subject to "rapidation." Alvin Toffler's otherwise unedifying *Future Shock* aptly describes the eroding waves of novelty that are experienced by this generation. The idea of stand-

Developing a Method for Public Theology

ing on the "front edge" may well have made sense when one believed there were three basic "periods" of human history and that the world was on the brink of transition from the second to the third. But what if "periodization," the discernment of periods or stages, is reduced from eras, or centuries, or even decades to a rapid succession of passing moments? This week the issue is the new fascism of the left, next week corporate (or state) capitalism, then racism, then sexism, then world hunger, followed by multinational corporations and ecology. The bearer of culture becomes trapped in a provincialism of time precisely at the "cutting edge." The crisis of the moment is elevated to ultimacy. But the ultimacy passes with the moment, and the bearer of culture is left with only a debilitating rootlessness, and the capacity for sustained education or critique is undercut. And should he or she suggest that one of these issues is the root historical experience for all the others, they are victims of the passé.

History may well have a direction and a meaning to be captured in a vision of the future, but direction and meaning are not so readily seen from the "front edge." They do not leap to the surface. The complexities and ambiguities of historical experience resist any simple formulation of meaning. Any attempt to speak of meaning or direction in history requires, more than anything else, a principle of interpretation. And that principle of interpretation cannot derive from the "front edge" itself. And there is the rub. We are to be bearers of culture within the turbulence of time and with no rock upon which to stand. Realism is without belief. There is no ground for vision. Ontology is a reification of existence; the divine, an objectification of the human; and culture, the product of human civilization. History becomes a matter of fate or accident. There is no objectively valid or knowable basis for theory except practice. The dialectic is broken. And there is no publicly ascertainable foundation for thought, artistic creation, or meaning that one can relate to a society, to a civilization, to a world community, or a world-historical process. Were this generation to write a new scripture, it might start out: "In the beginning people experienced. From their experience they created values, ideas, cultures, and Gods. These became reified and effected civilization. But they saw they were neither good nor true. Thus they knew that their paradise, where meaning existed, was a chimera."

Hannah Arendt pointed out some time ago in *The Human Condition* that the life of the *polis* in the ancient Greek world was the realm of creativity, freedom, and virtue. Public life could be in theory, in choice informed by the realm of serious public discourse, in contrast to private and family life, which were governed by the fates and by stereotyped, ritualized behavior. Fustel de

The Religious Basis of Cultural Activity

Coulanges's now classic *The Ancient City* provides a fascinating glimpse into this world also. Similar statements could be made about the ancient Hebrew world of the Old Testament prophets. To the present generation of intellectuals, the opposite is the case. A malaise about the public domain reigns, and meaning is found by carving out a space for private or interpersonal meaning that is judged genuine only insofar as it has a direct relationship to immediate experience.

II. Toward an Apologetic for Intellectual Life

If this situation is in any sense pervasive in our times, both the possibilities for serious intellectual and artistic work and the prospects for a vital civilization are surely questionable. If people can only bring themselves to concentrate on the immediate, the personal, and the experiential, the bases for ordering and gaining perspective on the immediate, the personal, and the experiential are compromised. Intellectual work is likely to become victim of the capriciousness of the immediate; and civilizational institutions are left to the vultures who live by devouring lifeless remains.

The question is whether we can articulate a compelling basis for what we, as ethically concerned intellectuals and artists, do with our lives.

The specific work of a bearer of culture is the clarification and communication, the exploration and reconstruction of image, symbol, and concept. These forms of expression bear within them the basic visions of meaning and value. They tell us how to perceive, how to hear, how to believe, how to act, and how to be. In ancient days these images and symbols were treated as gods, or as the residence or property of gods. To choose among images, symbols, or concepts was to choose among the gods, to allow oneself to be put under a commanding reality wherein one finds both creative freedom and the demand for disciplined obedience. Each placing of loyalties involved a sense of purpose, a scale of values, and a sense of the right ordering of the common life. Each was a truth claim. And the richer, the more profound the images, the symbols, and the concepts, especially if they were set forth with fervent simplicity, the wider the range of civilization these gods could claim as their domain. Only when choices are made for one or another set of images, symbols, and concepts can a civilization be established, sustained, or transformed. It is not by the voiding of loyalties, in the name of objectivity or rational scholarship, that bearers of culture serve society or truth, but by passionate and critical placement of loyalties in objective realities, and by disciplined mediation of their meanings. In this regard, civilization is dependent upon the bearers of culture, indeed on the "gods" of the bearers of culture.

It was through compelling images, symbols, and concepts as much as through organizational networks surviving a general collapse of institutional life that Christianity overcame "the metaphysical disease" of the ancient Greco-Roman world. It was through these same forms of meaning that Protestantism as much as the Renaissance shaped Northern Europe and America. It was through such meanings that Confucius and the Buddha shaped classical Asia. And it is through images, symbols, and concepts, as much as through political organization, that Marx has had such influence from the reading room of the British Museum. Thomas Kuhn's concept of the "paradigm shift" in his much-discussed *The Structure of Scientific Revolutions* and Ian Barbour's treatment of similar matters in *Myths, Models and Paradigms in Science and Religion* suggest that, indeed, modern natural science is itself rooted in similar developments. The content of these images, symbols, and concepts is, of course, variable; so that some, such as Professor Winich (in a summary article in Gould and Kolb's *Dictionary of the Social Sciences*), can speak of "cultural relativism" as "the principle that experience is interpreted by each person in terms of his own background, frame of reference, and social norms, and that factors will influence perceptions and evaluations, so that there is no single scale of values applicable to all societies." But the actual experience of the intellectual or artist suggests another possibility. When the artist paints, the composer works out a score, the dramatist writes a play, the scholar makes an argument, the judge renders a decision, or the believer tries to express a piety felt, there is a point where the images, symbols, and concepts with which they work begin to take on a life their own. The reality of what the images, symbols, and concepts represent exists prior to the work's completion and begins to work itself out on its own terms. The experience that evokes the cultural activity, and the images, symbols, and concepts by which it is expressed no longer remain merely "mine" or "ours" to do with what we will. They have their own terms to which we must be obedient. Our choices have to do with worthiness and integrity of the material we are representing, our willingness to place ourselves under these demands, and our marshaling of courage to bring these demands before the civilization.

All who have worked intensely on a cultural creation know of what I speak. It involves a concrete experience of ecstasy — of *ex-stasis* — of standing outside or beyond the particularity of intentional creation. It is distinct from, although it often occurs in the midst of, the grinding work of attention to detail and ordinary responsibility. At certain points one becomes aware of

The Religious Basis of Cultural Activity

what must be done; the "must" does not proceed entirely from our intention to do, yet the "must" evokes a passion to do. The composer "hears" the harmony before he can write it; the painter "sees" the outline before being able to paint it; the characters of drama and novel begin to play their parts before they are known to the author; the logic of an argument becomes clear before it can be worked out by the scholar. An urgency prevents apathy and transcends forced production. In such moments the religious basis for cultural activity is revealed.

We are sometimes deceived in this process. Fantasy creates its own pretentious worlds. Still, the authentic "creative soul" receives as well as produces. It is not an accident that great artists or scholars are called "gifted." The excellence of the "production," indeed, partially depends on the skilled diligence with which one heeds the integrity of the creative power beyond him or her by discerning receptivity. To force a cultural production in one way or another makes the artifact inauthentic, whereas the genuine artifact has an integrity beyond the author's wishes. It is for this reason that it is proper to use the term "*bearer* of culture" for intellectuals and artists. Something is there that is to be conveyed and not merely made.

While this experience transcends civilization, in that it is neither dependent on any specific civilization nor predictable on the basis of the patterns of a civilization, the reality to which it points is not irrelevant to civilization. The bearer of culture having such an experience *finds* meanings and values in it that force a stance vis-à-vis civilization as it is. Indeed, an intellectual or artistic work presents the civilization with a portrait of the fundamental decisions it has made, warts and all, as represented in images and symbols. Or it proposes alternative images, symbols, and concepts that call the civilization to alternative decisions that it can or ought to make. Such a representation of images, concepts, and symbols is no less real in a work of "minimalist" poetry or "optical" art than it is in a political epic or theological system. In any case, the actual processes of cultural life require a receptivity to a pattern, value, or meaning that has intrinsic worth and power prior to our efforts to represent it in image or symbol.

When a genuine cultural image, symbol, or concept is set before a civilization, it virtually shouts, "*This* is a major way to see, to feel, to act, to be." And all who come under its influence must decide: "Is it?" And to decide is not only to choose for or against the substance presented, but also for or against the civilization in which the cultural image or symbol is produced or received. Indeed, the civilization's survival or formation depends upon the cumulative power of such choices.

Developing a Method for Public Theology

III. Civilizational Responses

Civilizations respond differently to the fundamental reality presented by bearers of culture. In recent travel in Eastern Europe and in Asia, I saw how some societies recognize the power of cultural concepts, images, and symbols. But this power is a threat to civilizational patterns. Thus, political authorities restrict the range of choices by allowing only some to be produced and to reach the people. Bearers of culture may only send the "approved" images, symbols, and concepts. Only some "gods" may be represented. Thereby, any genuine dialectic between the basis for *theoria* and the actual *practice* of a civilization is frozen. But to maintain this condition, the conscientiousness of the artist and the intellectual has to be invaded and the living dynamic of a civilizational history must at least temporarily be repressed. Such a civilization makes war against itself, and its bearers of culture become divided against themselves. They cannot allow themselves to heed the sources of their own creativity.

Dramatic and dynamic images, symbols, and concepts can comprehend the major options. They present the most profound choices to civilizations because they point to the rich reality that is the source of all creativity. Such "gods" are not confined to the relativities of civilizations or to the secrets of the self. They stand beyond both, demanding social and personal choices and transformation. They issue in symbols, images, and concepts that bear the paradigmatic choices for humanity and allow the relative overcoming of relativity. These "gods" are rooted in the past but portend the future. They can either derive from the ecumenical encounter of times and spaces — from deep involvement with other times and other civilizations than the one in which they are produced — or plunge more deeply into the particularity one has at hand. Dennis Goulet in *The Cruel Choice* recently put the matter this way:

> Shakespeare is so very English, but he has plucked the heartstrings outside the British Empire. So with Lao-Tze: his masterful essay on The Way is thoroughly rooted in Chinese sensibility, yet it strikes a responsive chord in African or Western minds. And Dante, so profoundly Italian, has won rightful acclaim as a "universal" genius.

Of course the bearers of culture are civilization- and time-bound, but if they allow the objective and relatively autonomous powers that stand behind images, symbols, and concepts to emerge in them, they set before civilizations fundamental choices.

The Religious Basis of Cultural Activity

We are, it must be noted, on the brink of ultimate philosophical and theological questions. The bearer of culture may not shrink from such questions, though he or she may recognize that some theologians and philosophers have manipulated images, symbols, and concepts to baptize repressive or trivial forms of culture and civilization. At times they have taken recourse to a pure pietism that separates their message from civilization. More tragically they have sometimes absolutized and reified one set of images, symbols, and concepts and attempted to use the coercive powers of civilization in a "holy war" or "crusade" against all other choices. This pathology is as common among the ideologists of several secular philosophies as it is among the world's religions. Nevertheless, the bearers of culture have a role to play only insofar as they consciously assume the responsibility of standing on the brink of the ultimate philosophical, religious, and theological questions. Retreat from that vocation renders the work of the intellectual and the artist innocuous.

If the foregoing is valid, we may then suggest one final implication to the bearers of culture who are without, or are suspicious of, foundations for their own commitment to cultural work. Genuine intellectual and artistic work is most likely to occur where it is possible to conduct the "war of the gods," where fundamental images, concepts, and symbols may be posed in conflict with one another, with dominant cultural conventions, and with civilizational artifacts. Thus, bearers of culture must not only take responsibility for standing on the boundary of civilization in their intellectual and artistic work, they must also enter into the specific struggles of civilization in at least two ways. They must protect those relative "zones of freedom" wherein it is possible to pursue cultural activity. That is, the universities, the presses, the studios, the churches, and the various "guilds" of professional life have to be struggled for, supported, and sustained. It also means, as the ancient divines put it, that what one does or says has to be "understandable of the people." This latter point means both that there is a certain populist concern pertinent to the most esoteric forms of scholarly and artistic work, and that all of us are surely responsible for the edification of the people in such a way that a context of reception for images, concepts, and symbols is developed beyond the boundaries of our specific vocational, and especially career, concerns. In these ways, the basis for *theoria* can become an invigorating force in human civilization, and the prospect for cosmopolitan values can come within our horizons. Without them we not only become victims of our own doubts, we allow the mechanics of our work and the entropy of civilizations to overwhelm the foundations of all that we are about.

Public Theology and Ethical Judgment

The term "public theology" first appeared in the title of a 1974 analysis of the thought of Reinhold Niebuhr (1892-1971).[1] The main point of the article was that this leader of American Protestant ethics represented a deep strand of intellectual history, one rooted in the close interaction of religious insight, philosophical reflection, and social analysis. Rightly grounded and formed, they could form a basic conceptual framework capable of providing an accurate analysis of historical experience and of guiding ethical judgment in our common life. The term was used to stress the point that theology, while related to intensely personal commitments and to a particular community of worship, is, at its most profound level, neither merely private nor a matter of distinctive communal identity. Rather, it is an argument regarding the way things are and ought to be, one decisive for public discourse and necessary to the guidance of individual souls, societies, and, indeed, the community of nations.

The term was soon taken up by others. For example, David Tracy extended the term in a notable volume in 1981, connecting the idea to the Roman Catholic heritage as represented by John Courtney Murray, a contemporary of Niebuhr.[2] Tracy pointed out that it was once held that because religions are wildly variant, it was necessary to turn to the actualities of human experience to find a basis of common morality and meaning. But, as many came to recognize, experience turns out to be even more pluralistic — a "blooming, buzzing confusion," as pragmatist philosopher William James taught. Fur-

---

1. Martin E. Marty, "Reinhold Niebuhr: Public Theology and the American Experience," *Journal of Religion* 54 (October 1974): 332-59.

2. David Tracy, *The Analogical Imagination: Christian Theology and the Culture of Pluralism* (New York: Crossroad, 1981). Tracy was an editor of the journal in which Marty's essay first appeared.

Public Theology and Ethical Judgment

ther, experience does not interpret itself; various modes of public discourse are required to discern the meaning of particular experiences. We therefore turn to several "publics" to establish the relative validity of any serious claim.

Theology's Publics

One is the authentic religious public. It can be identified by posing this question: What can and should be preached and taught among those who seek faithful living and thinking according to the most holy, and thus the most comprehensive, righteous, and enduring reality to which humans can point?

Another is the political public. This too can be identified by a question: What can provide those in authority with a vision of and motivation for just institutions in society so that the common life can flourish? It is important to note, in this connection, that the term "public" does not mean "governmental," and even the word "political" is more directly related to the theory of "civil society" than to "regime." These are subtle but decisive distinctions that many miss. The evidence we have from the West suggests that theology is able to make its greatest contribution when it is not enforced or prohibited by governments. As I understand it, Christianity shares with most forms of socialism and democracy the idea that the "public" establishes, and is prior to, a "republic," and that its government is established to serve the public.[3] Public theology errs if it tries to usurp the role of government or politics, but it claims the ability to provide the moral and spiritual fiber that would allow just and responsive politics to function.

A third kind of public is the academic public. Here too is a key question: What can offer reasons and withstand critical analysis, offering convincing arguments, warrants, and evidence for the positions it advances in the context of serious dialogue among scholars?

To these three we must add at least one more: the economic public. What allows human life to flourish, to be relieved of drudgery, and to contribute to material well-being by encouraging creativity in production and distribution? Each of these — holiness, justice, truth, and creativity, which are correlated with the

---

3. The terms "public" and "republic" are drawn from the Roman Stoic philosophers. Christians use these terms but interpret them through ideas drawn from the biblical and Greek traditions. For example, the Hebrew *berît* (covenant) is understood to be prior to the formation of "empire" just as the Greek *ekklēsia* (an assembly of responsible citizens, or a worshiping community) is understood to be prior to the *"polis"* conceived as a "state." Thus, public theology tends to be suspicious of governmental efforts to establish a state cult or to forbid the public worship of God, known by Christians in Jesus Christ.

religious public, the political public, the academic public, and the economic public, respectively — involves intelligibility, moral integrity, and respect for others.[4]

Theology and the Common Life

The term "public theology," although still disputed, has been increasingly accepted, especially among those concerned about the ethical fabric of contemporary life.[5] In most current scholarship, it is recognized that although the term is new, the basic effort to develop what the term implies is not. It is well known that Christians, Jews, and, later, Muslims in the Middle East and in the areas around the Mediterranean Sea combined the religious insight of the biblical traditions with the philosophical analysis of the Greeks and the legal theories of the Romans to form the basic assumptions on which the West developed. These assumptions became more important as it became clear that the ancient civilization was, for all its power and glory, beset by a metaphysical-moral disease. The classical, pagan world could not explain its own basis. For all the valid wisdom it contained in many areas, it could finally not hold thought or life together. It could not inspire the people to creative living, guide the leaders to the reasonable practice of justice, or explain why things were the way they were. For Christians, the "Fathers of the Church" stand among the heroes of faith for their formation of a kind of thought, which we now call public theology, that saw in certain key religious insights the capacity to give new grounding and dimension to the most profound resources of philosophy and thereby also to the scientific, social, and legal reflection of their day. In short, they provided a moral and spiritual inner architecture to the emerging, complex civilization.

---

4. I first learned the term "public theology" from the noted student of Tracy and Marty, Dennis McCann. It applied not only to Niebuhr but to Ernst Troeltsch, Abraham Kuyper, Walter Rauschenbusch, Martin Luther King, Paul Tillich, James Luther Adams, and Paul Ramsey, all of whom, in my view, contributed to the contemporary development of public theology without using the term. However, as I and others adopted the term, we modified it also to apply to other areas of society, such as economic ethics. See, for example, my "Public Theology, Corporate Responsibility and Military Contracting," *Interfaith Center on Corporate Responsibility Brief* 12 (November 11, 1983); *Public Theology and Political Economy* (Grand Rapids: Eerdmans, 1986); and Max L. Stackhouse et al., eds., *Christian Social Ethics in a Global Era* (Nashville: Abingdon, 1995).

5. The most recent major treatment of the development of this idea is in Robert Benne, *The Paradoxical Vision: A Public Theology for the Twenty-First Century* (Minneapolis: Fortress, 1995).

Public Theology and Ethical Judgment

To be sure, other understandings of theology have been present in our history. For example, some claim that theology has nothing intrinsic to do with philosophical discourse or with social matters. It is essentially, they say, an articulation of revealed faith. Theology, in this view, is the clarification of dogma, of what in principle is not intended to be based on, justified by, related to, or assessed by anything (philosophical, scientific, social, or legal) outside of faith itself. In effect, revelation creates its own ethic, sociality, and intelligibility. "What," so goes the polemical question in this tradition, "has Athens to do with Jerusalem?" Or it is said, in another polemical repudiation of reasonableness, which is also a challenge to the linking of faith and philosophy, "I believe because it is absurd."

Public theology may draw from this dogmatic emphasis, may have polemical aspects, and may recognize the transrational aspects of faith and morality, but it also self-consciously draws from an equally strong apologetic emphasis.[6] While revelation, understood as a gift of God grasped by faith, is an indispensable ground of theological thought, ethics, and social life, not all claims about grace, God, faith, or revelation are of equal validity. It is not only possible but necessary to assess them, our own or someone else's, according to whether they are more or less compatible with the most universal human understandings of holiness, justice, truth, and creativity. Theology, in this view, is properly understood to be the philosophically and socially informed attempt to interpret what could be true about God and God's relationship to humanity, society, and the world, and is thus the most comprehensive and enduring public mode of discourse by which to assess claims about grace, God, faith, or revelation. Public theology engages philosophy and science, ethics and the analysis of social life, to find out which kinds of faith enhance life and which lead to contempt for all that is holy, to incoherence, injustice, or poverty and want. In short, public theology has seemed necessary to the contemporary world, for it reclaims the apologetic emphasis at a time when much of theology is dogmatic, and much of philosophy and science, as well as much of political ethics and socioeconomic theory, has simply presumed

---

6. It is useful to make distinctions between "dogmatic," "polemic," and "apologetic" modes of theology. Dogmatics seeks to clarify matters of faith and practice among those who already believe. Polemics attempts to unmask false teachings, to defeat opposing views, or to silence opposition. Apologetics seeks to speak in ways that can be grasped by those who doubt or do not share the faith. It thus tests the reasonability and morality of the faith and those who hold it by engaging those who are not already convinced. It acknowledges that if it is in principle impossible to make a case for the truth or justice of theology, others are under no obligation to take it seriously.

Developing a Method for Public Theology

that theology represents the polemics of groups claiming revelatory validity for insights that are incomprehensible by others or are nothing but the by-product of other, more real, cultural or social conditions.

Jewish and, later, Islamic scholars used many of these classic resources as well, although the idea of theology in its various forms has most frequently been identified with the Christian heritage. Jewish and Islamic scholars more often turned to philosophy of religion or to jurisprudence. Indeed, in periods when Christian theology became more dogmatic and polemical, and ceased to accent its apologetic side, Christian thinkers and jurists have turned to philosophy of religion, usually theistic in character, or to those modes of universalistic jurisprudence and social science that sought to identify comprehensive laws and patterns that could bridge conflicts between cultures and peoples and to clarify what views of justice could be defended in public discourse. These are all potentially allies of public theology.

In spite of intense conflicts, much of the history of the West could be written in terms of the relations between these forms of interaction of religious insight, philosophical wisdom, and social analysis as used in the ordering of the common life. Certainly, their interaction played a decisive role in the formation of both the great medieval synthesis at the hands of such major thinkers as Thomas Aquinas and again in the Reformation syntheses, as found, for example, in John Calvin or John Wesley or Jonathan Edwards or Abraham Kuyper. They and their scholarly colleagues, plus the preachers, teachers, philosophers, and jurists informed by similar convictions and the practitioners who actually built and managed the institutions of society, extended, revised, and refined public theology and thereby provided the intellectual resources to civilize the tribes of Europe. And, it is important to note, they drew heavily from humanist scholars who revived the study of nontheological classics. Although they did not necessarily believe all that the theologians taught, the humanists turned to the study of languages, the arts, and the sciences with a demand for intellectual integrity. These "Renaissance" thinkers were taken by theologians also to be as much allies as enemies, as the ancient philosophers, poets, and jurists had been in previous epochs.

The Modernist Critique

It is also true, however, that various social and political forces, recognizing the power and influence of theology, drew on dogmatic and polemical traditions to reinforce the legitimacy of their status or group. Combining particular traditions with this or that militant national or class loyalty and posing them against all outside or dissenting people or faiths, Europe was plunged into a time of war, with each side claiming that God was on its side. No small number of scholars and jurists, statesmen and artists began to doubt theology, and to wonder whether it could in fact deliver what it promised. Was it not so that wars of religion decivilized what religion had once civilized? And was it not possible that religion had civilized the West not because of its intrinsic merit but precisely because it had kept philosophy, art, science, jurisprudence, and social theory alive for a time? Was it now not time to recognize that these should be turned free?

These are the questions that modernity, as many today call the Enlightenment period of Western intellectual history, put to theology. The Enlightenment did not entirely deny the fact that religion or dogmatic and polemical forms of theology were powerful forces in people's lives. It simply relegated these to the private sphere of subjective, irrational preferences. This helped an intense examination of the subjective and irrational forces within the human personality, but it denied their public role. Insofar as a case for theology could be made, it would have to be made on secular-philosophical or social-utility grounds. Indeed, this raised a pressing question: Why is theology necessary to intellectual and social life at all, and why are philosophy and social analysis not sufficient to the task? All the questions that the ancient philosophers had put to pagan beliefs and all the issues that had been raised by humanists against medieval piety were posed again with great intensity.

Those of us who today claim the legacy of public theology point out that the "logos" (the logic/living word) of philosophical thought, social analysis, and moral judgment is unstable by itself. It bends easily to the unscrupulous interests that lurk in the very heart of the best of us if it is not rooted in a holy, true, just creativity that is greater than we humans can achieve in our subjectivity. Indeed, it tends always to be distorted if it is not ultimately grounded in God, for the human wisdom of philosophy, the ordering systems of societies, and the ethical judgments of individuals may express the irrational elements of human fantasy no less than does private religion; and all of them need to be seen as subject to standards, purposes, and an unconditioned reality greater than our wisdoms, systems, judgments, and religions can generate or discover alone. "Logos" requires "theos." Theology is required.

Yet, the questions of the Enlightenment force us to ask whether theology is not essentially the articulation of the presumptions of a particular religious tradition, which, if it is to be assessed, must rely on human wisdom and on a basic view of how the world works. After all, is it not so that, by the analysis of human nature, and especially the way by which we humans come to know what we know, and by understanding how the world works, we can understand also the way religions and theologies are formed? If so, these are matters to be explained by the more profound analysis of intellectual, material, and social forces. Modernity, indeed, is a period in which many efforts have been made to show that one or another form of "natural" theory could supply the foundations for thought, politics, and morality without the need for anything beyond "nature," such as "God."

In the place of theology as a mode of public discourse, supported by philosophy, jurisprudence, and social analysis, science became the basis of modern theory. Science was understood to be the rational and empirical interpretation of all things natural, and the basis for progress, democracy, and freedom — the chief virtue of modernity. It was presumed that scientific study would bring with it the capacity to understand the laws of the universe and to harness its forces in the service of humanity. Further, unlike the insights of tradition or revelation, which were presumed to be accessible only to some, science made knowledge available to all. Many said that it would promote harmony with nature, democracy, and human freedom. These, in turn, would provide a moral foundation for political life and the formation of national welfare.

Tensions were built into this view. Does harmony with nature really comport with freedom? And does democracy imply a will of the people that makes a solidarity out of individuals, as proclaimed by the contract theorists of France and Germany and their heirs, or a governance under law and natural rights, as claimed by the constitutional theorists of Holland and England and their heirs, or some combination of the two, as many argue in regard to America? In any case, it was presumed that people could, and should, reorganize life on moral grounds but without overt reference to religion or theology. The problem was the basis or foundation for this reorganization.

The Premodernist Critique

The reactions against this view of modernity have been several, and hosts of scholarly opinions stand behind each view. One view may be called "premodernism" or "traditionalism." It sees modernity's repudiation of the cultivated synthesis of religion, philosophy, and political authority over centuries as devastating, a pretentious denial that human thought and civility are cumulative, a pompous presumption that we can dispense with all that went before us, an arrogant conceit that the past is but prologue. What some call Enlightenment, it calls ruin.

Various premodernists date this "fall into modernity" in differing periods. Some see it at the dawn of modernity, when Machiavelli in the 1490s turned from political philosophy to a naturalist view of political science, and Luther turned in the 1520s from church consensus to individual conviction as a mark of faith. Not only, in this view, was the synthesis of the deep tradition broken as philosophy, politics, and religion each went its own way, but the world was plunged into a series of fragmented, anomic units, each claiming sovereignty. That, they say, is what led to the wars of modernity. Others date the "fall" of tradition from the French Revolution, when the goddess "Reason" was placed in the Catholic cathedral Notre Dame and traditional authorities were stripped of their power in intentional acts of secularization. Still others see the British or German Enlightenment, each connected with aspects of Protestant theology (one Puritan, the other Pietist) that challenged tradition, as the problem. The cure, in each case, is to return to premodern wisdom, to tradition.[7]

The Hypermodernist Critique

A second attack on modernity in its progressive, Western form was what we may call "hypermodernism," or "revolutionary humanism." This is the view that evolutionary progress was a bourgeois dream, and that change must be aided by the seizing of power and the mobilization of the forces that actually transform life — economic, political, and ideological power. The enemy of modernization, in this view, is not only traditionalism but all forms of popular religion, conventional morality, and elite social leadership. They are all pillars and symptoms of false consciousness. It is presumed that human will, aided by the power of material interests, can become the guiding power to change history and nature.

---

7. All these views can be found in what may well be the most profound text for the neoconservative revival in America today, Leo Strauss and Joseph Cropsey, eds., *History of Political Philosophy*, 2nd ed. (Chicago: Rand McNally, 1972). Other influential works that press comparable issues into contemporary discussions include Alasdair MacIntyre, *After Virtue: A Study in Moral Theology*, 2nd ed. (Notre Dame: University of Notre Dame Press, 1984); Richard John Neuhaus, *The Naked Public Square: Religion and Democracy in America*, 2nd ed. (Grand Rapids: Eerdmans, 1986); and Allan Bloom, *The Closing of the American Mind* (New York: Simon & Schuster, 1987).

In the West, hypermodernism has taken one of two forms — libertarian individualism and liberationist nationalism. The one became concentrated in individualistic economic theories, and the other in bureaucratic theories of state planning. What we know as democratic capitalism and democratic socialism are the moderate forms of these extremes. They often share the presupposition that interests, and the political will they generate, establish the contexts in which religious and ethical life develops, thereby determining the shape of that life, as an aspect of culture. They are secularizing movements, and their proponents tend to deny that religious, moral, philosophical, or aesthetic realities are independent causes in social life. They doubt that such realities could be decisive in political, economic, or technological development. Thus, they are suspicious of theology insofar as it attempts to offer the view of any or all of these as primary social forces, or as it provides a normative vision for them. Indeed, they are often also reluctant to grant an independent role to philosophy, jurisprudence, or social analysis that is not based on the material and political assumptions that they hold to be ultimately real.

In recent years, sharp questions have been put to the many forms of hypermodernism. While hypermodernism contributed to the dismantling of colonial and imperialist power, it is increasingly doubted that hypermodernism can construct a viable civilization, a compelling philosophy of life, and a profound culture. Where it has been most successful, it has tended to become a secular religion, demanding a kind of faith in human interests and material forces that the evidence does not seem to warrant. But it does not seem to evoke enduring loyalty or to provide the moral or spiritual foundations to guide souls or civilizations. For one thing, hypermodernism attempts to identify the progressive forces of history with some leader or nation or class. But this divinization of a particular group under no authority but its own power and interest tends to make it temporary and subject to the charge that it legitimates at least as much distortion, war, and disintegration as it presumes to replace. Indeed, many argue today that hypermodernism tends to compound the rationalization, elitism, and false consciousness that it attributes to traditionalists and contemporary radicals.

The Postmodernist Critique

Still a third critique of modernism is today widely discussed. It has taken the name "postmodernism" and is unwilling to identify with premodern traditionalism or with hypermodernist revolutionism, although it is in some ways related to them. Indeed, the chief insight of postmodernism is that none of these claims — premodern, modern, or hypermodern — is reliable. They are all nothing more than mental constructs imposed on a chaotic and fluctuating world. All reality is virtual reality, all morality is someone's preferences, and all truth is opinion. God, society, and the human self are all constructs.

The chief quarrel of postmodernism is with modernity and its claim that science, rationality, and social theory can supply their own foundations for meaning and morality, and thus the basis for thought and political life. This, say the postmodernists, is an intellectual fraud. Modernity, they say, is the dead end of the alliance of faith with the rational traditions, whether ancient, humanistic (at the time of the Renaissance), or scientific. It presumes an onto-theological view of reality — an interpretation of being, God, reason, and existence as integral one to the other — that on the one hand, simply cannot be sustained and on the other hand, should not be held even if it could. Such a view leads to "totalizing" impulses that seek to control freedom, creativity, independence, imagination, and the vital energies of particular loyalties, momentary passions, and precious (if fragmentary) insights by which life is actually governed. Is it not clear, they ask, that those peoples who embarked on the most radical efforts to modernize according to rational models of scientific progress have brought about the most visible terrors of our century, even if they dismantled the pretentious authoritarian systems of the premodernists?

There are several varieties of postmodern thought. One can be interpreted as a demand for a certain modesty in the modern, premodern, and hypermodern views of the world. The hopes for certitude, for agreement on all foundational questions because of science, have proven to be more dream than promise. Yet, we cannot return to premodernism; we left that for good reason. The critical thinking of the Enlightenment surpassed premodern traditionalism, as the hypermodernists also know. But both of these failed to turn their critical tools reflexively back on themselves. If anything, we need a chastised, cautious, moderate realism, slow to make big claims and fully aware of how contingent, fragmentary, temporary, and uncertain reality and our views of it are. Most of what people claim to know reflects the embedded, changing situations of which we are a part, and we must acknowledge this. To say more than that is to become "totalistic."[8]

---

8. This is the view of J. Wentzel van Huyssteen, winner of the Templeton Prize for his analysis of the influence of postmodern thought on the relationship of theology and the philosophy of science. See his "Is the Postmodernist Always a Postfoundationalist?" *Theology*

Developing a Method for Public Theology

However, the larger and more influential portion of postmodern thought has been less guarded. This strand derives from the critique of the Western intellectual heritage by the nineteenth-century philosopher Friedrich Nietzsche more than from any other source. As is widely known, he distinguishes two tendencies in Western thought. One, "the Apollonian" (named after the ancient Greek and Roman sun god, patron of music and poetry), was held by Nietzsche to have dominated the West. It is defined by its emphasis on order, measure, and balance. But the other, "the Dionysian" (named after the god of the harvest festival, patron of wine and ecstatic dance), was held by Nietzsche to have been the spirit of vital energy, able to create new possibilities. At certain points, the Dionysian impulses were able to include Apollonian elements, as can be seen in the arts. But this synthesis was subverted by the West, both in philosophy, when Plato dismantled the ancient stories for their irrational celebrations of the passions, and in religion, by the Christian use of philosophy and jurisprudence to develop theology and to refine and systematize sacred narrative. Indeed, the reassertion of the Dionysian impulses against Apollonian philosophy, theology, and all that resembles universalistic ethics is one of the most striking marks of postmodernism.[9]

It is more than interesting that postmodern thought is most pronounced in literary and cultural studies, and it is much engaged with issues of symbolic meanings, semiotics, the constructions and deconstructions of possible interpretations, and the display of style and expression. In fact, as premodern thought tends to turn ever and again to the classical thinkers, as modernism tends to turn to science and to read all evidence in terms of the basic theory, and as hypermodernism tends to turn to power analysis and the will, postmodernism too has its own mode of reduction. Indeed, it tends to view everything as a cultural-linguistic construal of consciousness. This impulse repudiates the very idea of anything being valid in an enduring or public way. All is relative to context, construal, and consciousness, all of which change. In the final analysis, this strand tends to nihilism.

An interesting public debate in America today illustrates this point. It

---

Today 50 (October 1993): 373-86. On quite different grounds, and in dialogue with the social rather than the natural sciences, see Seyla Benhabib, *Situating the Self: Gender, Community and Postmodernism in Contemporary Ethics* (New York: Routledge, 1992).

9. See, for example, Jean-François Lyotard, *The Postmodern Condition: A Report on Knowledge* (Minneapolis: University of Minnesota Press, 1984); and Michel Foucault, *The History of Sexuality*, 3 vols. (New York: Vantage, 1978-85). In my view, the key figure between Nietzsche and these contemporary thinkers is Martin Heidegger. See especially his *Nietzsche*, 4 vols. (San Francisco: Harper & Row, 1979-87).

concerns an essay by physicist Alan Sokal of New York University. He wrote "Transgressing the Boundaries: Toward a Transformative Hermeneutics of Quantum Gravity" and sent it to a postmodernist journal. The essay argued that science should become as postmodern as contemporary cultural studies. The essay quoted leading postmodern thinkers and suggested, for example, that pi was culturally variable. It also expressed doubt about the existence of "an external world, whose properties are independent of any individual human being." The journal published it as a serious piece of work; but Sokal published a second article in *Lingua Franca* exposing the fact that the first essay was a hoax to show that postmodern advocates cannot tell the difference between bogus and real arguments. The response was immediate and intense.[10]

While many of the current arguments have to do with whether science reflects truths about nature in some verifiable way or whether it is essentially the prevailing cultural-linguistic mindset of those under the spell of great imaginations or high positions of authority at a given time, another set of arguments is equally pertinent to our discussion here. In the debates as to whether the laws of physics are like the rules of baseball, which are a construct to make the game more coherent, all presume that when doing physics, umpiring a game, or writing articles for journals, one ought to tell the truth, give arguments for the positions one holds, change one's views if these arguments are falsified, and be trustworthy in the way one treats data, the public trust, and colleagues' views.

Such arguments have a parallel in some contemporary debates about theology. Several contemporary theologians have developed a constitutional hostility to modernity and to "liberal" Enlightenment philosophies.[11] They presume that the hypermodernist cries for liberation and revolution are based on accurate analyses of human rights, democracy, and modern economics,

---

10. See Alan Sokal, "Transgressing the Boundaries: Toward a Transformative Hermeneutics of Quantum Gravity," *Social Text* 14, no. 1-2 (Spring/Summer 1996): 217-52, and "A Physicist Experiments with Cultural Studies," *Lingua Franca* 6, no. 4 (May/June 1996): 62-64. See also Bruce Robbins and Andrew Ross (coeditors of *Social Text*), "These Culture Wars . . . ," *New York Times*, May 23, 1996, p. A28; and Stephen Weinberg, "Sokal's Hoax," *New York Review of Books* 43 (August 8, 1996): 11-15.

11. I have in mind here, especially, Stanley Hauerwas, *The Peaceable Kingdom: A Primer in Christian Ethics* (Notre Dame: University of Notre Dame Press, 1983), and *Dispatches from the Front: Theological Engagements with the Secular* (Durham, NC: Duke University Press, 1994); John Milbank, *Theology and Social Theory: Beyond Secular Reason* (Cambridge: Blackwell, 1993); and Brian D. Ingraffia, *Postmodern Theory and Biblical Theology: Vanquishing God's Shadow* (New York: Cambridge University Press, 1995).

Developing a Method for Public Theology

which they see as biases of the bourgeois West, having no more validity than a belief in unicorns. Further, they combine postmodernism in philosophy with premodernism in religion. Thus, they accept the views of the postmodernists that Nietzsche's deconstruction of Western philosophy is correct. Believing that philosophy, the natural sciences, and social theory lead us to the immorality of domination, violence, war, and destruction, they hold that the way is now clear to reassert their preferred traditional interpretation of Christianity against contemporary philosophy, science, and society. They do not give a public account of their convictions because they believe that one should not; the content and quality of faith is and must be entirely self-authenticating to all because it seems so to them.

What is most intriguing here is that these debates in physics and theology depend on ethical judgments. Of course, the obvious question is how these judgments are grounded and how they could be made if the postmodern viewpoint is valid. The very notion that postmodernism is obviously morally superior to modernity (and both the ethical principles and empirical data to which it must appeal if it claims this judgment to be valid) suggests that the advocates of the position live in a world of absolute consciousness but have a weak grasp on how this consciousness relates to the objective world. Yet, these advocates try to convince those who do not already believe them to believe them, citing what purports to be evidence about the way the world is. It appears that the absoluteness and objectivity they eschew are, in fact, not abandoned but simply relocated. But what is not clear is why we should trust their consciousness, their construal, their faith. If reality is simply a construct of those who compose perspectives, Sokal's prank to expose fraudulent thinking could not be distinguished from the claim of some that it was a "bad" joke because it violated public trust.[12] Why should anyone trust their moral assessment of human rights, democracy, and economic life if their views are based on a dismantling of public discourse in favor of highly particular, even idiosyncratic, construals?[13]

This, of course, brings us back to the question of what could be a reliable basis for religious assessment, ethical judgment, and public discourse. And it may be that all this struggle with modernity, by such premodernists, hyper-

---

12. See Stanley Fish (a leading postmodern author), "Professor Sokal's Bad Joke," *New York Times,* May 21, 1996, p. A23.

13. See Max L. Stackhouse and Stephen E. Healey, "Religion and Human Rights: A Theological Apologetic," in *Religious Human Rights in Global Perspective: Religious Perspectives,* ed. John Witte Jr. and Johan D. van der Vyver (The Hague: Martinus Nijhoff, 1996), pp. 485-516.

modernists, and postmodernists as I have sketched here, is less a contemporary Western peculiarity than simply another version of a longer and deeper and wider set of conversations that have gone on in many contexts over many centuries. Is it possible that China has its own modernizers who really do have complete confidence in reason, science, and progress? And does it have premodernist traditionalists in the form of some Confucians who protest this arrogant attitude and the way it dissolves society? Does China have its own hypermodernists who understand everything in terms of a liberating, materialist zeal to seize control of the future, either on an individualistic or on a collectivistic basis? And does it not have a history of ecstatic nihilism in those parts of Buddhism that see all as a construction of consciousness and that distrust not only modern science but premodern traditionalists and hypermodern activism? Perhaps not; or perhaps China's modernists, premodernists, hypermodernists, and postmodernists come in other forms than those I have suggested; but it seems likely that none of us can avoid the question of what it is that is, finally, most trustworthy, most true, most worthy of devotion. Indeed, it may be the case that every culture in every age has faced issues roughly comparable to what is here outlined. If so, we must all, ever and again ask this question: What, finally, is holy, true, just, and creative? To what shall we give our minds, our time, our energies?[14]

Resurgent Public Theology

One of the key problems in the West is the fact that proponents of all of these views tend to believe that modern thinkers understood their own foundations. The premodern traditionalists think that those foundations are false and that we need to repudiate them and return to sounder, ancient ones. The hypermodernist enthusiasts think that those foundations are absolutely valid, and thus they turn modernization into a secular religion. The postmodern nihilists think that those alleged foundations, and every other claim about foundations, are simply the imposition of conscious constructions on a chaotic context. All of these take their cues from what modernity says about itself.

---

14. A contemporary thinker who has posed sharp moral questions to postmodern thought in a comparable way is Gertrude Himmelfarb. See her *On Looking into the Abyss: Untimely Thoughts on Culture and Society* (New York: Knopf, 1994), and *The De-moralization of Society: From Victorian Virtues to Modern Values* (New York: Knopf, 1995).

Developing a Method for Public Theology

But it is more likely that modernity does not understand itself. After all, the Enlightenment of the West is not the same as the Enlightenment of the East, and the foundations of the former may be more deeply rooted in the presuppositions of the religious and philosophical traditions of the West than it acknowledges. If that is so, both the modernist and the traditionalist, who see the Enlightenment as the repudiation of the syntheses of previous epochs, are mistaken. The continuity may be greater than the discontinuity, and the difference may be that of profound foundation and superficial appearance. If that is so, then the hypermodernist who worships the presumptions of the Enlightenment is worshiping a set of very superficial gods, and the postmodernists are correct in saying that this sort of thing is, as it presents itself, groundless, without foundations — even though they themselves have no way to give a basis for the moral judgments to which they implicitly appeal when they judge others.

A deeper, more persuasive view is provided, I think, by the resurgent development of public theology. From this perspective, we may look again at what are purported to be the turning points in modernity and note that they rest on a more enduring basis than some have recognized. When, for example, the French philosopher Descartes tried to doubt all, he was able to discover a real self at the root of consciousness because the glasses through which he examined his own consciousness were ground by centuries of public theological discourse of a particular kind. He did not discover what the Buddha discovered when he plumbed his own consciousness. Similarly, John Locke, the British philosopher of religion and constitutional order, could speak of "self-evident truths and natural rights" of justice because he believed that all humans were endowed by their Creator with a conferred dignity and a capacity to recognize what was fair, and that these ought not be violated by political or religious authority. He did not discover what Lenin talked about when he spoke of these matters. So also the German philosopher of science and morality Immanuel Kant could speak of *a priori* truths in "the starry heavens above and the moral law within" because he thought within a framework of discourse that viewed both as established by a divine will. He did not understand these matters as did al-Ghazzali, whom some view as the fountainhead of Muslim fundamentalism.[15]

What is most remarkable is that when a new barbarism broke out in the

---

15. I offer here merely the briefest suggestion of an argument. Each of these figures requires more extensive treatment than I can provide here, and the history of thought requires much greater nuance than can be presented in this space.

West, at the hands of Hitler, it was the legacies of such Enlightenment thinkers, and even more the general framework on which they were dependent, to which the world turned. Indeed, the United Nations can enshrine such ideas as these in "covenants" because the social and intellectual heritage of public theology has generated a way of thinking about these matters that can be and has been recognized by many non-Christian peoples as containing something universally valid. In fact, if the development of contemporary global interactions of people has been possible because of the increasingly widespread actualization of certain universal principles that were first stated in biblical terms and were refined by theology through long, complex encounters with philosophy, jurisprudence, and complex cultures, then we cannot simply dismiss modernity or take it as the basis of a new secular faith or baldly claim that it is without grounding.[16]

But it is important to acknowledge that the public to which Western theology has spoken is still much too narrow and shallow. Today, if anything like a public theology is to be developed further, it must include a much-enlarged conversation; and the philosophy, law, and culture that it must engage are no longer confined to Mediterranean, European, or American (North and South) life. The modernity that theology in these areas generated has expanded and been adopted, and modified, all over the world. True, the West's contribution to it has sometimes been in ways that we now know to have been imperialistic, colonialistic, and exploitative. But we judge these as false, unjust, and unethical because the same theology that prompted expansion in these ways bears within it universal principles that demand both a self-critical judgment when its best contributions are distorted and a wider willingness to learn from other publics than those of the West. This theology holds that it is not true that there is nothing like a universal humanity, and it does not allow the belief that there are no moral laws under which the whole of humanity stands. Some things simply ought not to be done to people, and people ought not to do some things. If this conviction became most clear out of the contexts shaped by particular biblical insights developed in a particular history, it may nonetheless be valid for all and defensible on grounds recognizable in other contexts. It also implies, in our world, that the humanisms

---

16. Clarifying and assessing such claims has been a primary focus of my work for a quarter of a century. See, for example, my *Ethics and the Urban Ethos: An Essay in Social Theory and Theological Reconstruction* (Boston: Beacon, 1973); *Creeds, Society, and Human Rights: A Study in Three Cultures* (Grand Rapids: Eerdmans, 1984); and Max L. Stackhouse et al., eds., *On Moral Business: Classical and Contemporary Resources for Ethics in Economic Life* (Grand Rapids: Eerdmans, 1995).

of Confucius and Mencius, the religious philosophies of Ramanuja and Åankara, and the wisdom of Saicho (also known as Dengyo Daishi), of Ibn Rushd (also known as Averroes), and of those leaders in many fields who work out righteous ways of human dealing because of their considered convictions be taken as theological dialogue partners in the redefinition of a broader public. In this public, the great philosophies and world religions, which have demonstrated that they can shape great and complex civilizations over centuries, must have a place.

Among other things, this means that those of us who have been converted to the idea of public theology must reread our own traditions with new questions in mind. A model of what I am suggesting can be found in the impressive work of the Jewish scholar Daniel Elazar.[17] He shows how the biblical idea of covenant has given spiritual stability, moral form, and social focus to possibilities already present in other cultural traditions. What is especially interesting for us is that while he is not a Christian, he is convinced that aspects of Christian public theology in the covenantal tradition state something that can be acknowledged as universally valid.

In brief, it seems to me that not only Christians but all who struggle with modernizing developments and the critiques of those developments can, perhaps must, recognize that we can discuss matters of God, the world, humanity, and morality across many barriers. We are able to do so, I contend, because those modern developments that link us are, in significant part, the product of a public theology that, while unfinished, more accurately grasps aspects of the human condition, under God, in the world, than do the alternatives many today propose.

---

17. See Daniel Elazar, *Covenant and Polity in Biblical Israel: Biblical Foundations and Jewish Expressions* (New Brunswick, NJ: Transaction, 1995); *Covenant and Commonwealth: From Christian Separation through the Protestant Reformation* (New Brunswick, NJ: Transaction, 1996); *Covenant and Constitutionalism: The Great Frontier and the Matrix of Federal Democracy* (New Brunswick, NJ: Transaction, 1997); and *Covenant and Civil Society: A Constitutional Matrix of Modern Democracy* (New Brunswick, NJ: Transaction, 1998).

Ethics: Social and Christian

The moral conflicts that are experienced in contemporary society are, in some ways, matched only by the confusion that reigns in much of modern ethics and theology. The last several decades have brought forth a proliferation of fresh, absolutist moral claims and a simultaneous sense of the relativity of all our claims. Socially we seem to stand between a most secular society that has less and less to do with religion, and the sanctification of dimensions of personal and cultural sensibility that look more and more like new forms of religious effervescence. Theologically we seem to stand between the neo-orthodox certainties of a generation ago and the ambiguities of new idiosyncratic, socio-psychological interpretations of religion. And the reconstruction of our understanding of scripture and tradition by historians seems to undercut conventional ethical wisdom without providing new foundations for understanding whence we come. In this setting, where can we gain the tools to ground and to respond to moral experience?

It seems to me that any effort will have to be rooted in an articulate understanding of "religion and society," their effects on each other, their historical interaction, their contemporary state, and their prospects for the future. Thus, growing interests in sociology and psychology of religion and in theology of culture, politics, and society are reasons to rejoice. But in the churches, the seminaries, and many university departments of religion there has also developed a rather loosely defined field of Christian Social Ethics. In view, however, of the confusions in Christian theology, modern society, and ethics itself, it becomes necessary to look at the meanings of the terms in the title of this field and to see whether there is any sense in holding thems together. Should, indeed, *can,* theology, the social sciences, and ethics go their own way, or are there some existential and logical reasons that they should be held

Developing a Method for Public Theology

together? What follows is a somewhat programmatic or synoptic attempt to show that by looking at matters in a particular way, there can be a definition of boundaries that lends coherence to the field at least as it has developed on the American scene.

The noun in the term "Christian Social Ethics" is "Ethics." "Christian" and "Social" are adjectives that specify the kind of religion and the dimension of civilization and culture that are of primary concern. Each of these terms needs further definition if we are to see what it is precisely that stands at the core of this peculiar field of study.

I. Ethics and Ethos

Ethics is the disciplined study of obligation, its nature, its justifications, its consequences, its strategies. It is, in simplest terms, reflection on "ought." When we say that we ought to do thus and so, what on earth do we mean? How can we make such a judgment? By what authority? Everyone, in fact, makes such statements, and the sense of obligation or "ought" is built into the various relationships of our lives, although they are often articulated in substitute terms: "He *must* spend some more time with his family"; "I *have got to* send that contribution to candidate X"; and "The administration *should have* changed its policy on Indochina." Often, such judgments occur in negative terms: "They are not the most responsible parents," indicating that they "ought" to behave in a different way with their children; "The present abortion law is criminal," indicating that it "ought" to be changed; "He is a sick man," suggesting that he "ought" to be made well or that we "ought not" to take him seriously. It takes very little reflection to recognize the enormous variety of ways in which personal senses of obligation and socially patterned "oughts" penetrate our lives. Indeed, on the one hand, we are tempted to suggest that the sense of "ought" is a, if not the, distinguishing feature of humanity, and that man and society are most whole when there is a developed and refined pattern of obligation that evokes the distinctively human capacity to live under ethical conditions or make moral choices. On the other hand, the enormous variety of experienced "oughts" sometimes threatens our common life with moral Babel, a sense of such confusion that humanity and wholeness are lost.

But already in our examples of the way in which everyone uses moral language, we need to note two things. First, ethical reflection implies a distinction between description and prescription (or, as some prefer, between

Ethics: Social and Christian

indicative and imperative, or between "is" and "ought"). What "ought" to be is not necessarily the way things are. One may clearly and accurately describe how one spends the time away from his family, what the Indochina policy is, what people do as parents, what the abortion laws are, and what the pathological indicators are, and yet claim that they "ought" to be otherwise. Of course in making the "ought" judgment, one may appeal to something that "is" outside the judgment and rest the case of his "ought" on that. For instance, one may say that one ought to do this or that because it is the way the Will of God really is, or the way life actually is, or is compatible with natural law. But even then, there is a presumed distinction between the way things *empirically* are and the way they ought to be; and the thing that makes a concern ethical is the "ought" dimension. Therefore, ethical reflection or action inevitably involves prescription, imperative, and ought, beyond mere description, indicative, and is. The establishment of, clarification of, or calling attention to standards or values is part of thinking or acting morally.

Yet, most of the "oughts" about which we speak, and most of the obligations that are felt, derive from the social relationships in which we find ourselves. These "ought" claims reside in, even if they are not the same as, empirical facts. It is in response to the claims of family, political institutions, professional associations, friendship groups, religious groups, etc., that the sense of obligation is experienced. Human existence is often experienced as a network of competing claims telling us that we ought to do this or ought not to do that. Insofar as these competing claims are relatively stable, we can say that they make up an *ethos*. That is, they become organized into a subtle "web of values," a pattern of expectations, rewards, legitimations, and punishments that constitutes the operating norms of a community and gives it a peculiar social identity. It is into these that people are born; it is in relationship to these that people develop a sense of personal moral identity or "character"; it is in the context of these operating norms that moral problems arise; and it is in the midst of these that moral action takes place. Much of our life is shaped by the ethos in which we become ourselves and continue to have our selfhood. But the ethos is full of conflicts, and it is not always as it ought to be. Therefore we have to ask the normative question: To which "ought" claims should we give credence, and what "ought" claims should be built into the ethos so that they impinge upon us all? At this point we are at the brink of ethics proper, for its specialty is deciding between "oughts."

Developing a Method for Public Theology

The Right, the Good, and the Fit

Ethicists differ, however, on what is the best way to decide between the various claims of the ethos. They do not agree on what the organizing principle of our normative reflection should be, or how best to state the criteria of decision. But we can identify the three dominant ways of argument.[1] Some appeal primarily to categories of "right," some to "good," and some to "fit." In ordinary conversation, of course, these terms are almost interchangeable. To say "That's right" does not seem to be much different from saying "That's good" or "That fits." To make the judgment that such and such a claim is wrong does not seem to be far removed from saying that it is evil or inappropriate (unfit). But if we attempt to clarify the kinds of normative stance that can be taken vis-à-vis a specific problem of the ethos, it makes a great deal of difference whether we rely on categories of right, good, or fit, or some combination of them. Indeed, one can classify moral philosophies according to their relative dependence on one or another of these categories of ought. We should look at each of them briefly.

An ethic based on concepts of right (and wrong) attempts to state in a rational and clear fashion what *kinds* of acts are required, forbidden, or permitted in human relations. In its richer versions, it also attempts to articulate the warrants, procedures, or public criteria for making such statements. Its criteria, then, are rational clarity and universalizability. Thus, it tends to focus on such terms as duty or privilege, and to take the form of rules, principles, codes, or categorical laws. And its warrants tend to be rooted in a conception of the very nature of that about which it speaks. In technical terms, it is called a "deontological" ethic. By the very constitution of human relationships, for example, it is "right" as a universal *prima facie* duty to be fair, to seek justice, to tell the truth, and to keep promises, and not to murder, rape, or steal. In more restricted ways, we speak of civil "rights" or human "rights," of the rights of minority groups or women in an attempt to call to duty or to establish or retrieve lost privileges that can be articulated in clear principles or laws thought to be known from the very constitution of the civil community, or from the nature of humanity itself. Often, moral concerns of this sort are

---

1. There is not, at this time, a sufficiently common language in the discipline to satisfy many people working in the field. Indeed, there is the tendency to use terms in quite different ways in different schools of thought. Hence, what I am proposing here will surely be read by many as yet another idiosyncratic view. The purpose, however, is to invite the discipline to establish a language convention so that the boundaries of dominant ways of making moral arguments can be more clearly discussed and debated.

Ethics: Social and Christian

expressed in the negative: "You ought not to exploit your neighbor." Exploitation violates the neighbor's and the community's very nature. But these moral concerns may be stated in the affirmative: "You ought to guarantee to your neighbor the rights you claim for yourself." That produces fairness, justice, or "right order." Or, on even more restricted grounds, we speak of the rights and privileges that are part of a profession. It is just not right, and it is clearly wrong, whatever gestures or suggestions a patient might make, for a doctor to take sexual advantage of a patient disrobed for medical examination. That is, it is contrary to duty and privileges, for it is contrary to the essential nature of the medical profession and the ethics of the doctor-patient relationship. It is just not right, and it is clearly wrong, for a soldier to kill innocent noncombatants, for that is at least contrary to the nature of military duty or privilege and the laws of international warfare, not to mention the human rights of the victim. The facts that the soldier may have orders to do so or that he is under emotional strain that builds up in battle do not change the rightness or wrongness of the act. The Ten Commandments, the codes of ethics, the attempts to clarify a doctrine of "Just War," the arguments against abortion that say it is always wrong to destroy human life, are all examples of attempts to think ethically by focusing on the question of right. Unrelieved, that is, mere clarification of the *kinds* of acts that are required, forbidden, or permitted without simultaneous attention to other dimensions of moral experience, this mode of ethical reflection can end in oppressive legalism, vast systems of rational rules that box in every area of life. Ignored, it leads to antinomianism and the destruction of civilization. For, as Beckett said, "When the thicket of right is cut down, where then do we hide when the storms come?" Unrelieved legalism has been the occasional temptation of certain forms of Judaism, Catholicism, and Puritanism. Antinomian destruction of the concern for "right" has been the frequent temptation of their hedonistic and romantic critics.

An ethic based on "good and evil" is of a different sort. This kind of ethic focuses on purposes or ends. Usually it is worked out in terms of a vision of a desirable state of affairs. "On to Perfection," "the kingdom of God," "the perfect classless society," "the greatest good for the greatest number," "fulfilled personhood" are all examples of "good-oriented" ethics. Such an ethic often accents the potential that is present in a concrete situation and attempts to work out a calculus of direction or orientation. Such an ethic may be rooted in the subjective side of our moral experience, in which case we become greatly concerned about our moral intentions. In striving to be honest, or in desiring to be sincere, or in trying to direct our attention toward that which is most valued, one finds a sense of the good. "Nothing is good but the good will"; "Purity of heart is to will one thing"; "Love, and do what you will"; and "Faith, hope, and love abide" are characteristic forms of ethics that focus on questions of the subjective "good." Such accents are often called "dispositional ethics." This dimension of ethical reflection, however, also has its objective advocates, those suspicious of confining questions of the good to the subjective orientations of people or groups. Instead, they accent the objective consequences: "The road to hell is paved with good intentions." "Sure, you tried, but look what happened." "Obviously, a good action produces identifiable pleasure or happiness." "To be is to be directed to some end." "The logic of history presses ever toward a divine purpose." Technically, these are two forms of "teleological" ethics. (Some philosophers would dispute putting these in the same category, but I think it can be defended.)

When these two ways of being concerned about the good are joined, and one is sincerely disposed to get the desirable results, we say, "The end justifies the means." If, of course, we hold to a concept of right as well as good, we dispute that, for there are certain kinds of things that are "wrong" even if done for a good end. But ethicists who work primarily within the category of good alone say, "Only the end justifies any means." A second mode of joining the more subjective and objective understanding of good and evil turns to ontology and specifies the objective powers of good and evil that shape the disposition and the consequence: "Not I, but Christ in me"; "The Devil made me do it"; and "The inevitable progress of history." But whether subjective or objective in accents, or joined, an ethic based on "good" is teleological, purposive, or ends-oriented. When this dimension of moral experience is the exclusive center of all ethics, we end in subjective piety or objective cynicism. It is not accidental that historians of ethics often see Pietism and Machiavellianism as two sides of the same coin. They both ignore questions of the "right" and critical reflection on the "fit," allowing the intended ends to justify otherwise immoral means. Contemporary ethicists, similarly, identify psychologism and social manipulation as the modern versions of the same phenomena. However, when these "good" dimensions of the moral life are ignored, we have no way of taking the dispositions to moral action into account prior to that action, or of pragmatically calculating actual consequences after the act. Yet we praise or blame ourselves or others for these, and they are thus integral to any complete ethical view.

There is still a third way of understanding "ought." An ethic based on categories of "the fitting," sometimes called a contextualist ethic, is one that sees an analogy between ethics and aesthetics or critical interpretation. As striking an appropriate chord in a musical composition gives the whole its significance, so a "fitting" action sustains the whole context of life as a human enterprise. Indigenous to this ethical criterion is a sense of unique capacity that is in every particular human context but which must be interpreted according to more general models. We do not expect the two-year-old child to follow the same patterns of right and good that we expect of adults, nor can we expect a developing nation to sustain the same patterns of democracy, even if they be judged right and good, that we expect of the more developed countries. Here, a sense of proportion and balance, of richness and flexibility as aesthetic or interpretive ethical ingredients, must be acknowledged. The concern for the "fitting" puts the round cork in the round bottle; it tells the story that evokes the appropriate sensibilities; it captures the dilemmas of the everyday tissue of life by humor, irony, analogy, or hermeneutical model. In its conservative versions, the reliance on folk wisdom, tradition, habits, customs, and convention are taken as morally significant concerns. These elements are understood to render some relative completeness or "Gestalt" of meaning built up through long practical experience amidst the complexities of human crisis and frailty. In traditional cultures, the "fit" mode of ethical reflection is thus concerned about recognition of the validity of manners and morals, the styles by which honor and graciousness are exemplified, especially insofar as they sustain some quality of wholeness in the fabric of life.

Under the impact of the rise of historical consciousness and comparative cultural studies, however, this aesthetic-interpretive ethical dimension of moral discourse has taken a strikingly different turn. It has become linked with philosophical debates involving phenomenological, hermeneutical, structural-functional, and cultural criticism, often rooted in a philosophy or theology of history. In this, there is often a conscious attempt to recover biblical sensitivities about the dramatic character of human existence in history, trying to identify the mode of social or psychological perception, the varieties of consciousness, or the structures and functions of power and influence that touch the more profound reaches of mankind's ethical condition. In one sense, this can be seen as a striking recovery from its individualist distortions of the primordial meaning of "conscience," so that it comes to mean "systematized, practical moral sensitivity held in common." The decisive questions in this mode of doing ethics concern the forms of awareness, relationship, or sociality that sustain or create the capacity to be morally discerning and responsible in a particular context. When these do not obtain, it is frequently argued that it is fit to demand a therapeutic or revolutionary experience that transforms the consciousness or the context, which prevents the capacity for moral discernment and responsibility. At least what is required is a structure and a process of conversion or reconstruction that will make a person or a society "fit."

The apparent confusion in much of ethics, it seems to me, derives from the lack of consensus on the category "fit." After all, this dimension of ethics has, until recently, received little explicit attention in modern theory. And those who view ethics more exclusively in its more classic philosophical forms still find these concerns outside the range of the discipline. Yet, in fact, an enormous amount of the time of contemporary working ethicists is spent working through the perspectives of Camus or Dostoyevski, Marx or Weber, Freud or Mead, Piaget or Myrdal, and the like, not in order to become literary critics, sociologists, psychologists, or developmental theorists, but to select and relate the normative categories, metaphors, and models to render a fit interpretation of the moral world around us. It makes, to give just one example, a great deal of ethical difference whether we hold the conditions of ghetto-dwellers to be caused by racism, class exploitation, evolutionary inevitabilities, personal irresponsibility, or the tyrannies of urban bureaucratic society, for the choice we make will surely influence in a critical way which patterns of right and good ought to be invoked to deal with that situation.

When this category becomes the exclusive one in moral discourse, ethics becomes reduced to journalism or secondhand social science with a homiletical bent. But without clarity and precision on the question of the fitting, the categories of right and good seem to float in the air of lecture halls without rootage in the urgencies of human historical existence. Inclusion of the term "fit" in moral discourse makes explicit and conscious the normative role that is, and must be, played by our aesthetic-interpretive propensities and the import of sensibility, responsibility, and sense of the "Gestalt" that are necessary to view our contexts of life.

In any fully developed ethical position the questions of right, good, and fit are not seen in isolation, but in relationship and tension. Negatively we see this in condemnations of racism, classism, or sexism, for they are simultaneously wrong, evil, and inappropriate, though continuing, moral pathologies. Positively, in attempts to construct a moral covenant, the greatest moralists from Moses to Niebuhr are great precisely because they work with the tensions and yet try to hold them in relationship. They may use other terms, they may accent certain motifs more than others, and they may be in error at certain points, but they render a realistic moral vision that links together the duties and privileges of "right," the concern for intentions and consequences of "good," and the contextual-interpretive dimensions of "fit."

In the technical study of ethics, debate is often about the fuller defi-

Ethics: Social and Christian

nitions and the relationships of right, good, and fit. But no moral discourse known to this author escapes using one or some of these categories. In the modern Anglo-American traditions moral philosophy attempts to clarify and define the relations of these terms (or some similar set that makes the same kinds of distinctions). Such efforts reveal one crucial element for Christian Social Ethics: that to be clear, we must pay close attention as to how, in normative reflection on the ethos, we mix the deontological, teleological, and contextual aspects of our moral analysis. Failure to state which kind of moral claim is at stake in a particular concern, or a tendency to slide unwittingly from one kind of accent to another, makes our effort to evoke moral reflection and action shoddy and unconvincing. Without clarity, whatever ethical commitments we have or whatever actions we take will remain our private passion, unavailable to scrutiny by ourselves or others, and impossible to communicate or defend.

A second element in the heritage from this brand of philosophical ethics, however, is more problematic. Much of it attempts to develop a theory about ethics that shows, for instance, that right and fit are *really* part of the good, or that a full understanding of the duties and privileges (i.e., the right) already contains the principle that we should seek the good and the fit. Thus, there is a tendency to render a unified theory of ethics by inclusion of all "oughts" under one kind of "ought."

I must confess, at this point, that I tend to get bored by such debates for several reasons: they are tediously repetitious in the long history of philosophical ethics; such debates seldom come back to normative reflection on the ethos and remain focused on the grammar of normative reflection, often grinding the small end of very little all the way down to nothing; they persistently lack the genuine ring of moral authority and judgment; and they imply a neat unity of moral possibility that does not fit the complexity of moral experience. While it is both possible, and for me necessary, to affirm that in God, or in the kingdom of God, there will be a fully unified moral possibility, life as it is experienced is one of moral tension and tragedy. The good is often pitted against the fit, the right against the good, and so forth. And we must neither reduce one to another nor relinquish one in favor of another. That is why ethics is difficult and existential; and that is why morally serious positions may be in conflict. And that is why all arguments to the effect that ethics is really just elaboration of "love thy neighbor as thyself" or some other single dimension sound grossly like saying that all astronomy is "twinkle, twinkle, little star." The problem is less to try to absorb some moral categories into others than to identify, celebrate, and analyze those moments when in fact there is, or under what conditions there could be, some existential resolution between conflicting "oughts." We need to focus not on ideal unity, but on the actual ethos. If we do turn to the analysis of actual moral movements and institutions of life, we find that, in spite of the tensions, life is neither pulled totally asunder, nor prematurely simplified.

Ethos and Community

It was mentioned earlier that the experience of obligation derives from claims laid upon one by groups and persons with whom we are in relationship. These claims can place people in situations of enormous tension and insecurity, enrich their perspective, or become so confusing as to destroy any sustained moral sensitivity. The philosophers seldom in the twentieth century acknowledge this. They customarily treat moral claims as abstractions, although they resist that charge. But when the importance of the ethos is acknowledged, it is both logical and empirical to suggest that it is even more important for human life to have a moral ethos than to have a clear ethical theory. Conceptual clarity about right, good, and fit is important; but it is not the focus or end of ethics. A moral ethos, one would expect, would tend to produce theoretical clarity; but theoretical clarity does not always produce a moral ethos. The real practice and proof of ethics, then, is in the shaping of the ethos in concrete ways, for the ethos evokes existential integration of personality (conscientious people) and of institutional life (responsible and accountable groups) that operate in more or less right, good, and fit ways. The proper unity of ethics is found in patterns of relationships, an ethos, that sustains possibilities of life according to the best senses of "ought." For this reason, the more profound study of ethics in the West has been related to the structure of life in community, and the development of persons and groups who will be responsible to and for the community. Ethics was inseparable from politics in the thought of Plato and Aristotle. The quality of social righteousness was the core of Old Testament ethics, and the ethical materials of the New Testament were directly related to the life of the *koinonia*. In the post-biblical traditions, at least in those that evidence greatest ethical concern, namely, the Catholic, the Calvinist, and the "free-church" sectarians, ethics was directly related to ecclesiological concerns, to questions of polity and social relationships. And it becomes important to study these traditions, not as historians do to find out what happened and what it meant, but to find analogies, motifs, themes, sensibilities that tell what they mean today so that we can inform our ethos.

Ethics: Social and Christian

In all these traditions there is a sense that ethics has fundamentally to do with the shape of the common life. And when there is a relative agreement between the diverse ethical pressures of right, good, and fit so that a commonality of "ought" is formed that can sustain responsible and accountable persons and institutions, a "covenant community" can be said to exist. The formation of covenant, a community of moral commitment, discernment, and engagement, then, becomes crucial to the moral task, and the test of ethical theory is its capacity to shape or evoke such a community. That is the chief end of ethics.

And, if we draw on the biblical tradition for more than merely the term "covenant," we say that such a phenomenon is so rare, so precious, and so marvelous that it is revelatory, a gift of such worth and power that it imposes special obligation by its very existence. Even beyond the biblical traditions, we can claim that the sense of moral community is a "religious fact." Ethics, then, is inevitably social, religious, and related to the concrete structures of worth and power in the ethos.

II. Social Theory and Ethics

So far, however, we have really only dealt with the word "Ethics" in the term "Christian Social Ethics." But we have seen how one way of understanding that term leads to social categories and, indeed, theological ones. In a sense, thus, the adjectives are redundant, for in the final analysis sociality and religion, in at least a broad sense, are implied in the word "Ethics." But, preserving the terms "Christian" and "Social" in an explicit fashion forces us to make as clear as possible the nature of our sociological and theological assumptions.

I would like to suggest that every ethicist worthy of the name must have an explicit social theory by which he understands the ethos. It is, of course, conceivable that we should focus on "personal" ethics at this point, in contrast to "social" ethics. Indeed, some have tried to do so. But while this is a formal possibility, the content of every personal ethic known to this observer ends up dealing with qualities of relationship that transcend the self, and the exclusive focus on "personal" concerns merely inhibits the capacity to develop the categories to say what needs to be said about those relationships. Yet no social theory can deny or ignore the personal elements that must be taken into account in a social system.

In dealing with the sociological side of the ethical task, I have found it most useful to develop a classification of sectors of the social system that are necessary for the preservation of a moral ethos in a complex, differentiated society. Here the ethicist is partially dependent upon the sociologist, much in the same way that he is dependent upon the philosophers and historians at other points. But ethicists do not work as sociologists *per se,* for they ask particular kinds of questions about society that bear on their task. While it is not pertinent within the confines of this article to present all the reasons for adopting one as against another sociological model, it is possible to identify in a somewhat schematic fashion the chief variables that go into the social analysis that I have found most pertinent to ethics. There are two sets of variables, one relating to the decisive levels of power in a social system, and the second relating to the location of worth or meaning in society.

Patterns of Power

In sociological theory, there has been a long debate about what forces in human history are most powerful in bringing or resisting change, in forming or destroying communities. Of course, many variables enter into the process that makes a society move in one direction or another; but what kinds of forces seem to be most potent most of the time? Some have argued that change or resistance to change is due to the *ideas* that are dominant. Others have argued that it is the patterns of *association* and authority that govern. Still others have argued that it is the *material interests* that are dominant, the way in which we appropriate, organize, and are influenced by the forces of nature to meet primal, biophysical needs. Every sociologist, and every historian, and indeed every observer of the social scene who tries to deal with or interpret why things happen the way they do tends to draw on one or more of those perspectives. When one looks closely at these various theories, one finds that their advocates tend to choose one set of social institutions as the base points from which they interpret the whole of society. Thus, those who say that ideas are what makes things happen tend to draw their understanding from the realms of education, the arts, or jurisprudence. If you want to take the moral pulse of a society, so they say, look at the universities, the music, poetry, and painting, or the codes of law. Other sectors of society are understood as the outworkings, the "emanations," or "incarnations," of basic ideas. In contrast, those who see the kind and quality of society being determined by the patterns of human relations tend to draw their models from family, group, or political associations and structures of authority. In their view, the patterns of

Ethics: Social and Christian

human associations control material interests, and ideas are rationalizations of the human relations, the ways by which we express our sighs of repression or justify our domination. Ideas are not "true" or powerful in themselves, for the true power is in the pattern of association. Still others argue that what really makes for civilizational success or failure is dependent upon the material conditions, such as the physical or mental health conditions, the level of technology, or the modes of economic production and distribution. Ideas are ideology and projection of needs, while associations are the organized and rationalized forms of material interests.

Each of these levels of analysis has a moral strategy built into it. The cure for ill is in the intensification of the "decisive" level. Thus, if things go wrong and ideas are what makes things happen, the "idealists" say that a fuller dose of hard thinking is, therefore, what is most required. The "associationalists" on their presuppositions meanwhile turn to shoring up family life or political activism, while the "materialists" try to purify or satisfy the interests, instincts, or needs in various ways.

In fact, I think, although I cannot fully defend it here, all three levels have a certain cogency and that a "synthetic" view best accounts for a social system. In any fully developed social system all levels will be present and relatively organized at any given time. Furthermore, these levels are not totally dependent on one another, but each is at least partially independent. While there is clear influence and interpenetration between ideas and material interests, for example, we cannot reliably predict the one from the other. Thus, we may suggest that there are three levels of the social system that are relatively distinct: the ideational level, the associational level, and the material level. The idealist, the associationalist, and the materialist are all partially correct as to what has power in human affairs, at least within their own level of analysis.

Patterns of Meaning and Worth

From quite a different perspective, however, it is possible to argue as to whether the core meanings for mankind are to be located in the matrix of personal or interpersonal concerns, in the vast impersonal structures that govern so much of our lives and without which chaos would reign, or in the overarching patterns of culture and civilizational fabric that shape the general trends and define the limits of both personal meaning and institutional structure. Thus it is possible again and again to find those who, as a touchstone of social analysis, take the pulse of all ideational, associational, or material concerns by referring to their source in personal and interpersonal experience. It is personality and immediate interpersonal relationship that is the source and center of all meaning, and it is this that produces collective structures and cultures. Others, however, see the structures of social collectivities as the center and source of meaning. The objective structures of the civilizational, ideational, associational, or material patterns in a society engender distinct personality types, encourage or discourage characteristic forms of interpersonal relationship, and determine the course of the culture at large. In this view, we are all governed by the dynamics of collective existence that are borne by the processes of legal, political, and economic development. In radical forms, the first view becomes psychologism and the second sociologism, either of which taken alone is often criticized as being reductionistic. There is, however, a third option that suggests that the patterns of cultural achievement — as especially manifest in the forms of expression, in the forms of intentional and voluntary groups, and in the technological instruments devised by a culture — are what makes possible both the definitions of personal meanings and the construction of collectivities. Thus, cross-cutting the three levels of social analysis that have to do with assessments of what is powerful in social existence are three ways of locating the decisive patterns of meaning and worth: the personal and interpersonal relations, the collective structures, and the cultural patterns.

These variables can be shown in a diagram of the major sectors of a social system in a differentiated society:

(Location of Meaning and Worth)	Personal and Interpersonal Relations	Cultural Patterns	Collective Structures
(Levels of Power) Ideational Factors	Educational Institutions	Expressive Institutions	Legal Institutions
Associational Factors	Familial Institutions	Voluntary Institutions	Political Institutions
Material Factors	Healthcare Institutions	Technological Managerial Institutions	Economic Institutions

A diagram such as this cannot show in a simple fashion the actual dynamic interplay of influences or the continuous dynamic change that takes place over time in each area. But it can suggest that there is a set of institutions that makes an ethos concrete and sustains it. Such a set may simultaneously confuse and corrupt an ethos. In any case it implies that there are multiple centers wherein moral gains can be institutionalized and stabilized, where significant social change may take place, and where corruption occurs. Each shift affects, but does not completely alter, other centers of moral concern. Each sector of the social system has built into it a distinctive set of obligations, a constellation of values that is a specific rendering of a communally defined view of the right, good, and fit, and that is the necessary ethical core of any institution. Further, parts of various sectors sometimes combine in a specific institutional matrix to form a "complex," which also develops a value pattern at its core. (Cf. my *Ethics of Necropolis* on the Military-Industrial Complex.) We can call these value patterns "axiologies," some parts of which are proper to the sector itself, some of which are significant for other sectors of society, and some of which are pertinent to the social system as a whole. Thus, it becomes the responsibility of *social* ethics to analyze and evaluate the axiologies that are at the moral core of these institutions or complexes according to the categories of ethics — right, good, and fit. Such investigation requires intensive and detailed familiarity with the patterns that obtain in that sector of society, and the ethicist must gain, therefore, a measure of technical competence in that field. But his concern is not that of a political scientist, or a medical sociologist, etc. Rather it is the critical examination of the axiology of the institution or its policies and practices. The axiology of a particular institution or set of institutions working together ought not to violate the duties and privileges that sustain them; they ought not to pursue ends that destroy the prospects of good intention or consequence; and they ought not wantonly displace the fragile tissues of human intercourse and civility without creating new ones. Ethical analysis takes place in order to approve and strengthen those institutions or aspects of a sector of the social system that sustain the moral community, and in order to criticize, transform, or undermine those institutions or aspects of the social system that destroy such possibilities. (Hence, ethics must at certain points come face to face with strategic and tactical questions, although that is not its primary arena of reflection or action.) And the test is whether the sector, institution, or complex generates an ethos wherein the questions of right, good, and fit are dominant concerns. The task of social ethics at this point, then, is to focus on one or another of the major sectors of the social system, education, politics, law, etc., in order to sort out what is right, good, and fit in regard to the operating axiology of that sector of society or to resolve conflicts between sectors of society or between a sector of society and the social system at large.

Voluntary Associations

Perhaps it was noted by some readers that at the center of the diagram of the social system is "Voluntary Institutions." By this term is meant that whole range of groups that organize around some purpose by the choice of the members — friendship groups, caucuses, political parties, action groups, social service agencies, cultural associations, churches, unions, hobby, professional or interest groups, etc. In spite of the power of all the institutions in the other sectors of society, there is a good bit of evidence that it is from these groups that the basic possibilities of and perspectives on moral life are derived.

Further, it can be argued that the presence or absence of these groups is decisive for the ways in which the collective and cultural institutions develop. It was the destruction of these groups under Hitler and Stalin that made the worst forms of collectivism at least temporarily capable of overcoming any sensibilities of the moral community. Similarly, in Christian history the destruction of these groups by heretic-hunting and witch-burning reveals the lowest ebbs of the moral community. For these groups are the nexus in which the ideas, associations, and material interests of persons become voluntarily wedded to the cultural and collective possibilities, where more or less decent accommodations to the conflicting demands of right, good, and fit are experimented with and hammered out. Thus, the processes and problems and results of these groups are crucial to the understanding of the moral community, and are the model for it. Fragile and sometimes feeble though they often appear to be, they are the heart of the ethos. It is these that revolutionaries and reactionaries try to create when out of power and to control when in. Indeed, because of the apparent fragility of these groups, revolutionaries often underestimate their power, and reactionaries often overestimate their susceptibility to control. And, surely, there are many such groups who ideologically abdicate in the use of the power and influence they could have. In the view presented here, it is continually to remind us of these dimensions of experience that the term "social" is properly attached to "ethics." In dealing with social ethics, people feel free to offer normative reflection and to exercise morally informed power through concerted action in regard to education, legal, political, familial, and the other institutions. Sociologically, it is this focus and constituency that partially distinguishes Christian Social Ethics from its academic colleague in the university departments of philosophy; and it is the vitality of these groups that is decisive for the moral health of an ethos.

III. "Christian" and Social Ethics

But so far I have only spoken of "ethics" and "social," and I have not said much about the Christian part. I can almost hear the charges, "That is the trouble with ethics; it tends to tag on the Christian part almost as an afterthought." On the contrary, this kind of definition of ethics and this view of the power and worth of voluntary institutions as the core of the social system has been developed primarily in seminaries, churches, and departments of religion that are institutionally concerned about the community of faith. And that is not an accident. The definitions offered here as to what ethics is as it is related to society are inconceivable without the heritage of the Judeo-Christian traditions. Indeed, Judaism and Christianity, and to some degree their most closely related religious worldviews, Islam and Marxism, are intrinsically ethical and social (because of their concern with history) in contrast to other nonhistorical possibilities for understanding the meaning of the divine life. These concerns were, I believe, embedded in scripture and, later, in the liturgies, canon law, and dogma of the church where they were a part of a more organic ethos. But when urbanization and industrialization began to produce a more differentiated society, when modern criticism began to force reevaluation of our traditional uses of the Bible, when particular understandings of liturgy and canon law began to lose their potency, and when philosophy and the social sciences began to displace or challenge dogma, even if they contained their own dogmas, it was necessary to develop a distinct discipline that gathered up the fragments and construct the conceptual and social elements that could create, sustain, and evoke moral community in the modern ethos. Christian Social Ethics as a synthetic discipline was an invention to meet this crisis.

It is possible, of course, to develop a viable social ethic that is not explicitly rooted in a religious tradition. A theory of the right, good, and fit coupled to a social theory may indeed render a minimal interpretation of what must be protected to have an ethos, of what must be present to protect persons and institutions from wanton destruction or injustice. Many a voluntary association and much secular social theory in fact operates on such a basis. But such a view has three problems. First, its roots are often implicitly grounded in Judeo-Christian religious traditions, and failure to acknowledge this deprives it of some of its most useful tools. Second, it provides no focal point beyond established tradition, nature, or nurture, for making ethical judgments and thus accounting for moral freedom. That is, it does not have a concept of "God" that transcends empirical reality and prevents one-dimensional understandings of life. And third, it provides no vision of a divine ethos by which it can fundamentally criticize the existing one and envision a reconstructed one. Hence, in the long run, we are inevitably impoverished by attempts to avoid theological considerations in social ethics.

But there is another way in which the Christian element is directly pertinent to social ethics, a way that flows directly from the covenantal definitions of "ethics" and "social" above; namely, that among the voluntary institutions at the center of the social system, the church is the prototype. The Judeo-Christian tradition is, among other things, fundamentally a movement with an organized constituency and a sense of destiny in the undeserved triumph of the moral community as a gift of grace. There are many movements that form voluntary institutions around all sorts of purposes, often attempting to carry out for the whole community what religious groups once advocated for the faithful. But there is the audacious claim by the faithful that the Judeo-Christian movement is somehow *the* movement in human history, a claim held in fear and trembling, and sometimes in the face of empirically disconfirming evidence. It is, as I understand it, the main function of *Theological* Ethics to deal with that claim, to defend it against false criticisms, to criticize it where it becomes pretentious, to clarify what kind of religious, social, scientific, historical, and philosophical warrants might be given for such a claim, to reconstruct the theological tradition where it threatens to distort that possibility, to open up the possible ethical meanings of the symbols by which such a claim is articulated, and to confront in simultaneous charity and conviction those who identify other worldviews as decisive — such as tribalists, Hindus, Buddhists, naturalists, or, with a special sense of affinity, Muslims and Marxists. Here we may note again that at the boundaries of the discipline, we must not only have a social theory, but a fundamental and critical theory of "religion" that reaches universal dimensions in its concern for community.

But beyond the fact that the above definitions of "Social" and "Ethics" grow out of the Judeo-Christian heritage, and beyond the theological claims of the church as *the* organized "voluntary institution" bearing the decisive movement for human history, there is a third reason that "Christian" may properly be attached to the words "Social Ethics." The joining to form a moral community and to create a right, good, and fit ethos by specific engagement in the institutions of a social system demands an act of personal and social will. The will, it can be argued, is shaped by, legitimized by, and finds its principal expression in, symbols. The basic symbols of the Judeo-Christian traditions are fundamentally related to the voluntary capacities of people and institutions in society and

Ethics: Social and Christian

are laden with social ethical content: Creation and Fall; Exodus and Conquest; Law and Prophecy; Incarnation and Crucifixion; Resurrection, Communion of the Saints, and the Kingdom of God; Trinity and Ecclesiology. Nor are these symbols anti-historical, anti-rational, or anti-emotional as so many voluntaristic positions seem to become. While these symbols indicate that moral salvation does not derive primarily from tradition, intelligence, or feelings, they also accent the fact that no moral choice is complete without rootage in history, reason, and passion. Therefore, the Judeo-Christian heritage is one that both identifies the center of morality in the Will that is also rational, compassionate, and historically engaged in a way that supplies specific content to the categories of "ought" for a living community.

This profound theological insight of the Judeo-Christian tradition drives all who grasp it to establish an intentional moral community — involving, ultimately, all humanity — that brings the conflicting demands of right, good, and fit into a covenantal relationship and rejects three persistent pathologies of modern society: racism, sexism, and classism. Indeed, the awe inspired by the fact that there is any moral community at all in the midst of human life with mankind's tendency to place its faith in traditionalistic cant, pretentious rationality or dissipating emotionality, disembodied idealism or consuming material interest, and in the midst of a plethora of institutions going their own ways or institutionalizing society's pathologies, allows us to see glimpses of the grace of that ultimate power and worth that is beyond our ordinary comprehension but directly pertinent to the patterns of worth and power in institutional life. Thereby, we find a vision of ethical meaning at the brink of the ordinary experience of moral meaninglessness that allows us to be ruthlessly realistic about this world without becoming cynical. In short, the theological dimension provides a fundamental basis from which to engage in the task of ethics. This religious dimension of moral experience is intrinsic to each profound ethic — indeed, it is constitutive for it. And this dimension seems to have been most explicitly articulated in the Judeo-Christian heritage. Thus the attachment of the word "Christian" to what we have already joined, namely "Social Ethics," is neither special pleading nor accidental.

Implications

The religious dimension of social ethics has a double effect. On the one hand, we are fundamentally reminded that no traditionalistic moralism, no ethical theorizing, and no ecstatic experience of righteousness is sufficient to bring about a common fulfillment of the demand of "ought" experienced by all. On the other hand, rooted in a community itself rooted in a vision of ultimate worthy power, we gain an ethical foundation on which to stand. Hence, we are empowered to engage in a continuing and dynamic process of evaluation, blessing and support, criticism and transformation of the specific institutions in the social system that sustain or inhibit moral life. The specific *content* pertinent to these tasks is not the topic of this article, since we are focusing on the structural relations of "Christian," "Social," and "Ethics." But the symbols mentioned previously provide the clue to what that content would be. And these are the concerns of the religious community, confronted continually by the fact that all the various sectors of the social system at various times pretend to be *the* core of moral existence on earth. Who does not know those who see the family as *the* moral basis of society? Who can deny that for some the economic corporation has become their church? Who will doubt that particular political institutions have sometimes attempted to bear *the* moral life for the whole of mankind? Who has not encountered those who see the artist, the educator, the doctor, the lawyer, or the technologist as the bringers of salvation to the ethos? To be sure, schools, parties, hospitals, etc., do become agents of salvation, mediating ultimate worth and power to society at various moments. But these are "temporal" functions, and the tendency of all these efforts is to claim, on the basis of the relative moral coherence that they embody, special privilege instead of special obligation, because they do not see themselves continuously under divine judgment. On the basis of the religious dimension of a sound social ethic, we can expose these frauds without denying their importance to society or to the functioning of a moral community informed by a sense of the transcendent center of power and worth, and attempting to discern the common "oughts" of all of humanity.

Thus, to summarize, Christian Social Ethics attempts to provide a theological, covenantal basis for voluntary institutions, especially the church, to evaluate and act on the operating axiologies of the ethos according to what is right, good, and fit. Many who are doing Christian Social Ethics, in this view, are not consciously ethicists or consciously Christian, but they are doing what Christian Social Ethics sees as central. The discipline, as an academic enterprise, attempts to articulate the meanings of such activities and to give them conceptual guidance.

Christian Social Ethicists, in this mold, can begin at several points. They may want to begin by clarifying the distinctive motifs that derive from the Judeo-Christian heritage, apply those to the society at large or to some

Ethics: Social and Christian

sector of the social system, and show what those would mean for a compelling interpretation of right, good, and fit. They may wish to clarify some dimension of the right or the good or the fit and show how such a clarification aids the understanding of the tensions between those terms, especially as they represent conflicts between one or another axiology of society's institutions, and critically examine the religious worldview that one would logically have to invoke to legitimate such a view. Or, as I have found most useful, one may try to clarify the operating axiology of a specific set of institutions, bring them under the critical scrutiny of more precise understandings of the right, good, and fit, and show how a specific set of religious symbols gives impetus to the development of voluntary institutions to alter the axiology in particular directions. The test, in this view of Christian Social Ethics, is not whether one moves from one term to another in a particular order, but whether all bases are accounted for and whether therefore the possibilities of a moral ethos and a covenanted community are in fact enhanced in a way compatible with a cogent understanding of Divine Will and the social conditions under which man lives.

Of course, in a full treatment much more needs to be said about the nature of ethics, society, and perhaps, especially, the moral pertinence of Judeo-Christian theology (as I have attempted in my *Ethics and the Urban Ethos*). Nor have I attempted to present the full rationale for seeing the boundaries in this fashion. Instead I have tried to show how matters discussed in Christian Social Ethics do have a *prima facie* coherence.

But in short, Christian Social Ethics has at least a hypothetically coherent way of dealing with human moral experience, and of focusing the study of religion and society. It is, of necessity, interdisciplinary; but it does not get lost in cross-disciplinary study because it has a particular and important focus. Its focus is the formation of a right, good, and fit covenanted community rooted in the divine center of ultimate worth and power and actualized in society. Indeed, the capacity to develop a viable Christian social ethic will probably influence the survival potential of the Judeo-Christian heritage and modern society. It will certainly be necessary for any sustained attempt to give normative shape to our rather confused ethos.

Reflections on "Universal Absolutes"

On the grounds of an (essentially) Roman Catholic moral theology and political philosophy, Michael J. Perry states and argues for positions that vindicate the accent of recent popes on human rights as both a matter of faith and of reason, positions I believe to be largely valid and that could gain even stronger support from a Reformed Christian philosophical theology. This should not be surprising, for the Catholic tradition was the common tradition for centuries, it deeply stamped the legal structure of the West that gave rise to "rights talk," and those strands that led to human rights in its modern form were implicitly in it, even if they were strengthened by the struggles of Protestants to establish a right to convert and, later, to advocate the freedom of religion on spiritual, intellectual, and organization grounds. Perry knows, as most Catholic and Protestants believe, that social morality is unavoidably linked to religion, that these matters can be discussed in public discourse, and that it is fateful for politics, law, social well-being, and international relationships to do so. These matters are made clear not only in this book, but also in his earlier *Love and Power: The Role of Religion and Morality in American Politics*,[1] *The Constitution and the Courts: Law or Politics*,[2] and *Religion in Politics: Constitutional and Moral Perspectives*.[3] In the present book, as in the other remarkable products of this decade, we find Perry engaged not only with contemporary political philosophy and jurisprudence, which are largely

1. Michael J. Perry, *Love & Power: The Role of Religion and Morality in American Politics* (New York: Oxford University Press, 1991).
2. Michael J. Perry, *The Constitution in the Courts* (New York: Oxford University Press, 1994).
3. Michael J. Perry, *Religion in Politics: Constitutional and Moral Perspectives* (New York: Oxford University Press, 1997).

Reflections on "Universal Absolutes"

secular in outlook, but with a number of scholars who are concerned with what David Tracy has called "public theology," a term that several Protestants as well as Catholics have adopted — although in somewhat different ways.[4]

On these bases, he argues that the term "human rights," as it appears in the post–World War II debates about the United Nations Declaration and Covenants, is not only a new version of a functionally operating *jus gentium*, as John Witte has argued,[5] but a relatively new statement of the ancient Stoic-Christian idea of a God-given natural law.[6] The substantial moral content implied by the relatively wide consensus is that, in spite of many even ultimately fatal deficits and foibles and many differences of talent and capacity, every person is endowed with a "dignity" or must be seen as "sacred." On this basis, it is reasonable to argue that "certain choices should be made and certain other choices rejected; in particular, certain things ought not to be done to any human being and certain other things ought to be done for every human being."[7]

In arguing his case, he challenges those who wish to argue that religion is not helpful or convincing, especially against the argument by secular think-

---

4. David Tracy, *The Analogical Imagination: Christian Theology and the Culture of Pluralism* (New York: Crossroad, 1981); Robert Benne, *The Paradoxical Vision: A Public Theology for the Twenty-First Century* (Minneapolis: Fortress, 1995); Don Browning and Francis Schüssler-Fiorenza, eds., *Habermas, Modernity and Public Theology* (New York: Crossroad, 1992); Ronald Thiemann, *Constructing a Public Theology* (Louisville: Westminster John Knox, 1991); Robin Lovin, *Christian Faith and Public Choices* (Minneapolis: Fortress, 1984); Michael Himes and Kenneth Himes, *Fullness of Faith: The Public Significance of Theology* (New York: Paulist, 1993); Jose Casanova, *Public Religions in the Modern World* (Chicago: University of Chicago Press, 1994); and Max L. Stackhouse, *Public Theology and Political Economy* (Grand Rapids: Eerdmans, 1986).

5. John Witte and Johan Van der Vyver, eds., *Religious Human Rights in Global Perspective: Religious Perspectives* (Boston and The Hague: Martinus Nijhoff, 1996).

6. This, of course, is a disputed claim. While his view of the continuity between natural law theory and natural rights theory is supported by Brian Tierney, *The Idea of Natural Rights: Studies on Natural Rights, Natural Law, and Church Law* (Atlanta: Scholars Press, 1997); Knud Haakonssen, *Natural Law and Moral Philosophy* (New York: Cambridge University Press, 1996); Guenther Haas, *The Concept of Equity in Calvin's Ethics* (Waterloo, ON: Wilfrid Laurier University Press, 1997), and many others, another stream of scholars who oppose deontological ethics see human rights as a repudiation of natural law. See, for example, Ernest Fortin, *The Birth of Philosophic Christianity: Studies in Early Christian and Medieval Thought* (Lanham, MD: Rowman & Littlefield, 1996). Compare A. MacIntyre, *Whose Justice? Which Rationality?* (Notre Dame: University of Notre Dame Press, 1988).

7. Michael J. Perry, *The Idea of Human Rights: Four Inquiries* (New York: Oxford University Press, 1998), p. 5.

ers such as the neo-Kantian Jürgen Habermas, the neo-Pragmatist Richard Rorty, the neo-Liberal Ronald Dworkin, and the neo-Classicist Martha Nussbaum, all of whom say they want to support human rights but cannot supply a good reason for doing so. While he and I clearly respect aspects of their contributions to contemporary thought, his argument is ultimately devastating to other aspects of their ethical stances. His argument suggests that as thinkers they can only continue to hold the positions they set forth on this matter if they acknowledge that they are drawing on intellectual capital established by theological traditions that their own work does not acknowledge, cannot supply, and irrationally does not allow at the table of discourse.[8]

A closely related part of the argument, however, is today more widely accepted practically, but more widely denied on both philosophical and theological theoretical grounds. Behind the several parts of the argument that (1) all humans are endowed with a dignity or sanctity, and that (2) some things ought not be done to any human being, and (3) some things ought be done for every human being, is the fundamental issue: Are there any such things as "universal absolutes," religiously, philosophically, or ethically, and if there are, can we know them well enough to speak of them with confidence? The key terms — "all," "any," and "every" — signal a universality that appears to be absolute, and Perry certainly appears to think that, properly understood, we can say that there are such things, make a plausible case for them, and not only put a cloud of suspicion over those who deny that there can be such things or that we could know them if they were real, but also act in ways that assure that they make a significant difference in our politics and law.

This is today a demanding position, because to raise the issue of universal absolutes is seen by some to cross a line of intellectual impropriety, to become "totalizing," never mind that it was on the basis of such claims that the totalitarian movements of our century were most energetically resisted. Still, few today think in terms of "ethical universals," "moral laws," or "absolute

---

8. Perry, *The Idea of Human Rights*, pp. 43-56. I have attempted to make a similar case in several works. See, for example, Max L. Stackhouse, *Creeds, Society and Human Rights* (Grand Rapids: Eerdmans, 1984); Max L. Stackhouse and Stephen E. Healey, "Religion and Human Rights: A Theological Apologetic," in *Religious Human Rights in Global Perspective*, pp. 485-516 (cited in note 5); Max L. Stackhouse, "Public Theology and Ethical Judgment," *Theology Today* 54, no. 2 (1997): 165-79; and Max L. Stackhouse, "Human Rights and Public Theology: The Basic Validation of Human Rights," in *Religion and Human Rights: Competing Claims?* ed. Carrie Gustatson and Peter Juviler (Armonk, NY: M. E. Sharpe, 1999), pp. 12-30, with a response from Louis Henkin. That discussion is continued in "The Intellectual Crisis of a Good Idea," *Journal of Religious Ethics* 26, no. 2 (Fall 1998): 263-68.

truths," and in some circles to use such terms is close to admitting that one believes that the earth is flat or that unicorns exist. In either case, they suggest, one is close to imperialistic moralizing and fairy-tale theology, taking comfort in traditional idealisms or archaic narratives that can no longer be seen as related to serious thought or convincing argument — except possibly as a matter of historical curiosity. As a description of the present state of the argument in many circles, it is surely accurate to say that many believe that the whole idea of human rights, if one really means something like a universal absolute, is nonsense, and that we should scuttle it. Then, if we are premodern conservatives, we should remind people of the duties given by their social stations; or if we are modern liberals, seek to expand further the range of liberty if it is anywhere still restricted; or if we are postmodern anti-liberals, get on with the cultivation of our preferred version of virtue or proclaiming our preferred faith in our preferred language game in our preferred enclave.

To the contrary, Perry's argument implies (although it does not quite state it this baldly) that those who deny the idea of human rights, as well as those who accept the idea of human rights and fit it into one of the views sketched above without being able to supply reasons for holding that human rights are based in the theological understanding of the human as "made in the image of God," are in danger of simply asserting the sovereignty of their quite provincial sense of duty. They also back into the danger of claiming freedoms for their own benefit, displaying their own virtue, or making a leap of faith (often not in God, but in their own image of humanity) that is less defensible than the theological heritage to which he appeals.

To make a stronger case, Perry unclutters the issues. He is aware that when we speak seriously of human rights, we are not speaking of the whole of morality — an important point given that many common criticisms of human rights have to do with the fact that people are always claiming their rights without cultivating any visible virtue and seldom assuming the duties of responsibility in the common life. He agrees that other dimensions of morality may also need attention that are not always implied in the articulation, appeal to, or defense of human rights. But affirming this in no way invalidates the need for or cogency of human rights as a part of the larger moral picture and the basis for just international law. Human rights may involve, in some sense, universal absolutes, but that does not mean that they are exhaustive of the moral life.

Of course, much depends on what one means by "universal" and "absolute." If we define "absolute" in the way that one of my influential predecessors, Paul Lehmann, did, the idea is absurd. On the basis of a view that we are being led by a free and sovereign God, whom we know in Jesus Christ to be

Developing a Method for Public Theology

beyond all legalism, toward a "humanization" that overcomes all that is dehumanizing, he repudiated all talk of "universal absolutes." He believed that absolutist ethics ignores contextual realities and answers the question of what we are to do by supplying an abstract absolute:

> And what is an "absolute"? Ethically speaking, an "absolute" is a standard of conduct which can be and must be applied to all people in all situations in exactly the same way. The standard may be an ideal, a value, or a law. Its ethical reality and significance however, lies in its absolute character.[9]

However, no known theological ethicist or moral philosopher who speaks of universal absolutes holds the view he opposes. Of course, in both ethics and law, a governing principle is that we should treat like cases alike. But cases are not so very often exactly alike, and the principle does not apply to some demand that we force all the findings of the facts of all cases into a single mold. It says that in coming to a judgment about the particulars, we should invoke the same principles as a standard that we would properly use in other, very similar cases. Even those who hold to such absolute principles of right and wrong as "Thou shalt not murder," for instance, believe that the principle has to be applied to cases, and that this necessitates doing so in highly variant ways precisely in view of differing circumstances, context, and intent. That is why, in both morality and legal codes, every culture makes distinctions between, say, premeditated murder, manslaughter in varying degrees, accidental homicide, justifiable homicide by reason of self-defense, the use of coercive or even lethal force in morally justifiable actions of the police or military, etc.; every culture matches variant punishments to concrete conditions and probably consequences, and places those who bear arms under specific disciplines. Thus, if one has this "absolutistic" definition in the back of one's mind when one speaks of human rights, one must, of course, oppose what one has in the back of one's mind; but it

---

9. Paul Lehmann, *Ethics in a Christian Context* (New York: Harper & Row, 1963), p. 125. He and some disciples do not seem to recognize that insofar as they use the term "human" as a central criteriological principle in discerning what God is doing (in the various contexts of life) that is "humanizing" and what other forces are doing that is "dehumanizing," their view depends upon an abstract universal that is being applied as an absolute as to cases. In the process, they determine what is "right" and what "wrong," what is "good" and what is "evil," although they assiduously avoid such terms because they think these are normative and prescriptive in morally illegitimate ways rather than indicative and discerning descriptions, which they morally approve.

is not clear that the matter of "universal absolutes" with regard to human rights is eliminated.

It might, of course, immediately be noted that various cultures and societies differently define what counts as justifiable homicide or the morally justifiable use of lethal force, etc. From this reality, it can then be argued that since these cultures disagree, there is or can be no agreement about universals, or about what could be universal. And, indeed, if one understands "universals" as implying that every culture does or must immediately agree, this doubt is reasonable. There have been intense arguments as to whether, for example, "capitalist cultures" emphasize civil and political rights while "socialist cultures" accent social and economic rights, and which really comes first in lexical and historical priority. Also, there are questions as to whether "Asian Values" signal a moral system that is fundamentally different from "human rights," although the arguments for that claim grow thinner and constantly interweave with issues of capitalism and socialism; and it turns out to be more interesting that we can and do argue internationally, cross-culturally, and interreligiously about such matters and do not hold that we are arguing about nothing, simply talking past each other, or expressing our cultural differences, all of which are equally valid.[10]

The argument that people do not in fact agree on how to define certain features of human rights, thus, turns out to be less important philosophically, theologically, and morally than people who make a big point of it think it does, although the divergence does play an indispensable role in international diplomacy and in refining the formulations of international legal codes. People seldom find perfect agreement on scientific, historical, or artistic questions, and we should not expect greater immediate agreement on the ethical or theoretical ones that stand behind common legislation. The real issue is whether we can debate these matters in a way that points toward a normative moral order or ideal that we are trying to clarify and implement, and whether, in the context of debate, we think we can and should argue for certain moral constants and liberties that should apply to that category of intelligent, social, in-

---

10. See, for example, J. C. Hsiung, ed., *Human Rights in East Asia: A Cultural Perspective* (New York: Paragon House, 1985), and Wm. T. de Bary and Tu Weiming, eds., *Confucianism and Human Rights* (New York: Columbia University Press, 1998). Compare Christina Cerna, "Universality of Human Rights and Cultural Diversity: Implementation of Human Rights in Different Socio-Cultural Contexts," *Human Rights Quarterly* 16, no. 4 (1994): 740-52; Xiarong Lee, "'Asian Values' and the Universality of Human Rights," *Philosophy and Public Policy* (Spring 1996): 18-23; and Max L. Stackhouse, "The Future of Human Rights: Multiculturalism in Vienna," *Christian Century* 110, no. 20 (1993): 660-62.

evitably religious animals that we call "human," even if they (we) do not agree fully. This issue makes both theoretical and practical differences: Is there any way by which we can, without cultural imperialism but with a secure enough sense of justice to act, say that if this or that group does not stop enslaving people, torturing them, "disappearing" them, or "dehumanizing" them, we are justified in mobilizing opposition to the perpetrators?

A related argument points out that no known culture is without terms for murder, rape, lying, stealing, and the like — all terms laden with the understanding that such things are wrong and known to be wrong, and that the victims of such behaviors have a right to resist them and to demand some sort of restitution if they occur even if some try to justify them. Of course, there is disagreement about to whom they apply and what kinds of restitutions can be claimed — matters that are culturally variant and subject to historical and social conditions. Often, for example, the prohibition "do not murder" (etc.) is only applied to the "in-group." But that merely means that we have a debate over the sociological boundaries of the in-group, not over the moral wrongness of murder, the moral right to resist being murdered, or the duty to establish a society as inclusive as possible in which tendencies to murder are constrained. Human rights imply that in some meaningful sense all humanity is part of the in-group, even if some seek with all their might, demagogic rhetoric, or even deep religious fervor to define a smaller "us" as the only "true" in-group. Not everyone agrees. Yet all who oppose racism, tribalism, nationalism, and other forms of chauvinism, and hold that others ought also to do so, must logically hold that something is more "honorable," "valuable," "dignified," or "sacred" than these "in-group" centers of loyalty. They may not like the language of "rights" for some reason or other, but they are more in accord with the universal moral standards that human rights discourse requires than those who support racism, tribalism, etc.[11]

    11. In this connection, it is important to note that those who defend a theological basis for human rights often distinguish between kinds of "in-group/out-group" ways of thinking and thus have two boundaries of inclusion and exclusion. Theistic (and panentheistic) religions usually have an inclusive recognition of "all humans" to whom human rights apply, and an exclusive recognition of "those who belong to our religious community due to shared convictions and practices about that reality," to whom rights of membership apply. Some rights apply to "all" and others to "us." Those who acknowledge the moral and spiritual rights of all, but reserve other particular rights, duties, and loyalties to an "us," would differ from a definition that considered the "us" to be the only "all," denying rights, even the term "humanity," to any outside the "us." The best defense for human rights, I think, is provided by those theological traditions that see themselves under a theistic reality that governs the universal "all," since nothing else is fully inclusive, and defends the rights of multiple particular

Reflections on "Universal Absolutes"

To such arguments as these we could add the observation that many believe we are presently in a new historical epoch — one in which the various possibilities of discourse about universal principles are simply outmoded. They hold that generalizing modes of discourse have been shattered, and that we now live in historically and culturally enclosed fragments of systems, each with its own language games, guided only by our own tradition's narratives, which are incommensurable with other systems, linguistic patterns, traditions, and narratives.[12] This, however, is an argument based on the "naturalistic fallacy" — seeking to establish a normative perspective on the grounds of empirical evidence, in spite of the fact that what is is not always what ought to be. In this particular belief about our present state of affairs, indeed, the view that our age is different from all other ages is questionable on both empirical and normative grounds. The view presumes some correspondence between their description of the increased fragmentation of society and morality and the way things really are, as compared to some previous time (which is seldom specified). It is a correspondence for which there is anecdotal and journalistic evidence, but there is also anecdotal and journalistic evidence to suggest that those who make such arguments are often reflecting their own de-provincialization as they move from a small homogeneous social horizon to a world that has been quite diverse and heterogeneous for centuries.

Perry touches on, but does not sufficiently develop, in my view, the notion that many widespread postmodern theories that speak of the fragmentation of moral understanding in our midst simply do not seem to grasp the most important dynamics of our time, although they may point to the psychological effects that beset many. It is likely that we are aware of greater pluralism due to greater media, travel, education, and migrations that make us aware of wider reaches of human cultures. But what is more remarkable is the fact not only that more international law has been made since World

---

groups of "us" — religious, political, ideological, educational, etc. — to organize and set forth their specific views of truth and right practice in public. See Max L. Stackhouse and Deidre Hainsworth, "Deciding for God: The Right to Convert in Protestant Perspectives," in John Witte Jr., ed., *Sharing the Book: Religious Perspectives on the Rights and Wrongs of Proselytism* (Maryknoll, NY: Orbis, 1999).

12. It is one of the oddities of our time that Amnesty International, one of the great human rights advocacy organizations, invited a large number of scholars who hold such views to speak of human rights, and they did so in ways that in fact undercut the possibility of holding to them. See Stephen Shute and Susan Hurley, eds., *On Human Rights* (New York: Basic Books, 1993). Compare Max L. Stackhouse and Stephen E. Healey, "Religion and Human Rights: A Theological Apologetic" (cited in note 8).

War II than in any half-century in human history, but that more common agreement about matters of government, trade, and morality is at hand than ever. "Globalization" is the most plausible candidate for the "real postmodernism," one that is bringing the prospect of a world-comprehending culture, with a new recognition of certain common moral standards.

No doubt, much of globalization is carried by an American or Western cultural neocolonialism; but we condemn that when it occurs, even if we are beneficiaries of it, because we know (or can recognize when pressed; or believe, with compelling reasons for believing) that it is wrong and unjust. It is contrary to the highest and widest standards of human rights and justice that we do not fully grasp but can, together, point toward and acknowledge as not subject to dissolution according to various changes that are taking place in history.[13] In short, real postmodernity may demand the intensification of the quest for articulate universal absolutes.

Further, for many the issue is not a matter of the shock of changing social locations, but a matter of the fundamental loss of, or doubt about, faith. No few have rebelled against the simplistic confidence of their youth and have, in their learned sophistication, adopted the Nietzschean view that since God is dead, all is permitted, as Perry knows. Such a view, however, does not account for the resurgence of the world's great theistic religions in our time, and it overlooks the more significant fact that people can and do learn, in some significant measure, each other's languages and do find commonality with the stranger, the other, and the foreigner — recognizing when they are mistreated or neglected by powerful forces at home or abroad. Such observations suggest that there may be, in humanity, some deep structure of commonality that allows us to use the word "human" without embarrassment, to discover and recognize commonality when we encounter other humans who are very different in many ways, and to seek moral ways of relating to them, although Perry does not take up this issue to any extent.

We may debate, of course, whether it is some innate capacity for rationality and moral commonality that best accounts for this, and we may debate

---

13. The concept of "globalization" and all that it may entail is hotly debated, especially in relation to postmodernity. Perhaps the best half-dozen resources are Roland Robertson, *Globalization: Social Theory and Global Culture* (London: Sage, 1992); John Witte, ed., *Christianity and Democracy in Global Context* (Boulder, CO: Westview, 1993); Peter Beyer, *Religion and Globalization* (London: Sage, 1994); Mike Featherstone, Scott Lash, and Roland Robertson, eds., *Global Modernities* (London: Sage, 1995); Hans Küng, *A Global Ethic for Global Politics and Economics* (New York: Oxford University Press, 1997); and David Marpel and Terry Nardin, eds., *International Society* (Princeton: Princeton University Press, 1998).

whether the Greek term "nous," with its capacity to recognize a "logos," or the theological implications of the Hebraic expression "image of God" given with the breath of life, or the Hindu understanding of the "atma," or some other concept of "soul" or "human self" best identifies what is at the root of this capacity. But we are in each case seeking to point toward something that is universal and absolute and common to all. At least we can say that when believers, theologians, and international jurists talk about such things, they are in a realm of discourse that has universal implications and are pointing to a reality that does not dissolve in the tides of history.

Perry seldom takes up the more empirical and cross-cultural issues that I have signaled here, although his argument does seem to be compatible with them. Instead he argues that some relativist challenges to the idea of human rights are plausible. He acknowledges that no feature of our human nature eliminates all but one ideal for humanity (he does not discuss a need for "salvation"), and he argues that insofar as there is such a thing as a fixed human nature, invariant from social environment to social environment, it is not sufficiently determinate to legislate a single determinate good for humanity. This is not controversial, although it leads to a certain awkwardness of argument, as we shall see, for at this point he shifts from a concept of Right and rights to a concept of teleological good. He writes:

> Universalism about human good is correct: Human beings are all alike in some respects.... But pluralism about human good is correct, too: There are many important respects in which human beings are not all alike... intraculturally as well as interculturally....
>
> Undeniably, then, any plausible conception of human good must be pluralist. A conception of human good, however, can be, and should be, universalist as well as pluralist: It can acknowledge sameness as well as difference, commonality as well as variety.[14]

He is surely correct, but this raises a most interesting, and in some ways the most ambiguous argument that he makes. It is not with regard to "universality," but with regard to "absoluteness." He knows that "no one argues that every human right — every 'ought' and 'ought not' — established by the international law of human rights is or even should be absolute," and he acknowledges that real social conditions and possibilities limit what can be fulfilled in many situations, and that this fact is recognized in human rights covenants.

---

14. Perry, *The Idea of Human Rights*, p. 65 (cited in note 7).

Developing a Method for Public Theology

Indeed, some of the rights that most interest theologically concerned people — the rights to freedom of religion and expression — are "conditional rather than unconditional," and that some are "derogable" while others appear to be "not derogable."[15] In a complex analysis, he argues for the view that "it does make sense for international law to make some rights nonderogable even if the rights are not, as moral rights, absolute."[16] And, in fact, he concludes his book with the following sentence: "Even if no human rights are, as moral rights, absolute, some human rights, as international legal rights, should be — and happily, are — absolute."[17]

The complexity of this final argument is, at first, puzzling. What kind of "should," if not a moral "should," could he mean as the warrant for absolute legal rights? It seems to me that in this section of this marvelous book (the fourth chapter), he makes arguments that are more overtly laden with Roman Catholic presumptions about natural law, presumptions that remain critical for continuing disputes in Catholicism and between Protestants and Catholics. Much that is at stake bears on the definition of "absolute." I have already argued that the issue does not rest so much on whether or not something is exclusive — that is, whether it must be taken to be the sole or only consideration to be taken into account in moral decision, and I have suggested that Perry agrees that exclusiveness is not what is at stake in the term "absolute." I have also agreed with Perry that a more basic issue is whether a purported absolute norm, principle, or ideal is subject to dissolution, by conditioned circumstance or derogation in time and history. On the whole, Perry says "no"; but then with regard to human rights specifically, he divides the question so that these rights stand as absolutes in law, but not in morality. What is going on here?

It appears that what has happened is that he has unveiled his rootage in one view of natural law, a teleological one held largely by Catholics but shared

15. See Perry, *The Idea of Human Rights*, pp. 89ff.
16. Perry, *The Idea of Human Rights*, p. 93.
17. Perry, *The Idea of Human Rights*, p. 106. Much of this chapter has to do with a critique of the moral absolutism of John Finnis, the noted natural law advocate. Compare John Finnis, *Moral Absolutes: Tradition, Revision and Truth* (Washington, DC: Catholic University of America Press, 1991), pp. 12, 20. At the end of Perry's last sentence, one finds a very interesting and complex footnote with references to Kent Greenawalt's influence, especially in regard to his "Natural Law and Political Choice: The General Justification Defense: Criteria for Political Action, and the Duty to Obey the Law," *Catholic University Law Review* 36 (1986). Compare also Kent Greenawalt, *Private Consciences and Public Reasons* (New York: Oxford University Press, 1995). He also refers to Jean Porter's "Direct and Indirect in Grisez's Moral Theory," *Theological Studies* 57 (1996): 611, 627-31.

by some Protestants and theistic philosophers, to supply the basis of "rights." And, in this perspective, of course, the chief end of moral development is not the cultivation, actualization, or fulfillment of human rights. Thus, rights are not the absolute end or goal of life, and they are not such that we must (or even may) claim them before God to bring our internal moral propensities for the good to highest realization. However, at the social and political level, the common good is decidedly served by installing human rights as "absolutes" — in the sense that they are necessary principles to assure the fulfillment of the common life. A cultivated, actuated, and fulfilled society cannot be reasonably imagined that would not contain the basic principles of human rights as a civil reality. But since civil realities are essentially instrumental to the moral and spiritual development of persons, human rights are proper to civil order but not necessarily to the persons that order serves. Thus, while human rights are regulative for the common good, they are essentially instrumental to persons and personal morality. In short, it appears that human rights are best understood in terms of a "rule teleology" that functionally requires something like human rights that can be jurisprudentially formulated as absolutes. If that is so, claims about their "absoluteness" are and must be modest.[18]

While some Protestants share these views, more of Protestantism and indeed, some wings of Catholicism and some philosophers of jurisprudence have used a related, but distinctive logic when speaking of "absoluteness." This view centers on a deontological view of the universal moral law (what believers often identify as the "Laws of God"). These laws may be specified in several ways. Some see them as those laws propagated by God, others as those that are a part of God's inner constitutional character as can be seen in the way God deals with the world, still others as the "law which is written on the heart of all" by God so that even the nonbeliever cannot deny it if intellectual honesty is at hand. Ordinarily these are held in combination and they all point in the same direction. However much human life, will, and knowledge are distorted (by sin), the imprint of God's intended right order of things is not totally effaced from human consciousness or the way things

---

18. I do not take up the debate between Perry and his adversary, Finnis, in this chapter, except to say that from the standpoint of a Protestant it appears to be a debate between the more modest semi-Pelagian view of Perry and the more Pelagian perspective of Finnis. The latter seems to believe that we can both know and attain the good in both personal morality and civil order by the exercise of our rational will as directed to its natural ends. I mention this also to indicate that certain classical theological debates and findings often provide accurate access to critical ethical and social debates otherwise remaining obscure.

Developing a Method for Public Theology

are in the world.[19] These manifestations of the Laws of God are, in some measure, knowable by virtue of the fact that they are both partially discernible by reason and confirmed by revelation — by, indeed, that kind of revelation that does not violate reason's demand for plausibility, but which also recognizes that love of neighbor is a regulative principle for justice. In this view, the universality of moral law does not depend on the fact that it actuates the good ends of the common life and thus aids personal morality, although it may well do so. Rather, it establishes the first principles by which persons and societies may pursue an enormous variety of ends. There is, after all, no guarantee that things converge to some common good. Persons, peoples, cultures, institutions, and complex civilizations have a multiplicity of ends, and they may not easily converge in social history.[20] Lurking below many calls to solidarity for the common good may well be divergent but proper purposes that are prematurely repressed if they are jammed into some integrated view of the common good. After all, what we call "common" is usually quite limited — to our tribe, our nation, our period of history, for instance. And what we call "good" is often identified with quite feeble human achievement, a matter that easily can lead us to all sorts of false optimism, utopianism, and arrogance about our own virtue and how hard we can work to become virtuous.

Looked at another way, we are not seldom plagued with guilt or shame or a sense of failure because we think that we could really do better, yet know that we will not and perhaps in fact cannot. What is most pertinent about this awareness is that we implicitly know a standard that is not manifest in present action or in attainable goal, and we know that both present experience and future possibility are to be measured by it. In spite of the fact that the knowl-

---

19. See, as a twentieth-century restatement of a very long tradition from St. Paul through the reformers and the Puritans (such as Jonathan Edwards), Reinhold Niebuhr's *The Nature and Destiny of Man*, vol. 1 (New York: Charles Scribner's Sons, 1941), especially ch. 10, where he treats the residual effects of *justitia originalis*. This is a quite different way of understanding what others call "natural law," which allows (among other things) believers and nonbelievers to recognize that the policies and ideology of the Nazis are wrong, whether people are Christians or not, or part of the Western cultural traditions or not, even if they disagree about human ends. On this basis, even fascist believers would have some awareness of moral self-deception and have no excuse. Compare The Paul Ramsey Colloquium "On Human Rights: The Universal Declaration of Human Rights Fifty Years Later," *First Things* 82 (1998): 18-22. These views represent Augustinian, or better, semi-Augustinian perspectives.

20. In fact, in most theological views, it is not even clear that all persons will be "saved" beyond history. Insofar as they may converge in some ultimate salvation beyond history and society, the matter is outside of the range of either personal or social morality. It is best treated by the poetic imagination of John, Dante, or Milton.

edge of this "moral law" is obscured by bias, interest, egocentric interests, or pride, it is by this awareness that we know something of the limits by which to assess the widely variegated ends that people pursue. In this view, thus, it is more accurate to the moral life to say that the deontological aspects of moral life are regulative for the teleological ends we pursue and the means by which we do so. Human rights are one part of the larger deontological moral logic, that to which we may appeal when some end measured favorably by this standard is being pursued and someone (person or group) seeks to deny that possibility (perhaps by demanding that our action conform to this or that common good and denying, for example, freedom of religion, free speech and assembly, conversion to another faith in good conscience, experimenting with another way of organizing material or social resources, or actively advocating a policy or agenda that some would rather not hear about, etc.).[21]

On these grounds, we can suggest that Perry has his argument backwards. Human rights are absolute as moral first principles of right and wrong, guiding and governing how we ought to treat others while precisely recognizing the variant contexts in which people live and must be permitted to live as their right, and ends which they may pursue and must be permitted to pursue as a right.[22] Because of these variations, there will continue to be disagreements about how best to clarify and specify the absolutes in concrete codes, and we can recognize that some moral rights are, tragically, almost impossible under some conditions. But they still hover over these situations, and to utterly ignore them because they are impractical in the immediate press of this or that crisis is wrong. They judge precisely the crisis situations and prompt us to alter the conditions so that the moral norms can be more fully recognized and actualized, and can shape the policies of specific groups — churches, families, corporations, nations, international organizations — to pursue ends that are not incompatible with these moral rights without presuming that all will, can, or should harmonize in this life.

---

21. See Stackhouse and Hainsworth, "Deciding for God" (cited in note 11).

22. It is this which many of the "liberal" philosophical heirs of Locke and Kant have developed in modernity, even if they, as Perry and many postmodernist thinkers show, cannot give self-sustaining grounds for what they — for example, Habermas, Rawls, Nussbaum, etc. — argue. But that does not mean that they are entirely wrong about rights, only that they are limited with regard to the compelling quality of the arguments they give as to why humanity should hold to them because, as I mentioned, of their irrational, anti-theological bias.

The Fifth Social Gospel and the Global Mission of the Church

The American social gospel, I believe, was not and is not a fixed set of doctrines, a single social program, or a passé period piece, so much as it is a set of particular expressions of an enduring recognition that a biblically grounded faith requires an engagement with the social and political issues of the age, a view that was given fresh articulation at the end of the nineteenth century and the start of the twentieth. It is the demand that we acknowledge that the dynamics of the common life need the moral and spiritual guidance of a discerning theology, that Christian theology can amply meet that need, and that the internal impetus of that theology drives the truly faithful to engage public issues.

The periodic recovery and restatement of this dimension of what Christianity is about is necessary because of the fact that the inevitably fluctuating variables of social change and the always dynamic developments of doctrine, both with many false starts, detours, and occasional disasters, can easily obscure any sense of a stable ethical architecture for human life together. The experience of rapid social change as we have come to experience it in the last two centuries can, in fact, render a radical sense of moral relativism on the one hand or a militant sense of fundamentalist reaction against the relativism on the other. And the development of doctrine can become an end in itself, a dogmatic unfolding of the inner meanings of the faith that focuses so intently on those meanings that the dogmas neither learn from any wider wisdom nor inform the wider world. Moreover, the fact that the Christian faith has profound meaning for the individual human soul and for the life of the worshiping community can invite a private piety or an enclave fideism that can easily obscure the wider implications of the faith. The genius of the American social gospel at the beginning of the last century was that it drew from the depths of

The Fifth Social Gospel and the Global Mission of the Church

the biblical and theological traditions in a way that prompted simultaneously a reconstruction of the guiding themes of that heritage so that they could speak normatively to the burning, dynamic issues of the day.

It had been done before, to be sure, although it seems like slow motion, long ago, and far away. Who can deny that Moses and the Hebrew prophets shaped ancient Israel, drawing on traditions that went before them as they faced new conditions? The church fathers did the same in the context of the Roman Empire. The scholastics did so at the height of late medieval civilization. The Reformers did the same in the context of the rising cities and the new humanism of early modernity. And the Puritans, Pietists, and Evangelicals did likewise in the New World's frontiers and later in the world missionary movements. Indeed, it is doubtful that it is possible to understand the history of Christianity, the course of Western civilizational history, or the simultaneous continuity and repeated novelty of Christian social ethics if this is not recognized.

As the American social gospel movement began to take conscious responsibility for the earlier indirect and unintended effects of the Christian faith in its impact on society in the last quarter of the nineteenth century, so its heirs developed their contributions and modulated them by attending to the legacy and newer conditions in the twentieth. The founders of the American social gospel movement were, of course, most notable for the ways in which they faced the crises of the Industrial Revolution, especially as it had a major impact on labor. That revolution had been prompted by the Civil War, which accelerated America's late entry into the industrial age, and even more by the Spanish-American War, which made the United States something of a world power for the first time. This is the period in which Francis Greenwood Peabody, Washington Gladden, Shailer Mathews, and Walter Rauschenbusch, among others, developed their enduring convictions.

The message as these "fathers" of the movement developed it (with some variations) continued to be a formative influence from World War I to the Great Depression. They strongly supported the growing labor movements and advocated both voluntary and government programs to aid those whose lives were shattered by the transition from an agricultural-rural to an industrial urban society.[1] The fruits of this movement arguably generated the moral and spiritual ethos that legitimated if it did not generate the New Deal

---

1. See my "Jesus and Economics: A Century of Christian Reflection on the Economic Order," *The Bible in American Law, Politics and Political Rhetoric*, ed. J. T. Johnson et al., SBL Centennial Series, no. 5 (Lanham, MD: Scholars Press, 1985), pp. 107-52.

Developing a Method for Public Theology

policies of the 1930s, when the Depression hit full force and it appeared that more materialist, anti-religious, and more authoritarian movements might capture the loyalties of the working classes. After all, that is what happened with the rise of both a neo-pagan, premodernist, racially oriented national socialist and a militantly secular, hypermodernist, class-oriented proletarian socialist movement in Europe.

The social gospel leaders were alert to international issues in a way. They believed in the universality of their message. Many came from or ministered to immigrant churches and thus were allergic to the temptations of "Americanist nativism" — the view that those European Protestants born in America had a special destiny to preserve "White, Christian" culture from both the degradations to which it had fallen in Europe and from the corruptions of misogyny to which it was tempted in the multiracial United States.[2] Those who were rooted in the ancient Catholic traditions had a sense of the wholeness of humanity, and those who became deeply engaged in the Evangelical mission movements sought to reach out to all peoples and also resisted that "nativism."

Yet it must also be said that a decided inclination to pacifism born out of their idealism and optimism made many unable to deal with the terrors on the international front that the national socialist movements took under the ideologies of fascism, and the proletarian socialist movements took under the influence of Soviet Communism after World War I. The pathetic and seemingly pointless sacrifice of millions in the trenches of Germany between 1914 and 1918 for only a few yards reinforced the pacifist tendencies. Thus both conviction and experience disarmed the movement from its capacity to face more devastating perils that were soon to follow. In both cases, one on the radical right, the other on the radical left, the state sought to use its military prowess to control the world. The depths of human identity, of freedom, and of justice were threatened. To preserve them, the pacifist impulses of the social gospel had to be modulated by the deeper and longer Christian teachings about the depths of sin in human affairs and the sometimes justifiable use of coercive force in a just war that would have as its aim the establishment of a more lasting just peace.

Thus, a second, modified embodiment of the social gospel, Christian

---

2. See the new introduction to the republished volume by Walter Rauschenbusch, *The Righteousness of the Kingdom* (Lewiston, NY: Edwin Mellen, 1999). There, I credit Ronald C. White Jr., *Liberty and Justice for All* (San Francisco: Harper & Row, 1990), and Ralph E. Luker, *The Social Gospel in Black and White* (Chapel Hill: University of North Carolina Press, 1991) with clarifying previous questions about the relationship of the social gospel to racial issues.

The Fifth Social Gospel and the Global Mission of the Church

realism, carried much of the burden of Christian witness from World War II through the Cold War. In spite of the often sharp critique of the social gospel by advocates of Christian realism on matters of the depth of sin and the immorality of irresponsible pacifism,[3] there is more continuity than discontinuity in what they were about. Both saw modern constitutional democracy, the protection of the rights of the exploited, and the reformation of the dominant institutions of society as demands of the gospel and the legacy of Christian influence as it intersected with social realities and philosophical reason.[4]

Neither the primary nor this second form of the American social gospel was oblivious to the oppressed status of minority groups and women in Western society, but they did not make these issues their central focus, and have sometimes been criticized for that lack of emphasis. Still, in the first social gospel, several leaders openly supported women's suffrage, more of them advocated laws to protect women and children in factories, and a number saw Prohibition as a way of defending women by upholding Christian "family values" (as they were understood in that Victorian age), even if other priorities seemed more immediate. The biases of that period have been much corrected by more recent feminist thought. Still, it is not wrong to say that the social gospelers were among the first public "authorities" who became advocates of the early feminist movements. And their heirs, the Christian realists, were deeply involved in defending American blacks, Jews, and, later, Hispanics and Asians. Moreover, the racism and classism of those who opposed them made their disciples more alert to other evils lurking below the surface of American life and Euro-American thought. Thus, as World War II wound down, the descendants of both early forms of the social gospel joined hands in supporting the movements for civil rights and, more widely, for human rights. They were among the first to support the movement headed by Martin Luther King Jr. Whatever their other disagreements, they jointly and eagerly embraced this new phase of the American social gospel. Indeed, they both

---

3. See Reinhold Niebuhr, "Why the Christian Church Is Not Pacifist," in *Christianity and Power Politics* (New York: Charles Scribner's Sons, 1948), and his earlier *Moral Man and Immoral Society* (New York: Charles Scribner's Sons, 1932).

4. See Charles Howard Hopkins, *The Rise of the Social Gospel in American Protestantism: 1865-1915* (New Haven: Yale University Press, 1940). These motifs had parallels in Roman Catholic Christian thought, as can be seen in Paul Misner, *Social Catholicism in Europe: From the Onset of Industrialization to the First World War* (New York: Crossroad, 1991). For a "Neo-Conservative" effort to recover these motifs through conversation between Protestants and Catholics, see R. J. Neuhaus and G. Weigel, eds., *Being Christian Today: An American Conversation* (Washington, DC: Ethics and Public Policy Center, 1992).

Developing a Method for Public Theology

reappropriated a modified form of the earlier social gospel's pacifist instincts, augmented by Gandhian ideas of "active nonviolence," some for principle's sake, some for strategic reasons. Both also adopted a realist reading of class and race relations in America.[5] The result was the civil and human rights movement that turned out to be the third incarnation of the social gospel in America — one that expanded to include not only women but other groups who were discriminated against.

This development was paralleled by decolonialization movements around the world, backed heavily by missionaries who had themselves been motivated to undertake their vocations by the influence of such representative figures as Walter Rauschenbusch, Reinhold Niebuhr, and Martin Luther King Jr., and their colleagues, heirs, and disciples. It made many who did not go abroad sympathetic to liberation theology as it developed among the indigenous anti-colonial movements, often using many of the categories of Marxist-Leninist social analysis. One way or another, under various names (Dalit theology in India, Minjung theology in Korea, Black theology in South Africa, etc.), this became the major form of the social gospel in the "Third World." They did not doubt the depths of social sin or eschew the use of coercive power in revolutionary movements. Indeed, some saw revolution as the only cure for social sin. This became the fourth form of the social gospel of the twentieth century, and, like Christian realism and the human rights movement, made the social gospel less a peculiarly American phenomenon than a worldwide development.[6]

Indeed, American Protestants became also more and more aware not only of the contributions of voices long silent, but of the Roman Catholic "Social Encyclicals," which paralleled many of these developments. By the Second Vatican Council of the mid-60s, Protestant and Catholic thought increasingly converged on many of these issues of public moment. The earlier, harsh polemics between Catholics and Protestants were muted and cooperative programs and conversations were expanded, even if profound disagreements remained in regard to authority in the church, teachings about birth control, and the nature and character of sacraments.

Each of these incarnations of the social gospel had its great successes

---

5. Martin Luther King Jr.'s *Stride Toward Freedom* (New York: Harper, 1958) is a kind of commentary on the two sides of the earlier legacy. His analysis of the power realities in the Montgomery City Council is fully "Niebuhrian," while his strategy for mobilizing the movement without provoking violent reaction is "active pacifism."

6. Perhaps the meeting of the World Council of Churches in Africa in 1965 was the chief emblem of that.

and failures. All called for a renewal of the heart and a new relationship to God through Christ; each also sought the revitalization of the mission of the church at the hands of the Holy Spirit manifest in the renewal of the prophetic and priestly offices of the church. Each identified the struggles they saw as part of the ongoing manifestation of a kingdom ethic in the common life of humanity. Moreover, in many ways, these movements accomplished their goals — they helped bring about a greater dignity for labor, former slaves, and women. They contributed to the defeat of Nazism, the collapse of Communism, the expansion of constitutional democracy under more just laws around the world, and the decolonialization of subject peoples. We can surely rejoice at what they left as a legacy to the faith, to the church, and to society, even if they did not solve these problems once and for all.

In fact, as we enter the first decade of a new century, we find a continuation of all the issues with which the social gospel, in its various forms, struggled. Economic inequality and manifest suffering among those caught up in urbanizing, industrializing, and now globalizing processes are notable in every region — and are devastating for those left out of these developments, even if the middle classes are expanding in most lands. The viciousness of ethnic conflict and discrimination is present on every continent, even if it is not of the same scope as the twentieth-century wars. Violations of civil rights and both theoretical and practical resistance to human rights are present among every people, even if more countries have adopted rights constitutionally than ever before. The residues of neo-pagan nationalist violence and of militant secular revolutionism explode at the margins of civility in the North and South, the East and the West, even if their main international centers are gone. Women and minorities have not yet found full acceptance, whatever gains they have made; and both old forms of tyranny and new fantasies of grandeur appear out of the disarray of broken societies and shattered dreams, however much the world seems to have sobered. The "superpersonal forces of evil," as Rauschenbusch called them, are with us still — even if they have changed their masks and lurk only as the side-eddies of life.

Indeed, in some ways, several social problems have become more threatening precisely because they have become global in scope and are related to great and complex civilizations. What we do not have is either a social analysis or a theology large enough to match the dilemmas we face. Many of the institutions on which we relied in the past — the ecumenical churches and councils, the alliances of religion and labor, the missionary agencies, the "programs" for this and against that, continue to struggle with these issues, for they rightly know that they are not solved; but they often seem tired, using

Developing a Method for Public Theology

ideological frameworks to interpret what is going on, and exhausted slogans without compelling visions, precisely because they do not grasp the wider context in which we face such issues. Many seem fixated on an essentially liberationist view of the world, not recognizing that it was but one expression of a much wider and deeper heritage. Indeed, it tends to isolate the church from public discourse because it has not and perhaps cannot become a genuinely public theology. The particular incarnation of the social gospel that pertained to the decolonializing period could help deconstruct some oppressive and corrupt old orders under some conditions; but it cannot reconstruct just and viable new ones any more than the Marxist-Leninist social analysis, on which it largely depended, could.

Our New Global Situation[7]

Today, the world cannot so simply be divided into first, second, and third worlds, or into a new version of the old class struggle, "the West and the Rest," "the North and the South," or "the East and the West." It is at once a more integrated and a more variegated historical interaction of people and societies undergoing a dynamic transformation that is called globalization, one that has many implications also for the world as biophysical planet and for the world as a philosophical-theological realm of meaning, precisely because it is creating a new public that surpasses the one addressed by previous forms of the social gospel. While sometimes seen as essentially, or only, an economic development, globalization is in fact a vast social, technological, communications, and structural change laden with ethical perils and promises as great as those brought about by the ancient rise, and subsequent fall, of the ancient empires, the later development and then demise of feudalism, the still later rise of modernity with its nationalisms and recent industrial revolutions, and their decline.[8] While it is true, as some fear, that the multinational corpora-

---

7. Portions of this section of the paper are drawn from my "General Introduction" to the four-volume study *God and Globalization: Theological Ethics and the Spheres of Life* (Harrisburg, PA: Trinity Press International, 2000).

8. The remarkable new volume by British scholars David Held, Anthony McGrew, et al., *Global Transformations: Politics, Economics and Culture* (Stanford: Stanford University Press, 1999), joins the more journalistic treatment by Thomas L. Friedman, *The Lexus and the Olive Tree: Understanding Globalization* (New York: Farrar, Straus & Giroux, 1999), as summarizing the state-of-the-art work on globalization from the standpoint of nontheological perspectives.

tion is a chief vehicle of many of these changes and is particularly suited to take advantage of the processes that make globalization viable (in part because it is less politically accountable than other institutions), the extent of the wider process is so monumental that no area of life will be untouched. Globalization in the broader sense invites, almost demands, a reassessment of those traditions that have not only contributed to the dynamics now reshaping what we have, but may enhance or inhibit the capacity to participate in, avoid victimization by, and constructively guide what appears to be the creation of a new encompassing and highly complex civilization. Some Roman Catholic scholars working with the idea of "subsidiarity," some Reformed and Evangelical scholars, working with the concepts of "sphere sovereignty," some Jewish and Protestant scholars working with federal-covenantal theory, and some secular scholars advocating communitarian ideas of the "common good" are already seeking fresh ways of drawing on and recasting classical traditions to guide our future.[9]

Many, of course, take up these questions from more limited points of view. Many public protests against globalization in the United States and around the world are quite strident, fully convinced that the data are clear and that globalization is having devastating effects everywhere. But in a summary of current social scientific literature on the changes brought by globalization, Giovanni Arrighi and Beverly Silver review the current state of research with an eye to the effects on politics, national economies, working peoples, and minorities. They write:

> [There is] little consensus on anything but the fact that an era of history has ended. There is no consensus on which state, if any, benefitted most from the confrontation of the Cold War and is now poised to replace the United States as the dominant player in the global political economy. There is no consensus on whether the proliferation in the variety and number of multinational corporations and the formation of global financial markets is undermining state capacities and, if so, how generally and permanently. There is no consensus on whether the world's working class is an endangered species or simply changing color and the countries of its residence. There is no consensus on whether modernization is shoring up civilizational divides, melting them down, or restoring the intercivilizational balance of power of modern times. Above all, there is no

---

9. Examples of all of these motifs are present in Scott Paeth, Timothy Dearborn, et al., *The Local Church in a Global Era* (Grand Rapids: Eerdmans, 2000).

consensus on what kind of world order, if any, we can expect to emerge from the combination of whatever changes are actually occurring in the global configuration of power.[10]

In spite of the lack of consensus, people have very strong views about these issues. Many are locally affected by the changes and are not unwilling to project local experiences and interests onto a global screen. Kofi Annan, Secretary-General of the United Nations, pointed out that many see globalization less as "a term describing objective reality" about the creation of a new social or civilizational possibility than as "an ideology of predatory capitalism," which they experience as a kind of "siege." Against it, they join a "backlash" that takes at least three major forms.[11] One is a growing nationalism, sometimes threatening multiethnic states. The second, more troubling in view of the history of the twentieth century, is the call for strong leaders — seldom democratic, often overtly anti-democratic — who seek to mobilize these national interests against internationalism. And the third is the attempt to use globalization as a scapegoat for all the ills that in fact "have domestic roots" of a political and social nature.[12] To many, globalization has nothing to do with religion, theology, or ethics except the changing of the way they used to live. They do not know how to control it or to join it. Appeals to religion, religious ethics, or religiously shaped cultural attitudes are then used to mobilize sentiment against global trends. Local elites who find themselves swamped by developments they do not understand and cannot negotiate are particularly negative.[13]

10. G. Arrighi and B. Silver, *Chaos and Governance in the Modern World System* (Minneapolis: University of Minnesota Press, 1999), p. 21.

11. Kofi Annan, "The Backlash Against Globalism," *The Futurist* 33, no. 3 (March 1999): 27.

12. Annan, "The Backlash Against Globalism," p. 27. We can sometimes see this abroad before we recognize it at home. See Mark Juergensmeyer, *The New Cold War: Religious Nationalism Confronts the Secular State* (Berkeley: University of California Press, 1993); and Peter van der Veer, *Religious Nationalism: Hindus and Muslims in India* (Berkeley: University of California Press, 1994).

13. This is true of Christian voices as well as those indifferent to religion. See M. D. Litonjua, "Global Capitalism," *Theology Today* 56, no. 2 (July 1999): 210ff.; F. Jameson and M. Miyoshi, eds., *The Cultures of Globalization* (Durham, NC: Duke University Press, 1998), or Paul Hellyer, *Stop: Think* (Toronto: Chimo Media, 1999). Hellyer lists the best available bibliography of Western attacks on globalization, understood as the increasing influence of the World Bank, the IMF, and all who cooperate with "the multinationals" and "capitalism." "Third World" attacks can be represented by J. Mohan Razu, *Transnational Corporations as Agents of Dehumanization in Asia: An Ethical Critique of Development* (Delhi: CISRS/ISPCK, 1999).

The Fifth Social Gospel and the Global Mission of the Church

Such views, however, seldom help understanding even if they are understandable, and even if they do point to some necessary reforms and cautions in a number of areas. It is more likely that globalization has promising as well as threatening possibilities — possibilities that cannot be clearly seen without attention to the larger picture and to certain kinds of "public theological" matters. Thus, one of our responsibilities is to assess the degree to which various reactions are justifiable, and to chart responses that are more likely to address the realities we face. In doing so, we must remember the realistic forms of the social gospel legacy.

We must not obscure the fact that globalization is disrupting many aspects of traditional religion, ethics, culture, economics, politics, and society, but we must work from that side of the social gospel that does not see religion only as a force to mobilize against things as they are, but as a force capable of aiding and guiding the transformation of things as they are changing. Indeed, we shall repeatedly find that a deeper analysis demands that we acknowledge that people do, or can, know something about what is holy, and can recognize that holy possibilities are not entirely absent from globalization. Neither part of this hypothesis is universally accepted or decisively proven. However, they have not been decisively refuted or universally rejected either. In spite of a widely held view that the future is inevitably and increasingly secular, the resurgence of religious vitality has puzzled various secularizers to no end, and it is again becoming clear to a great number of scholars that religious insights and traditions are a permanent feature of human life, clearly evident in global trends, and the locus where questions of righteousness — of truth, justice, and holiness — take their most intense forms.[14]

However, since not all religious insights are in agreement, and all cannot be equally valid, the various claims that are made about truth, justice, and holiness must be subjected to critical examination. Thus, comparative philosophical theology, comparative ethics, and comparative social analyses, and not only appeals to this or that particular religion, are indispensable in inves-

---

14. Peter Berger, ed., *The Desecularization of the World: Resurgent Religion and World Politics* (Grand Rapids: Eerdmans, 1999), represents a major trend in current scholarship on this point. From the standpoint of the philosophical and historical analysis of cultures, see also the remarkable *The Human Condition,* ed. Robert Cummings Neville (Albany: State University of New York Press, 2001) and *Ultimate Realities,* ed. Robert Cummings Neville (Albany: State University of New York Press, 2001); and the discerning review of major new studies in anthropology that signal a return of interest in religion after several generations of nonreligious or anti-religious focus by Sarah Caldwell, "Transcendence and Culture: Anthropologists Theorize Religion," *Religious Studies Review* 28, no. 3 (July 1999): 227-32.

tigating the relative validity of various religious claims about how we should live in this life and the role in this life of that which transcends it. Issues of justice and responsibility, righteousness and compassion, truth and holiness are thus intrinsic to this assessment, for no one can authentically give loyalty or credence to a view or lifestyle that does not evoke, ground, manifest, or sustain these qualities. In an emerging global civilization, theological ethical issues are thus again unavoidable. Insofar as we can know these things with any degree of confidence, we must come to an informed judgment, as many traditions would put it, about how God wants us to live in it, respond to it, and shape it.

We are faced with a complex question in a complex situation. Obviously, the question demands the joining of ethics and theology. In concert with most classical traditions and in contrast to many modern trends that divorced or even opposed the two, we hold that theology and ethics are mutually supportive, even necessary to each other. Still, we must acknowledge the validity of the modern insight that the two are analytically distinct in a way that allows them to correct one another. Thus, we may use ethics critically to inquire into and assess the assumptions and implications of every theologically approved practice and every dogmatic claim. We may demand further that valid ethical criteria must find their ultimate sanctions in what is truly universal and enduring and not only in what is religiously and temporarily "mine" or "ours" at the moment. This is one of the characteristics of public theology, which works with, but also beyond, confessional dogmatics.[15] Without these critical principles, theological ethics is tempted to be little more than another species of idiosyncratic subcultural folkways and taboos, and theology is tempted to be simply the ideological megaphone for what this or that group wants to believe or practice.[16] It must be said that, like the gaps in social gospel thinking filled by the Christian realist, civil and human

---

15. See my "Public Theology and Ethical Judgment," in *East & West: Religious Ethics: Proceedings of the Third Symposium of Sino-American Philosophy and Religious Studies*, ed. Zhang Zhegang and Mel Stewart (Beijing: University of Beijing, 1998), pp. 132-47; English edition in *Theology Today* 54, no. 2 (July 1997): 165-79; and "Human Rights and Public Theology: The Basic Validation of Human Rights," in *Religion and Human Rights: Competing Claims?* ed. Carrie Gustafson and Peter Juviler (Armonk, NY: M. E. Sharpe, 1999), pp. 12-30.

16. See Peter Byrne, *The Moral Interpretation of Religion* (Grand Rapids: Eerdmans, 1998), and Franklin I. Gamwell, *The Divine Good: Modern Moral Theory and the Necessity of God* (San Francisco: HarperCollins, 1990). These volumes not only review the contributions of mutually critical thinking in theology and ethics since the Enlightenment, but show the contemporary state of their discussion.

The Fifth Social Gospel and the Global Mission of the Church

rights, and liberation movements, public theology may well be required in our global era as the fifth incarnation of the social gospel — drawing on, expanding, and modifying what has gone before.

The theological ethical questions can be pressed by inquiring not only into the inner mechanics of the spiritual life, but also into the decisive issues that have been pressed into contemporary consciousness by the emergence of global business, technologies, ecological awareness, the struggles for universal human rights, and a host of related developments after the defeat of militant nationalism in World War II, and the collapse of international socialism at the end of the Cold War. These developments are rooted in long, historic trends that seem to many to now be leading humanity toward the possible creation of a global civilization that will alter every community and tradition.[17] Of particular interest to theological ethics as it inquires into such issues are the often implicit key moral assumptions and metaphysical convictions that form the moral ecology, the "ethos" of the worldwide social environment in which we increasingly live. The ethos conditions the minds of ordinary people more than they know, as well as the thinking of the theologian and ethicist more than they often admit. Further, since every viable social context is constituted by a network of interactive, interdependent spheres of activity, organized into various practices and institutions, we must pay attention to the various spheres of activity that shape life, and to the question of what holds these various spheres into identifiable units of common action. Thus, theological ethics tries to understand, evaluate, and help guide the various spheres of the common life in which the social ecology is manifest as ethos, and to discern how theological ethics should interact with various nontheological forces and fields of study beyond ethics that also influence these spheres of life, for these "other" areas are always also bearers of values and norms.

---

17. When globalization began is an open question and laden with tensions between naturalist and historical perspectives. Jared Diamond, *Guns, Germs and Steel* (New York: W. W. Norton, 1998), suggests that it is built into the universal evolutionary process; while David Landes, *The Wealth and Poverty of Nations* (New York: W. W. Norton, 1998), treats it as a European phenomenon, rooted in the deep social and cultural history of the West — often resisted by political decisions in other parts of the world; and Saskia Sassen, *Losing Control? Sovereignty in an Age of Globalization* (New York: Columbia University Press, 1996), sees it as the wider empowerment of the United States after the collapse of the USSR, obvious in the global hegemony of U.S. popular culture and in the new instruments of world governance backed by the United States and its closest allies. These are not the only, uncontroverted, or mutually exclusive theories.

Developing a Method for Public Theology

The Special Problem of the World Religions

The social gospel authors knew that those perennial institutions of the common life — family, politics, economy, and culture — were always necessary and necessarily influenced by religion.[18] Indeed, that was their essential program to make the religion they knew and loved an effective influence to reform the institutions of the common life. They also knew that how they were held together was fateful for the well-being of persons and civilizations as a whole. That is why they resisted the Roman Catholic tradition of their time, which seemed to them to be based on the coercion of belief and on the forms of conservative, evangelical piety that celebrated the conversion of souls but resisted the conversion of society. Thus, they sought to use religious resources to reform these perennial areas of life. Moreover, they suspected and sometimes commented on the distinctively modern spheres of activity, particularly the classical professions of education, medicine, and law, and occasionally touched on the marvels of modern technology as well. But they rarely saw how these too were framed by religion, although they were frequently much engaged in establishing schools and colleges for education, hospitals and clinics for healthcare, and more just laws for the protection of workers and children.[19]

In our day, migration, travel, the media, and education have brought everyone into contact with the various world religions. People in the West may not know a single Hindu, but they have heard not only of Gandhi, but of karma, yoga, and transcendental meditation. They may not know a Buddhist,

---

18. I have elsewhere identified the ways in which a great number of the social gospel authors utilized a set of categories to define the foundational institutions of society as necessary to the common life — religion, family, economy, politics, and culture (sometimes also, science), and did so in ways that accorded with liberal Lutheran, conservative Calvinist, Roman Catholic, and humanist attempts to identify the main spheres of life (see my "Introduction" to Rauschenbusch, *The Righteousness of the Kingdom*, especially pp. xxiv-xxv, mentioned in note 2 above). Today, a number of scholars prefer to rely on Niklas Luhmann's treatment of the various social systems of communications media: truth, love, money, power, and art (see his *Religious Dogmatics and the Evolution of Societies*, trans. P. Beyer (Lewiston, NY: Edwin Mellen, 1984). I prefer, following Rauschenbusch's treatment of the "superpersonal forces of good and evil," to speak not only of religion, but of eros, mammon, Mars, and the muses as "powers" in globalization today. See *God and Globalization*.

19. In fact, Rauschenbusch was quite alert to these professions and their significance. He does not treat them very extensively in his major books, but they appear with nuanced awareness in his *For God and the People: Prayers of the Social Awakening* (Cleveland: Pilgrim Press, 1910).

The Fifth Social Gospel and the Global Mission of the Church

but they have heard of the Dalai Lama, and possibly of Aung San Suu Kyi, and of the concepts of compassion and nirvana. Most people in the West know Jews, and increasingly they have come to know Muslims, or at least bits and pieces about Islam, and know that they do not eat pork and they have a profound sense of religious law. They also know something about various forms of spiritual healing, Native American practices, and new-age religions, most of which are retrofitted versions of ancient cults. In brief, the world religions are not only long ago, far away, or beyond our horizons as options, they are present in the mix of the common life.

There is enormous historical evidence that religion always has been a decisive influence on the shape of social life. Can Africa be understood without some knowledge of tribal life, loyalties, and traditions? Can the Middle East be understood without reference to Islam? Can the social-political shape of South Asia be analyzed without dealing with Hinduism? Can East Asia be understood without noting the various syntheses of Tao, Buddhism, and Confucianism? And if it is also true that we are forming a global civilization in which everything in the West will be influenced by everything in the East, and vice versa, and those in the South will find their destiny tied to those in the North, and vice versa, the question of what kinds of religion will become more or less influential will be fateful. No civilization has ever survived without a religion at its core, although in the twentieth century the programmatic atheism of Marxism and the functional agnosticism of liberalism in politics, libertarianism in economics, modernism in the arts, and postmodernism in cultural analysis have been the most extended efforts to test whether that is a possibility. Still, behind these developments, religious or secular, most versions of the social gospel have presumed an essentially Christian theological perspective and conducted most intellectual and organizational battles on an intramural basis.

In a global environment, however, it is not simply a question of whether the Baptists or the Catholics, the Reformed or the Anabaptist versions of the Christian faith would be the most influential, or how they might relate to Jews; it is a question of what religions are in contention to define the moral and spiritual center of the global common life. After all, the primal religions, which we sometimes identify as "tribalism" in Africa, Hinduism in India, Buddhism in Southeast Asia, Confucianism in East Asia, and Islam, from North Africa through the Mideast to Indonesia, have, with local variations not unlike the branches of Christianity in various regions, distinctively stamped whole civilizations. Indeed, the various cultures of the world can easily be treated as the outward and visible signs of various inward spirits.

Developing a Method for Public Theology

This has been recognized by Samuel Huntington in his much-discussed *The Clash of Civilizations and the Remaking of World Order,* which has the virtue of acknowledging the formative role of religion in society and culture, and the vice of not asking whether deeper unifying moral and spiritual realities are possible to discover and cultivate.[20] When we, if we, move toward a global civilization, how shall these religions relate, and, more importantly, how does each of the great world religions shape the social, political, legal, and cultural environment it stamps with its moral and spiritual genetic code in regard to the treatment of other religions, the basic human rights of all, the possibilities of intermarriage, conversion, economic opportunity, and so forth? This is an area that the social gospel and most of its heirs simply did not face.

During the twentieth century, the earlier versions of the social gospel faced the acids of the laissez-faire capitalism of the robber baron era and the rising power of the neo-paganism of the Nazis and the secular materialism of the Communists. Then the more recent versions attempted to confront the deep legacies of racism, sexism, classism, as we have seen. In all of these, the question of the relationship of Christian thought as public theology to the other religions was not on the agenda — except for the occasional recognition of the fact that religions might cooperate to overcome certain recognized evils. Thus, from the Parliament of Religions of 1893 through the formulation of the United Nations Charter and Bill of Rights, the religions of the world cooperated (more or less) against various forms of grotesque barbarism.

Still, a certain view, derived from the Enlightenment, tended to reign — that ethics, especially as it dealt with public issues, could be separated from any and all religious and theological grounding. Various doctrines and dogmas may be held by anyone and freely taught by various religious groups; but people could know right and wrong, good and evil, without any need of religious appeal. God was essentially irrelevant to public morality. Indeed, religion, especially in an "orthodox" form, was often seen as the cause of violence, discrimination, hate, ecological damage, and war. Not only must we have the institutional separation of church and state, but religiously grounded ethics and theologically warranted morality had no place in public discourse. This, of course, tended to silence the religious bigots of the world and to dis-

---

20. S. P. Huntington, *The Clash of Civilizations and the Remaking of World Order* (New York: Simon & Schuster, 1997). A great number of highly informative volumes on globalization ignore religion or treat it simply as a subordinate function of culture. Huntington's argument, not beyond criticism by any means, has forced religion onto the table of discussion of social and political life in a global era, much as has already been the case in global discussions of human rights and ecological concerns.

The Fifth Social Gospel and the Global Mission of the Church

enfranchise the multiple heirs of the social gospel. The very idea of a public theology, especially one capable of critically and comparatively evaluating various religions, was considered dubious.

It was in this context that the concerns of the various versions of the social gospel began to converge with certain other developments. The Christian foreign missionary movements, both Protestant and Catholic, were at their heights precisely during the early years of the American social gospel, and, indeed, two of the great leaders of the early social gospel, Washington Gladden and Shailer Mathews, were presidents of the American Board of Commissioners for Foreign Missions. Walter Rauschenbusch himself wanted to become a missionary, but was turned down because of his "unorthodox" interpretation of the message of the biblical prophets. The experience of other religions and cultures by missionaries abroad and the struggles to redefine social ethics in the face of industrializing and urbanizing developments at home mutually influenced each other.[21] Further, the children of missionaries became the founders of the new discipline of anthropology, just as the children of the social gospel pastors became the founders of the new discipline of sociology, and these too informed each other — both with an alertness, at least for several generations, of the decisive role that religion does and can play in shaping society.[22] All this was deeply disrupted by the world wars, hot and cold, that dominated attention from World War I until the fall of the Wall, and predictions of inevitable secularization dominated the field for many years; but with the new global openness, it turns out that religions are not fading from view, but reasserting their vigor. Islam is obviously reasserting itself in many ways throughout North Africa, the Mideast, to Indonesia, and is a major voice in the African American community. Hinduism has captured the government of India, and a missionizing form of Hinduism has influenced many in the West. Buddhism has reestablished itself in several countries of Southeast Asia, and is sending missionaries into China, even if Tibetan Buddhism is under threat. A rebirth of Confucian studies is taking place especially among "overseas Chinese." Evangelical and Pentecostal forms of Christianity are reshaping the Americas, Africa, and Korea, as the pope calls for a reinvigoration of Catholic missions and the "reevangelization of Europe."

---

21. I have documented some of these convergences in my contributions "Christian Social Movements" and "Missionary Activity" in *The Encyclopedia of Religion*, ed. Mircea Eliade et al. (New York: Macmillan, 1987), vol. 3, pp. 446-52, and vol. 9, pp. 563-69.

22. This is amply documented in, for example, Arthur Vidich and S. M. Lyman, *American Sociology* (New Haven: Yale University Press, 1987).

Developing a Method for Public Theology

It is in this context that several have recognized that we need, above all, a "theology of religions." This is presently taking three forms. The first is most clearly represented by Wilfred Cantwell Smith, a child of the missionary movement, who argues that faith is a universal feature of human existence, and that the various religions and theologies are expressions of this underlying reality.[23] What is interesting to him, however, as a historian of religion, is the variety by which this is articulated and the multiplicity of forms by which it is expressed. A second approach is best represented by the former Catholic missionary Paul Knitter, who artfully surveys the current Christian attitudes toward other religions and argues for a nonexclusive pluralism of religions, all of which have a validity, even if each may be assessed accordingly as it does or does not promote a liberating movement against social oppression — a criterion, of course, that sets one incarnation of the social gospel as the universal standard for both Christianity and all the world religions.[24] The third form, the one that is most likely to converge with the public theology promise of the social gospel in a global era, is best represented by the renegade Catholic theologian Hans Küng, the maverick Protestant social theorist Francis Fukuyama, and the highly independent Jewish political scientist Daniel Elazar.[25] What these scholars share is a deep commitment to comparative and historical studies, a recognition of the role of religion in the formation of a social ethic, and the necessity of evaluating various religious traditions according to their capacity to form and sustain a viable, just, pluralist, open, and culturally and economically flourishing civilization. They know that any encounter with the world religions involves a social, cultural, and intellectual encounter, and the possible reconstruction of every institution in civil society. In my view, they could each include aspects of the views of Smith and Knitter in what they offer, but they will not only affirm a deep common humanity or an inevitable pluralism, they will invite the many members of the

---

23. See especially W. C. Smith, *Towards a World Theology* (Maryknoll, NY: Orbis, 1981), part III. This commonality, of course, is directly opposed to both Huntington's sense of inevitable "clash" and to Christian dogmatic approaches, such as that of Karl Barth.

24. See especially P. F. Knitter, *No Other Name? A Critical Survey of Christian Attitudes Toward the World Religions* (Maryknoll, NY: Orbis, 1985). He is especially critical of Evangelical Protestant and Catholic Exclusivist approaches, but also of positions such as Smith's, which are prematurely inclusivist, as though real differences are simply incidental, historical accretions.

25. See H. Küng et al., *Christianity and the World Religions* (New York: Doubleday, 1986); F. Fukuyama, *Trust: The Social Virtues and the Creation of Prosperity* (New York: Free Press, 1995); and Daniel Elazar, *The Covenant Tradition in Politics*, vol. 4 (New Brunswick, NJ: Transaction Press, 1994-98).

emerging global civilization to participate in the reformation of the common life, and will do so on the basis of what is, ultimately, a biblical view of justice, righteousness, and holiness.[26]

I am, in brief, proposing a fifth incarnation for the social gospel, one that will substantially de-provincialize it of its Americanist roots, bring it more clearly into dialogue with the world's religions, and risk the attempt to construct a biblically based and theologically rooted, but broadly ecumenical social ethic, one intentionally open to interfaith influences and able to give guidance in and to the emerging global civilization. Of course, other voices with other roots will also be involved; but at least those who find meaning and encouragement from the social gospel traditions will be prepared to participate in one of the most important missions to the human future.

---

26. With contributions from Lamin Sanneh of Yale, Diane Obenchain of Beijing, Thomas Thangaraj of Emory, John Mbiti of Bern, Kosuke Koyama of Union, Szekar Wan of Andover Newton, and Justo González of Columbia, I have edited a volume that will attempt to extend, refine, and integrate such perspectives. See *God and Globalization*, vol. 3, *Christ and the Dominions of Civilization* (Harrisburg, PA: Trinity International Press, 2002).

Civil Religion, Political Theology, and Public Theology: What's the Difference?

I am grateful to the editors of *Political Theology* for arranging this event and for extending the reach of this publication to these shores. It not only represents another manifestation of the Anglo-American alliance at a time in which it is apparently suspect on the part of many; it also provides a chance to reflect on some of the continuing commonalities and differences between two democratic political orders deeply stamped by Christian principles. To be sure, one is shaped by a royal tradition, an established church, and a history of both imperial power and Laborite socialism; and the other echoes still of Puritan resistance to such institutions, but today appears to be tempted toward a new imperialism backed by corporate capitalism as well as a dedication to expanding human rights and democratic governance. Putting the matter this way, of course, obscures the fact that these traditions have come to share many basic principles over the years — a limited state, governance under law, a wide range of civil liberties, and, most decisive, freedom of religion. When we compare them to the defeated neo-pagan fascisms of the Continent of the last century, the now-faded secularist militancy of Marxism-Leninism in the East and South, or the post-Christian secular statist democracy that derives from the French Revolution, they seem quite similar indeed. They share even more if compared to the new theocratic movements of Hindutva in the Indian subcontinent and of the Islamist resurgence that extends from Morocco to Mindanao, and the still-dominant residuum of Jacobin revolutionism that reigns in China and the sad effects of tribal traditionalism that still shape Africa and several other regions. Yet there are some important differences that need to be identified in the trialogue between the Continent, Great Britain, and the United States, whose influence, together, is influential in generating the forces that have produced the rather chaotic "new world order," as we all in the West encounter a postcolonial world on new terms and face the prospect of a highly diverse global civilization.[1] And since it has never been the case before in human history that an enduring civilization has been formed without a basic religious or a theological vision at its core, it may be useful if we, here at the American Academy of Religion, attempt to sort out the role of religion in the common life of our common future.

The central thesis of this article is that the public role of religion, specifically the Christian religion, can be clarified if we recognize the differences between three often-confused terms: "civil religion," "political theology," and "public theology," each of which has a distinct pedigree and entails a particular set of assumptions and implications.[2] Moreover, each of these differs from, even if it draws at points on, the confessions and practices of church religion, usually articulated in various creeds or liturgies and given extended, rationalized articulation by the dogmatic theologies of these specific Christian traditions.

We should also want to distinguish these three terms from the constructions of systematic theology. Any one of them can be studied in a systematic fashion, of course; but systematic theology is primarily a work of the modern academy, which attempts to elucidate the insights of revelation in the light of critical thought, especially as these insights encounter, respond to, or adopt from and adapt to developments in various methods of philosophy or science. Public theology is surely also developed with attention to these

---

1. Peter Berger and Samuel Huntington are surely correct in arguing, along with others, that there are *Many Globalizations* (New York: Oxford University Press, 2002), due to "Cultural Diversity in the Contemporary World," as the subtitle of the volume says. The idea that globalization is essentially "Americanization" or "Westernization," or simply "individualistic capitalism" tends to fall apart when one sees how much each society selectively appropriates what it wishes to take of several high-potential capacities developed in the West on the basis of both material interests and an ongoing set of cultural, usually religiously rooted values. And yet, it is also the case that each society is forced to decide what parts and how much of these high-potential capacities — technology, mass communication, corporate organization, democratic polity, human rights, etc. — they want to accept and on what terms, which is why it can be recognized everywhere as "globalization." Failure to incorporate these high-potential capacities leaves the resisting societies out of the interactive community of nations and often in previously existing states of poverty and tyranny. At the same time, their incorporation both alters the interior fabric of the adopting society and provides new resources for interaction with others.

2. This paper is intrinsically related to "What Is Public Theology? An American View," presented at a conference on "public theology" in Prague in May 2003, co-sponsored by the Theological Faculty of Charles University and the Center for Theological Inquiry of Princeton Theological Seminary.

modes of study, but its main reason for coming into being is that a new and wider public is in formation. The projects of civil religion, political theology, and public theology take the world's religions and cultures more seriously than most systematic efforts. The goal of finding a more inclusive, genuinely ecumenical and catholic way of identifying a valid, viable inner convictional and ethical framework on which to build the moral and spiritual architecture of our increasingly common life is indispensable.[3]

To speak of ecumenical, even intrareligious dialogue and communication, raises still another point of inquiry in the midst of a postmodern mood, when many despair of, and others delight in, the presumed impossibility of finding any commonalities in a fragmented, multicultural, and pluralistic world. The temptation of neo-sectarian religiosity and localistic neo-tribalism as particularist groups reassert subcultural values as a form of self-celebrating religious idolatry is a present danger in the churches and in the world. It is true, as many recognize, that the age of national creeds established by political regimes, once a practice in the ancient world, reasserted in modernity in the legacy of Westphalia, and resurrected in the nationalist movements of the decolonialization period, is over. To be sure, it lingers in Europe, as one can see in the difficulties in forming an EU Constitution. That difficulty is compounded by the reluctance to put any reference to religion in their proposed constitution; yet people know that Italy or Ireland cannot be understood without reference to Catholicism, or Germany or Sweden without Lutheranism, or Holland or Scotland without Calvinism. And, even more, none of them can be understood without reference to the Christian heritage. The echoes are there in influential ways, and they reappear in the decolonialized nations, including America, in the various "civil religions" of national identity and cultural idolatry, as we saw also in the recent vicious holocausts of the Balkans and Central Africa, with all sides invoking their own religio-cultural identity to justify ethnic cleansing. I

---

3. This view differs from three of the most important current understandings of globalization. For instance, Immanuel Wallerstein interprets globalization almost entirely in economistic terms in *The Capitalist World-Economy* (Cambridge: Cambridge University Press, 1979). David Held et al., in contrast, uses a three-level analysis of economy, politics, and culture, with politics basically determining both the economic and cultural developments, in *Global Transformations* (Stanford: Stanford University Press, 1999). In contrast to both, Samuel P. Huntington, in his famous *The Clash of Civilizations* (New York: Simon & Schuster, 1997) and even more in the collection he edited with Lawrence Harrison, *Culture Matters* (New York: Basic Books, 2000), argues that cultures shaped by religion form irreconcilable civilizations that are decisive for political and economic development. None of these see theology as decisive for the critique or reformation of religion, culture, political, and economic life.

Civil Religion, Political Theology, and Public Theology

shall argue that this dynamic differs not only from dogmatic and systematic theology, but also from "political theology" and "public theology," although there is some confusion about the differences.[4]

We know the marks of civil religion in this land as "Americanism," sometimes called the "Shinto" of the United States. We are not alone in having such a religion, and there is surely a place for a limited patriotism in the repertoire of human loyalties, even among those most faithful to their theological tradition. Yet, it may be a particularly weighty issue for the U.S. since it has, today, so much political, military, economic, and cultural influence around the world, and has apparently not quite decided whether or not it should become a new empire to fill the power vacuum left by the successive collapses of the old Roman Empire, the Germanic Holy Roman Empire, and the pluralistic empires of the Turkish Ottomans, the Chinese dynasties, and the wide-flung attempts at imperialism that issued in colonialism by the European powers — of which the British generated the greatest and most enduring of them all, with comparatively better legacies left in colonialized lands when colonialism ended. But these are not all that has collapsed. In the living memory of many still today is the collapsed pretense of the Third Reich, the collapsed, temporary, but nearly worldwide empire of the USSR, and the failure of the United Nations to respond effectively to the Balkan and Central African genocides, residual forms of Communism as in North Korea, the challenge of resurgent and militant forms of Islam, or, for that matter, fundamentalist Hinduism in India and militarized Buddhism in Burma and Sri Lanka.

Besides, Americanist civil religion is often baptized — usually sprinkled, not immersed — by the symbols of the world's largest faith, namely Christianity, and currently of a distinctly evangelical type. This baptism seems to many Americans to legitimate a Christian view of national policy. This current evangelical emphasis is a two-edged sword. On one hand, it typically transcends the kind of sectarian pietism that besets the neo-Anabaptist camp, so popularized in the U.S. by Stanley Hauerwas. But it is doubtful, on the other hand, if it can constrain, and may even enhance, an imperialistic impulse, and if it does encourage that impulse, it does not seem capable of guiding it toward the formation of a *Pax Humanitatis*. The reason is simple. Current evangelicalism in the U.S. lacks an articulate political or social theory except for a generalized pa-

---

4. E. Harold Breitenberg Jr. has documented the variety of uses of the term in his extremely useful essay, "To Tell the Truth: Will the Real Public Theology Please Stand Up?" *Journal of the Society of Christian Ethics* 23, no. 2 (2003): 55-96, from which I draw with the permission of the author.

triotism. In contrast, both "political theology" and "public theology" do. They draw from certain indispensable aspects of theology that have been neglected and that have within them both critical analyses of populist, chauvinist religion and constructive visions of basic political and social matters — today often neglected by many scholarly observers, and overshadowed or even shouted down by a number of recent theological developments.[5] It is, indeed, a major ideational conflict, fateful for the world, as to what kind of American civil religion — one sprinkled with evangelical piety or one that is marked by the deeper public and political implications of Christianity — comes to guide U.S. policy.

But before we turn to the comparative analysis of these two terms and their structural implications, we should note that the discussion of "civil religion" rose in the United States especially after World War II and note why it is suspect. While, in one sense, America had emerged as a world power while opposing imperialism in the Spanish-American War in the nineteenth century, it only became a world leader in the last half of the twentieth century. This highly pluralistic nation, long ago founded on the basis of theological orientations that supported religious freedom, constitutional democracy, human rights, and open economic opportunity, had to clarify its core values again. (A *New Yorker* cartoon shows two Puritans on the ship about to land on the shores of old New England. One says to the other: "Well, first I am going to establish religious freedom and democracy, then I am going into real estate.")

But as the fervor of World War II settled down, and it became manifestly clear that the USSR was no longer an ally against a common enemy, but a serious adversary itself, backing regimes or revolutionary movements in China, Korea, and the southern hemisphere, and the European nations were too weakened to resist its blandishments alone, the United States had to redefine its principles and its purposes. It was the great Jewish sociologist, Will Herberg, who published a widely discussed sociological essay that spoke of the shared values held by believers in the United States. He wrote of the ways in which Protestantism, Catholicism, and Judaism were, after World War II, more and more to be seen as sister denominations, branches of a single religious family that converged politically and socially at reunions as in times of tragedy or cel-

---

5. The attempt to challenge contemporary scholarship in the West on these matters (as well as to provide an alternative vision for the future to the "liberationism" worked out in the "new nations" in their decolonializing period, nearly all of which generated ethnic- and class-oriented "civil religions" by combining socialist theory with traditionalist values and a primitivist reading of the Bible) is a primary purpose of the project on *God and Globalization*, 4 vols. (Harrisburg, PA: Trinity Press International, 2000-2007).

ebration.⁶ Herberg used the term "civic religion" to describe what they shared as the religious aspect of "Americanism," a catchier term than what a number of social historians were already treating as "the religion of the republic." Herberg was clearer than several others that each pillar of this shared canopy of conviction retained its own distinctive faith and practice.

Soon thereafter, another well-known sociologist, Robert Bellah, published one of his famous essays on "civil religion."⁷ He drew not only from Alexis de Tocqueville, but also from Émile Durkheim's adaptation of the term from Rousseau's *Contrât social* (ch. viii). And when we look closely at Rousseau's treatment of it, we find something not unlike Herberg's argument, but with an exclusive reference to one view of Christianity. There is a religion that many people hold, which Rousseau says is "truly Christian" (that is, "purely spiritual" and thus "private to the soul"), but something else must govern the life of the nation. And that, in fact, is the view of Cicero, to whom he refers. In *De Legibus* (Book II), Cicero treats the kinds of religious beliefs and practices that should be accepted or forbidden by political authority to ensure the sacred solidarity of the citizenry, so that loyalty to Rome should not be undercut by the worship of any non-native or transnational deities. Rousseau, of course, had adopted this idea of civil religion shortly before the French Revolution, and spoke of the necessity of each nation cultivating its own symbols to express the primal freedom of "the people" and cultivating a "general will" (a concept against church dogma that puts belief on a voluntarist basis forming a national collective consciousness). The displacement of all transnationalist, indeed transcendental, religion by the Revolution made Christian conviction a matter of private preference only, by law.

The ideologues of the revolutionary tradition then constructed for political purposes a "civil religion" built out of the presumed distinctive character of the people's ethnic unity. It is the sort of thing that caused Augustine to call the civic virtues spelled out by Cicero, "splendid vices," and that allowed Barth to be so hostile to natural theology and religion, which he understood to be a kind of culturally manufactured idolatry. Bellah, by the way, later modified his reliance on this history, ceased using the term, and became more overtly theological.⁸

---

6. W. Herberg, *Protestant, Catholic, Jew* (New York: Doubleday, 1955, rev. ed., 1960).

7. Robert Bellah, "Civil Religion in America," *Daedalus* 96 (1967): 1-21.

8. See the debates over this by R. N. Bellah et al. in *Christianity and Civil Society*, ed. R. L. Petersen (New York: Orbis, 1995).

Developing a Method for Public Theology

In Europe, especially the Germanic and Scandinavian lands, but also in England, a different kind of tradition developed after World War II. It is the tradition of "political theology," one that has its deepest philosophical roots in Aristotle who had influenced all higher education in Catholic and Anglican lands since St. Thomas, and in Lutheran ones since Melanchthon. Aristotle saw the political order as the comprehending and ordering institution of all of society. That view was, of course, later modified by St. Thomas because of his Augustinian understanding of the central role of the church and theology in society, distinct from the political order; nevertheless the Aristotelian view became dominant in most post-feudal European states and the primary pattern of the aristocratic politics of the Continent. It was present not only in the Austro-Hungarian Empire in Central Europe, and the Catholic establishments in Italy, Poland, Spain, and Ireland, but in the later history of politically established Protestant churches after the Westphalian principle of *cuius regio, ius religio*. This not only established national churches, it also tended to subordinate those religions to the political order in an Erastian fashion. Every princely state had its own "confession," "catechism" or "articles of faith," and mandated "book of worship."

When European society began to secularize and religion became more and more like a public utility, other forms of political theology were developed. While the deepest roots of political theology are in Eusebius's view of Constantine, in the development after the Reformation of "national creeds or confessions," and in Spinoza's *Politico-Theological Treatise*, the term was brought into modern usage by Carl Schmitt, following Machiavelli and Hobbes, on the right, and used by Ernst Bloch, following Münzer and drawing on Marx, on the left. One side saw the use of coercive force at the will of the sovereign as the defining characteristic of regime (on the analogy of the will and omnipotence of God), and the other saw economic power and private property as the primary social issue, disrupting the natural order of things and needing revolutionary political action from below that would issue in a recovered communal harmony (a utopian vision of the future that is also a return to Eden). Both the right and the left offered a political program for finding a final solution to the crises of modernizing society.

After the defeat of the Nazis on the right and the rise of Stalinism on the left, a generation of revisionist political theologians turned to Gramsci, Blondel, and the Frankfurt School of critical theory. They both fed and drew from the anti-colonial movements that overthrew the world dominance of European powers and established a host of independent nation-states around the world. They did not foresee that many of these would become one-party

Civil Religion, Political Theology, and Public Theology

regimes with religion still playing the Erastian role of subservient subordination to and ideological support of cultural identity and national interest.

The statist idolatries of this heritage were of course challenged theologically in the European context during the last half-century under the powerful influence of Karl Barth's return to church- and dogma-centered theology, as articulated in the Barmen Declaration, as well as by the honoring of the martyr Dietrich Bonhoeffer. And they were informed by American pro-democratic theologies in the tradition of Ernst Troeltsch, already mobilized during World War II by such voices as Reinhold Niebuhr and Paul Tillich, as well as by ecumenically oriented Catholic leaders who became convinced that democracy and human rights are not, as the anti-Catholic French Revolution had claimed, purely secular. Indeed they came to see that they are implications of the deepest reaches of the Christian tradition, and had to be defended and extended, by political and even military means if necessary.[9]

The new wave of political theology advanced on the Continent was represented by the reformist and overtly democratic political theologies of Catholic Johannes Metz and Reformed Jürgen Moltmann. They became influential, respectively, in Vatican II and the World Council of Churches. Their work signaled a form of political theology guided by the idea not only that the pastor, believer, and theologian may address public matters, but in fact must do so, since the policies of every political order need direct guidance and transformation at the hands of theological-ethical insight. And yet, all the heirs of these developments remained committed to a rather centralized state, a state not focused on colonial expansion or military conquest or nationalist solidarity, but on an integrated and politically managed economic policy. Scott Paeth has argued, on this point, that the crises of the Continent at the hands of twentieth-century totalitarianism forced democratically oriented political theologians such as Metz and Moltmann to be more statist than other aspects of their theology would suggest.[10] A similar argument could be made that the same is true for the progressive advocate of political theology, Duncan Forrester, and the more conservative advocate of it, Oliver

---

9. See Elisabeth Sifton, *The Serenity Prayer: Faith and Politics in Times of Peace and War* (New York: W. W. Norton, 2003). As the daughter of Reinhold Niebuhr, she gives an "inside account" not only of the piety of the Niebuhrs, but of the religious and political leaders who gathered around her father to mobilize public religious sentiment to resist the Nazis and overcome American isolation and fundamentalism.

10. I am indebted to the work of my doctoral student, Scott Paeth, on these points. See his "From the Church to the World: Public Theology, Civil Society, and the Theology of Jürgen Moltmann" (Ph.D. dissertation, Princeton Theological Seminary, 2004).

O'Donovan, in Great Britain,[11] and of Reinhold Niebuhr in the USA in certain stages of his thought.

In contrast to both "civil religion" and "political theology," which remain in wide usage, a number of scholars and church leaders have turned to the term "public theology." This term was first used in America by the well-known historian of religion, Martin Marty. For some time, he had written about "the public church" or "public religion,"[12] which shared with the concept of "civil religion" the recognition that religious influence often becomes institutionalized in general sets of cultural convictions of the people, and reinforces patriotic values. But, when writing on Reinhold Niebuhr and the developments of "Christian Realism," after World War II, he specifically tied the term "public theology" to the American experience.[13]

This shift of terms of course raises many questions about the relationship of theology to religion. Is theology basically the more systematic statement of religious experience and belief, as Schleiermacher argued? Is theology, at least Christian theology, opposed to religion, especially civil religion, because it focuses on faith and revelation, and not on any cultural creation, as Barth claimed? Or is theology a critical and reconstructive discipline that is developed to assess, reform, and guide religious belief so that it issues in what is true, just, and cross-culturally fitting to the human condition and historical existence, as Niebuhr sought to do it? Marty, in speaking of Niebuhr, pointed not only to the fact that political realism demanded the public invocation of a radical doctrine of sin, but to the fact that we can recognize that the reality of sin implies an epistemic realism — one rooted in those streams of thought deriving from the Platonic tradition that appeared not only in Augustinian motifs, but in certain branches of the Renaissance, Reformation, and Enlightenment. Humans have some principles of right and wrong "written on their hearts," as St. Paul stated. It is thus possible for all to recognize that there are norms of faith, hope, love, and justice in spite of the fact that they are inevitably obscured by ignorance, self-interest, and willful distortion — as acknowledged in various liberal notions that grew out of a long tradition of idealistic philosophy that interacted with the biblical traditions.

---

11. See D. Forrester, *Theology and Politics* (London: Blackwell, 1988) and *Christian Justice and Public Policy* (Cambridge: Cambridge University Press, 1997); and O. O'Donovan and J. O'Donovan, eds., *From Irenaeus to Grotius: A Sourcebook in Christian Political Thought* (Grand Rapids: Eerdmans, 1999).

12. For example, see Martin E. Marty, *The Public Church* (New York: Crossroad, 1981).

13. See Martin E. Marty, "Reinhold Niebuhr: Public Theology and the American Experience," *Journal of Religion* 54, no. 4 (1974): 332-59.

Civil Religion, Political Theology, and Public Theology

The context to which this view spoke resonated due to the historic influence in the U.S. of the "self-evident truths" of which Locke wrote, knowable by believing citizens of society prior to the formation of a state, of the "consent to being" of the Puritan theologian Jonathan Edwards, of the developmental patterns of faithful understanding to which Christian educator Horace Bushnell pointed, and of the sense of basic justice appealed to by the social gospel leader, Walter Rauschenbusch. All of these had influenced the American public, and used overtly theological language to interpret and to reform the basic social ethos. Many, if not all, saw the social fabric of ordinary life as both beset by sin and revealing the providential care, truth, and justice of the living God. Moreover, as Marty noted, several of the founding fathers, plus Presidents Abraham Lincoln and Woodrow Wilson, saw things quite similarly; but they did not subordinate religion to either the projections of the social realities, as was frequent in civil religion, or subordinate the theological first principles to the ruling political authority, as was frequent in the Erastian motifs of much European political theology.

The term "public theology" was new; but it gained currency rather quickly, not because of its novelty or because the theological concerns to which it pointed were new, but because it seemed to capture one wide and deep, but widely neglected, strand of the classical theological tradition, often found in the "free church" traditions. It was rooted in the interaction of biblical insight, philosophical analysis, and the responsibility of the ecclesial community to engage in historical discernment of and constant reformation of the social order because it believed that certain kinds of progress could be made in human affairs. Religion that is tempted to idolatry or cultural chauvinism could be brought under critique, those forms of dogma that did not offer guidance in regard to the formation and inevitably necessary reformation of society could be refuted, and the wise combination of social realism and ethical realism could mobilize movements to constrain injustice and improve the prospects of a more just society.

This tradition in America had long honored those who built not only the churches and the missionary societies, but also the schools and the hospitals, the industries and the unions, the stores and the banks, the railroads and steamships, the museums and the concert halls — plus the leaders of those institutions dedicated to the reform of all of these. Niebuhr's generation were extremely suspicious of capitalism during the Depression, but became more critical of socialism in the second half of the century. Unlike the heritage of "civil religion," this kind of public theology did not celebrate the social system and its culture as it was — it changed things. And, unlike political theology,

Developing a Method for Public Theology

it neither sought political power nor called for radical transformations with a utopian vision; it rejoiced at modest improvements, for it knew the depth of sin. It was and is a reformist movement more than a conservative or revolutionary one, and it takes this stand for it believes that an authentic theology is by necessity realist. Indeed, in recent history, Martin Luther King Jr. became a worldwide exemplar of public theology in its activist and optimistic mode.

The deeper roots of this tradition had long presumed that theologians, clergy, and committed laity could and should draw on theological resources to teach, preach, and organize publically to advance issues of truth, faith, and justice in society. They saw themselves as agents of Christ, the prophet, priest, and king, who had inaugurated the kingdom of God that works within and among the church and the civil society, often under the radar of political authority. They were convinced that they must take responsibility for the spiritual and moral architecture of the common life as the medieval church had done with the collapse of the Roman Empire, as the Reformers had done in the free cities of early modern Europe, and as the Puritans and Pietists had done with regard to the formation of a society in the wilderness of America, and as the social gospel did with the advent of modern industrialization.

Today, throughout those parts of the world that we used to call the "third world," before the "second world" collapsed, and it became recognized that the "third world" lives also in the "first world" and the "first world" in the midst of the "third world," Evangelical and Pentecostal movements often also support social agendas that are altering the common life and even the political contours of the region — less by direct political means than by altering the fabric of the institutions of the common life and changing the inherited culture.[14]

In light of this history, we can identify two main reasons for using the adjective "public." One is very simple: it is a modest protest against the

---

14. See, especially with regard to Latin America, the work of David Martin, *Tongues of Fire* (Oxford: Blackwell, 1993) and *Pentecostalism* (Oxford: Blackwell, 2001). See also, with special reference to Africa, Philip Jenkins, *The Next Christendom: The Coming of Global Christianity* (New York: Oxford University Press, 2002), and in regard to East Asia, David Aikman, *Jesus in Beijing: How Christianity Is Transforming China and Changing the Global Balance of Power* (New York: H. Regnery, 2003). These movements have no doubt about the fact that life is beset by sin, or that certain truths of morality and faith are universally valid and capable of constraining or changing sinful life in personal and social ways. This alters the perception of political life (and of economics, family patterns, cultural values, education, etc.) and limits all statist tendencies. They tend to ignore or repudiate both political theology and its cousin, liberation theology.

Civil Religion, Political Theology, and Public Theology

dominant understandings of political theology. This protest is based on the conviction that the public is prior to the republic, that the fabric of civil society, of which religious faith and organization is inevitably the core, is more determinative of and normatively more important for politics than politics is for society and religion. Politics in human affairs makes great waves, like a hurricane or typhoon on the top of the ocean — often with great and fateful consequences; but these massive storms seldom change the deeper tides, currents, or dominant wind patterns. At deeper social levels, fundamental alterations of the structures that channel the flows of energy, the powers and principalities of life, make a much greater difference over time, and even determine what political storms get played out.

Yet, public theology cannot be said to be anti-political. It is well aware that arrangements for the building of police, military, judicial, medical, educational, and infrastructure (roads, bridges, harbors, etc.) institutions are inevitably necessary and that all citizens have to be willing to pay appropriate levels of taxes to do collectively what cannot be done separately. And it is aware that principles developed in the theological tradition to guide choices about the just and unjust use of coercive force are required for there to be any viable political structures to do these necessary things. It is simply that it wants politics to be the limited servant of the other institutions of society, not their master. A people tutored to see the possibilities of sin and the reality of truth and justice by a serious theology will find ways to organize and to control political institutions so that they do not seek to comprehend or dominate life.

The idea that the faith can and should not only address believers in the church in ways that touch their souls, but empower the faithful to address the world in its wider structures and dynamics by developing the kind of reasonable moral theology that is able to assess and reform the institutions of civil society, is often represented by certain themes in Catholic theology, both in its classical heritage and in its more recent developments as it gradually overcame much of its deep suspicion (since the French Revolution) of democracy, human rights, and, later, "Americanism." The term "public theology" was not in currency, but the idea that certain doctrines held and taught by the Christian faith can and should address "all people of good will," and are in principle clearly understandable by all was routinely stated in official documents. Moreover, the several notable Catholic thinkers who became public voices and unofficial representatives of theology in public discourse made a major mark. Let us not forget such major twentieth-century figures as the French philosopher Jacques Maritain, whose writings did so much to advance the cause of human rights during the drafting of the UN Declaration of Rights, or the American Jesuit John Courtney Murray, who defended the ethical validity of democracy and pluralism in ways that shaped Vatican II. Murray is especially interesting, for in his early writings he had little sympathy with the ways in which Protestant theologians dealt with social matters theologically and wanted to treat these issues strictly by the use of natural law theory. But later, he questioned the possibility of a society existing without combining philosophical reason with the biblical heritage, which implies a public theology. In fact, he began to question whether Western society can exist without just such a "religious" base. One of his major interpreters summarizes his views:

> If there is no consensus as to the core direction and meaning of humanity, and no public discussion of that reality, then "society is founded on a vacuum; and society, like nature itself, abhors a vacuum and cannot tolerate it. . . ." Can society live without a public religion? "The historical evidence would seem to argue for a negative answer." It may be possible "that an individual can live without religion, but a society cannot." [Thus] . . . after years of defending the adequacy of natural law religious discourse. . . . Murray even suggested, or more properly cried out, that perhaps an explicitly Christian religious public discourse is necessary for social survival. Quoting John of Salisbury, Murray . . . asked "Whether or not civilization, that is civil order, civil unity, civil peace, is possible without what he [John] calls in a beautiful phrase 'the sweet and fruitful marriage of reason and the Word of God.'"[15]

This Catholic accent was cultivated further by a number of contemporary progressive Catholic thinkers such as theologian David Tracy, theological ethicist David Hollenbach, social ethicist Dennis McCann, and political philosopher Paul Sigmund, among others. They have drawn not only from the legacies of Maritain and Murray, but from a close encounter with Protestant theology and with the widening scope of Catholic teachings in the social encyclicals, from *Rerum Novarum* on labor by Pope Leo XIII, through *Quadragesimo Anno* on the ideas of subsidiarity and of solidarity by Pius XI, to *Pacem in Terris* by John XXIII, and perhaps most powerfully in *Centessimus Annus*, by Pope John Paul II. This reading of the tradition influenced Vatican

---

15. Leon Hooper, *The Ethics of Discourse: The Social Ethics of John Courtney Murray* (Washington, DC: Georgetown University Press, 1986), pp. 113-14.

statements to the UN on racism, war, human rights, and pluralism, drawing on philosophical-theological traditions and shaping the message to wider civilizational issues. The theologian David Tracy sought to find the basis of a truly catholic theology, and used Troeltschian modes of thought to grasp the sense of pluralism in social and theological history. Various modes of analysis are needed to discern meaning. He identifies three: one is the church, another is the wider society, and the third is academia, where the intellectual community tests the possible validity of every proposal.[16]

Implicit in the remarks about the various publics that are emerging as dominating influences on a global scale, is the prospect that a highly pluralistic global civil society may be emerging, what some believe could become the basis of a worldwide, complex civilization. And the most notable fact about this development is that it is developing without an integrated political order to guide it, and there are competing conceptions as to how a civilization can and should be ordered. With the United Nations in relative disarray and unwilling to act to enforce its own resolutions, America is tempted to become a new imperial power, a very odd one, I must say, for nothing in the tradition of the U.S. approves of imperialism, and its several interventions in other societies have been justified by its opposition to imperialist and tyrannical tendencies on the part of others. Even in the attitudes of those who support the present policies in Iraq, the belief is widespread that America is not only interested in protecting the oil of the region from monopolistic control by tyrants, but deeply concerned for ethical reasons with extending the principles of freedom of religion, a pluralistic civil society with human rights, and a constitutional democracy with a limited state in areas where dominant religio-cultural traditions make these possibilities unlikely.

If we are to avoid the danger of a more malicious imperialism — a danger to the USA and to the world — we will need to see how it is that the various publics of an increasingly complex and worldwide civil society can be ordered into a viable system. It is a major empirical and theoretical issue of great practical consequence: whether the various public spheres are and should be prior to or the result of a regime. At stake is whether these spheres exist in ways that require a political order, and whether they can reconstruct a political order. To put the matter another way, public theology differs from

---

16. David Tracy's *Blessed Rage for Order* (New York: Crossroad, 1991) shows dependence on the work of the liberal Lutheran, Ernst Troeltsch, as well as on Catholic sources. His subsequent *Analogical Imagination: Christian Theology and the Culture of Pluralism* (New York: Crossroad, 1998) articulates these three areas of "public" that must be addressed by theology. See note 3 above.

political theology precisely because public theology tends to adopt a social theory of politics, and political theology inclines to have a political view of society. Public theology is, oddly, more like socialism is in theory, for it too sees the fabric of society as decisive for every area of the common life. It differs from socialism, however, in that it does not see the polarization of the classes as the fundamental characteristic of society — either in theory or in fact — and does not expect the state to control economic life by centralized planning and capitalization.

This contrasts with political theology in that it tends to see politics, focused on a centralized government, as the comprehending institution of society and the primary manifestation and guarantor of public justice. Politics, in this view, is dedicated to the accumulation, organization, and exercise of the kind of power that sees itself as responsible for the control and guidance of all the social institutions within it. It may be more or less benevolent, authoritarian, or totalitarian; but it is always deeply concerned with the power to guide, limit, empower, or command every subject or citizen and every other institution in a geographical territory, and the threat of the use of force stands behind its actions. In this, it is closer to the way socialism actually works. This is the model that was adopted by most governments — gently in Sweden and Greece, harshly in Russia and China in the past, with many European countries in between, and it is the model that was exported to the "new" nations in the decolonializing period. Indeed, it was advocated by a number of American "developmentalists" and political theologians who sought major capital loans for economic development to the centralized governments of the decolonializing states, presuming that a well-financed government could build a good civil society. But when the funds were siphoned off for all sorts of family favoritism, corrupt cronies, and political payoffs, economic development stalled and the borrowing governments could not pay the loans. The "debt crisis" hit many of the poorest regions, and the people, still living in undeveloped societies, suffered.

A nonsocialist social theory of politics sees every political order as subject over time to the more primary powers in society — those spheres of life that embody those moral and spiritual orientations that become embodied in social and ethical tissues and associations of the common life and that are prior to the formation of political orders. In this view, political parties, regimes, and policies come and go; they are always necessary, but they are also the by-product of those religious, cultural, familial, economic, and social traditions that are prior to government, and every government is, sooner or later, accountable to them. If political leaders attempt to control these sectors

Civil Religion, Political Theology, and Public Theology

of social life, they will foment resistance and reform movements to transform the ruling parties or the form of government altogether. Thus the most decisive questions are how the pre-political organizations of life are ordered and, behind that, what religious or ethical presumptions they seek to incarnate — basic questions for every public theology. For this reason, a public theology has a preference for certain social theories of life and history and thus of politics. It turns to those social theories that hold that cultural, familial, economic, and intellectual traditions are deeply shaped by religion, and specifically to those that believe in the possibility of conversion. Such matters are more comprehensive than any political order.

One key question, in view of these factors, is what Christians might have to offer as a public theology for a world situation in which a civil society is now being formed — without a clear and centered political order (although with a dominant political hegemony that could become imperialistic, as I have already suggested). Does Christianity have normative models of how to order complex civil societies that reach beyond any single nation-state? I think it does. Should a public theology based in Christian doctrine assume the responsibility of helping give shape to "the new world order," and can it do so without cultural imperialism? I think so, as others and I have argued elsewhere.[17]

Sometimes named "that order which is called freedom," Christian public theology points toward a social order that is as close to how God wants us to live together as humanity has yet discerned. It often appeared first in ecclesiology, then in civil society, and through the influence of these as carried by ordinary believers into the political realm. A key example of this way of viewing matters is represented by the thought of Althusius, who saw society as a "consociation of consociations," a "federation" of "covenanted" communities. Another example, a more recent one, is Abraham Kuyper, who developed the basic theory of the relative sovereignty of the "spheres" of life.[18] And, in an-

---

17. This contrast was drawn by James Hastings Nichols, *Democracy and the Churches* (Philadelphia: Westminster, 1951); F. W. Dillistone, *The Structure of the Divine Society* (London: Lutterworth; Philadelphia: Westminster, 1951); William J. Everett, in his *God's Federal Republic* (New York: Paulist, 1988); and a Jewish political philosopher who has a high appreciation of the Reformed tradition, Daniel Elazar, *The Covenant Tradition in Politics*, 4 vols. (Piscataway, NJ: Transaction Publishers, 1995-98).

18. See his famous *Lectures on Calvinism* (Grand Rapids: Eerdmans, 1931); and the essays written for the 100th anniversary celebration of them, edited by Luis Lugo: *Religion, Pluralism, and Public Life: Abraham Kuyper's Legacy for the Twenty-First Century* (Grand Rapids: Eerdmans, 2000). Cf. also one of the best current treatments of these themes: James

other way, Emil Brunner's Gifford Lectures of 1948, sadly neglected, engaged these issues in a most imaginative way. All of these Reformational Protestants depend on the basic doctrine of the sovereignty of God, a doctrine that implies that all areas of life are under God, and thus no earthly power can be sovereign over them all. Such doctrines pose the key question as to how we should seek to order their relationship while keeping maximum freedom, under God, for each area of life, yet work with other religions, cultures, and traditions since they too share the basic capacity to discern the principles of right and wrong and live in societies also built on analogous spheres of social life — even if they have differing views of ultimate salvation.

I am encouraged in this view by the new research conducted by John Nurser, who has written the very significant new study, "A Global Ethos for a Global Order: The Ecumenical Movement Churches and Human Rights 1938-1948." In brief he argues that when Hitler and Stalin were on the prowl, certain wide-visioned ecumenical church leaders saw not only that they must be stopped by the use of force, but that a revised, nonterritorial, and non-coercive interpretation of "Christendom" could help shape a new global order on the far side of the conflict. It is not so much the familiar story that some of the most famous theological leaders from that period (Niebuhr, Bonhoeffer, Barth, Tillich) made major contributions in resisting tyranny. Rather it was that a host of lesser-known figures, led by theologians Fred Nolde and Searle Bates, plus half a dozen others who worked with a number of Catholic and Jewish leaders, translated the basic presuppositions of the wider tradition into terms that could be endorsed on interfaith, cross-cultural, and international bases. From the early consultations at Dumbarton Oaks where the first plans were laid for the United Nations, the World Bank, the IMF, and the UN Declaration of Human Rights, these leaders supplied the intellectual firepower and the zeal for the cause that tirelessly prodded believing leaders of diplomatic corps, and mobilized notables in religious and ecumenical institutions to think about the articulation of an ethical vision and the formation of institutions that could most likely prevent the neo-pagan barbarism of Fascism and the hypersecular utopianism of Communism from terrorizing the world in the future. It may be that the institutions they envisioned need, already, reexamination and reform, and it is clear that they did not fully foresee the challenges that Islamic and Hindu fundamentalism could later pose, but they generated the first basic designs behind the most important international in-

---

Skillen and R. M. McCarthy, eds., *Political Order and the Plural Structure of Society* (Atlanta: Scholars Press, 1991).

stitutions of today — the capstone of which was the Declaration of Human Rights that has now become the *jus gentium* of most of the world.

In brief, then, civil religion is, essentially, as Rousseau in one way and Durkheim and their American followers (like Feuerbach in Germany) in other ways argued, a projection by a civic order of its experiences and values onto the cosmic order for the sake of social solidarity. It is, so to speak, society worshiping the image of itself, from the bottom up. A political theology, in this respect like a public theology, claims that its origins are essentially divine, from the top down as it were, and not simply a human construction of those seeking power. However, a political theology also tends to see the political order as the only comprehending one, and seeks to use governmental power to shape the policies of all "subordinate" organizations so that they aid the whole — as defined by the political order. This means, however, an ever-expanding rule by a centralized power that takes all political, economic, military, educational, cultural, legal, and eventually religious authority in its own hands.

A public theology, as I understand it, agrees with political theology in that it is not simply the religious sentiments or experience of a particular community, projected into the artifact of a cultural self-celebration, that is the source of normative thought and life, but that it is a revelatory source that stands as the norm. However, it sees this "top-down" reality as not having implications for the political order in the first instance, but first of all for inner personal convictions, the communities of faith, and the associations that they generate in an open society — and these will inevitably be plural and in contention. The principles and purposes they advocate, however, do not stay in the religious community or in private associations. They work their way through the convictions of the people and the policies of the multiple institutions of civil society where the people live and work and play, that make up the primary public realm. Indeed, it holds that these convictional-commitment-incarnate multiple centers in the lives of the public are, together, the most decisive core of civilizational life. With the proper cultivation and development, they are refined as they work their way not from the bottom up, nor from the top down, but from the center out. They show up eventually in the formation of a limited constitutional political order that serves the people, protects their human rights, and allows the multiple institutions and spheres of a pluralistic society to flourish in the glory of God, and by their constantly prophetic, priestly, and princely mutual correction, serve the well-being of an unavoidably sinful, but morally and spiritually edified, community of communities.

Covenantal Justice in a Global Era

The idea that justice has a covenantal form is not new; but it has taken on a renewed vitality in theological and political circles. A number of studies of the biblical idea of covenant have been published in the last century, and the idea has become common in international law since World War II, as we can see in the efforts by the United Nations to establish a series of covenants on human rights. Further, several remarkable cross-cultural analyses of the role of covenantal thinking have been published in political theory and history, especially as the idea has shaped contemporary thinking about constitutional government, social compact, pluralistic civil society, and international federations. Indeed, covenantal thinking has become more prominent with the end of the Cold War, with the new crises in totalitarian and authoritarian societies around the world, and with a quest for viable models of an emerging global civilization. The purpose of this paper in view of these developments is to review the biblical roots of the idea of covenant, to identify some of its key transcontextual structures, and to suggest how it pertains to peoples who hope to participate in shaping the emerging global society beyond the crises of totalitarian and authoritarian regimes.

The Roots of the Idea

It is well known that the idea of covenant is rooted in ancient mid-Eastern social and religious history, and most often took the form of a suzerain treaty between a stronger political leader and a weaker one in which divine powers were invoked to witness the treaty. An agreement was reached, often with one party specifying the terms and the other acquiescing, which entailed the enumeration of the duties of the parties (X will protect Y, but Y must honor the edicts of and give tribute to X). Other forms of the covenant were mutual pledges between more equal partners, and often had commercial-contractual or marital engagement characteristics. In all genuinely covenantal cases, however, God was invoked as, at least, a witness to such binding agreements.

This basic "mutual," oath-bound creation of responsible relationships was taken by some of the ancient Semitic sages and prophets to be, in some ways, a close analogy to the way the one, true, righteous, and merciful God relates to humanity, and a model of how humans can and should relate to each other under this God. This theological adaptation of the idea shifted it from a matter of the human establishment of domination by coercive force or threat to a fresh unveiling of the character of a just and merciful God who directly engages in the formation and sustaining of human life in community — although it was also believed that the loss of a relationship with God due to human injustice would threaten the well-being of the human partners and of society at large.

The remarkable thing about this idea of a divinely established covenantal justice, as it appears in both the biblical record and in the history of social theory, jurisprudence, and political history, is that it is both stable and dynamic, pre-given and unfinished. It is stable in that it depends upon the basic character of the God who inaugurates covenants with humanity that manifest a holy justice, who reliably keeps these covenants, and who is not subject to caprice. Yet the God who is disclosed as constant and trustworthy by both abiding fidelity and in enduring laws that transcend the passing contexts of history is also the dynamic God who responds to persons in all sorts of conditions and seasons, and redemptively participates with humanity in the struggles for justice of human history. This God's commands and laws do not change from age to age, even if our understandings of them may change. This God limits the divine capacity for infinite freedom and does not alter the basic pattern of existence whereby life for human partners is sustained, yet this God also may freely blot out human failures to live up to and obey this law, and reaches out to humanity again and again, dynamically renewing the social covenants of life whereby we can live more responsibly in relationship to God and neighbor and more in accord with that basic, just, and merciful pattern. This is the God who hears the cries of the oppressed, who calls both wicked rulers and wayward peasants to account through prophetic judgment, who walks with the lonely through the valleys of the shadow of death, who forgives those with a contrite heart, and tempers the wind for the shorn lamb.

The justice of the covenanting God is not only simultaneously stable and dynamic, it is pre-given and unfinished. It is pre-given in that it is constituted by a standard and an ultimate end that humans can neither construct nor deconstruct; but it is unfinished in that the standards of right and wrong, good and evil are neither fully recognized nor completely fulfilled in life. Most importantly, the ultimate end cannot be fulfilled, only approximated, in history. It comes to us as promise, and the systems of positive justice by which we in all our societies attempt to actuate God's standards and ends in the world are ever imperfect. No human society can fully establish justice; all are under judgment; every society needs repeated reform; each can only reflect degrees of God's holiness.

Let us note that what is pre-given to us to guide the conduct of life is both standard and end, both *nomos* and *telos* as the philosophers noted long ago — both law and purpose. Both the overarching right order of things and the ultimate destiny of creation have to be interpreted, of course, and neither is easy to read off the raw data of life. This is due in part to the limits of human understanding, in part to distortions introduced into life by the sinful failures of humans to use the freedom available to us to choose for the right and the good, and in part because the full data of creation and history are not in yet. But those who believe in this God hold that enough is known that we can believe with good reason that life is governed by a moral law and that existence is not without purpose. Ultimately, human existence is governed by first principles that we do not construct and cannot deconstruct, and directed toward an ultimate end that we cannot know in detail or attain without divine aid and guidance.

To note the distinction between the right and the good is, to be sure, to introduce one of the deepest debates in the history of ethics, jurisprudence, and social life, for it is simply not clear to all that universal laws and ultimate purposes make full sense in either theory or practice. And, even if they do, some wonder how the first principles of right are to be accurately related to the divine purposes in view of the historical actualities that people daily face. The issue can also be put as a reverse, negative, question: How is wrong related to evil intentions and consequences and bad circumstances? Philosophers over the centuries have demanded that theologians, jurists, and politicians be clear on the grounds for which they argue for a "deontology" or a "teleology," and the way they specify the relationships of these two subdisciplines that, respectively, study the bases on which we might best know right from wrong and good from evil. Philosophers have also noted a constant temptation to try to reduce the right to the good or the good to the right. Subtle combinations of "rule-teleology" and "act-deontology" have been proposed; but whether the right is to defer to and can be defined by the good, or whether the good is to defer to and can be defined by the right in particular systems of thought or particular cases where judgment is required is a never-ending issue. The problem is that both the right and the good must be fulfilled for a fuller justice, and in human systems of thought as well as in human judgments they rarely are.

The biblical way of posing this issue has to do with the relationship of the laws of God to the purposes of God, and the relationship of them, as aspects of the kingdom of God, to the actual living of life. Those who worship the God of the biblical traditions are to live obediently under the laws of God and to live actively in the world as agents of that God toward the fulfillment of God's purposes. We are able to recognize and seek the Kingdom for it is commensurate with our own deepest nature, precisely because we are made in the image of God. Humans have some residual capacity to recognize the right and to seek the good in spite of the fact that we live under conditions that are neither fully right nor altogether good. That capacity may be deeply defaced by sin, rebellion, and ignorance, but it is not utterly destroyed. Indeed, when we are drawn into a relationship with God, we find these capacities revitalized. We are called by God to be defenders of the right and active instruments of the good, co-creative covenant partners with God to enact the righteous principles and the ultimate ends God intends for humanity — as confident agents of justice.

However, even faithful believers recognize the tension between obedience to the right and active agency for the good as these interact in the actual conditions of social life. It creates painful conundrums in the moral life. One of the deepest implications of "sin" and "the Fall" is that the right and the good almost never join to make perfect justice in human life. The achievement of the relative and proximate justice that is possible in the complexities of sociohistorical life, glorious as they may be, often seems to require some compromise with one or another of the first principles of the moral law under which we are to live or with some feature of the ultimate purpose toward which we should strive. On the one hand, we willingly or unwittingly sacrifice what is right for the "larger" good. On the other hand, a rigorous obedience to the righteousness of God leads, not seldom, to bad consequences for ourselves or our neighbors. Who has not bent the law for a greater good; who has not appealed to the right while wounding a neighbor? Thus, our confidence must ever be muted by realism, modesty, and contrition.

The laws of God and the purposes of God are united in the kingdom of God; but they rarely are in human experience. This is one of the indications

Developing a Method for Public Theology

that humans, in spite of an original goodness intended by God, experience life as morally anguished, a condition we think is inevitable but not eternal. The moments in life that hint of the Kingdom offer a hope of ultimate salvation, when righteousness is fulfilled and God's purposes are realized, when the right and the good coincide perfectly. This is the hope that drove Abraham, Sarah, and their heirs as they sought a city that has foundations, whose builder and maker is God. Indeed, Abraham, and Noah before him, were able to recognize that they were to obey God's commands and laws, and were called to do the work of the Lord on earth, not only because they were made in the image of God, but because they were parties to a covenant of promise and hope beyond the despair of moral conflict, one clarified at Sinai and fully renewed in Jesus Christ. This too is what is pre-given in a view of covenantal justice.

But what is pre-given is also unfinished. It grew more complete, according to the biblical record, after this covenanted people fell into slavery and found liberation under the leadership of Moses. But the liberation is not the central point of the story. It is the covenant renewal, with the giving of the law — a vast and subtle clarification of the first principles of right and wrong, the disclosure of the moral law that governs human life, a disclosure that was so remarkable that a religion is founded on the marvel of that event. It reconstituted a people, gave a renewed national identity, and called them to a new, universal mission to be a light to the nations.

Later on, it became clear that this people could not carry out its mission in the face of exterior threat without complex social institutions. In the course of a noble history, not only prophets and priests, but kings were identified as belonging to anointed offices, and multiple other forms of vocation were developed, from craftsmen to judges and healers, from merchants to poets and musicians. In these developments we see not only the more abstract dimensions of covenantal justice — the deontological right and the teleological good — but the relative social embodiments of covenantal callings and institutions as spheres of the common life. These vocations and spheres of practice indicate that not only the ultimate principles of right, and the ultimate ends of the good are part of covenantal living, but so are to be the concrete relationships of life in civil society — both in person-to-person relationships with and under God, and in the interacting associations and institutions of the common life whereby relative approximations to the right and the good enable community life to flourish on an ongoing basis. Not only the Hebrews at the mountain but also the people building a city on a hill, one that anticipates the New Jerusalem for all the nations, are among the great synthetic

Covenantal Justice in a Global Era

moments in which that people was called to be a light to the nations. Those moments, with Moses and David, like those with Noah and Abraham, made contributions that remain valid. The clarification of the content of the moral law, a law given when there was no state and thus no human legislators, is one of the greatest covenantal moments of human history. It is to these that the later prophets, priests, and kings returned again and again, renewing the covenant as enabled and demanded by their faithful leaders. But their capacity to be a light to the nations was compromised. Their mission to the world could not be carried forward, for the greatest insight they gave to humanity became too closely associated with legalistic detail, ritualism, ethnic particularism, and nationalistic identity. The walls that were built to protect their treasure became a tomb that had to be opened for the treasure to become manifest to the wider world.

Something like the ancient Hebraic view of covenantal justice, and often its encased shells, can be found in many of the great cultural traditions of the world. However, those rooted in theistic religious traditions differ from the nontheistic ones in this respect: they believe that nothing that humans can do can either hide the justice toward which the covenants point forever or accomplish its full realization. Relative gains can be made, the most vicious forms of injustice can be modulated, incremental approximations to the first principles of righteousness can be habituated by human virtue and social practice, and greater awareness of divine good and human well-being can be cultivated. Many of these convictions are held also by great philosophies that grasp the depths of human existence and morality. But theistic religions hold that the full actualization of the right and the good in our inner lives, in our human relationships, and in the matrices of social life cannot be attained on humanistic grounds alone. These great religions know that, beyond human wisdom, valuable as it is, a divine initiative must be taken. A redeemer, a messiah, a revealing act of God is necessary.

On the nature of this revealing act, however, the God-based traditions disagree among themselves, whatever commonality they have with philosophy and with each other on other points. These disagreements and relative agreements are complex, but they can, with only modest distortion, be summarized briefly: A number of Hindu and tribal religions hold that saviors in the form of heroic avatars come often in the cycles of time and that their epics are parables of this ongoing process. The Jewish tradition denies that any Messiah has come, but looks forward to the coming of a messianic renewal. Christians believe that Jesus is the Christ, the very Son of God, the one and only Messiah, who has come and has inaugurated the final covenantal renewal, which will be perfectly revealed only in a coming age beyond history. And Muslims believe that all these are superseded by a final revelation of the very thoughts of God in the Qur'an, which promises, in covenantal fashion, final redemption for those who submit to its divine author and message — which Hindus, Jews, and Christians may respect, but do not believe to be the final revelation. The final confirmation as to whether the Hindu, the Jewish, the Christian, the Islamic, or some other possibility is correct about God's final unveiling of covenantal justice remains in the future. Believers in each of these traditions may live by faith in the meantime, but no final certainty is possible at this point in time. In this way too, most basically, the idea of God's covenantal justice is unfinished, and divergent religious traditions press us toward divergent visions of the good life — whatever else we share.

The Structures of Covenantal Justice

Although we have no final certainty about the teleological end of justice, we are without neither insight nor the capacity to make moral judgments with regard to certain other aspects of justice — recognizing that these may be subject to revision if and when fuller understanding of God's purposes are disclosed. Peoples and nations, cultures and religious traditions are often covenantal in some respects, and that is why we can find agreement on many things that are morally wrong. Every language has terms for sacrilege, disrespect, lying, cheating, stealing, murder, rape, exploitation, etc.; every nation has laws against these, every culture disapproves of them, and every known religion recognizes these as opposed to divine law — even if there are some differences of tradition as to how these are applied to particular cases. Further, people know when they are treated by authorities in wrong or evil ways, even if they are unsure about how to make things right or what good should be pursued personally and socially, and what the best methods for that might be. In brief, every people and culture knows some of the boundaries of covenantal justice and thus both the deeper levels of a culture's moral tradition, and the more immediate voices of the people experiencing wrong must be allowed to inform the common life and to set limits on what is socially tolerable.

Moreover, the very lack of certainty about the good implies that we must allow a range of rights in those areas where the ultimate issues of the right and the good are at stake. This implies a provisional pluralism, one in which people must be free to pursue the visions of the good that grasp their loyalties, so long as this free pursuit does not destroy the ability of others to seek their vision. Above all, thus, religious and intellectual freedom in regard to the ultimate warrants for what is held to be good must be guaranteed until the final confirmation arrives — that is, until all of history is finished and God's final reign is fully and clearly visible, and all that is truly good is fulfilled. The denial of religious and intellectual freedom and the demand for ideological conformity is often the first betrayal of right and human rights: it demands a lie in the heart and an ingenuous participation in public life. It leads inexorably to the systematic violation of the image of God in the neighbor and thereby destroys covenantal justice and thus the fabric of social trust.

This implies that the open discussion of religious and ethical issues must be protected in the positive sense. Public discussion and debate, public preaching and teaching, the possibilities of conversion and social reform, and therefore the open publication, distribution, and broadcast of religious, ethical, and social opinions about the right and the good in and for society are of fundamental importance to persons and to the common welfare. Where these are mature, they help bring about the capacity to find relative agreement and cooperate in common projects. It is through social deliberation and open, mutual correction that people come to convictions about what can be affirmed without compulsion, and what ought to be made a part of the common life without coercive threat. In these contexts, in spite of diversity of views about social morality that is inevitable, the prospect of covenantal agreement about critical aspects of justice is discovered as a voluntary option — something that people can adhere to and seek to enact without soldiers standing at their backs or spies looking over their shoulders. Indeed, this openness is so indispensable to the long-range well-being of society that coercive authority ought to be deployed essentially to keep the social processes of such public discussions open, and to protect the rights of persons to seek the truth about the right and the good, and about the divine roots of their possible combination, through the exploration and advocacy of the most important questions. This leads directly to social rights: the rights of people to develop those religious, educational, and political organizations that allow them to search for, discover, set forth, and exemplify their best versions of what the right and the good might be, what their basis is, how they can and should be related to each other, and how they might become embodied and enacted in all spheres of life.

We should not neglect to note that while individual persons, made in the image of God and thus blessed with a capacity to reason and choose, need to be protected, an individualistic understanding of human rights is only partially valid. Individualism does recognize the spiritual and moral dignity of each person, as one endowed by the Creator with the image of God and thus with a right to have rights, but it sometimes fails to recognize and often functionally denies that persons are inevitably relational beings, called to live in groups and associations, to cultivate communities and traditions, and to have responsibilities that are built into complex relationships. Thus, while the fundamental structures of covenantal justice involve a respect for basic aspects of personal freedom and dignity, the freedom and the rights that these imply are best realized when they are used to fulfill responsibilities in interpersonal, community, and societal arenas of life.

Those who have advocated "communitarianism" and opposed "individualism" in the last few decades have recognized the fact that people do live, and in some senses must live, if life is to be meaningful, in various forms of morally embedded social interdependence. They demand the recognition of mutual moral bonds of obligation and responsibility more fully than the advocates of individual rights have acknowledged. We must recognize, however, that some have set forth "communitarianism" in collectivist ways that unjustly suppress the rights of various groups and associations, and some have appealed to "common" values to violate the human rights of persons.

The world has just been through a century in which several forms of communitarianism were taken up and radicalized in ways that brought great tragedy to many. Some took up the matter of national identity, combined it with ethnic definitions of peoplehood, and generated great horrors. The Nazis of midcentury Europe are particularly notable precisely because they made the covenantal peoples of the biblical tradition, the Jews and their faithful Christian brothers and sisters, the victims of their distortions, denying that all people live under universal first principles and raising their own national values into a neo-pagan idolatry. But it was not only they who did this. The phenomenon has parallels in many other locations. Replications of precisely these motifs appear today in efforts at "ethnic cleansing" that threaten to drown covenantal justice again in the blood of nationalism.

Others took up the vision of an ultimate good future and made it a program for utopian, revolutionary justice, presuming that they knew the ultimate end of human existence — the perfect classless society. The Marxists of our century rightly recognized the evils of the oppression of some by others, and they radicalized the notion that the slave must overthrow the master. They also opposed the evils of nationalism in favor of an international coalition of the oppressed against the oppressors; but they made several fatal moral errors that distorted their partially valid insights. For one thing, they held that all the world was divided into two classes — one good but poor, one rich and evil. They thought they could eliminate evil by eliminating a class of people, in part by violent revolution, in part by eliminating the social conditions by which that class gained wealth. The result was a failed economy and a new class of bureaucratically privileged elites.

Further, they did not understand that right and wrong are pre-given, but understood both injustice and justice to be nothing more than the social artifacts of particular, victorious classes. Thus, they undercut the standards by which they could have held themselves accountable. Nor did they understand that the good we know is only provisional and that no theory about the logic of history can construct the human future and reconstruct fallen human nature without divine aid. Because they did not understand these basic elements of covenantal justice, they held the view that the oppressed class, relieved of their idealistic and religious illusions and working in solidarity, could construct a new destiny for humanity out of their own will, reason, and needs. Thus, in the name of class solidarity, they blotted out both a vertical covenantal relationship with God and the horizontal multiple covenants of civil society by which the tissues of creative participation in God's purposes under law are maintained and enhanced in history. Both individual persons and the mediating institutions by which people everywhere seek to enhance the right and the good in a host of humanizing organizations and relationships were swallowed — this time not into a nationalism of blood and steel, but into a dehumanizing collectivism of regimented and dispirited mediocrity.

In highly indirect ways, the nationalism of one movement and the ideology of class solidarity of the other combined in a recent theological movement against the modern colonialism of the West, often taking the Exodus of the Bible as its model. This produced a powerful set of liberation movements that brought national independence and mass movements toward equality around the world. However, these movements have not fully acknowledged how deeply their efforts were dependent on fascist-like nationalism and Marxist class analysis, and that justice is neither national identity nor class solidarity. No few of these movements ended in essentially one-party states that actually brought new forms of authoritarian or totalitarian oppression — along with economic disaster.

Of course, the problem is complex: every human attempt to enact covenantal justice is synthetic and temporary. It must not only draw together what we can know about fundamental standards of right and wrong under God with a dedication to the ultimate good end which we can know only in part and by faith; it must also demand the open and pluralistic reconstruction of the basic social institutions of the common life through particular covenantal agreements. That is, it must inform all those aspects of life to which the prophets, priests, and kings long ago directed our attention — family and sexuality, business and economic development, law and political life, education and cultural life. Even more, it must allow for the freedom of religion, so that every community of faith may pursue and practice the faith it knows, and offer its insights openly and without compulsion to the whole of humanity.

In brief, the structures of covenantal justice are both internal to ethics and external in the organizational life of society. They are internal to ethics in that they become the internal horizons of reference for the morally just person and community; and they are external in that they join, so far as possible given the limits of human history, the right and the good to the necessary value-bearing institutions of the common life — all those institutions that stand between the individual as an isolated being and connect the person to responsible associations without letting him or her get lost in some collective herd or hive. Where these are well developed they can prevent anarchy, challenge tyranny, and provide the federated networks of associational life where specific covenants may be enacted among the people with freedom and equity. These form character and establish a viable, flourishing civil society.

We know the shape of some of these institutions, as they have developed under modern conditions. First of all the free church — that is, the community of faith seeking to know and embody the right and the good without internal coercion and with neither dependence on the state nor seeking to control the state, although the church to be free must be able to preach and teach openly about justice in the operations of the state. Second, we may speak about various organizations and means of communication that will spring up around religious organizations seeking what is right and good for the smallest units in society, especially the family, the school, and the workplace. These are the building blocks of society, and if the partners in a marriage are mistreated, or if children are exploited or neglected, or if there is no way to earn the daily bread, a whole society will suffer in the future. If these flourish, charitable care for those in need follows.

But the bigger lesson of this past century is that civil society demands constitutional democracy with protections under law for the rights of persons and minorities. Indeed, constitutional democracy is one of the key covenantal forms that have come to be the most just manifestations of political life known to contemporary humanity. Governments that are to manifest covenantal justice will be constitutional in that they will operate under just laws, laws that defend human rights and thereby approximate the right and the good so far as humans can know and implement them in contemporary society; and governments will be democratic in the sense that they will enable the people to organize and rule themselves through the multiple associations and organizations that constitute civil society. Of course, just as churches, families, and schools will differ from case to case and culture to culture, so we can expect democracies to vary. The democracy of England is not that of the United States, that of Australia is not that of India, and that of the Philippines is not what is taking shape in South Africa. Still, we can see in their similarities their difference from colonialism and imperialism, from national or class tyranny, from religious or ideological conformism, and from individualist or ethnic anarchy.

Implications for a Global Era

We have traced the biblical roots of the idea of covenantal justice. It has, over the ages, engaged, learned from, and stabilized those aspects of justice that were already present in various cultures. It has also reformed, revised, deepened, and broadened other aspects of life that were less just and not fully covenantal as the biblical heritage was recontextualized in various societies and cultures. We did not here trace, but it has elsewhere been shown, that this idea modulated the Greek and Roman cultures of the ancient Mediterranean society, revised the Gallic and Germanic communities of Northern Europe, became central to Anglo-American civilization, transformed many tribal societies that were converted in the last two centuries of missions, and is now facing both the great world religions and a new global era in a new way. At each stage it has fostered the founding of communities of faith able to bring new levels of freedom, equality, righteousness, and mercy into the social ecology of human relations' arid institutional order, creating new syntheses of organizational life and pressing for a federation of the sectors of the common life. These transformations have been most notable in ecclesiology, politics, and law. It has pressed for religious communities and charitable associations independent of the state, for democratic procedures and open debates by multiple parties under constitutional protections in politics, for guarantees of civil liberties for persons and groups under just law that protect the rights of minorities, and for the protection of children and the equitable treatment of women and men in church, society, and family life.

It must be admitted, to be sure, that the history of the idea of covenantal justice is not all glorious and wonderful. Many distortions have entered human history. Some understandings of covenant have not been just. They have been used in condescending, exclusivist, and prejudicial ways. We must also admit that some conceptions of justice have not been covenantal. Not only have we experienced movements that have been statist or classist, as already mentioned; but we have seen ontocratic notions of justice so deeply ridden with concepts of caste and status that no place is left for voluntary bonding, for equality and freedom, or for the constant, and constantly necessary, formation and transformation of human social institutions. Still more, the idea of covenantal justice has sometimes degenerated into ideas of self-righteousness among those who are convinced that only they are privileged to be called into the covenant of redemption by God, or degenerated into a contract among those who hold that morality consists of whatever humans consent to, with no need for either a relationship with God or a higher moral law to guide them. These are, perhaps, the greatest temptations in the West.

Nevertheless, the history of the idea of covenant is extremely rich. It can be extended and it can be renewed. It presses us at each moment in human history to wed the ideas of the right and the good to the actual conditions under which we live. It demands that we recognize that we cannot bring a full integration on earth without God's promised intervention. Yet, it also gives us confidence that, under God and with God's help, we are not powerless to more nearly approximate the relative degrees of justice possible in human life. We can at least modulate the particular institutions of civil society in which we live so that gross wrongs are constrained and enable people to pursue worthy ends in particular and concrete spheres of life that more nearly approximate the right and the good of God's justice.

This is particularly important at two levels. We stand at the brink of a global era, which means that the nation-state, the chief instrument of modernization and development in many places for the last several generations, is finding its power to mobilize resources compromised. The technological, economic, communication, and educational possibilities reshaping our world are at once beyond and below the capacity of states to develop or constrain. They develop on local levels outside state planning and in transnational organizations that states need but cannot control. All societies are going to have to modulate their sense of national sovereignty. Those countries where the state has played the central role of development in recent history are having, and will have for the foreseeable future, the most difficult time, for the cultural, moral, social, and economic institutions outside the state's leadership are not well developed. In fact, strong centralized governments in the nation-states of our recent history — right-wing, left-wing, or moderate-technocratic —

Covenantal Justice in a Global Era

had quite strong reasons for keeping these institutions weak. When these are weak, the people are better controlled, and thus easier to exploit, control, or, if one thinks that the state must take full responsibility for the development of the people, mobilize. In consequence, both the organized sectors of civil society below the state and the transnational organizations beyond the state are weak precisely at the moment when they must play roles that demand their leadership and creativity. It is too much to say that the age of the nation-state is ended; but it is not too much to say that any state that hopes to preserve itself must, in some measure, lose itself in the wider world of international interdependency and as servant of institutions that it once tried to control.

Beyond the political issues that are at stake, great economic changes are at hand. The multinational corporations are the overwhelming agent of international interdependence and are providing the means of production, technological transfer, jobs, consumer goods, sense of professional excellence, and centers of operational identity that national, ethnic, and regional identity can no longer supply. They also opportunistically turn to the lowest bidder on various contracts and are oblivious to the local needs of whatever location can supply the needed workers or services at a lower price. Thus, they foment a new international competition for cheap labor that, on the one hand, exploits whatever opportunities are available and, on the other hand, draws more and more poor people into the orbit of a global economy. Subsistence economies, traditional means of production, centralized planning, mercantilist policies, and socialist schemes are utterly surpassed by the productive and marketing powers of contemporary developments.

I am well aware that many see these developments as simply a new economic imperialism of the West. There is some truth to that charge; and that is part of the reason that globalization needs further and extended cross-cultural discussion. It will not halt these developments to say "stop," and it is no more helpful to say "stop talking about them," as if they will disappear when we deny their reality. But if we do talk about them, we find that they are not all that is going on.

We find that local businesses, if they are going to be productive, provide jobs for people, and gain income from trade and export, must emulate these developments in some measure. If the young are to be educated for the likely future, they will have to have not only the means to pay for an education, but well-equipped institutions for education at a time when the nation-states are cutting spending to remain solvent. If we want hospitals with doctors, nurses, and medicines, we shall have to attend to international standards of medicine. If we want cultural institutions with a capacity to offer the music, art, novels, and TV programs that we can appreciate, we must develop institutions for the development of talent. If we want political parties in power that will defend human rights and control corruption, legal institutions and talented people dedicated to just laws must be cultivated and supported. And so on. One could go through the various sectors of society. In every area, I believe, the most effective way to form and sustain a viable society is to turn again to the model of covenantal justice as it derives from the Bible and has developed over the centuries. That model now needs renewal and extension. It needs renewal in those areas where it has been effective in the past, and is now forgotten; it needs extension into those areas where it has not been actuated in the past — most particularly in formerly authoritarian and totalitarian states, in areas where ontocratic religions or cultures have diminished its possibilities, and internationally where it can, we pray, bring a new federal commonality and participation to peoples feeling that they are being swept away by the new global developments.

To carry this forward, there is no substitute for developing a wider and deeper mission of the churches based on a public theology, one that will study, extend, and refine the applicability of the ideas of covenantal justice to the contexts in which we find ourselves. This we must seek to implement within every human relationship, every sector of society, and especially in the new institutions that are creating the new global civilization of the future. This can, of course, only be done if our efforts are God-dependent and subject to correction both by our continued discovery of the open future and God's purposes for it, and in encounter with and mutual correction from the world's great religions and philosophies that, themselves, are willing to undertake a quest for covenantal justice.

PART THREE

Constructing a Global Public Theology

A Post-Communist Manifesto:
Public Theology after the Collapse of Socialism

Co-Written with Dennis P. McCann

The specter that haunted the modern world has vanished. That specter is communism. Nobody who has been paying attention takes it seriously anymore, although a few will echo its slogans for generations. To be more specific: no one thinks anymore that the route to social justice and prosperity necessarily lies in the political control of the marketplace and the means of production. Along with Soviet communism, forms of Marxism, even the gentler forms of European socialism, are under pressure.

We can neither ignore this fact nor deny its implications for Christian social ethics. The Protestant social gospel, early Christian realism, much neo-orthodoxy, many forms of Catholic modernism, the modern ecumenical drive for racial and social inclusiveness, and contemporary liberation theories all held that democracy, human rights, and socialism were the marks of the coming kingdom. For all their prophetic witness in many areas, they were wrong about socialism. The future will not bring what contemporary theology said it would and should.

This is not like other recent crises. The current crisis in the Middle East makes American complacency impossible. The upheavals in Central America have chastened American paternalism. Vietnam struck at national arrogance. The civil rights era demanded the repudiation of racism. The defeat of fascism vindicated democracy. And the crash of 1929 demanded the reform of the industrial order. All these altered the social landscape. But they did not require repentance of modern Christianity. Indeed, they clarified before the world deep though obscured social principles held by the ecumenical church.

The failure of the socialist vision, where it does not bring a crisis of faith, demands repentance. All too many religious leaders still cling to the belief that capitalism is greedy, individualistic, exploitative, and failing; that socialism is generous, community-affirming, equitable, and coming; and that the transition from the one to the other is what God is doing in the world.

The truth is: no system has a monopoly on greed; modern capitalism engenders greater cooperation; socialism is more exploitative; and no one who has experienced "really existing socialism" now believes that it was God's design. What we now face is more than a delay in the socialist *parousia*. It is the recognition that this presumptive dogma is wrong.

If we can no longer affirm the socialist decision, must we now become enthusiastic neoconservatives? The answer is No, for questions of social justice are a necessary part of modern economics, not an intrusion into it. The economies of the future cannot be based on eighteenth-century theories or a return to nineteenth-century practices. Is it possible that, in face of the new evidence, everyone who holds to a "preferential option for the poor" must now embrace capitalism, since socialism itself impoverishes? In some measure, the answer is Yes. But it must be a reformed capitalism — one that uses law, politics, education, and especially theology and ethics to constrain the temptations to exploitation and greed everywhere.

Whenever capitalism rapes the earth or becomes a pillar of racism, sexism, classism, or nationalism, it must be resisted. But if the age of individualist greed is past, so is the age of collectivist protest against it. Aggregates of possessive egos, each making bottom-line decisions by the utilitarian calculation of cost and benefit, are as false as command economies where political and military leaders control the whole society.

Of course, socialism and Christianity are in theoretical accord on one key point: society is and must be prior to both government and business. But on the issue of what constitutes the core of society the differences appear immediately: more important than class conflict is theology and communities of faith. These transcend political economy both logically and historically and provide the model for the common life.

All politics and all economics must be conducted under the context-transcending principles of truth, justice, and love. Concretely understood, these protect the moral and spiritual rights of persons and groups and disclose purposes for living that are not of this world. Such principles and purposes are, and must be, the formative force in all public life, as well as in personal piety. They must enhance the salvation of both souls and civilizations.

At once more personal and more cosmopolitan than any political ideology or economic interest can be, a genuinely theological vision must constitute the ethics of our post-socialist economic order. Every authority and every policy that is deemed legitimate must recognize the integrity of both material and spiritual matters, of both historical consciousness and the awareness of eternity, of both humanistic interests and metaphysical-moral visions.

Theology is indispensable to the analysis of the human condition and the historical ethos. Interests not guided by theology and channeled by covenanted communities of faith march through the world like armies in the night; but they do not build civilizations and cultures that endure. Communities of intimacy and ultimacy, not class consciousness; institutions of affection and excellence, not revolutionary cadres; organizations of creativity and cooperation, not bureaucratized control mechanisms; and associations dedicated to what is true and just and loving before God, not quasi-scientific dialectics, are what shape social destiny in the long run.

Any account, including a Marxist one, of why things are the way they are that does not speak of theology and ecclesiology errs. It is doomed to fail. But where the political economy honors these, society can become open to a redemptive spirit. Modern theology and ethics have not said this clearly enough.

Yet it is one of the providential aspects of this moment in human history that the failure of communism, and consequently the doubt now thrown on all forms of socialism, cannot justify triumphalism in the West generally or among Christians particularly. The fact that "they" are sick does not prove that "we" are well. The new situation merely means that we can and must examine the relations of theology to political economy with a new openness that does not simply sprinkle holy water on materialist theories, outdated ideologies, and special interests.

The ensemble of problems that we confront is formidable. A full repertoire of solutions is not at hand. Optimism is soured by the nation's growing addiction to debt, a dependence on oil, recurrent hunger in far too many parts of the world, the peril of ecological disaster, the probability of a recession, the high visibility of ethical rot (as in recent junk-bond trading and the savings-and-loan crisis), a lack of commitment to educational excellence, the growing disparity between conspicuous consumption for some and conspicuous poverty for others, and the loss of hope and talent due to discrimination and drugs among far too many.

Even more, many contemporary forms of theology — fideist, fundamentalist, and liberationist — are so alienated from modern science, technology, culture, and especially business that they cannot discern where, in the midst of these sectors of our contemporary life, God is accomplishing something new. And now that the socialist forms of analysis have proven empty, even modern ecumenical thought will have to struggle to provide the framework of meaning, the principles and purposes, necessary to face the new situation.

Any theology able to address the future must reach beyond confessional particularities, exclusive histories, and privileged realms of discourse. In constructing a cosmopolitan social ethics, certain dimensions of theology are more important than others. If theology is only the proclamation of personal sin and redemption, of course, let some continue to preach to their choirs. This message has partial validity, and the old songs replenish the soul. If theology is essentially narrative or metaphor, let others take time to write a novel or a poem. The world needs good ones. If theology is essentially a tradition's confession of faith, still others will want to study their catechisms. People ought to know what their communities believe. And if theology is primarily the reflected experience of some particular gender or race or support group, let them serve the needs of their sectarian enclaves. This, too, is a valid ministry.

But a theology adequate to the cosmopolitan challenges that await us must have another dimension as well: it must develop a social ethic for the emerging world in which democracy, human rights, and a mixed economy are acknowledged as universal necessities. It must address a world linked by technology, trade, and a host of new interdependencies.

This agenda for Christian thought requires a "public theology," a way of speaking about the reality of God and God's will for the world that is intellectually valid in the marketplace of ideas and morally effective in the marketplace of goods and services.

Of course, there are some aspects of Christianity that stand as perennial constraints on every effort of this kind. On the one hand, the Bible knows no economic blueprint. Further, it tells us that to take economic matters too seriously is to miss the point of the lilies of the field, to decline the invitation to the banquet, to turn away sadly, indeed, to worship mammon. This prevents all Christians from identifying any economic system with the kingdom of God.

On the other hand, the Bible also calls us to be responsible stewards — not only of our talents and personal possessions but of all that is the Lord's until he returns. We are to labor in the vineyards of the world — even when the vineyards reach around the globe in new patterns of corporate capitalism.

We dare not shrink from this task. We cannot say that the new economy now taking shape globally is without theological roots. Nor can we say that it needs no theological help. We must not give the impression that Christianity has nothing to offer it other than condemnation. Islam, and for that matter Hinduism, Buddhism, and the host of secular humanisms and neo-pagan spiritualities that seek to capture the soul of our times, should not be allowed to shape the future by default. They need a Christian theological perspective to fulfill them and, where necessary, to correct them.

If we refuse the challenge to which providence has called this generation, we betray the gospel. Any pastor who does not preach on these matters, any congregation that does not study them, any seminary that does not teach about them, or any baptized Christian who does not pray about them with a depth that can overcome old ideologies and alter common practices denies that God is Lord over all of creation and history.

What issues, then, are central to this challenge?

1. The Stewardship of Capital

Vast amounts of capital are necessary for the twenty-first century. We must invest in research and development, in new equipment for robotic production, in the development of nonfossil fuels and biotechnology, and in the training of a highly skilled workforce. Failure to capitalize means not only economic stagnation but environmental destruction, unemployment, wider hunger, and further homelessness. The undercapitalization that results from policies directed against economic growth inevitably compounds social injustice. The challenge is to capitalize in ways that reflect our responsibilities as faithful stewards. How ought we do it?

Precisely because capitalization by state fiat under socialism has failed to promote economic development and has worsened most of the evils it intended to correct, contemporary Christians must think more deeply about the morality of profits in a world oriented toward markets, corporations, and global competition. Creating wealth is the whole point of economic activity, as known to folk wisdom: "If your output is less than your intake, your upkeep is your downfall." What is true of the body's energy level and the family budget is true of every economic effort.

If profits are made by honorable means, we must recognize that working to serve people's needs in the marketplace may be a holy vocation in and for the salvation of the world. We are bound therefore to help businesspeople discover how to exercise this vocation with due respect for employees, customers, and suppliers. Further, public theology must insist upon a regard for the larger social and natural environment. In these ways, the disciplined pursuit of profits within a responsible strategy of capitalization can be a modern form of stewardship — one finding much precedent in the biblical record.

Constructing a Global Public Theology

Indeed, a new form of Christian mission today emerges precisely at this point. Converting hearts to God through the grace of Christ is paramount, of course. But outward and material signs of this grace are required. If we care for people's material conditions, the churches should send out to the poorer regions people who can teach others how to develop their own resources — how to form corporations and manage them, how to find markets, how to develop technology, how to work with employees, and how to make profits for the common good.

Enhancing the capacity for capitalization in responsible corporations is as much the new name for mission as development is the new name for peace.

2. The Covenant for Corporations

The corporation has already become the social form distinctive of every co-operative human activity outside the family, the government, and personal friendships. It is historically based on the patterns of association worked out by the church beyond tribe, patriarchy, and nation. The modern business corporation could become a worldly ecclesia no less than hospitals, unions, parties, schools, voluntary organizations, and cultural institutions, virtually all of which are incorporated.

Further, the business corporation has, as much as any other institution, leaped cultural and social boundaries and broken down the walls that divide people. It has found a home in societies far from its roots. Where the opportunities to form corporations are constricted or the skills to sustain them are absent, people remain in an underdeveloped condition. Societies stagnate and people die for want of the ability to form corporations.

Businesses need all the spiritual and moral guidance they can get. The financial environment is in constant flux. Accountability to investors requires a devotion to efficiency that may threaten other principles and goals of covenantal association. Moreover, businesses increasingly operate in a context of global competition. Comparative advantages can make selling out, closing down, or moving to other lands imperative. The failure to move is in some cases a manifestation of a misplaced patriotism, and may fail to aid underdeveloped regions.

Further, such pressures put corporations in a moral bind. On the one hand, the corporations that focus most directly on short-term, bottom-line considerations are those least able to sustain the loyalty of their employees and the trust of the communities they serve. On the other hand, those that spend the most resources on benefits, promote community service, and encourage the personal and social development of their employees are often least equipped to defend themselves against hostile corporate takeovers. For them, liquidation can bring a greater immediate return than quarterly performance. For businesspeople to resign themselves to either alternative, and for the church not to address such questions, is to fall short of the covenantal implications of public theology in corporate life.

If the modern business corporation is to fulfill its calling as a secular form of covenantal community, Christian leaders must assist businesspeople to understand the fateful choice between building an association of interdependent persons seeking to produce goods and services that benefit the commonwealth, and being reduced to an instrument with interchangeable parts, seeking maximum immediate advantage.

If public theology can help us overcome our contempt for corporations as mere money machines, then Christians can begin to articulate what we expect of these institutions. We can even learn to love them as we have learned to love our churches, neighborhoods, nations, schools, and hospitals — although we must not be tempted to seek from them the loves that are proper to other relationships.

We can demand moral responses from them, put a decent measure of loyalty and trust in them, be alert to the strong possibility of sin within them, judge them, forgive them, and convert them when we find them snared in corrigible error. Further, we can encourage church people to work in them and find their callings there, precisely because they may discover valid moral principles already operative there.

While rejecting as both false and unjust the view of the corporation as an inhuman piece of organizational machinery, public theology also must be aware of the limits of this form of covenantal community. Corporations become idols when we become married to firms, when our loyalty is to them only, when we bend all politics to their service, when their distinctive modes of operation get confused with the ideals that must govern healthcare, education, and culture. Corporations become idols, in short, when we think that they can bring salvation to human life.

The question of limits, however, is not simply one of public ecclesiology. The modern business corporation is not only a voluntary association but an economic institution designed to achieve a degree of control over markets. To the extent that corporations are successful, markets cannot be relied upon exclusively to control corporations. The voice of labor, the demands of government, the rule of law must also be developed.

Furthermore, dramatic increases in corporate mastery of the latest advances in technology enormously enhance any industry's capacity to have a decisive impact on its environment, both culturally and ecologically. While affirming the corporation as a covenantal community, a public theology fully resonant with our emerging world will have to collaborate in developing new systems of public accountability to ensure that corporations respect God's gift of creation.

3. The Vocation of Management

Business managers have not yet become members of a genuine profession in the ways that clergy, teachers, doctors, lawyers, and architects have. There were many reasons for this in the past. They are less valid now, and will become increasingly less so. Managers, no doubt, are already professionals in the way that baseball players, rock stars, and talk-show hosts are: they are experts at what they do, they work at it full time, and they make big bucks. And many do what they do with personal standards of integrity at least as high as those of the clergy. But management itself has not yet developed the rich texture of public responsibility that emerged from the sense of "high" calling historically characteristic of the traditional professions.

In the emerging world of global economic interdependence, management can and should be professionalized. Christians should come to regard it as an honorable and specialized ministry of the laity. If we can no longer dismiss corporations as inhuman machines, we must also confess that it is false and unjust to categorize managers only as bosses. A public theology that is open to the experiences of those who exercise responsibility in modern business corporations will soon discover that managers have more in common with community organizers, pastors, and teachers than they do with impersonal systems of mechanical control. Granted, they must measure performance, both personal and corporate, by standards that aspire to objectivity; but ultimately so must all those who genuinely empower others. There is no longer any reason to deny the holiness of a vocation to business management.

4. A Public Theology for a Global Civilization

Capitalization and profits, the corporation as a covenanting community and worldly ecclesia, the professionalization of management and technology? As theological topics? Yes. These are key examples of a public theology that respects the ordering principles of Trinitarian thought, with its fundamental commitment to the inclusive community of persons and its dynamic reconception of the biblical message in nonbiblical social and intellectual environments. In a post-socialist world, these are among the decisive areas where the righteous sovereignty of God, the sacrificial presence of Jesus Christ, and the dynamic novelty of the Holy Spirit must become concrete.

Such topics are at least as important for the human future as today's theologies of sexuality, literary criticism, and biomedical ethics. The biblical and doctrinal, the ethical and interpretive resources of the ecumenically open traditions have more to offer this new world than we have yet seen. To rediscover these resources is the first requirement for those Protestant and Catholic communities of faith that hope to speak socially and ethically to the momentous changes of our times.

Christians of the world, awake! Now that the specter of communism has vanished, cast off the spell of economic dogmatism! There is nothing to lose but ideology and irrelevance.

The Moral Roots of the Corporation

As the Christianization of the Germanic tribes recentered civilization from the Mediterranean to Europe, as the triumph of canon law transformed the jurisprudence of modernity,[1] as the Cromwellian and later the French revolutions established modern constitutional democracy and then secularized it, and as the idea that nature is fallen and must be transformed to be fulfilled brought waves of industrial revolutions and lifted peasants from drudgery to cybernetics, we are in the midst of an economic turning point in history. I do not mean only the collapse of Communism, although that is obvious and important. I mean the fundamental transformation of social organization that has taken place in the last century: the corporation is no longer only the instrument of production and distribution; it has become the governing social form of our period. Nearly everything is organized as a corporation — educational institutions, hospitals, law firms, missionary societies, political parties, and unions. All have to remain solvent, but some are given over to the explicit purpose of increasing wealth, the chief purpose of the economic corporation.

To be sure, various forms of partnerships and firms have been present in society for centuries; but the triumph of this mode of association is a novum. The corporation, unlike family or regime or language or even religion, is not a "natural" institution. It cannot be found in every society. Some economic or-

---

1. I am persuaded of this by Harold J. Berman's monumental *Law and Revolution: The Formation of the Western Legal Tradition* (Cambridge, MA: Harvard University Press, 1983).

This article is based on research done in cooperation with Dennis McCann of DePaul University, Shirley Roels of Calvin College, and Preston Williams of Harvard Divinity School. See *On Moral Business: Classical and Contemporary Resources for Ethics in Economic Life* (Grand Rapids: Eerdmans, 1995).

ganization is always present for production, distribution, and consumption. The modern corporation as a distinct institution for production and distribution is a striking exception in the array of possibilities. Where it appears, it displaces and reorders those "natural" institutions that, in most societies and most of history, are seen as the centers of moral formation and loyalty as well as the primary centers of production, distribution, and consumption. Indeed, the corporation has been identified by some social commentators as the force destroying the moral fabric of the family, corrupting politics, disrupting genuine communication, and commercializing religion. On the one hand, it is accused of destroying family farms, moving people around with little regard for spouses and kids, and invading the household through media images; and on the other, it buys politicians, seeks profits over the common good, and corrupts the political sovereignty of smaller nations. Some see the corporation as the reincarnation in our day of Baal's altar or Mammon's temple, corroding every relationship and piety.

Yet, the household, following the decline of the clan, the manor, and the family farm and family firm, cannot be said to be the center of economic organization of the future. Certainly, the survival of the household in an age of dual-career families is a matter of considerable importance, in part because the nurture of a responsible next generation has always been indispensable to the future. Contemporary confusions about sex and roles, indeed about the nature and character of love, are rampant; we simply do not know how we are going to organize the family in the future. In any case, the household is unlikely to become again the decisive economic unit in society.[2]

Further, the state is unlikely to be the chief instrument of capitalization or the primary engine and organizer of the economy, both because centrally planned economies have proven to be such miserable failures and because contemporary economic systems have outgrown all national methods of control. To be sure, the state will still play a role in shaping aspects of economic life, but it appears that regimes will be evaluated on whether they can create the conditions wherein viable transnational corporations can flourish.

Nor is it simply enough to study the market as the chief characteristic of our society, although that is the arena in which corporations act. The market, however, is an impersonal mechanism that reflects the conscious decisions

---

2. It is possible that distinct examples of household-based economies may persist for some time in parts of Asia and the Hispanic world — as we see in the quasi-feudal "Samurai corporations" of Japan, the "*jati* cooperatives" of South India, and "Hacienda subsidiaries" in former Iberian colonies.

of myriads of actors, and the greatest degree of coordinated, integrated action today is found in the corporation. We should talk less about a market economy and more about a corporate economy, simply to call attention to that with which we wrestle. It now seems clearer than it did a decade ago that economies fail if one cannot predict the price of things or people's desire for them, and that a market is necessary to both of these; and it now is evident how devastating to the human spirit and to ecological health, as well as to the economy, was the state control of individualism and initiative in Eastern Europe. But the chief economic agent today is less the individual, state, or market than the corporation. It is as if corporations are a newly discovered "order of creation," or at least a new invention that has become so much a part of the "second nature" of modern civilization that we cannot imagine a modern economy without them. Workers want them even when they resent them; politicians, even if their rhetoric opposes them, compete to get them in their territory; law allows them as it seeks to control them; economic well-being demands them; peoples without them remain undeveloped; those who do not know how to form and, in certain ways, conform to them stay poor; and those who cannot sustain them go broke.[3]

Such a description is not a matter of praise. It is an attempt to identify what the actualities of our situation are. The problem is that we do not quite know how to assess what we have ethically. Elders around the world, including clergy and professors and journalists and politicians, suspect that it is a conspiracy of greed. Nobody really loves it, and forms of inflated corporate enthusiasm seem corny and contrived when they are not psychic manipulation to control the souls as well as the bodies of the workers, or manifestations of the totemic cults of those who have given their lives over to Mammon. The enthusiastic singing of the company song to start the workday, as we hear about in some Japanese firms, seems comical, even if we decry the loss of modern corporate loyalty in America. Few believe that this *persona ficta* has a spirit, and yet it is not simply a piece of organizational machinery. The corporation only works when there is something like an *esprit de corps* with a distinctive culture and character. It is a moral as well as an institutional reality. If there is no spirit, culture, or character in a social institution, people leave or psychically drop out.[4]

---

3. Recent writers on the new economic situation who draw on several fields include Peter Berger, *The Capitalist Revolution* (New York: Basic Books, 1986), Robert Reich, *The Work of Nations* (New York: A. A. Knopf, 1991), and J. W. Kuhn and D. W. Shriver Jr., *Beyond Success: Corporations and Their Critics in the 1990s* (New York: Oxford University Press, 1991).

4. I developed this particular argument in *Public Theology and Political Economy* (Lan-

To inquire further into the nature of this institutional form demands recognition of the fact that the corporation has arisen in the context of a distinct "ethos," that is, from an operating web of values — expectations, principles, rewards, punishments, and operating norms that have been built into the common life over long historical periods. And in this specific area of human life, religion has played a much greater role than is commonly thought.[5] Indeed, if the many factors that have influenced the development of the corporation are not pushed to their religious roots, we are unlikely either to discern the actual shape of the ethos or to transcend it sufficiently to reshape it and guide its future.

Why We Live as We Live

If we inquire into the transformations that brought us the modern corporation, we will not be surprised to find that the most serious decisions about business are precisely those that expose the religious roots and evoke the question of what to preserve and what to leave behind.

At the most basic level, the deepest roots of the corporation are in the synagogues and burial or mystery cults that set the organizational models the early Christians took over, modified, and turned into the church. These are the institutions that established a range of organizational activity outside the family and the state as centers of meaning. Before that, and in most of the world even today, the two centers of organization mentioned above — family (which means, in most historic cultures, kinship organizations such as clan, tribe, and caste) and government (royal, imperial, republican, or democratic) — tend to control both economics and religion. The household is the center of production and consumption, as well as of initiation and religious nurture. The regime is the center of allocation of all other resources — most frequently land or water; often of mining and metallurgy; sometimes of shipping and international trade;

---

ham, MD: University Press of America, 1991), ch. 7. I found, in a recent trip to the former German Democratic Republic, that this is one of the major reasons for the downfall of that regime. See my "White Candles vs. Red Flags: Religion and the Fall of the Berlin Wall," *Occasional Papers on Religion in Eastern Europe* 12, no. 5 (October 1, 1992): 1-18.

5. On this point, I commend the new work by Robert H. Nelson, *Reaching for Heaven on Earth: The Theological Meaning of Economics* (Savage, MD: Rowman & Littlefield, 1991). He argues that the main disputes in economic theory are secularized forms of the debate between Roman and Protestant versions of Christianity, even among those not personally interested in religious issues or acquainted with theology.

Constructing a Global Public Theology

and always of taxes to provide defense and common improvements, such as dams, bridges, and roads. The regime is nearly always also the center of a cultus, either because it establishes a religion or claims divinity for its own powers. Not infrequently, household and regime were combined, as we see in all dynasties and patriarchies east and west, ancient and modern.

But the formation of the synagogue, the mystery cult, and then the church altered that. They claimed the right to have an organization outside either family or state connections, in part because they dealt with another world. Persons could join, whatever their birth or citizenship or, for that matter, mother-tongue. Baptism is distinct from these. The church drew into itself, of course, many outsiders — not because they were necessarily the poor and the oppressed, as the Liberationists claim, but because people saw a higher purpose in life, one that could bring, indeed, a fresh moral and spiritual content to the whole of life, to the familial and political, that is, to all cultural and economic existence. Because the church was held to be more holy than either family or regime, it rejected the authority of both to determine people's most important memberships. That fact did not go unnoticed, and the official reason for the persecution of the early church by the early emperors was that it had no legal right to exist. The church formed an organization that was neither identical with nor approved by "gene-pool identity" or "political governance." The members here lived under a "covenant," a *"testamentum,"* that was autocephalic and understood itself to be the "corpus Christi" (who never married or aspired to political domination). For the first time in human history, an enduring model of a third center of organization, what today sociologists call "voluntary associations" or, less elegantly, "NGOs" (non-governmental organizations), was formed.

To be sure, the church itself was not fully aware of what it was creating civilizationally, and no few of the church fathers also wanted the true "household of God" and "kingdom of Christ" to be guided by due regard for household and regime. Others wanted to turn it the other way around, with household and regime controlled by the church. Sex and power as well as wealth were at stake, and a full consensus as to how these were related to holiness was not at hand. Tensions mounted. Finally, the orders, and eventually also their hospitals and schools, managed to secure a right to exist by denying connections with the family (through celibacy) and with the state (by obedience to religious authority only) and promising to ignore wealth (in taking the vow of poverty). The deepest roots of the corporation are here; although they did not arise smoothly or evenly in all parts of Christianity, and the nature and character of these relations remain in dispute within Christianity.

Further, even where the church did gain a degree of relative sovereignty for an independent sector in society, there was great suspicion of property and wealth. These were considered to be corrupting influences, for outside of family and regime, they, like sex and power, distorted values. That presumption, of course, was dominant in most of the world religions: lower, material interests must be controlled by higher forces, and we become more spiritual the less we concern ourselves with filthy lucre — a sentiment shared still by no few Hindu sadhus, Buddhist monks, Islamic Sufis, and Confucian sages. In Christianity, even where the relative independence of some communities was affirmed, we find also a powerful sentiment against commerce and trade.[6]

But these matters remained unsettled. A recent translation by Br. Allan Wolter of *Duns Scotus' Political and Economic Philosophy* reveals that this famous Franciscan took up one of the most disputed questions of economic history in the early 1300s, namely, whether Christianity could approve the idea of private property, and specifically of private groups holding property.[7] Scotus argued that the distinction between "mine" and "thine" was necessary in a world afflicted by the Fall, for one had to have a system of accountability for things; but property was best administered under agreements based on reasonable principles. Contract law that formed communities of accountability, we might say, made property morally acceptable.

Of course, the idea that property is personal yet best administered in a communal mode by agreements under law is an idea that had to win its way. In much of history and many parts of the world, property is communal — that is, controlled by leading families or the state, or to put it more baldly, by patriarchal violence. That still happens, but that is not all that happens, and modern business life could not have developed if that were all. This is a historic dividing line between those traditions that led to such organizations as the Mafia (which have very deep historical roots and which can be found in most cultures) and those that led to the corporation. Scotus anticipated what we find in the Jesuit Suarez, the Lutheran Puffendorf, the Calvinist Althusius, and became most familiar to modernity in the Puritan Locke and the Pietist Kant: economic life can only flourish when all are under an accountability system that includes clear understandings of what is "mine" and what is "thine," with duties to the neighbor. Complain as we might about living in

---

6. Lester K. Little, *Religious Poverty and the Profit Economy* in *Medieval Europe* (Ithaca, NY: Cornell University Press, 1978), pp. 35ff.

7. John Duns Scotus and Allan Bernard Wolter, *John Duns Scotus' Political and Economic Philosophy* (Santa Barbara, CA: Old Mission Santa Barbara, 1989).

a litigious culture, economic development may not be possible unless a fabric of law is developed.

Private property, corporate management, and common law are not, however, the only great forces defining the modern ethos. It is very much an ethos defined by time, by schedules, by punctuality, and by a disciplined attitude toward the organization of tempo and sequence, with regular and predictable rhythms to each day and week. Indeed, business depends on a social psychology of time. Business people are busy; they constantly check their watches; idleness is shameful. If they do not punch in and out on the time-clock, they get to work "on time" and know what it means to "quit early" or to "work late" (either one, too often, induces guilt and indicates that something is wrong). The first mark of responsibility is being where one is supposed to be when one is supposed to be there.

In cross-cultural encounters, those from more-developed economies and those from less-developed ones are frequently struck by different cultural senses of time. For some, life is ordered by this sense of punctuality, planning, and appointments that is identified with responsibility. Daily tasks (even for the young) are organized into scheduled units, each with its programmed number of minutes or hours. For others, life is measured by seasons or the moon or the sun. Life, after all, in this view, is not about scurrying to meet the demands of production or efficiency or date-books or calendars. Being is more important than doing. Time is the sea in which we swim, not the master of our days nor the servant of some higher meaning.

Every culture, of course, has had its own way of reckoning time. But the motivations for doing this vary. One reason for trying to calculate the movements of the stars or the changing of the seasons was so that the human community could more easily fit into the natural and cosmic rhythms. This motivation contrasts with the effort to divide the time in such a way that humans could all the better control nature and transcend the cosmic forces in action for spiritual and moral reasons.

The idea that the efficient use of time is an ethical and theological matter and thus decisive in the basic pattern of the good life had to be developed, as much as did a sense of private property guided by reasonable and agreed-upon communal principles of justice. It reflects a certain orientation toward meaning, God, and the world. Such a notion is important only where people believe that the timeless and eternal is in some basic way related to the proximate, the temporal, and transient, and that we humans ought, therefore, to order the latter for the sake of the former.

In a major book on this subject, Harvard historian David Landes traces

The Moral Roots of the Corporation

the development of time-keeping devices in cultures where they were most extensively developed — China and Europe. In China, the purpose was to discern the fitting times for aligning social and cultic life with cosmological events. In Europe, the time technology in the Christian monastery reflected the attempt not to fit into the cosmos, but to triumph over the fallenness of the world and the temptations of the flesh. Landes shows not only the intimate connection between a pre-Protestant sense of the relation of discipline to time and the technology of clocks, but also the way in which that informed the commercial world and began to make post-agricultural senses of "non-natural" time decisive for production. In the process, the theological grounding of the sense of temporal discipline was lost, and the economic advantage of precisely timed speed — now symbolized by the nanoseconds of advanced computer programs — influences how we conduct business.[8]

Still other dimensions of the formation of the ethos of modern corporations are revealed to us by Max Weber. I will not, here, turn again to debate about the much-misunderstood *The Protestant Ethic and the Spirit of Capitalism*. On the whole, however, it is increasingly clear that those social analysts who recognized that Weber's argument is essentially about the power of religion as an independent variable in the formation of modern social history, and not about the differences between socialism and capitalism, have proven to be more accurate predictors of historic developments than those interpreters who ignored his writings and turned to Feuerbach, Marx, and the host of secular reductionists who see religion as the result of "real" social and economic forces.[9]

I shall, however, draw attention to a neglected section of Weber's work that may well be as fateful for the modern ethos and corporation life as the work ethic. This development followed historically well after the newer definitions of property, and the formation of the time consciousness of the monasteries, if well before the asceticism of the Reformation period. In his famous work on "The City," Weber argued that pre-Reformation forms of Christian-

---

8. David Landes, "Of Time, Work, and Prayer," an excerpt from *Revolution in Time* (Cambridge, MA: Harvard University Press, 1983), pp. 58-78.

9. See, for example, Ehrhart Neubert's "Die Revolution der Protestanten," in *Nach der Wende*, ed. R. Schulze (Berlin: Wichern-Verlag, 1990), pp. 23-50, which suggests that Weber is the only major social theorist whose categories are able to grasp the complexity of developments in East Germany; David Martin's study of recent developments in Latin America, *Tongues Afire* (London: Blackwell, 1990); and a parallel study in India by L. Caplan, *New Religious Movements in South India* (Madras: SCM Press, 1991).

ity decisively influenced the development of modern economic life.[10] The city is where new middle classes arise that are neither nobility nor peasantry. It is where fixed "stations in life" are left behind as new occupations are created, and the opportunity to form new, self-governing associations blossom. It is where business is most fully developed, where factories, labor pools, administrative offices, educational resources, technological skills, financial institutions, and communication centers are born. The city is the model of civilization. If cities are alive, business and culture flourish; if cities die, they fail.

What, then, is the organizing principle of the city? What has to be maintained? What has to be transferred to or evoked from new people when they come to the city? Although the cities are ever plagued by poverty, homelessness, crime, and despair, people see in the city chances for riches, a place for decency and hope — compared to other options. What, in short, is at the core of the city that prevents it from becoming *only* "concrete jungle" or a crossroads for warring clans, or a highly organized set of mutual exploitations (although these exist in every city)? Weber, in his characteristic if awkward way of thinking about such questions, sorts through the several possible definitions that people have in their minds when they speak of "the city." Then he draws on his vast cross-cultural studies to test the idea. Is it a high-density area? Yes, but some rural areas have higher density. Is it a political-military center, a fortress or garrison? Often, but some are not cities and some cities are not those. Is it a market? Usually, but one formed where definitions of community and citizenship have developed, where ethnic, occupational, and status differences, although always present, are not sanctified.

The city, Weber argues, is rooted in a kind of fellowship that was formed by the "secular" appropriation of egalitarian principles communicated by the mass. Historically, it was the religious service, specifically the mass where people ate and drank together, that formed the sense of fellowship. Where that is not present, the city, and the civilization, reverts to tribal, feudal, or garrison centers of high density and much exploitation. Legal definitions of citizen membership, mutual responsibility, and civil rights grew out of such soil — but it is not clear whether they can be sustained without such rootage.

It is said that in-group/out-group relations are best seen at table, in bed, and at work — with whom one feasts, marries, and does business. Christian Communion destroyed pagan legitimations of food and marriage barriers between the peoples and the levels of feudal society, if Weber is correct, and

---

10. The only decent translation is in Max Weber, *Economy and Society*, vol. 3, trans. E. Fischoff et al. (Totowa, NJ: Bedminster, 1968).

this created the preconditions for modernization; but it also heightened barriers between Christians and non-Christians, especially Jews.

It may be difficult for some today to imagine what it means to live in an environment in which every relationship is defined by ethnicity and inherited social status. Today's resurgence of consciousness of ethnicity and tribalism has something frightening about it where it is not merely pathetic; but many human groups in history and much of the world today still believe that racism, sexism, nationalism, and "classism" are moral duties. Battles about the "other" remain. Economic interests but also "natural orders" and "our gods (or culture)" are thought to be at issue.

One area where a number of these tensions are visible, and where a transformation fateful for business was made, is "usury." The battles — religious, moral, and social — that were fought around it are not over and have to be fought in new terms, it seems, in every generation. But in his chief legacy to our understanding of the modern world, Benjamin Nelson, longtime editor of the *Psychoanalytic Review*, traces how a particular biblical text prohibiting usury among members of "one's own kind" was applied over the centuries — until a theological shift altered the idea of communal "brotherhood,"[11] and legitimated the use of credit with moderate interest. In effect, this shift made every "other" a brother or sister in moral terms, and every brother and sister an "other" in business relationships. A banker ought to exercise fiduciary responsibility in regard to the resources of each customer, and ought not give special rates to those to whom she or he is related. A business should trade with all who will do so peacefully, and should not discriminate racially. These are ideas that had to be established in long and painful battles.

Nelson's analysis is closely related to two other issues, one more philosophical and one more ethical. The first is the notion that money, as a social artifact, is not "fecund," as Aristotle, Thomas, and Martin Luther along with most of the premodern world argued, and as we still find in much of the Islamic world. In its broadest implications, the issue is whether what is moral is what is natural, and whether making money from "artificial exchange" should be viewed as "unnatural" and thus as immoral. If it is "unnatural," banking and finance will be assigned to those who are only allowed to be marginal to the society.

A related issue is the fact that, for much of history and in parts of the world still, no distinction was made between "interest" and "usury." Stan-

---

11. Benjamin Nelson, *The Idea of Usury: From Tribal Brotherhood to Universal Otherhood* (Princeton: Princeton University Press, 1949).

dards of "just price" and practices of "fixed price" for any goods and services, including money-lending, were not well established. High rates meant inability to pay, and debt meant perpetual servitude. Both creditors and debtors were reviled on all sides. Nelson shows how modern business practice, with its distinction between these two, until quite recently depended on a now-forgotten religious change.

One additional study should be mentioned here, for it too points to developments that have decisively shaped the ethos of the contemporary corporation. In a most intriguing study, Colin Campbell has asked how it happens that many of the great changes that brought about the modern economic ethos had to do with discipline and production. Yet the face it presents is one of consumption. In *The Romantic Ethic and the Spirit of Modern Consumerism*,[12] he traces how the romantic era, with its close attentiveness to feeling, to the inner experience of felt-need and impulse, was paralleled and spread by Evangelical movements that indicated that salvation and all questions of heaven and hell depended on the question of personal experience of Christ. It too focused all attention on the inner sentiments, with the implicit notion that failure to heed the deep inner voice — beyond law, beyond book, beyond doctrine, beyond church, beyond any external authority — would lead one to unauthentic commitment. When the transcendent reference and salvific urgency of the revival is past, the emphasis on personal experience quickly fades into the romantic need to meet one's innermost, felt needs. The worst thing one could do was to repress an inner impulse that might be authentic. Campbell traces the convolutions this motif takes as it was grasped and cultivated by advertising, which not only teaches people what is available, but what to want and what to need.

What I have surveyed here is, obviously, not the whole of the complex of forces that have shaped the modern corporation, but rather a selection of historic themes that have decisively shaped what we have that are either neglected or under dispute today. What are we to make of these? If it is true that these are among the critical historic, social, and religious forces that have produced our high-performance, high-tech, high-consumption, complex business world of the corporation, what shall we do with these deep structures in our ethos? No small number of people have lost contact with the deep theological principles that guided the developments of these institutions. Many more are convinced that since the Enlightenment, theological principles are not needed.

---

12. Colin Campbell, *The Romantic Ethic and the Spirit of Modern Consumerism* (New York: Blackwell, 1987).

What Are We Living For?

We have been told, for some two hundred years by "serious" intellectuals, that everything other than theology is at the center of social change, for religious faith was privatized or treated as a poeticized expression of pre-scientific opinion. But whether we want to affirm or to transform the civilizational patterns we have now and the ethos on which they rest, we must inquire again as to the nature of this inner guidance system and evaluate its adequacy. And for this, there is no enduring and profound way to proceed than to raise again the theological questions out of which these developments were birthed.

It is not possible here to resolve the issues on each of the fronts that have been touched. Yet, it should be clear that the moral core of the corporation, and of the ethos that produced it, is derived from profound theological-historical roots — roots that if not recovered and recast for our times will leave our civilization adrift. Religion and business, church and firm, ethic and economics, spirituality and materiality, the gospel and the ethos of corporative civilization are not the same; but one is the necessary foundation for the other, and the other can embody some values of the one and thereby become an agent in salvation, or at least a sign of grace.

It is my conviction that the great Catholic and Protestant traditions already have this insight deep in their traditions — although they have squandered parts of it in recent years. It is also my conviction that neo-evangelical, fundamentalist, neoconservative movements grasp (often, I think, on inadequate grounds) the fact that modern models of economic life, with which many ecumenical and "liberal" theologians operate, are neither profound nor accurate. In many ways, theologians and ethicists who attempt to address the public issues of our day are challenged to come clean about the role of religion in the fabric of modernity and postmodernity.

What then is the moral core of the corporation? It is not in economics, nor alone in the relative efficiencies it can introduce. It is in the ethos, and it appears in the practices of many who live according to the deepest principles already incarnate in business. But these practices themselves are framed by theological and social forces that are extrinsic and prior to business. The guidance of modern economic systems, the renewal of our political economy, the moral fabric of the twenty-first century toward which we are limping and lurching will depend in substantial measure on whether we can grasp and refresh the theological foundations on which the ethos and these practices rest — especially since they have now become nearly universal in secular form, without consciousness of their moral and spiritual roots. Without this consciousness, the roots dry up; Baal triumphs and Mammon wins — at least for a moment. But with this guidance, the moral and spiritual foundations for moral business practice can become self-conscious and thereby self-critical and self-reconstructive once more, to the glory of God.

Spheres of Management:
Social, Ethical, and Theological Reflections

For the most part, we live in a democracy. The constitution of the United States, and of more than 150 other countries around the world, calls for those patterns of political order that we today identify by this term: regular popular elections of representatives to various legislative, executive, and some judicial positions; rule by the majority, as constrained by laws that guarantee rights and liberties to all; and opportunity for the organization of associations — churches, parties, businesses, unions, and so on — independent of the ruling party or the state. This is not, of course, the democracy of the elites imagined by the ancient Greeks, nor is it the populist democracy of the masses, *à la* French Revolutionary attempt to form an egalitarian solidarity based only on "the will of the people" — a motif that led in one case to Napoleon and in another (as adopted by Marx) to Stalin. "Democracy," in the usual sense, is a way of forming a limited authority with power to govern some areas of the common life.

Its roots lie in the biblical idea of covenantal order, where people and rulers are called to live under moral law for moral ends that they discern, not construct. Democracy recognizes both the dignity of the individual person, for each is made in the image of God, as well as the tendency of all to distort that dignity (thus a system of social checks and balances is needed). Still, it recognizes that humans, if inspired by the deep sources of moral insight and the use of reason, can form viable, community-serving associations in a civil society.

In our contemporary ethos, the various associations and organizations that make up civil society, however, are only in an indirect sense democratic. Most of them are, in fact, managed. Democracy lets them be; but it does not rule them. If anything, a democratic political order is formed by them and lets them inform it. Much of society, as a complex of associations, organizations, and interest groups, is managed by a leadership that is not elected and is only indirectly governed by the constitution. This is somewhat true of governmental bureaucracies; it is truer of the non-governmental organizations of civil society. Nowhere is this clearer than in the area of the economy; but the issue is much broader. Most of the institutions that constitute the fabric of daily life — families, schools, local businesses, corporations, hospitals, media, and religious organizations — are managed by authorities with whom we may choose to work, but whom we do not usually elect. Moreover, the internal patterns of governance in these institutions are rarely democratic, and the theological or ethical principles by which they are ordered are seldom articulated. Indeed, some want to keep everything theological centered in the church and its internal narrative, while others are simply unaware of the depth of the theological, ethical, and cultural principles, values, or virtues that are at stake in the managed world of civil life, although the nature and character of these social institutions have all been deeply shaped by the theological tradition and are laden with implicit theological motifs. This essay offers interpretive reflections on issues of management in a globalizing, capitalist era.

Political Management

What we say in regard to the ethos of our local communities is increasingly true in other venues as well, with the emergence of a worldwide civilization, one of the greatest events of our times. We do not yet know whether the world's only remaining superpower will use its power to become, by policy or default, a new imperial power, recolonizing the world in an arrogant and exploitative way or, instead, to become the agent of a new *Pax Humanitatis*, following in the train of the *Pax Romana*, the Germanic Holy Roman Empire, and the more recent British Empire, all of which established a semblance of international peace over several centuries, allowed several cultures to flourish, supported the arts and the sciences, encouraged the spread of Christianity, fostered dramatic changes in healthcare, education, human rights, and economic development, and encouraged new definitions of the nature of freedom and justice — by management more than by democracy.

Most Americans, however, do not seek to become an empire managing the world — either solo or in a coalition with close allies, unless it is for a short term and aids in the formation of a free society with a democratic polity. If anything, we are a nation that resists imperial designs. Yet many around the world believe that there was no basic reason for the war with Iraq other than an economically driven, neo-imperialist desire to control the vast oil reserves of the Middle East. And, surely, control of the oil reserves is a matter of great interest both to the people in and beyond that region. If the price of oil were to double or triple at the hand of some regional autocrat, the great world economies of the G-8 nations and of the greatest global population centers — China, India, Indonesia, and Brazil — would falter dramatically. Millions, even billions of those around the world already living in marginal conditions would be plunged into worse suffering. Thus, it may be good for the world's economic development that a "regime change" in Iraq took place, even if that is not one of the reasons given for the conflict and would not have been accepted as a good one at the time had it been offered. Still, plans for the use of revenues from oil to rebuild the country and to form a new infrastructure for the region by keeping international industries supplied with a low-cost energy source seem reasonable. But who is to manage this effort and on what basis? A nationalized Iraqi oil industry would replicate the Baathist design; a program run by Americans would reinforce perceptions of neo-imperialism; and the formation of a new, independent oil company would force a host of decisions about how to order it, what kinds of principles would, should, or could guide its management, and how it would relate to either the existing oil cartel or other oil companies.

These issues of management are not easily addressed, and it would not be too far afield to argue that our democratic values are being challenged by neo-imperialist temptations and the problem of oil as a needed world resource. These issues do not come to us naked, of course. Interests may prompt actions, but interests alone do not legitimate them. Everyone wants to have some assurance that the interests are legitimate morally. Thus, there are other issues at stake in the imperial temptation, including the "clash of civilizations" and, less overtly but more powerfully, the clash of religions that have formed and legitimated competing patterns of social life. Few of the dominant patterns in the Middle East are democratic in any formal political sense, and most are suspicious of pluralistic institutions in a complex civil society that is distinct from theocratic control and is so on theological grounds. Issues of polity in economic life were central, of course, to world events in the clash of socialist and capitalist systems; but they were not finally resolved by the demise of socialism as a living option. They appear again when we ask how a world resource is to be administered in a context where Islamic and Christian understandings of a just society are unlikely to coincide.

Ecological Management

Closely related to the issue of energy resources and the dependence of the world economy on fossil fuels is the ongoing, even wider debate about how we should manage natural resources more generally, and, indeed, nature itself. It is one thing to manage "the world"; it is another to manage "the earth." Many are plagued by a nagging worry about the environment. Of course, no one is in favor of making life in the world "unsustainable"; but how to manage the biophysical world wisely is not a settled issue. From the protests against the failure of the USA to sign the Kyoto treaty, against the opening of federal lands to drilling and logging, against the marketing of SUVs, and so forth, we can see that a large number of people view degradation of the environment as a direct result of the increasing role of market forces and their managers around the globe. Protesters want somebody to do something to stop it.

Of course, strong arguments can be made that the chief threats to an ecologically viable world are most severe where poor, underdeveloped, and technologically ill-equipped peoples struggle for subsistence and that an open, pluralistic society with a variety of corporations working in a market system overcomes poverty, fosters development, and cleans up its messes more efficiently with less enduring damage to the environment than any other known system. Moreover, people choose this system over every other if given the choice, not only because it is more possible to become rich, but also because the living conditions are better. Still, we must acknowledge that ecological well-being demands increased, not reduced, management of nature in ways that could limit democratic preferences, productivity, and an open-market system.

The conflicts between ecologists and advocates of corporate development are well known. But what is less often noted is the fact that nowhere on earth can we find "nature" as a zone of animal, mineral, and vegetable existence that does not already bear the marks of human intervention. Not only have hunting, gathering, and centuries of agriculture altered the dominant forms of flora and fauna in given areas, but humans also have slashed and burned, bred animals, dug canals, dammed rivers, and killed pests to expand these options — all of which have altered the ecological order, even in the most remote areas. It is, in a sense, our nature to do so. We tend to manage our environments by technological means. The technological developments that have allowed ever-deeper alterations of the systems of nature have also allowed population growth and a corresponding geometric increase in the subjection of the biophysical universe to human designs. Some specialists in industrial ecology now speak of an "anthropogenic world" in which nothing purely natural can be found — or left any more to itself. The earth has to be managed to preserve, restore, enhance, or reconstruct what we have, if we are to have a viable and desirable habitat.

That "nature" is no longer simply natural is already obvious in urban planning, park services, and land management, but it is also the case in "wilderness" areas. We are in an age of the humanization of the biosphere. Humans now define the boundaries of a "natural preserve" — we breed eagles, wolves, and bobcats and introduce them into areas where they have become extinct, so that they will control other species. We now decide how many beaver can dam how many parts of a stream, until some must be captured and moved to new places. We legislate what fishing banks may be trolled or dragged and what salmon runs may be fished and by whom. We plan for the optimum size of an elk, deer, or bison herd to roam in a designated space and when and where they can be fenced in, hunted, harvested, or culled. And we determine which forest fires to let burn and which to extinguish — to preserve "nature" as we think it could work out best for an inhabited biosphere. Troubling as it is to the "deep ecologists" and many "green advocates," nature is already more like a city park than a primeval forest, veldt, or swamp.

This leads us to a second major set of questions. It is not only a question of managing the institutions of a civil society, near at hand or on a world scale, or of finding the principles to manage the world's energy sources; it is an even more cosmic question: Where shall we find the principles and purposes to manage nature, if nature has been, is being, and must be more fully transformed? Many, of course, hold that nature is the source and norm of the right order of things, and that to alter it is to destroy existence itself. Thus, we humans, when we intervene in the given structure of the biophysical order, become the source of destruction. This perspective, however, presumes a two-factor analysis — nature and humanity. But it could be that a three-factor analysis is more accurate. Many, indeed, hold it to be a more profound opinion that God, more than nature and humanity, is the creator of nature and that nature in itself (including humanity) is flawed, threatening, and, while ever re-creating itself, is also ever decaying and self-destroying.

Those who hold this view often also think that humans are made in the image of God in a way that other parts of creation are not. Thus, in principle, they (we) can be drawn into a relationship with God that calls us to become caretakers, stewards, and cultivators of nature, having dominion over it on behalf of those divine laws and purposes that promise salvation from nature's own flaws and threats. If this is a more realistic possibility than the binary thesis about nature and humanity, then certain forms of technological intervention in nature may be seen as a part of the human theological task of being God's stewards of the earth. We are to manage the biophysical world in accord with God's laws and purposes, a mandate that demands considerable theological reflection and moral seriousness.

Managing the Markets

But our perplexity at wanting a democratic society and in fact having an ever-increasingly managed one is not only a matter of the unsettling involvements in war or oil and the lack of clarity about our international role; nor is it only our worries about ecology and the dangers and duties of our technological management of it. We are on the brink of other basic changes in technology that could further increase the need to manage our future. The gains brought by computerization and the cybernation of manufacturing have been digested by many centers of advanced production and distribution. The bubble of dot-com speculation reached its limits of expansion and popped, leaving residual but ambiguous traces. All of this triggered what was called an irrationally "excessive exuberance" by our economic czar, Alan Greenspan, some time ago. Its demise led to an unwarranted pessimism, so far as I can see. But changes brought about by fusion physics could allow the extension of energy resources to fuel further alteration of the environment, and others in bioengineering could involve alteration of the laws of genetics itself. Such changes may be only on the more distant horizon; still, the direct effects could be dramatic and make the questions already posed more urgent.

These several issues are related to globalization, for much that was possible in one place is now possible in many others — made so by modern communication and transportation, as these have developed over the last century and a half, yet obscured by previous nationalistic wars and the rise and fall of colonialism. Globalization involves not only the expansion of markets and the new availability of lower-cost labor as it draws millions of people around the world into new patterns of productivity and participation in the world economy — even if many join at the bottom of the wage scales in poor working conditions. Globalization also means a civilizational shift, so that those who learned over the past couple of centuries to think in terms of the political economics of one nation now must study their lessons again. Many feel very ambiguous about this, and it does bypass the great national debates of the last century about policies that would protect the workers as citizens of "our" land by controlling the corporations who employ them, by taxing those corporations and their managers. States then took the responsibility of managing the capital of the society and of redistributing the wealth by providing services or benefits to all who shared the national identity, even if that was rarely done equitably.

Now, it seems, the corporations have escaped the control of state authorities and found ways to take their capital and operations across every border. Many political leaders and the nationalist populations of newly emerged lands may resent the incursion of "foreign" economic influence just as they are developing "modern" nation-states of their own and seeking to control their own economic destinies. But the dominant attitudes of people from these countries are often more mixed. They want national dignity but, simultaneously, they want the goods, services, and jobs that come from these international firms. Young people resent being denied Coca-Cola, McDonalds, blue jeans, or the Internet; and those who are older want less corruption and the better working conditions that the multinationals bring.

Meanwhile, the ability of nation-states (whether highly developed or newly emerging) to plan and manage their own economies is reduced. Functionally, we find a growing gap between two words that once seemed parts of a single phrase: "political" and "economy." Politics increasingly has become the forming of a stable government able to establish and maintain the kind of law and order that assures those conditions whereby a viable economy can function effectively. And economy means the forming and sustaining of self-managed corporations, owned and operated cross-culturally and internationally, beyond any single state's control.

The massive spread of corporate capitalism to a global scale is especially troubling both to all those who have, for the last hundred years, understood capitalism as the progenitor of individualism and to those who have understood it as the creator of polarized classes, views that remain pervasive in segments of academic and religious leadership. However, an apparent majority of those who are supposed to be victims of contemporary capitalism seem not to feel victimized by it. Almost nowhere can anyone get elected by being against capitalism. Most people do not believe that capitalism generates either a class polarity that turns each class into a solidarity or works simply by the triumph of individual selfishness. They seem to know that modern capitalism thrives on the formation of effective teams of those with diverse abilities and skills who can work well with each other in well-managed corporations that have "fair" systems of stratified rewards — and they want to be a part of it.

Moreover, people seek (often by migration) those centers of business activity that invite corporations to do what they do best — create wealth and jobs where people can use their energy, develop their talents, and earn enough to meet their obligations and be responsible members of civil society. Both workers and managers at the several levels of work and pay want to benefit by becoming a part of such organizations. It is doubtful, thus, that contemporary forms of capitalism lead to the polarization of classes or the atomization of alienated individuals. Rather, they tend to generate new middle classes that contribute to both local and global civil society — as can be seen quite obviously in every country where capitalism is embraced.

It is true, however, that, since the decline of governmental capitalization by mercantilist and socialist systems and the increase of deregulation and privatization, there has been a spike in the number of super-rich, as capitalization processes are more and more assigned to corporate management, which handles a greater portion of the world's wealth. And, it is also true that management is more highly rewarded for its efforts, sometimes absurdly so, thus creating a greater gap between the highest and lowest quintiles of the population, even if the lower levels are moving up on average. But the increased percentage of the world's population that now participates in the common economy and thus has joined at least the lower and increasingly the median ranks of the middle classes is the more remarkable story. A graph of income and wealth distribution would tend to look more pear-shaped than pyramid-shaped or bell-shaped, compared to past economies. This is what causes a growing pattern of inequality in many lands and between various parts of the world. Some are approaching Western standards of living, while other parts seem mired in premodern levels of subsistence. And some nations seem to be making significant strides, while others are riddled with disease and constant fighting, with low educational and technological levels and a pervasive sense of despair.

Yet, beyond these realities, we can say in general that higher percentages of the world's population than ever before, including those at the lower economic levels, are gaining in both income and wealth, which reflects and enhances at least modestly increased access to healthcare and education. It is simply that the higher levels of the population, those in the management of the institutions of the society, are gaining much more rapidly and are reinvesting their gains at higher levels in future economic development. It is also true that some portions of the population are basically left out of either rapid or moderate growth; but those portions, while still large, seem to be a smaller fraction of the world population than ever before. For the most part, this difference is due to the presence or absence of resources that foster those independent institutions that develop quality management.

Spheres of Management

It remains a question whether all of this does or does not promote individualism. In some senses it clearly does. People from tribal or caste backgrounds, where identity is determined by gene-pool solidarity or given communal status, often find their identities shattered by the impact of the new modes of relationship in civil society or corporations, managed by quite different principles than those they know. Others find that, with the wages from participation in this system, they become freer than those without them.

One implication of this, of course, is that many, many women have been able to leave stereotyped, dependent roles and move into areas of individual achievement in the wider world of paid employment; and they, like the men who left the drudgery of subsistence farming or the dependency of serfdom to enter the industrial and technological worlds of work outside the household a generation or two earlier, want to be regarded as people who carry their own weight and to be rewarded fairly for their work. Further, many men and women alike now judge their value as persons in part according to the level of rewards they receive — a marker of how others assess their contributions to the commonwealth. But it is difficult to argue that this is all driven by some individualist greed that makes alienated atoms out of people. Most people are involved in committed communities — family, church activities, networks of friends, clubs — and want to be known more by their personal qualities and capacity for caring than their wealth.

Moreover, as a system of investment, capitalism arguably is driven less by private attempts to get rich by short-term gains — some live for that, but most leave that to the drug traffickers — than by steady, if slower, growth in reliability and choices. Wealth is gained by the ownership of real estate that usually increases in value rather slowly and by the behavior of larger corporate units — retirement funds, mutual and money market accounts, insurance policies, and other forms of "institutional investment" (some 70 percent of the stock market, according to the best estimates I have seen) that are concerned about long-term growth. Individuals entrust their personal (and familial) capital to these managers because their judgment is more trusted and accompanied by more services than persons can manage by themselves. As TIAA/CREF, one of the larger retirement funds, says, they are "for people who have other things to think about."

Still, some say that all these developments in a nonpolitical, but managed society and economy are, through their indirect effects, damaging to indigenous cultures and are generating poverty at record-breaking speed, with the support of what I have elsewhere called the "new transnational regencies" — the International Monetary Fund (IMF), the World Bank, and World

Trade Organization (WTO). Their policies, it is held, make it impossible to develop stable governments that help people. There is no doubt that these new regencies, when they are called in because some political-economic system is faltering, set policies that demand changes in traditional cultural patterns, attitudes, and practices that have made local economies dysfunctional. In doing this, they have made some blunders and sometimes have seen their economic recommendations in altogether too narrow a framework. But both popular protests and scholarly critiques have made these transnational regencies aware of the need for greater sensitivity, and they are, by all reports, seeking to sort out the valid from the specious critiques and are revising a number of these policies.

The data, however, do not support the more severe accusations: that they are causing poverty, even though the perception is widespread because there are shreds of evidence that lend themselves to this interpretation. Most of the countries where poverty is at a record level have been poor for centuries, and their present distress has been exacerbated first by bad colonial administration and then by worse administration by indigenous kleptocracies. What the regencies are doing is introducing new demands for the accountable management of funds donated or loaned by others to governments in crisis, usually in contexts where corruption, favoritism, and the propping up of inefficient and nonproductive industries run by friends of the political elite is rampant.

Managing Civil Society

There is also still the question of what principles should guide the newer global developments. The privatization of more and more economic functions means that more of the management of public life is shifting from government to civil society, increasingly organized on a corporate model. Of course, those who do become the managers of the growing instruments of production and distribution have access to greater opportunities of all sorts, for corruption as well as for constructive contribution. These managers are highly rewarded when they are successful in making these technological and social institutions function well and are given very generous settlements when they leave after even marginally successful service. But we must realize that privatization is taking place because the known alternative systems are unable to perform as well. The lesson of earlier feudalism, where local royalty ran the economy, and of modernist state capitalism of either the mercantilist, fascist, or socialist kinds is this: Governments make poor managers of the economy. True, the authoritarian governments of the "tigers" of East Asia seemed, for a time, to provide the productive umbrella for rapid economic development, but they did so by subsidizing favored corporations, protecting a mostly free domestic market, encouraging exports, providing technically oriented education, and curtailing labor unrest. Now, all are engaged in various degrees of privatization and deregulation, and, in the process, are realizing that they must face the challenges of a global economy that they cannot politically control. All are also facing pressures to democratize their political institutions and allow more independent social organizations.

The problem is this: Governments tend to make a centralized plan that cannot easily keep pace with the local variations and changing circumstances of a fast-moving economy. And when they do attempt to make nuanced plans, it becomes difficult to do so without allowing political factors to guide economic decisions. Considerations of political power, party loyalty, and crony solidarity override economic logic and prudence. Then, as tax bases or popular support or the insider knowledge of the business and financial elites begin to see a crisis coming and start to pull out, the leading officials feel compelled to take further command of the economic processes — which reduces private investment, voluntary formation of new businesses or industries, and economic efficiency. Of course, no economy can function without boundaries drawn by a legal order, and some health, safety, tax, and contractual constraints will always be necessary. But the range of justice and law, now extending systems of international law exponentially, and the extension of more equal access to economic opportunity to many around the world increase as the world's economic life is removed from the direct control of the nation-state. In other words, we have identified another area of transpolitical management that is fateful for the future, if anything like a global civil society is to expand. At its deepest levels, it could portend a new catholicity and a new ecumenicity that is little understood by religious and theological leaders.

Managing the Corporations

Contemporary corporations reflect a model of organizing the common life that can be found not only in the great multinational firms, but also in local and regional for-profit businesses and, indeed, almost every other area of civil society — hospitals, universities, media, art centers, missionary and advocacy organizations — each of which fiercely protects its independence from direct governmental control, even if it is directly or indirectly subsidized in part by it. Yet, we must also note that widespread public confidence in corporations has been shaken by the disclosures of obviously corrupt practices in a few of them. I refer particularly to the fraud perpetrated by previously respected firms, including communications, energy, accounting, investment, and banking institutions who were trusted to manage large portions of the nation's and the world's wealth. The mere mention of the list — WorldCom, Enron, Anderson, for example — with new names being added with each passing month — Citigroup, J. P. Morgan, Deutsche Bank, Vivendi, and Telecom — suggests the presence of an interior moral rot precisely in those contemporary economic institutions to which the world is now turning for management as it further privatizes and deregulates the economy.

There are doubtless many other factors influencing our economic situation, but if management of the world's economic well-being is to be located outside of direct political control, then those concerned about the moral fabric of civil society in a global era will have to take a deeper look at the nature and character of management. The American and European corporations failed not because of the post–Cold War, world-shaking, international developments already mentioned; they failed because of corruption within. Those specifically charged with the responsibility to manage other people's resources in the modern corporate economy lied, cheated, conspired, covered up, and exploited their workers, suppliers, customers, and the general public. The people who trusted them and worked for them were betrayed, giving rise to grave doubts about the quality of society in which we live and the quality of people who manage it. Whether we speak of the external circumstances that presently shape our world economy or the internal life of our businesses and our capacity to trust them and their leaders, we are in a complex of crises that demand ethical and theological attention. Here is still another area where we must inquire into the principles, values, and constraints that should guide management.

Perhaps the most amazing feature of this situation is that almost no arguments are being put forth in public to change the system in any fundamental way. One hears no calls for a political or economic revolution, although there are echoes of the 1960s in the rhetoric of gray-haired radicals; one reads no manifestos in favor of reform, although there are proposals put forward for discussion by cynical pundits; one sees no demonstrations calling for systemic changes, even if there are episodic disruptions at the meetings of the G-8, the World Bank, the IMF, or the WTO. Instead, we hear of modest changes in accounting procedures and in rules concerning disclosures of conflicting interests that will make the actual financial conditions of corporations more transparent, so that people can invest with greater knowledge of the real circumstances. We get a greater willingness of reporters who write in the business sections of the newspapers to expose shaky, but glossy press releases from the companies. We also get a series of business schools doing background checks on applicants to see if they have shaded or overstated their qualifications. And we get hosts of acquaintances who fulminate at the slightest mention of the present administration, but who have no idea how realistically to modify the developments sketched here. None of these are likely to alter the basic system we have.

What Can the Churches Do?

Why are the religious voices essentially silent on these issues? It is clear that some thinkers focus entirely on doctrinal questions, but have little interest in relating them to the ethos we actually face. We also know that Roman Catholics have been preoccupied by problems related to child abuse, and mainline Protestants have been bitterly divided over questions of homosexual marriage and ordination, and both have had their most vocal advocates embrace liberation thought in the last several decades — a sermon that all should have preached during decolonialization, but which has little to say about the reconstructive management of viable social or economic orders under globalizing conditions. Indeed, many of these advocates have a deep contempt for the corporation as an institution, for capitalism in general, and for the Reformed-Puritan history that generated the dynamic institutions that changed the world democratically, technologically, and economically, producing the present ethos in which we live. It is unlikely that these can be guided without a retrieval and reform of the chief motifs of this history.

Such accents in theological leadership have brought on severe problems of credibility and have deflected the bodies who were at the forefront of the social gospel, Christian realism, and the civil rights movements from cultivating a public theology for managing those areas of civil society now at the center of global development. To be sure, the pope has called upon advocates of globalization to acknowledge that it has not yet delivered on its promises of resolving the problems of poverty, social inequality, and environmental damage, and no one can reasonably deny that this is so. Today, mainline Protestant and ecumenical leaders show little interest in developing a theology that could guide the managers of a new world order on how to carry out their vocations in that world.

It is also true that evangelical churches — including some on the fundamentalist and Pentecostal wings — have not developed a public theology that deals with such matters. Indeed, although many of the leaders of the postliberationist countries and of the indicted corporations in recent American scandals are evangelicals, I have yet to discover evidence that the pastors of corporate managers who recently were exposed have said anything to them about a theology of calling, stewardship, or covenantal responsibility.

Laura Nash has identified one of the main problems: the seismic difference in the worldview of leaders in religion and business about economics in general. Clergy do not see the questions as an issue of management, but of the meaning of capitalism and profit in the first place:

> For the clergy, profit is a clear sign of "me-first" self-interest, materialistic and therefore not Christian. To the business person, profit was a result of actions that were partially other-oriented combined with the legitimate pursuit of (other-focused) self-interest, like serving a customer or creating jobs or donating part of the proceeds to charity. The second major difference was present in their language. The clergy's language reflects . . . a subtractive approach. They would solve problems by emphasizing taking away things, such as money, from the "haves" as means of providing benefit to the disadvantaged. The business people use an additive language. They would speak of providing jobs and creating valued services and products to increase the standard of living.[1]

What, today, do the churches have to say about the classical understanding of "vocation," of "calling," as it can and should lead to a response of "profession" — of profession of faith and the cultivation of the excellencies of talent God has given, including the talent to be a "steward," a manager of that which belongs temporally to others, and ultimately to the Lord? And what might this imply for one who is a "trustee" of, say, a multinational, for-profit corporation? What about the idea of "covenant," that we must be engaged in real-world communities of commitment in, but also beyond, the church that are equally holy because we are under obligation in all areas of life that we did not construct and cannot deconstruct and have purposes that do not derive

---

1. Laura Nash, "Toward Integrating Work and Faith" (interview), *Religion and Liberty* 12, no. 6 (December 2002): 1-2.

Spheres of Management

only from our desires or hopes for rewards? It simply is not sufficient that the churches worship on Sundays or even take political stances on a great number of issues, including those having to do with the poor, if they do not also think about how to generate a viable civil society for the world. The question is how to think faithfully and with due care to the best evidence and theory about ministry to and formation of those who are to be the leaders of the global future, a world deeply shaped by modern management.

And here the issues of managing institutions within our democracy, managing international conflicts where religious differences are sharp, managing global resources such as oil, managing the ecological order in the face of modern technology, managing the civil society, and managing corporations when they are no longer subject to any single political economy are before us. They come down to issues very fateful for our global future. On one side, they are personal issues. People in many professions today are frustrated with what they find in their professional schools and places of employment. They love their work, in a way; but the moral and spiritual roots of why they do what they do are often ignored or blocked out of view. The management of a global resource like oil or the transformation of nature as a duty of the quest for redemptive possibilities is hardly mentioned in debates about today's technology. Covenantal patterns of responsible relationship are frequently lost in treatments of the corporation, and the trustee-stewardship model of management is seldom discussed. It is an open question whether we can cultivate an inner sense of meaning in our time, one that can guide us as we move increasingly toward a global society, which has as yet no overarching political order. Especially important will be the question of whether the managers of today and tomorrow can capture a moral and spiritual vision of what they do and why they do it — under what principles of right and what sense of the good they can and should organize the common life. It is not at all clear that a purely secular vision can recapture and recast these themes under the changing circumstances of today.

It is equally unclear whether clergy who minister to believing business executives can offer anything to them that is fundamentally helpful and whether they can offer a theological and ethical framework of understanding that will convince nonbelievers that faith has anything basic to offer their world. Seldom do clergy find management in the church or in society a topic of interest. But it is likely that, where morally rich corporations and spiritually fed managers are not cultivated, democratic political orders, open market economies, vibrant civil societies, and corporate leaders will lose their character, close in on themselves, and constrict, by nationalistic priorities,

Constructing a Global Public Theology

coercive constraint, or outright corruption, the most promising and productive forms of life that are on the horizon today. No social institutions live forever, and new patterns of social life may evolve. Still, for the foreseeable future, those concerned about viable political, economic, and social systems, the well-being of the people, and faithful living will surely have to engage these issues.

Globalization, Faith, and Theological Education

The topic of globalization invites theological educators, who work in a faith tradition that treasures learning and the formation of leaders, to engage the structures and processes of contemporary life without succumbing to the secular rationalism that is associated with the modern*ism* of the research university. The topic also invites theological educators to encounter postmodernity without adopting the celebration of antinomianism that dominates many fields in the postmodern*ist* multiversity.

At the same time, facing issues of globalization prevents both the retreat into the sectarianism that attends many theological perspectives today and the slide into fundamentalism that is evident in many of the world's religions. Both sectarianism and fundamentalism isolate faith from the wider world and from those disciplines that are necessary to grasp and guide the massive new developments that are on the horizon. Indeed, a collegium committed to the highest standards of learning, and dedicated to the service of God and humanity, offers a rare but precious context for taking up the decisive questions of what can only be called *the other postmodernism* — the one that opens the door to a new cosmopolitan vision without imperialism and colonialism, the one that recognizes that issues of human rights, ecological sanity, international trade and finance, and worldwide communications that lock us into a new interdependence beyond the presumed incommensurability of our local traditions and confessions. This alternative postmodernism could contribute to the formation of a new global society where learning can flourish more widely, life can become more graceful, justice can be more widely spread, and we can inch closer to the realm where every knee will bow and every tongue confess the lordship of Christ — white knee, black knee, red knee, yellow knee, male knee, female knee — Indo-Aryan tongue, sinaitic tongue, click tongue, rich tongue, poor tongue.

Fredric Jameson and Masao Miyoshi begin their book *The Cultures of Globalization* (1998) with these words: "Globalization falls outside the established academic disciplines, as a sign of the emergence of a new kind of social phenomenon, fully as much an index of the origins of those disciplines in the nineteenth-century realities that are no longer ours."[1] They go on to quote Roland Robertson, dean of the theoretical study of globalization, who defines it as "the twofold process of the particularization of the universal and the universalization of the particular." That sounds almost Christological. But Jameson and Miyoshi are critical of Robertson. They are not having it. Not complementarity and integration, but conflict and disintegration, are what globalization is about, a repolarization of old conflicts and the regeneration of ideologies of control by elites who benefit from economic and social developments.

It is likely, however, that given the complexity of globalization, more than one point is valid: globalization is a new phenomenon. Not brand new, as we shall shortly see, but very recent in its pervasive character. It also demands new forms of transdisciplinary thinking, beyond the Holy Grail of interdisciplinary studies, which many have attempted and few attained. Globalization requires a new convergence of universalist and particularist motifs with theological overtones, and simultaneously provides a new occasion in which the tensions that have haunted the past are being exacerbated and could become dominant. The battles continue between realism and nominalism, idealism and materialism, theory and experience, optimism and pessimism, the traditionalists and the *Zeitgeistlers,* the locals and the cosmopolitans, the libertarians and the liberationists — all projected on a wider screen where there is much evidence that there will be winners and losers. But that may not be all, and theology may have some indispensable insights about the whole.

Globalization is new, but when it became so is a question of considerable debate. The idea of *the whole world as one place,* as an inclusive field of spaces and peoples, is actually quite old. Teachers of the great world religions, including the Hebrew prophets, knew long ago of a single material realm where many peoples lived under a universal law and with a sacred purpose. Further, when Crates of Mallus (about 150 BCE) made the first globe symbolizing "the world," the Greek concept of *kosmos* already entailed a mystical-mathematical view of the universe in Pythagoras, a spiritual-cosmological vision in Plato, and a socio-cosmopolitan awareness in Aristotle. Moreover, the Stoic notion of *oikoumene* referred to the whole inhabited earth.

---

1. Fredric Jameson and Masao Miyoshi, eds., *The Cultures of Globalization* (Durham, NC: Duke University Press, 1998), p. xi.

The "ization" part of "globalization," however, suggests not only that some whole can be conceived, but that a historical process is taking place whereby some different whole comes into being. When "global" and "ization" are joined, the result points to a systemic alteration of what already is, in a manner and degree that brings a *novum* that has not been before. The New Testament conveys such views with an idea of "the world" as something that is, but which is fallen and thus is something to which we are not to conform. Yet "the world" is something that God so loved that it is being redeemed. Those who know God are sent to aid in the process of redemption of the world, even as it groans in travail toward a new creation and the new cosmopolitan civilization.

A consciousness of the world as a whole with a divine destiny was voiced, in a modern key, at the Parliament of World Religions a century ago, at the Hague Peace Conference of 1899, and at the later Carnegie Endowment for International Peace. Shortly thereafter, at the World Missionary Conference of 1910, the great scholar of Hinduism, J. N. Farquhar, said: "We have entered a new era. . . . The nations have become one city; we buy each other's goods; . . . we think each other's thoughts . . . we begin to hear the music of humanity."[2] The music was soon to become a cacophony of military marches accompanied by the screeching sounds of steel shells, discrediting the lovely hopes for modernity and automatic progress. But it was partly true: history is now planetary, no culture is now self-contained, and every war becomes worldwide in scope or effect — a novelty of our times.

The term most used to describe what brought all this about is "modernization," a term developed by a generation of social theorists who thought that they knew the stages of development. They see in globalization a "western" modernization of the world, a new form of sociocultural imperialism that has come to reign everywhere in a purportedly postcolonial era. Many hold that these developments are driven essentially by neocapitalist interests, and many critics have published diatribes against the export of an exploitative bazaar of greed where American consumerism produces a "McWorld" supported by Western-dominated institutions such as the World Bank and the International Monetary Fund (IMF).

Some years ago, the radical Dutch theologian Arend van Leeuwen, a contemporary of the modernizationists, offered a deeper perspective on what that generation almost saw. In his *Christianity in World History* (1966), he

---

2. Quoted in Olav Guttorm Myklebust, *The Study of Missions in Theological Education*, vol. 2 (1910-1950) (Oslo: Forlaget Land Og Kirke [Egede Instituttet], 1957), pp. 13f.

recounted the slow but steady adoption of rational modes of technology and science and of democratized political, legal, and economic institutions by the East and the South as evidence of the providential spread of socially embedded theological themes, of which neither the indigenous enthusiasts of modernization nor its Western agents were aware. Yet, these developments were inconceivable without the background beliefs of Christian theology, and their spread was a kind of *preparatio evangelicum* that would eventually have to be acknowledged by those who adopted them, for they would sooner or later have to inquire into the convictional base that makes them viable.

Although it became unfashionable to mention such an idea in the period in which all religions were viewed as equal and any cultural transfer from West to East or North to South was viewed as imperialistic, I think there is more to this theory than is acknowledged in most treatments of modernization. Nevertheless, the term "modernization" continues to be associated largely with the efforts by "underdeveloped" societies to achieve "advanced" development by rationalizing the means of production and governance on models like those developed in the West since the fifteenth century — almost always without knowledge of or reference to the role that Christianity played in shaping the souls, societies, and employments of reason that brought these patterns into being.

Those who view globalization only as an extended form of modernization generally remain convinced that what we have is a product of post-theological developments, and that we are now driven by individualism, autonomous reason, and nationalist interests. Ironically, this view is shared by two groups. Secularists are pleased to be beyond all that religious stuff, which they never believed could be a cause of much of anything, because they see it as the epiphenomenon of real factors. On the other hand, traditionalists hold that modernism's profound sense of the individual person, its high regard for a reasonable faith expressed in its aversion to magic, mysticism, chance, or esoteric gnosis, and its support of governments that recognize and protect the independence of the church from state intervention are all symptoms of the acids of secularization. In fact, it is theological causes more than secular symptoms that these modernist nostrums represent, and if we do not see this we cannot grasp or sustain some of the good things that contemporary life brings.

The reference to governments also points to one reason why the term "globalization" is often used instead of or in contrast to internationalization. "Internationalization" acknowledges increased interaction between nations, but preserves the notion that the primary unit of identity and action is the nation. Saskia Sassen, in her *Globalization and Its Discontents* (1998), is probably right when she argues that we are not seeing the end of national governments. They will no more disappear than states disappeared when federal governments were formed. There may even be times when agency will again devolve to them. However, not states but cities, especially the urban clusters of corporations and communication channels, are becoming the ganglia in a global net of interdependence, and nation-states find that they are not the sovereign agents they once were. They must act in ways that fit them into systems that are simultaneously more metropolitan and more cosmopolitan than the systems of sovereign nation-states that had dominated the common life of the West for centuries. Sassen focuses on the urban laboring classes that serve the cosmopolitans, the educated, technological and managerial elites who are constructing these new global interactions, and she shows no interest in religious factors in society. But her evidence fits with what several political historians today argue. We are at the end of the age of Westphalia, the accords that brought the so-called "religious wars" to a tolerable settlement, established the notion of the sovereignty of the nation-state, and fundamentally brought the idea of a Holy Roman Empire to an end — although its lingering death took much longer.

Today, the nation-states continue to exist, but are partly superseded by the gradual formation of a global civilization that entails a "new catholicity," as Robert Schreiter has argued so well. The context in which we now think, work, pray, and contextualize our convictions is increasingly a comprehending context, one that includes many specific locales and subcultures within it. Life is "glocal," simultaneously global and local, in part because we live in a period of the "compression of the world," which is not only multipolar politically, but unified economically.

How are we to respond to such a situation in theological education? One of the ways to do so is to turn again, as we must repeatedly do, to basic theological reflection and ethical research. A team of eighteen, mostly Protestant, scholars is presently taking up this challenge at the Center of Theological Inquiry in Princeton, New Jersey. (Catholics already have a stronger sense of universality than today's Protestants.) Of course, each scholar will bring his or her own stamp to this effort, but I would like to share briefly my view of the architecture of the whole. It is based in a socio-theological exploration into three areas too much neglected in contemporary thought:

1. The perspectival shift from orders of creation to the spheres of relative sovereignty.

2. A fresh analysis of the meanings of the powers, authorities, thrones, and dominions.
3. A recovery and recasting of the covenantal-federal view of the story of salvation.

Spheres of Relative Sovereignty

The idea that we live in various "spheres of life," each having its own sense of justice, as Michael Walzer[3] says, is surely rooted in the older Reformation notion of the "orders of creation," the view that from the beginning of the world, God established certain institutions in which humans are to live — especially familial, political, and ecclesiastical. Here was a divinely ordained natural-law view of institutional life, designed to help us serve humanity and praise God. This view was fundamentally challenged by Rousseau and the French Revolution, where it was held that "man is born free" and is chained by the institutions of civilization. It was further challenged when Darwin taught that there was never a time when humanity lived in the dreaming innocence of a pre-fallen, institutionally ordered state. More than a generation before the Nazis tried to recover the idea of the "Orders" to claim a divinely appointed total authority, and two generations before Barth, Bonhoeffer, and Thielicke began arguing for terms like "orders of preservation," or "mandates of God," the Dutch conservative Calvinist Abraham Kuyper turned from "orders" to the idea of spheres. This notion is close to the idea of "departments of life" developed by an interesting, if (in some ways) odd group of his friends, including the quasi-unitarian Max Weber and the liberal Lutheran Ernst Troeltsch. This view is also close to the idea of "sectors of society" developed by the Catholic socialist Antonio Gramsci while he was imprisoned by the Fascists. In the idea of "sectors of society" Gramsci sought to integrate Leo XIII and Karl Marx.

This brilliant idea of spheres implies that the functional requirements of stable human living demand our participation in and maintenance of viable institutions. But the stability of human living does not derive from a form fixed in creation to which we shall someday return. The spheres change in number and contours; they expand or contract in role and import. The Reformers did not clearly see the arts, science, medicine, or the media as spheres, nor could some see an economic sphere as distinct from family and

---

3. Michael Walzer, *Spheres of Justice* (New York: Basic Books, 1984).

state and in some senses regulative of them. Thus, we have to acknowledge not only that the spheres change, but that each must respond to developments in other spheres, and there is always something of a human construction about them. They are as much historical as creational. They have to be redesigned in each generation, preferably under theological and ethical guidance, even if they are in some sense built into the unavoidable necessities of human society. Thus, the peoples of God must tend the pluralistic areas of responsibility, forming and reforming them as part of the *missio dei*.

Powers, Authorities, Thrones, and Dominions

Globalization brings us a new, wider context where we must engage in that task again. We must renew and reform those viable institutions in our communities, cities, nations, and those international alliances that have been formed on presuppositions that derive from our knowledge of God's sovereignty over creation and history. The globally interdependent world into which we are thrust today is a veritable cauldron of brewing spheres, old and new, in need of a formative, dynamically pliable vision, lest chaos and conflict utterly dominate. Each sphere needs its own housing in a viable, humane institution.

This is a problem for some. After all, we live in a generation that is "spiritual" but not "religious," committed to a circle of friends but only sometimes to a church, concerned about community but skeptical of society, involved in relationships but dubious about marriage, eager to have a job but cynical about corporations, morally sensitive but suspicious of anything like ethical absolutes, believers in God but doubtful of any characteristics of God that smack of an order that limits liberty. We live in an era that is anti-institutional, but all the efforts of recent generations to throw off the tyrannies of racism, classism, sexism, colonialism, etc., have not shown that they can reconstruct a viable social ecology. This is true largely, I think, for this reason: recent generations cannot grasp, contain, or guide what the Bible calls "powers," "authorities," "thrones," or "dominions." When they overthrow some, they unleash others, for they really do not believe in institutional formation as a duty and reformation as a constantly necessary strategy. They do not believe that we live in a world of "fallen angels" — vital, intelligible, spiritual forces that could be good, but are now so separated from their original source, form, and purpose that they distort everything around them. The loss of a vocabulary to deal with such a phenomenon has impoverished our capacity to grasp part of reality.

Constructing a Global Public Theology

In some cultures, people seem to live in a world of enchanted powers — a world populated by spirits that can be invoked, demons that must be exorcised, or charms and curses that may be used. Elaborate systems develop around these concerns, and every religion has followers who use their faith in such ways, even if the great religions discourage it. Other superpersonal forces of good and evil are identified by modern social sciences. Some speak of "complexes" or "stereotypes," of "totems" and "taboos," or of "isms" and "ideologies." They come to dominate persons or peoples, who do not know quite how. Ordinary people also use terms from various religious traditions to express uncontrolled dynamics in their lives. "Fate," "fortune," "karma," "kismet," etc., suggest cosmic forces that seem to determine behavior, although today genetics and social conditioning are favored explanations of powers that make us do what we do. All tell us that we have no choice but to live out what the powers dictate. Concerns about the powers vary from person to person, culture to culture, and epoch to epoch, but they are always present. Theology must face the issues they pose.

In our time, a number of primal powers seem to be of special significance. How we deal with them will be fateful for humanity. For instance, every society has to cope with the threats of violence within and without. Organized violence is required to hold those threats in check, and people ready to kill and be killed are necessary. But it is always possible that they can themselves get out of control, obsessed by their own importance, blinded to the limits of their roles in life, and tempted to identify their own powers as those that can save humanity and establish a spiritual and moral civilization. Fed by an insatiable greed, a lust for power, or even a desire for spiritual glory, this self-idolatry deploys death and destruction. It generates a fanaticism that in turn renders the terrorism of bombers and rebels — not seldom also unleashing unfettered reactions that become a terror too.

This kind of power, as the ancients knew, is "Mars," the idolatrous form of skilled violence. Mars is always necessary, always a danger — today all the more so because weapons of mass destruction have reached a new level of capacity, and firepower unimaginable to World War II heroes is available to militiamen and schoolchildren. Mars may save us from some perils, but it imperils us also. It needs institutional constraint — around the world.

"Eros," the symbol of sensuality and sexual desire, is a much more personal and intimate, but also a more pervasive power. No family, no society could live without it for more than a generation. Yet, persons and cultures can become obsessed with it. It can command our lives far beyond its own proper sphere, partly because it can simulate the experience of religious ecstasy. Then it prompts the betrayal of familial loyalties and social duty, for not only does it identify with political potency and image, it also seduces business relations and advertising, penetrates educational relationships and judgments, exploits medical care and decisions, and invades religious entrustments and practices. When it is deified, much is distorted; it is best confined and celebrated regularly and joyfully in marriage.

Mammon, too, distorts greatly. Money is a convenient and useful means of calculating cost, value, and gain. It may take all sorts of symbolic forms, from coinage to electronic signals, and these symbols are important in life. It is better to have some reasonable access to these symbols than not — people die for lack of it, and people with more of it are freed from the calculations of subsistence to live for larger purposes. Yet, like Mars and Eros, money can become an idol. It becomes Mammon when it is taken as the means of salvation, the source of security, or the purpose of life. The worship of "the almighty buck" brings terrors of its own; it needs disciplined institutions of accountability.

And what shall we say about the power of the media in our day? The muses have long been recognized as a defining reality in culture. The bard, the artist, the dramatist, the poet, the teller of tales have all been seen as the creators of culture, the refiners of social life, the conscience of humanity that not only exposes its foibles, but clarifies its virtues and celebrates its approximations to them. No society is without its "muses." Every culture has its distinctive forms of poetry and song, painting and sculpture, dance and ritual, its particular sense of beauty, and its temptation to worship its own creativity or creations, even if the arts are a kind of universal language. But our collective consciousness is deeply influenced by today's media. What is in our living room also reaches around the world. Like Mars, it is ever a force; like Eros, it is ever present; like Mammon, it is ever a temptation — in a global world it has become the virtual reality.

Every sphere of life — the sciences, sports, administrative methods, and not only political forces, sexuality, business, or media — has potencies that are spiritually and morally creative and that can become distorted and destructive authorities unto themselves. The cumulative effect of the regnant powers does more to determine the role that government plays among us than government does to determine the role of these powers in life, although the "thrones" of the world will always be a factor. Thus, it is not only a political duty to sustain a context in which social institutions may be formed to guide the powers, it becomes a theological responsibility of academia and ecclesia to expose their spiritual pretensions, and to convert them into forces that serve the larger vision.

Constructing a Global Public Theology

In our time, in our global environment, it is not only these perennial powers that are a potential problem; various authorities and dominions also challenge us. The cultivated professions — Law, Education, Medicine, and Technology (Architecture, Engineering, etc.) — are among the most honored and compelling authorities in contemporary life (only in some places is Ministry included as it historically was). Each is driven by a distinctive "spirit," but any conscious relationship to the Holy Spirit is rarely traced. All of these have been deeply stamped by theological history, but most today are largely unaware of their own roots. The wider availability of education — much of it decidedly nonreligious, some of it anti-religious in character — puts specialists at the peak of authority in each subdiscipline, but only some identify any connection between what they do and theology or ethics, even though many professionals have high standards of integrity, or are personally religious. These authorities are critical to the globalizing process, but if they do not serve God's law and purpose, they will serve only the interests of demonic forces, or become demonic themselves.

Still another level is decisive. We dare not neglect the profound contributions and challenges of the great world religions. Christianity as a religion and, even more, as a theology and ethic, cannot fail to recognize that it is in simultaneous contention and cooperation with the world religions. Religions shape the "powers and authorities" of culture, and where they have done so, they have formed an enduring "dominion" — a distinctive culture and societal pattern in a given region, of which the ordering core is inevitably religious. If Christ is not Lord, some other Lord will reign.

A complex set of questions must be asked in regard, at least, to the great, civilization-forming religions — Hinduism, Buddhism, Confucianism, Islam, and likely some tribal traditions — for they have already long engaged the powers, thrones, and authorities, and have come to arrangements with them. Because no enduring civilization has ever developed without a dominant religion at its core, it is unlikely that a global society can develop in creative directions without one. But it makes a great difference which religion becomes dominant, how it does so, and how it treats other traditions. Today, the commonly accepted study of religions is "nontheological" and "nonevaluative," yet one of the tasks of theological ethics in our era will surely be to seek to identify the valid and the nonvalid forms of religious belief and practice not only within the Christian tradition but in the world religions, specifically as they shape the spheres and institutions of the common life. How to do so is one of the greatest issues of our time.

Christianity is increasingly present to these "dominions" in non-

Western societies — as a faith, a theological ethic, a principality, a social and religious threat and challenge. These great religions are also present to the West in similar ways. The question of how the catholic traditions of Christian theology and ethics, shaped by the recognition of the perennial need for reformation, do, can, and ought to face these complex traditions in their own contexts has been much discussed in the past. But these complex traditions are no longer safely in their own contexts. The dominions are here as well as there, now as well as then. The new context of a global society demands a revisiting of the issues once thought settled and the posing of questions not yet clearly acknowledged.

How can we develop a faithful theological ethic to interpret and guide the common life in a situation where we must interpret and assess, embrace or resist, tolerate or critique what other religions assume, imply, advocate, or demand in regard to the ordering of the powers, thrones, authorities, and dominions in the common life? What can we do about all these forces that are simultaneously natural, historical, and spiritual? Shall we avoid them? Shall we attempt to destroy them? Shall we simply recognize that they are part of the nature of society — at least of our society, as other kinds of angelic/demonic forces seemed to be accepted in other times by other peoples? In our day, the institutions that frame and guide, confine and channel these powers are in fragile condition. The forces threaten to burst the channels of creativity and become forces of destruction.

Some powers may simply have to be condemned, confined, and contained by counter-forces that hold them in check, even though they writhe in their bonds. But other powers, thrones, and authorities, and perhaps some of the dominions, may be drawn into communities of responsibility and accountability. Just as we seek to bring persons — so alienated from God and themselves that they wreak havoc among their neighbors — into covenanted communities of spiritual and moral discipline by proselytism, evangelism, or catechesis, so we now have a mission to draw some powers, thrones, authorities, and dominions into the domain of disciplined service to God.

Covenantal-Federal View of the Story of Salvation

It is a deep conviction of mine that the best way to do this is to extend the covenantal understanding of salvation history. A covenant, like a contract, is a binding agreement between two or more parties. It binds persons in accord with the desires of their will and it creates communities of cooperative action in accord with mutual principles, rights, and duties. However, a covenant is different from a contract in that the terms for agreement and mutual promises are established by God, and not only by the human parties. God is always the party to covenant and sets its terms. Thus, a covenant also has sacramental characteristics. When it is enacted, recounted, or renewed, ritual symbols of life and meaning — water or blood, fasting or feasting, prayer and sacred song — signify the formation, celebration, or reformation of a just, faithful community of commitment under a holy law and with a common purpose.

In the history of salvation, we find that God continued to try to lure Israel to righteousness and faithfulness as a light to the nations. Isaiah is inspired to speak of a Messiah in which prophet, priest, and ruler are combined into a One who could reconcile the people to God. The people began to look for such a redeemer who could renew the covenant by God's grace and power. And when Jesus used the setting of the last supper to proclaim the final covenant renewal, he inaugurated a new epoch, not yet ended, that anticipates a triumph over death and meaninglessness, a reconciliation of God and people, a justice and rejoicing in a cosmopolitan city, and a hope for the fulfillment of life.

We do not know how the results of such research and writing about such matters will come out, but the implications of such a view for a theological faculty and the various disciplines — given our world situation — may well be weighty. Indeed, it may be that only a theological perspective can make sense of the complexities at hand. It is not yet clear, however, that we are theologically ready for a world that is being pressed toward a new catholicity, a new ecumenicity that is wider than Rome or Geneva imagined, or even to admit that only a God-rooted pursuit of the disciplines can form a generation of leaders able to relate the faith to all the fields where the global future will be framed.

Seminary faculties have, at least, a new challenge before them: to form the clergy with a new sense of mission and an appreciation for the ministry of the laity in this kind of world. Pastors must be enabled not only to nurture the inner, personal, convictional side of faith, but also the outer implications of that faith as worked out by believing laity in their vocations in a now-global civil society. In short, theological education must form leaders who are able to form the people of God for their ministries in the world, and not for only the ministries in the church. If we do this, the global civilization aborning in our midst may become a blessing to humanity, not a curse.

A Christian Perspective on Human Rights

More than a quarter-century ago, I was invited by my church to participate in ecumenical discussions and to serve as a visiting lecturer in the theological academies of sister churches in the German Democratic Republic and in southern India. I became fascinated with the way in which different ideational and social traditions treated human rights, including the interpretations of the United Nations Declaration of 1947 and its subsequent "Covenants." Resistance to "Western" definitions of human rights was intense in the Marxist parties of Eastern Europe. Such resistance was also intense in India, both in the leadership of the Congress Party under Indira Gandhi, when she declared her "Emergency" in 1976, and in the then-emerging Hindu nationalist parties that now form India's current Hindu nationalist government. On the basis of these extended exposures to non-Western interpretations of human rights at that time, I engaged in a comparative study of the roots and conceptual framework that made modern human rights discourse possible. The invitation to contribute to this symposium is a welcome opportunity to rethink the issues in view of new conditions.

The new conditions are probably obvious to all. Beyond the judgment against the inhumane barbarism of Nazism, which triggered the United Nations Declaration, the great struggles facing issues of human rights and pluralism of the last third of the previous century had to do with racial justice, the rising parallel movements of equal rights for women, and the worldwide movements for decolonialization. All these took place in the context of a life-and-death confrontation of the "free world" with "world communism," and the development of the idea of the "Third World." The question was whether human rights were in any sense universal, especially in view of the fact of pluralism. It is not, of course, the case that the world became pluralistic all of a sudden — it had been so for as long as we have recorded history; but the direct awareness of cultures, traditions, customs, moralities, social orders, and religions, brought to us by modern communication, transportation, urbanization, and immigration made the pluralistic world more present to us.

In some ways the consensus has grown that human rights are universal, at least with regard to the issues of race and sex. Racism and sexism are widely condemned although they have not been abolished, and a number of regions are experiencing new diversities that evoke new forms of ethnic consciousness and conflict. Still, the suspicion remains that human rights in other areas of civil and political rights are an invention of the bourgeois West, in spite of the fact that the Soviet world has collapsed, and with it the chief advocates of this view. In some ways, their place as been taken by the rise of Islamist militancy, with it a theocratic rather than a humanistic hope for a revolutionary change that will overthrow the influence of the world's largest religion and of the remaining superpower. This has happened in the context of massive globalization in technology, science, democratic ideals, the increased power and range of professionalism, ecological consciousness, media influence, and economic interaction, all of which also bring a fresh encounter of the world religions.

To be sure, many people think about globalization only in economic terms. But this narrow understanding of our present situation, as if the economic challenges were not themselves largely a function of educational, technological, legal, communication, and, indeed, moral and spiritual developments, blinds us to one of the most difficult problems of universalistic principles in the face of pluralism, the conflict of values, of definitions of what is human and what is right held by the world religions. On the whole, globalization is the forming of a new and wider human interdependence, extremely complex and highly variegated, that nevertheless raises the prospect of a new world civilization, and the now unavoidable encounter of the world's cultures and societies, and the religious values on which they are based, requires us to think again about universalistic ethical principles, and whether they are possible and real, what difference they make and whether they inhibit or enhance the prospects of a genuine and principled pluralism. After all, to speak of "human" rights is to speak categorically, irrespective of social and cultural differences.

On this point, those who defend human rights as global principles have reason to be cautiously optimistic. We can be optimistic, for the wider vision of human rights ideas has, at the least, become a part of the *jus gentium*, the operating consensus as to what constitutes proper behavior by states and other formal institutions, and what counts as compelling moral argument in contemporary international discourse. Although it seemed in the middle years of the twentieth century that a neo-pagan nationalism and a militant anti-liberalism of socialist secularism, both backed by radically historicist philosophies that denied any "essentialist" normative order, could not be contained by theological, ethical, or social wisdom, and would bring only holocausts, gulags, and violence to the future, it was too-often-obscured Judeo-Christian ethical principles, frequently in their religiously neutered Enlightenment formulations, that the nations have increasingly adopted.

The background story of how this definition of human rights came to enter the official, cross-cultural, international definition of standards, however, is only now being told. In fresh research, the British scholar-pastor Canon John Nurser has documented in extended detail the ways in which, from 1939 until 1947, leading ecumenical Protestant figures worked not only with key figures in developing the Bretton Woods agreements, anticipating a postwar need for economic stability and development, but formed the Commission for a Just and Durable Peace, the Churches' Commission on International Affairs, and later the Joint Committee on Religious Liberty, all under the auspices of the Federal Council of Churches, with close connections to the emerging World Council of Churches and the World Missionary Conference. These organizations, notably led by Lutheran O. Frederick Nolde, Congregationalist Richard Fagley, Baptist M. Searle Bates, and Presbyterian John A. Mackay, among others, were dedicated to shaping what they then called a "new world order" that would honor human rights. They worked closely with Jacob Blaustein and Joseph Proskauer of the American Jewish Committee and with twelve bishops of the Roman Catholic Church to encourage the formation of the drafting committees of the United Nations Charter Committee and the committee that composed the Universal Declaration on Human Rights and deeply shaped their results. Furthermore, they worked through their church and synagogue contacts at the local level to build the popular support for what they were doing. In fact, the more of this history that is dug out, the clearer it becomes that they supplied much of the intellectual and ethical substance that formed these so-called "secular" documents. Such data is of particular importance, for it helps correct the secularists' slanderous treatment of religion as the cause of human rights violations.

The results of such efforts are what, at least, the leaders from most of the world's great cultures have now endorsed, and what oppressed peoples appeal to for justice, functionally recognizing principles of universal justice in the legacy of these particular traditions. Moreover, there are, at present, more people living under democratically ordered constitutions that seek to protect human rights, there is a broader public constituency interested in defending them than at any point in human history, and there is little evidence of their fading from normative use soon. Indeed, even those who violate human rights plead special conditions, temporary delays, or hermeneutical differences regarding the relative weight of some as compared to others; they seldom deny their validity as ideals or goals.

Yet if these facts give us reason to be optimistic, it must be a cautious optimism, not only because the rights of so many people continue to be savagely violated in so many places, and the exigencies of earlier battles by colonialized peoples against domination and now against threats of terrorism in many countries seem to justify the use of means that threaten the rights of groups and persons in ways that are more than "collateral damage." For those who seek to defend civil rights and liberties and see them as a way to love their neighbors near and far, the potential erosion of the legal protections of civil rights and liberties is a matter of immediate and pressing practical concern. This is so because it denies that there are inalienable human rights that stand beyond and above civil rights, which are granted by a state and thus can be withdrawn by civil authority. It makes human rights a function of state policy, not a matter of universal principle.

This points to a deeper threat, for it takes human rights outside the realm of universal, meta-legal norms that cannot be repealed by political authority, no matter how powerful. It is a refusal to see human rights as the same as the prohibition against murder. The world, after all, has known that murder is wrong for many centuries, and all peoples have laws against it. People know that murders occur, with very few "justifiable homicides." But they also know that the empirical fact that things happen does not negate the normative principles by which we judge them. Today, the threat to human rights is deeper than their sometimes violation; it is a profound intellectual and spiritual problem, for many today doubt that we can have or defend any trans-empirical principles to judge empirical life. And human rights ideas were formulated historically by those branches of the biblically based traditions, especially Jewish and Christian, that were willing to recognize, learn from, and selectively embrace philosophical and legal insights from other cultures if they saw them also living under universal principles of right and wrong that they did not construct and could not deconstruct.

Most Christians hold that this adoption or "baptism" of nonbiblical ideas that are compatible with the universalist, moral, and spiritual insights of the gospel is quite possible, and that these ideas are sometimes able to refine what the tradition held reflexively, anticipated in earlier portions of the Bible itself, especially in the Wisdom literature. It was extended in the traditions that developed after the fuller formation of Judaism and Christianity in the selective embrace of Greek philosophy, Roman law, and, later, certain insights from other cultures. It is being further extended today as people from many cultures bring other philosophical, moral, social, and religious insights with them into contemporary theological and ethical understanding. The famous passages in the book of Acts that speak of all having "the law written on their hearts," and of all those gathered from many regions understanding the preaching "each in his own language," are being reenacted. Certainly we cannot say that all of Judaism or of Christianity has supported human rights; it has been key minority traditions that have argued their case over long periods of time and that have become more widely accepted. Nor can we say that even these traditions have been faithful to the implications of their own heritage at all times, and the horror stories of our pasts also have to be told to mitigate any temptation to triumphalism. Still, intellectual honesty demands recognition of the fact that what passes as "secular," "Western" principles of basic human rights developed nowhere else than out of key strands of the biblically rooted religions. And while many scholars and leaders from other traditions have endorsed them, and found resources in their own traditions that point to quite similar principles, today these views are under suspicion both by some Asian leaders who appeal to "Asian Values" and by some communitarian and postmodern philosophers in the West who have challenged the very idea of human rights. The deepest threat comes from those intellectual leaders who have adopted anti-universalist, anti-principle perspectives.

Those who doubt the validity of human rights do so on the ground that there neither is nor can be any universalistic moral theology, master narrative, or *jus naturale* to support the idea. That, of course, is a universalistic claim in itself, one that ironically presses toward a universal moral relativism. Thus, they see "the West's" pressure to affirm human rights as rooted in a positive *jus civile* of a particular civilization or (in some versions) in the philosophical or religious "values" of distinct traditions or historical periods of thought, and doubt that either humanwide "first principles" or universalistic ends can be found if one turns to particular traditions, especially in the face of religious variety and cultural multiplicity. The fact of the diversity of religions and cultures is taken as an argument for relativism in normative morality. Thus, human rights are seen as a matter of sociohistorical context. While some lament that more universal principles cannot be found, many celebrate the fact, making diversity, multiculturalism, and religious distinctiveness themselves universally positive moral values, although on their own grounds it is difficult to see how they could defend the view, except as a cultural preference. In this situation, to insist that all people be judged according to principles of human rights is seen as an act of cultural imperialism. In addition, some argue that such "values" are altogether too individualistic, and that since abstract individuals do not exist, only concrete persons-in-relationship do, we need an ethic based essentially in the particularities of specific community-embedded practices and duties.

Politically, such arguments can be seen to feed the interests of those states that are the least democratic and the most likely to violate the rights of their own citizens, as recognized by the interfaith Project on Religion and Human Rights. Nearly a decade ago they recognized that:

> To date, governmental claims that culture justifies deviating from human rights standards have been made exclusively by states that have demonstrably bad human rights records. State invocations of "culture" and "cultural relativism" seem to be little more than cynical pretexts for rationalizing human rights abuses that particular states would in any case commit. (Some) . . . emulate China in appealing to . . . national sovereignty. . . . (Others) . . . such as Saudi Arabia, . . . maintain that they are following Islamic human rights norms, while failing to adhere to the norms that they officially deem Islamic. . . .[1]

Yet these critics have one valid point that fuels their argument. They are partially correct insofar as they know that abstract principles and abstracted autonomous conceptions of human nature do not and cannot supply a full ethic for humanity or provide the general theory to guide a just and peaceful civil society in a global era. They also know that particular kinds of ethical obligations, rooted in specific traditions of duty, are authentic aspects of morality and identity and that the most significant of these are rooted in commitments that have become joined to religious loyalties, and that something precious would be lost or betrayed if these were denied.

But these critics are only partly correct. They are also partly wrong when they view the matter as a situation where we must turn *either* to first principles of an abstract universalistic kind *or* to concrete networks of culturally, historically, and biographically gained commitments, loyalties, and

---

1. John Kelsey and Sumner Twiss, eds., *Religion and Human Rights* (New York: The Project on Religion and Human Rights, 1994), p. 38.

expectations that shape our senses of responsibility, especially if that is how they view the highest level of religious or theological truth. In fact, most ethical issues, including those of human rights, require a synthetic judgment, one in which we must join normative first principles to the concrete matrices of experience by which we know events and read the existing ethos of our lives — that concrete network of events, traditions, relationships, commitments and specific blends of connectedness and alienation which shape the "values" of daily experience and our senses of obligation. The classic traditions of case-study, codified in the "responsa" literature and in classic casuistry as well as the modern strictures of court procedure, exemplify this joining: they require both a finding of law, which involves the critical reflection on juristic first principles behind the law, *and* a finding of "fact," which requires reliance on the experience-gained wisdom, often having to argue before a jury of peers. Moreover, they require an anticipatory assessment of the various consequences of various courses of action implied by a judgment about the interaction of principle and fact.

Indeed, it is theologically paradigmatic that following the accounts of the Decalogue in both Exodus and Deuteronomy, surely prime examples of universalistic abstract principles, the next several chapters are repositories of the casuistic results of the blending of the implications of those principles with the situations that people experienced concretely in their ethos. This joining rendered judgments that are held to contribute to the well-being of the common life and to the development of a morally righteous people. Similarly, much in the prophetic tradition makes the case against the infidelities of the people and/or the people in power by identifying the enduring principles in the covenants of old, the experience of social history in the present, and the prospects for a bleak, or a redeemed, future according to human deserts and divine mercy. And, for Christians specifically, to deny that any absolute universal can be connected to the realities of concrete historical experience in ways that lead to a redeemed future is in fact a denial of the deepest insight of our faith: that Christ was both fully God and fully human, and that his life fulfilled the commands of God, was concretely lived in the midst of a specific ethos, and nevertheless pointed to an ultimate future that we could not otherwise obtain.

This should be our first lesson in understanding the bases of human rights. First, they foster specific kinds of pluralism because theologically based moral judgments are, in principle, demanding of a universalistic reference point, but are simultaneously pluralistic in their internal structure. Second, they demand critical reflection on the first principles of right and wrong, plus both the repeated analysis of the actual events and experiences of life as they occur in particular contexts, and a vision of the ultimate future — one that anticipates a more final assessment of what is right, judging what is wrong and affirming what is already good as we live toward the future. The philosophies and politics of "either/or" are inevitably lopsided.

The first implications of this brief excursus about "abstractions" for our question are these: do not trust theologians, philosophers, or social critics who repudiate first principles or advocate positions or policies that encourage humanity to ignore them in favor of a view that accents only the concreteness of historical experience. Similarly, do not trust those philosophers or religious leaders who do not take into account the complex matrices of experience that people have in the concrete contexts of life. Moreover, we should place both under scrutiny on the question of whether their proposals regarding the prospects for the ultimate future form a horizon in which we shall be able to discern an assessment of our proximate synthetic judgments.

Not only do I want to argue that the affirmation of such "universal absolutes" as those stated in the Ten Commandments and less perfectly embodied in human rights provisions of our historic constitutions and such documents as the United Nations Declaration is compatible with, and in fact seen most profoundly by, certain strands of the deeper theological heritage, I want to claim that without the impetus of theological insight, human rights concepts would not have come to their current widespread recognition, and that they are likely to fade over time if they are not anchored in a universal, context-transcending metaphysical reality.

I want to suggest also that there is another way in which "abstraction" is required by the best of Christian and ethical views. At the practical level, persons are sometimes abstracted from their concrete historical situations and need the protection of abstract laws and rules and procedures of enforcement that say: "This person may already be alienated from his or her context of ordinary moral relationships, but the dismantling of this person's integrity must not proceed beyond specifiable limits: it is 'indivisible.' Thou shalt not torture, abuse, violate, exploit or wantonly execute even the most miserable and guilty specimen of a human being!" We can see this in one way when we are dealing with someone accused of a crime, imprisoned, subjected to slavery or forced labor, victimized by rape or torture, forced to submit to arranged marriages or liaisons, or denied the ability to participate by voice or vote in familial, political, or economic institutions that decide their fate. In these imposed situations, persons are functionally alone, abstracted, as they face a dominating power they cannot control and to which they do not give honest assent. Without knowing what the race, gender, nationality, cultural background, social location, political preferences, character, or network of friends of a person are, we must say, abstractly, "some things ought never to be done to them"; and if persons, to live and sustain some shred of dignity in the midst of someone or other of such situations need help, "some things ought to be done for them," as Michael Perry has put it. This implies that other people and institutions must limit their powers with regard to persons, and not to define the whole of the meaning of a person by the communities, traditions, and habits in which they are embedded. This means also that, in some ways, a profound individualism, in the sense of the moral inviolability of each person, in contrast only to communitarian regard, is required.

At other points, people abstract themselves from the matrices of life in which they dwell ordinarily, when they choose to leave home, get married (especially if the partner is one whom the parents do not approve for reasons, say, of ethnicity or religion), seek access to a profession other than that of the "station in life" into which they were born, decide to have or not to have a child by the use of pregnancy technology, and, most critical for our discussions, decide whether to follow the faith in which they were born and raised with dedication and devotion, or turn to another by overt rejection or positive conversion — that is, by joining the inchoate company of atheists or agnostics or joining another community of faith. Here, in quite a different way than in some humanly imposed violation of personhood, one stands as an individual before the deepest levels of his or her own soul and before God or the emptiness of nothingness. People may be informed by other persons' advice, arguments, or threats, and a person's community of origin may have rules and regulations about such things, but in the final analysis the individual person stands sociologically quite alone in such moments.

All the current debates about "proselytism" and hence of the freedom of religion at the personal level are at stake here. Moreover, this fact of personal freedom implies the necessity of the right of people of like "chosen" faith to associate and form "voluntary associations" on religious grounds and to engage in free speech and press to seek to persuade others to join their faith. In these two areas of life, when people are under coercion that alienates them from their communities of life, or when they choose to leave their community of origin to join an association of conscientious, committed orientation, they must have the right to do so. These two areas illustrate a certain "soul sovereignty" with regard to individual human rights that, if denied, leads to the dehumanization of humanity. From a normative Christian point of view, not always recognized by all in the tradition, each person must be free from the miseries of oppression and the threat of arbitrary destruction, and must have, at least, the basic rights to form families, to find a calling, and to convert to a worldview or religion that is in accord with a personal understanding of the "best light." Christians hold that these matters ought not to be matters of coercion, and that the use of it to force or restrict persons' decisions in these areas issues in a lie in the soul and the corruption of society. In this regard, a second level of pluralism is fundamentally affirmed and advocated by this tradition.

Christians and many Jews hold this view because we believe that each person is made in the "image of God." That is, we have some residual capacity to reason, to will, and to love that is given to us as an endowment that we did not achieve by our own efforts. And while every one of these areas of human life is at least imperfect, often distorted by sin, obscured by false desires or corrupted by exterior influences in sinful circumstances, the dignity conferred on us by the gift of the "imago" demands both a personal regard for each person, and a constant drive to form and sustain those sociopolitical arrangements that protect the relative capacities to reason, to choose, to love that are given with this gift. Moreover, Christians hold that each person is called into particular networks of relationships in which he or she may exercise these capacities and to order these networks with justice, as God guides us to be just and loving agents in the world. We believe that in Christ, we learn how God wants us to reorder the institutions of the common life — sacramentally, or as others say, covenantally — that are necessary to preserve humanity, and how to make them and ourselves more nearly approximate to the redemptive purposes God has for the world. Those Christians who know the history of the development of the social and ethical implications of their faith, believe that the historical and normative defense of human rights derives from precisely these roots and that this particular tradition has, in principle, in spite of many betrayals of it by Christians, disclosed to humanity something universally valid with regard to human nature and the necessities of just social existence.

Still a third implication of this tradition for pluralism and human rights is signaled by the direct mention of the term "church." The formation of the Christian church, anticipated in certain sociological ways, of course, in the older traditions of the synagogues and, to a degree, in the ancient Mediterranean mystery cults, was a decisive influence in the formation of pluralistic democracy and in the generation of civil society with legal protection of the rights of free association. One of the greatest revolutions in the history of humanity was the formation of institutions differentiated from both familial, tribal, and ethnic identity on one hand and from political authority (as under the Caesars, Kaisers, and Czars of history), as happened in early Christianity by slowly making the claim stick that the church was the Body of Christ with an inviolable, divine sovereignty of its own. This was gradually made more actual by those now obscure, ancient struggles between Pope and Emperor, Bishop and King, Preacher and Prince, and again, more fully, in the modern Protestant, especially Puritan and Pietist, demanding of the right to form congregations outside of state authorization, and in the struggles for tolerance. These developments have generated a social fabric where multiple independent institutions can flourish.

This has not only generated a diversified society in which colleges and universities, multiple political parties, a variety of economic corporations, and a mass of self-governing charitable and advocacy groups flourish, it has established the legitimacy of their claims to rights as associations with their own purposes. Indeed, it has made those parts of the world where these influences are most pronounced the safest havens for nonestablished and nonmajoritarian religions, including non-Christian ones, to enjoy. The empirical consequence is that the Christian faith and its concrete social embodiment, for all the ambiguities, foibles, and outright betrayals of Christianity's own best principles (this faith did not abolish original sin, after all), has opened the door to the development of dynamic pluralistic democratic polities that are both protected *by* human rights ideals and laws and provide the organizational infrastructure for the protection *of* human rights of both persons and of groups.

Two related problems in this area face us as we face a global future. One is the basic question as to whether we can form a global civil society that does not have a theologically based inner moral architecture at its core. Historically, no society has ever existed without a religion at its center and no complex civilization capable of including many peoples and subcultures within it has endured without a profound and subtle religiously oriented philosophy or theology at its core. Yet some civilizations seem to have been repeatedly renewed by the development of doctrines and innovative social institutions based in their deepest heritage while others seem to have been incapable of perpetual self-reformation. The present worldwide rhetoric and legal agenda of human rights, with its several "generations" of rights, is, I believe, most deeply grounded in a highly refined critical appropriation of the biblical traditions; but many of the current activists on behalf of human rights have little place for religion or theology in their conception of what they advocate. Can it endure without attention to its roots and ultimate legitimations? Doubtful!

Constructing a Global Public Theology

However, if human rights are universal in principle and the biblical, theological, and social legacies here identified provide a strong, possibly the only, grounds for recognizing and enacting them in the midst of a highly ambiguous social history, as I have suggested, we still have to ask what this means for those religions, philosophies, and cultures not shaped by this legacy. I am personally convinced of the fact that the theological motifs here discussed are, in this area of thought and action, scripted into the deepest levels of the human soul, even if they are overlaid and obscured by other doctrines, dogmas, practices, and habitual ways of thinking in many of the traditions of the world's religions, including some branches of Judaism and Christianity. Thus our task is to identify where, in the depths of all these traditions, that residual capacity to recognize and further refine the truth and justice of human rights insights lies, for this is necessary in order to overcome what, otherwise, is likely to be a "clash of civilizations." And if, God willing, we are able to survive such a clash, should it come, it is these that could, more than any other option known to me, at least provide a model for a just reconstruction of a global civil society.

Living the Tensions: Christians and Divorce

Divorce deeply troubles Christians. They know that both scripture and tradition condemn it, and the evidence mounts that it is hard on kids, yet nearly everyone today has been touched by it, either personally or through families and friends. Not to face the issue openly in our churches would be a failure of moral nerve. But to be legalistic about divorce would align us with those who tried to trick Jesus by asking him, "Is it lawful for a man to divorce his wife?"

Jesus recognized the trap in the question and answered these lawyers by referring to the law. He appealed to the ancient law of Moses, which permitted divorce under certain circumstances. But he went further, citing the very foundational design of God's creation: "'God made them male and female,'" he quotes. "'For this reason a man shall leave his father and mother and be joined to his wife and the two shall become one flesh.'" In his own words, he concludes, "Therefore what God has joined together let no one separate." The ideal for marriage is the heterosexual, monogamous lifelong union. That is what God intended; any departure from it is problematic.

But in the actual living of life, the people of God have had trouble with this hard saying of Jesus. Various sections of the Bible seem to present other arrangements, such as polygamy, as permissible. The laws of Moses allowed divorce and remarriage, and Jesus himself forgave the woman taken in adultery. Throughout its history, the church has allowed various procedures for annulment and separation. John Milton, the great Puritan poet, was one of the first to publish a theological defense of divorce. But all these compromises recognize that the necessary decisions of life do not always match what God wants for us — and what, at the deepest levels, we want for ourselves.

There are other sayings of Jesus that are equally hard to live out. The New Testament admonishes us to live peacefully with our neighbors. "Blessed are the peacemakers," Jesus says. Yet when Christians are confronted by murderers, rapists, or tyrants like Adolf Hitler, they may feel forced to respond with coercive force. Though war is wrong, it is sometimes the justifiable lesser of two evils. Similarly, though the biblical tradition presses us to trust in God's capacity to provide for us and to take no thought for the future, Christians have developed doctrines of responsible stewardship that involve careful financial planning, insurance, and retirement funds.

In these matters, the Catholic approach has been somewhat different from the Protestant. The Catholic tradition set up a two-level morality, one for priests, monks, and nuns and another for the laity. Those in religious orders are to avoid worldly activities that could result in divorce, require the use of coercive violence, or involve them in economic calculation. They take vows of chastity, poverty, and obedience to church authorities.

The Protestant tradition has not made this kind of distinction. Our tradition does not differentiate between clergy and laity, between a higher and a lower morality, as Catholicism does. We all confront equally the tensions between the ideal and the actual conditions of life. All are called to live in but not of the world. Protestants realize that some people will live all or most of their lives unmarried, and honor and include those who remain single. Through baptism and confirmation, we join the church, our most significant community, as individuals rather than as families. Protestantism demands perfection of all and yet acknowledges that none is perfect. Jesus tells the rich man who addresses him as "good teacher" that "no one is good but God alone." When the shocked disciples ask, "Who, then, can be saved?" Jesus replies that it is possible only with God. It is only through God's forgiveness and mercy that we can live amidst and engage the tensions of this world.

Everyone who has been divorced already knows something of this. No one thinks that divorce is wonderful; no one gets married in order to get divorced. When they marry, people hope and plan for a stable, constant, faithful relationship of mutual support and care. When the marital relationship begins to break down, when it becomes intolerable or even vicious, no moral person can avoid feeling shame and guilt. Even if each partner becomes convinced that the spouse bears most of the blame, each is still haunted by the feeling that perhaps "I, too, am guilty."

Sometimes, instead of blaming the spouse, one partner will take all the blame, condemning herself or himself to a dark pit of despair. Such a person has a hard time imagining forgiveness. Usually, when we probe the feelings of people whose marriage is ending, we find exactly what the Bible tells us: an ideal has been compromised. The ancient cries of the faithful surge from our hearts: "God help us. Lord have mercy."

Those who have stable marriages must not cast stones at those who divorce. Happy marriages are a precious gift that we should celebrate with thankfulness, for few if any deserve this gift. Those who hold troubled marriages together through sacrifice and determination are even more to be honored, for the courage to face daily difficulty is surely a sign of grace. We are all tempted to put our trust in activities that strain marriages: the drive for success, the lust for money, the pursuit of career, the deceptive solace of liquor, the fascination of sexual novelty, the quest for self-fulfillment. Jesus tells us that we must strive after the ideal, but that since our lives are often less than ideal, we dare not judge others, "lest we be judged."

We must also remember that though we bear individual responsibility for divorce, our society is also at fault. Economic conditions put pressure on many marriages. And our culture's expectations and visions of marriage are such that many people are not aware of the effort it takes to sustain the joy of love. Only after painful failures or near failures can many of us think of marriage realistically.

Some of us are still influenced by stereotypical conceptions of gender roles that seem to leave little room for our particularities and peculiarities. Others are so misled by our culture's overvaluing of autonomy that we undervalue covenant, commitment, and enduring relationship. Christians are responsible for challenging and changing social structures that constrict the possibilities for happy and stable marriages.

Most people who have been divorced are seeking new relationships and responsibilities. Let us rejoice with those who find them. Many do not, and are frustrated in their longing for love and partnership. In the face of divorce, Christians must neither lower the standards set by their faith to suit the convenience of the times, nor let themselves be trapped by legalistic applications of the ideal. We must live in tension between our ideal of what marriage should be and the harshness of experience in a sinful world.

Divorce is never absolutely right. But by the grace of God people can be forgiven and given another chance in those situations when divorce is the lesser evil. Just as Christians hold that there is life after death, so we hold that there is hope after divorce.

The Pastor as Public Theologian

Some aspects of ministry properly focus on the relation of the soul to God. Every pastor knows that the vibrancy of faith depends, in substantial measure, on the quite personal sense of a living relationship between the deepest core of human selfhood and the living God whom Christians have come to know through Jesus Christ. It is a faith relationship that touches heart, spirit, will, and energy. It is the "God Connection," as some of my students call it. According to traditional Christian teaching, the *imago dei* makes this relationship possible; and God's providential will enlivens the relationship by evoking a sense of vocation. The personal "God Connection" means that no one is ever ultimately alone, although we often feel lonely; that no one is without resources, although we often may be penniless and exhausted; that no one is without a dignity, although we may feel worthless; and that we have a basis for fidelity, even if much in our feelings and context presses us toward faithlessness.

Different traditions express the vitality of this faith relationship differently — some speak of "knowing Jesus," others of a "feeling of absolute dependence," and still others of experiencing a *mysterium tremendum,* of "forming a spirituality," of developing a "vital prayer life," or of "coming to conviction." In these, and dozens of other formulations, Christians express the inner sense of relation to the living power that is greater than any in the world. This is an indispensable vertical awareness that every pastor must have, and must be able to nurture in others. It is the root of faith. Where it is absent, the pastor burns out, the ministry goes stale, the community of faith loses confidence.

Some aspects of ministry correctly focus on hope. The moments of immediate, faithful awareness of God may seem timeless. Yet even if they pass quickly, they remind us of the eternal, and they empower us both to address moments of hopelessness and to live in disjointed times in expectation. Every current intimation of God has a past that points toward and promises a future when we despair of other evidences. It is one of the key aspects of ministry to cultivate the lore of such moments so that we can gain perspective on what is important in the present and be reminded of the prospects of a promising future. Indeed, our capacities to understand the dynamics of the present and to prepare for the future are as proportional to the amplitude of our memory of the past as they are to our vertical sense of the "God Connection." That is why every seminary prepares people for ministry by requiring substantial familiarity with the history of the Hebrews, of the early church, and of the development of doctrine, ethics, liturgy, and missions over the ages.

Pastors are, among other things, custodians of that memory, recorded in scripture and tradition, for these allow us to encounter and convey the vision of a new heaven and a new earth. The core of the past provides renewed and renewing hope even in the face of suffering and the threats of loss, death, nuclear holocaust, or cosmic entropy. Where this rooted hope is absent, people allow the memories of family, class, or tribal experience to determine their understandings of the present, and anticipate a future that extends no longer than the reading of their wills. Trapped in ghettos of temporal immediacy, people simply endure, without vision. The ends of life are narrow and short.

Still other aspects of ministry correctly demand attention to the horizontal relationships we have with other people. A deep faith and a long hope prompt a wide reach. Reinhold Niebuhr once wrote that "nothing we do, however virtuous, can be accomplished alone. Therefore we are saved by love." Love, like faith and hope, is rooted in the grace of God. It nurtures the capacity to listen to, care for, and share with other people. Love seeks involvement with the neighbor and reaches toward compassionate inclusion of the neglected and the despised. It draws into its scope those whom we could not otherwise stand; it builds enduring bonds of trust and mutuality with all whom it embraces. Love makes every human relationship a co-archy; it resists both domination and subordination. Love invites to service, yet it refuses subservience. This, too, is indispensable to ministry. Where this is absent, leadership becomes managerial, paternalistic, servile, or condescending.

Pastors who already know that faith, hope, and love are radically real are potential members of the communion of the saints — although all of us know ourselves to be less than saintly. But the locus of ministry is not only in the *communio sanctorum*. It takes place among those specific collections of sinners, housed in quite material buildings, besieged by ideological, material, temporal, and affectional conflicts, that we call "the church." And to deal practically with churches we must add to faith, hope, and love, "wisdom" — the kind of wisdom that is wiser than serpents. It is a kind of prudence that, in the mix and mess of daily life, is able to discern the relative concretions of faith, hope, and love already present and evoke longings for them when they are absent. This entails the craft of ministry, one that structures the common life of worship and witness with the resources at hand, that builds of broken lives a temple to God. Such craftiness demands not only an awareness of the theological virtues, but also a specific kind of graceful shrewdness whereby pastors can see, without becoming cynical, potentialities for faith, hope, and love in the midst of pride, greed, and lust, where they frequently appear.

Ministry, thus, lives in the service of those times and places in which the vertical, the historical, and the horizontal genuinely intersect, and an *ecclesia* is formed. Then we find a lively sense of the holy in the midst of unholy life. We find people touched by a vital spiritual strength; we find horizons expanded by vision, and relationships of grace and equity. When these are organized, celebrated, and acknowledged as gifts of a gracious God, we find that churches become centers of holiness. The wisdom to know how the vertical, the historical, and the horizontal dimensions of holiness can be brought to organizational form, and how they become embodied on earth, is also indispensable to ministry.

The Larger World

In one sense, however, these authentic and indispensable dimensions of ministry, and their centers of intersection, are not the end of ministry. They are complicated enough that it is understandable that much of what ministers do is focused only on such matters. But from another perspective these are only the beginning, the point of departure, for faithful and effective ministry. For not only churches, but also civilizations — in other, more complex ways — are concrete embodiments of relative intersections between the vertical, the historical, the horizontal, and the communal dimensions of existence. A public world, which personal spirituality may neglect or flee, is the context of faith. The memories and expectations of peoples, nations, religions, and cultures, which our traditions may not include, are the context of our hope. And neighbors whom we shall never know, but whom we are called to love in impersonal ways, are the context within which our particular affections are bonded. Organized centers of trust, service, and excellence that shape the beliefs, receive the commitments, and preoccupy the people surround the churches we serve.

I am saying nothing that pastors do not already know. We are not oblivious to the fact that when we drive down the street we see not only churches, but homes, schools, shops, factories, police stations, clinics, theaters, and monuments as well. And when we pick up the paper we find sections on business, sports, politics, television, medicine, learning, and law — as well as religion. Do we not, ourselves, turn to the universities when we want education; to the hospitals when we are ill; to the courts to resolve conflicting claims; to the corporations when we want goods or services or jobs; to the concert halls, ball parks, or films when we want entertainment; and to government — even with its instruments of coercion — when we seek the constraint of crime and violence? Such institutions constitute the public world, and those whom we gather in our communities of worship to speak of faith, hope, and love often find their senses of fidelity, purpose, and mutuality in such institutions.

Each of these institutions is constituted by a complex set of trusts, memories, and hopes, by complex networks of affections, and, of course, by communal embodiments of regularized rituals, rites, doctrines, and polities, although they seldom speak of anything theological. Do these institutions not also have, at least potentially, a vertical relation to God, a historical sense of roots and destiny, and a horizontal relation to neighbors near and far? If these public worlds are the larger context of our ministries, we need a public theology to deal with that reality.

We have a name for that which speaks of, invites us to have, and enhances a personal conviction about personal faith: "piety." We also have a name for those normative streams of memory that shape our present and bear promise for the future: "tradition." Still further, we have a name for the kind of bonding, in mutuality, that seeks to secure co-archic human relationships of love: "covenant." And we have a name for the distinctive beliefs that are held by specific religious communities when these are joined: "confessions." All these may be necessary to the formation and preservation of Christian identity; but as my colleague Eleanor McLaughlin pointed out in a recent sermon, identity is frequently nothing more than "individual self-fulfillment at the institutional level . . . [a manifestation of] exclusive individual or tribal values." What we seldom have is a way of critically connecting these to the structures of life in the world, a way of speaking with and to the world, a way of discerning where in the fabric of civilizations the divine may be present, and a way of making the case, in the world, for the significance of that to which we point when we testify to faith, invoke traditions that engender hope, form covenants in love, and make our confessions. Few have a public theology.

The term "public theology" may be new to some, but it has been around for at least a couple of generations, and it applies to a kind of thinking that has deep roots in Christian history and that intentionally attempts to overcome the relegation to irrelevance the word "theology" often provokes. Indeed, the case could be made that "theology," in its systematic and critical-reflective senses, did not even appear in Christianity until the confessional foundations of faith, hope, and love, as we see them in the Bible, encountered public worlds beyond its own — in Greek, Roman, and (subsequently) other cultures. In many contexts biblically grounded faith, hope, love, and wisdom have had to make the case, in public discourse, that its deepest concerns were reasonable in the face of, pertinent to, even decisive for, the patterns of thought and structures of civilization in which believers found themselves.

The term is as much a symbol as a concept. That is, it has several levels of meaning that need to be sorted by comparison and contrast with modes of thought to which it is allied but from which it is distinct. Public theology is not, for one thing, "biblical politics," a particular temptation of those branches of Protestantism that take the Reformation doctrine of *sola scriptura* in the direction of bibliolatry. Public theology does not attempt what some fundamentalists and liberationists try to do. For example, it does not take the creation story or the references to Armageddon as the basis for political movements to alter government policies in regard to education or nuclear weaponry. Nor does it take the exodus story or the references to the Jubilee as the basis for political movements to alter governmental policies in regard to the Sandinistas or welfare legislation. Public theology takes the witness of scripture more seriously than these selective distortions, for it notes how lopsided such uses of scripture are. Instead, it points out that later scripture uses earlier scripture in a much subtler way, and it reminds us that then is not now, and there is not here.

Political Theology?

Nor is public theology identical with its closest relative, political theology, which both historically and among modern advocates such as Catholic Johannes Metz and Protestant Jürgen Moltmann finds its locus in countries where religion is officially established or, as Frederick Lawrence points out, in lands were religious leadership is part of the unofficial political establishment.[1] Like political theology, public theology does recognize the "crisis of legitimacy" brought about by the attack on traditionally held beliefs at the hands of those modern "masters of suspicion," Nietzsche, Marx, and Freud, and it does recognize that no theology is complete that does not address political responsibilities. But public theology does not begin the approach to the crises of common meaning in modern life through political means. It is instead an attempt to say that political problems are not the primary ones, and that we make an error if we allow the word "public" to be used in a way that makes all decisions about the common life matters of state.

The differences between public theology and political theology are these: Public theology has a social theory of political life, one that understands religiously rooted metaphysical and moral convictions to be integral to the formation of societies and their constituting institutions, of which one aspect, but not the whole, is necessarily political. Political structures can change and be changed accordingly as they *serve* the other institutions in a civilization, and are obedient to the warranted claims of justice and truth implicit in the governing metaphysical-moral vision, as borne by the nongovernmental institutions. Political theology, in contrast, tends toward a political theory of social life, one that understands political structures to be the *master* of all other institutions in a society. Thus all other institutions are subject to change by the use of political means. Organized religion is tempted to become an instrument of state, or an ideology to seize and guide the state. In short, it is a question of whether the "public" is prior or secondary to the "republic."

At a different level, what is at stake between political theology and public theology is a question of the meaning of the noun that both "public" and "political" modify. What is it that theology offers life and thought beyond the community of worship? Political theology tends to view theology as organized reflection on our faith as we confess it. Theology clarifies dogmatic themes to which a community of believers adheres, and spells out implications for political action. Political theology, in other words, is the modern form of the priestly adviser to princes — in its current radical forms, to pretenders to the thrones of the world.

Public theology, in contrast, is apologetic, not confessional, in approach. It intends to offer to the world not "our confessional perspective," but warranted claims about what is ultimately true and just that pertains to

---

1. Frederick Lawrence, "Political Theology," *Encyclopedia of Religion* 11 (New York: Macmillan, 1986), pp. 404-8. See also in same volume Max L. Stackhouse, "Politics and Religion," pp. 408-23.

all. It attempts, therefore, to ask: What aspects of the many confessions that religious groups make, including our own, are true and just, as measured by an epistemologically and ethically defensible understanding of what humans can reliably know about truth, justice, and God? It is willing to submit the specific contents of its own confessions, of its own faiths, hopes, and loves to public scrutiny, and to engage in those public forms of discourse by which truth and justice are recognized ecumenically and cross-culturally. What theology sets forth, thus, is not in the first instance addressed to political powers, established or anti-establishment, on the basis of "our religion," but to the people through those communities of discourse — scientific, jurisprudential, economic, cultural, technological, etc. — by which people find glimpses of true and just meanings in their lives. When theological claims are made, thus, they are to be filtered through the consciences of the people and linked by them, if by anybody, to political matters.

Several implications follow from this. Insofar as public theology has direct implications for politics, it implies the necessity of "democracy," in the sense that every state or use of political authority is to be limited by the obedience of all state power to publicly discerned first principles. Such discernment has both cross-cultural and populist elements. It presumes that there are interfaith, constant, and intercultural standards of truth and justice to which every regime must be subject; and it presumes that the people within a given society can sufficiently transcend their own cultural biases to grasp these principles and demand that their own governments be accountable to them. We call these "human rights." Public theology is, thus, not to be confused with any "civil religion," or any "social spirituality" that derives only from the cultural and historical experiences of a given people.[2] Even should these contain universalistic principles, a transcontextual understanding of truth and justice would be required to recognize them.

Public theology has a prophetic streak that invites it to engage and evaluate every religion and every sociocultural context. But unlike those understandings of prophecy that presume a "divine zap" theory of revelation, a public theology presumes that the truth and justice of God can be, in some measure, reliably known through philosophical theology and ethics. What prophetic theology and ethics are about is not privileged, esoteric, or confined to specific confessional identities. In this regard, public theology is closer to certain classic understandings of prophecy that linked it to "natural

---

2. I have dealt with these at some length in *Creeds, Society, and Human Rights* (Grand Rapids: Eerdmans, 1984).

theology." This can be seen in Augustine, when he linked the biblical tradition to Neoplatonic thought; in Thomas Aquinas, when he used Aristotle and Augustine to join faith and reason; in Calvin, when he spoke of "common" or "general" grace and used Stoic motifs to explicate it; or in Jonathan Edwards, who used Locke to speak of a "Consent to Being." None of these, to be sure, end up being philosophical only, for they recognized that metaphysical or moral speculation based only in human reason becomes rudderless. Philosophy requires a God-centeredness to render a genuinely universal sense of truth and justice.

To be sure, such models put an enormous burden on the pastor, one that many would gladly neglect, and that more feel ill-equipped to accept. It is my central contention, however, that the pastor is to be not only one who wisely nurtures Christian faith, hope, and love in specific congregations, but also the philosophical-theologian of universally valid truth and justice in residence among the peoples of God, and to equip the people to discern how and where, *in the world,* the traces of God's truth and justice may be unveiled. Perhaps Whitehead, Tillich, Brunner, Niebuhr, Lonergan, and Panikkar can draw the harvest of modern philosophical, scientific, cultural, social, psychological, and comparative-cultural theories into dialogue with Christian concerns; acknowledge that something of the truth and justice of God may be found in the "secular" modes of understanding; and restate the deepest sensibilities of Christian claims in ways that allow the world to see their truth, their justice, and their pertinence in the world; but to expect pastors to do the same will be seen by many as simply too much. My argument, however, is that it is precisely this "too much" that must become woven into the fabric of what pastors do.

Some Difficulties

I recognize that this presents difficulties to many modern pastors. One difficulty we have to face is the fact that secularization has shaped us all more profoundly than even our immediate forebears. *Homo religiosus* is, for many in our churches, for some in the ministry, and for more in our culture, intellectually, emotionally, and institutionally segregated from *homo intellectus, homo economicus, homo faber,* and *homo legis.* On the one hand, this has meant that clergy sometimes come to believe that they do not have to think about, systematically study, or be theologically responsible for or to scientific, economic, artistic and technical, or legal structures of modern life. Some, to be sure, preach that *homo religiosus* must become more relevant. But they prescribe only one course: liberation; that is, as Christ overthrows the principalities and powers, so we must act to liberate everything from the prevailing structures of authority.

But the people do not believe us. Clergy proclamations about the horrors of American imperialism or the terrors of multinational corporations are met with the same responses that Catholic laity give to magisterial proclamations about birth control: laity tend to ignore what the pastors say because they do not believe pastors know what they are talking about. They may indulge pastors they love, but they will often try to get them to avoid "politics" and stick to "religious stuff." Current prevalent views of what it means to be relevant and faithful trap the ministry today. If we see "relevance" as "liberation" only, clergy can either "speak out" and be ignored or keep quiet and manicure people's psyches. In either case it means that spiritual, relational, scriptural, and ecclesial matters, which clergy do take seriously, simply become all the more cut off from cultural, social, and civilizational aspects of life wherein the people spend most of their time, energy, and money. "Real life" is therefore set outside the domain of theology and ministry.

A second difficulty we have to face is that today, and in spite of the secularization of many arenas of life, we have no choice but to engage the world's religions in new ways. The religions of the world are not only "long ago and far away," but also in the news every day, among the relatives of people we pastor, and woven into the inchoate beliefs of church members. Magic and most of the ancient heresies are well entrenched in some segments of our churches, as are Hindu views of the soul, Islamic views of the divine dictation of holy writ, Buddhist views of "release," Confucian senses of filial obligation, and pagan views of tribe or clan. Often we cannot recognize them. Max Mueller was surely correct when he said that those who understand only their own religion understand none.

But it is surely also correct that every attempt to encounter other religions introduces the problems of an epistemological, metaphysical, and moral pluralism in new ways. Similarly, much of modern philosophy has become increasingly dedicated to the proposition that there is nothing that can be reliably known about transcendence. Human experience and rationality are on their own; all universalistic claims are historically, psychologically, or linguistically idiosyncratic and perspectival. The foundations of the common life, and of common human understanding, have no warranted bases in, and none for, anything like "God."

These difficulties are reinforced by our daily encounter with the belated fruits of the Enlightenment's rationalistic skepticism about all religious matters, and the Romantic movement's skepticism about both institutional religion and the Enlightenment's rationalism. The echoes of religious skepticism, anti-intellectualism, and anti-institutionalism resonate still in our churches, in our communities, in our human relationships, and in our hearts. As heirs of the Enlightenment and of Romanticism, whether they know it or not, many doubt that faith, hope, love can be connected with truth and justice, in anything like an "objective" sense, in the first place. We have perhaps capitulated too much when we allow the view that between profound faith and profound reason stands a great gulf, that there are no reasonable grounds for being a believer, or that only a faith that is beyond reason can supply insight for life.

One of the greatest temptations of our time is "confessionalism," especially as it tries to be socially relevant on the basis of contextually derived insights. Confessionalism is the view that theology is not a "science" in which there can be any reliable knowledge about God's truth and justice. Rather, it is an expression of personal or group opinion based on what the experience of our social context presents to us, or on what we are acculturated into believing, or on what we choose to believe. Thus what is true or just for some may be quite different for others. Theology then becomes little more than the rationalized clarification of inchoate convictions, and ethics becomes the expressive clarification of values into which we are socialized or for which we arbitrarily decide. Each person, each little group, each corporation and union, each party, each caucus and interest group, and indeed each church asserts what it wants to pursue on the basis of its own confession, often without supplying the warrants as to why anyone not already committed should take us seriously.

Is it not odd that we no longer speak of "Christian persuasion"? The phrase, indeed, sounds quaint today. But I suspect that this signals a profound and dangerous development, especially since we do hear a good bit about who has "power" — clout. Modern intellectual leadership today, including many clergy, has lost confidence in the possibility that we can *know* anything about the most fateful matters for the future of humanity, about what is basic and universally valid in regard to truth and justice, pertinent to the salvation of civilizations as well as souls, and capable of being persuasively argued in the public forums of life. If this is so, clergy have, in fact, no reliable word for the world, no warranted claims to which all should attend, no message for modernity, nothing for those who hear us preach to carry into worlds of work except personal piety, individual hopes, and private affections. For the public world all we have, like every other enclave of special interest, is the possibility of pitting power against power, and interest against interest. But the power of persuasion is not considered to be real power in the ways of the world.

The problem is this: Theology, which is the only thing pastors have to offer the world not already better offered by others, becomes the rhetorically ordered proclamation of what some deeply believe on irrational grounds. But it is something cut off from public discourse, frequently presented in such a way as to suggest that no public warrants for it could be given in the world. Such a view of theology presents at least two problems.

First, in the pluralistic religious world in which we live it is already believed that all religious convictions are a matter of personal or group preference. Some may be into this or that confessing church, others into Sufi meditation, others into Orthodox Judaism, others into the "human potential movement," and still others into Christian pacifism or post-Christian feminism. *All these confessional stances are easily tolerated because they make no basic difference to public life.* Each confessional stance is a curiosity unto itself. "Personally," said a *New Yorker* cartoon figure, "I'm a Zen-Presbyterian."

Second, confessionalism allows the world to wallow in its own pseudo-realism. The medical professional is not pressed to struggle with the relation of body to spirit. The legal professional is not prompted to inquire about the relation of substantive to procedural justice. The artist is not called to create or perform under the norm of beauty. The worker and the manager are not called to see their work as a vocation from God, but can be satisfied with a job or a career. The historian, the scientist, and the journalist can compile facts and correlate data without attentiveness to meaning and value. And public figures can worry about public image, but ignore public virtue. All may, in their personal lives, embrace one or another confession and be "good people," but the fundamental claims of faith about what is ultimately true and just do not form or inform the way "real life" is conducted.

Today we might better take our models from those Christians in such places as India, China, Indonesia, and Korea, who, as tiny minorities, are struggling to make the case as to how and why certain Christian theological understandings of God's truth and justice might well be valid foundations for the transformations of ancient personal loyalties and of ancient, if now rapidly modernizing, cultures. These are among the pastoral theologians of our day whom we should emulate. They refuse to be merely confessional; they refuse merely to oppose Christianity to the structures of complex civilizations; and they refuse to limit the meanings of faith to "private" matters. Instead, they seek to discern where in their cultures the universal living God is present, to state persuasively, in dialogue with non-Christians, something of the nature of truth and justice by which the common life might be transformed. And in the process they find both that many discover the foundations of faith, hope, and love in new ways, and that their own confessions are altered in wider directions.

The Agenda for Pastors

We are badly in need of a new *apologia* for normative public theology and ethics in our day, one that can make the case for the fact that Christian theology and ethics are sciences — art/sciences perhaps but sciences nonetheless — by which we can know that what we teach and preach in churches and enact in the world about faith, hope, and love involves a reliable approximation to the truth and justice of God.

I have referred several times to "truth and justice." I recognize that this is not the most frequent juxtaposition of terms used by clergy today. More frequent are references to "praxis." Indeed, if there is one sacred arrow in the quiver of those who believe themselves to be in the battle for a relevant contemporary theology, one supposed to be the benchmark for ministry today, it is "praxis." The term, however, is not a simple one, and it is, in some ways, one of the most abstract terms of contemporary thought. Orlando Costas, a noted Latin liberationist, is among those who have tried to give it precise definition. He defines "praxis" in this way: "action that provokes reflection and is corrected by it, and reflection that is verified by efficacious action."[3]

It is clear that everything in this definition begins and ends with action. Action is to provoke reflection, and reflection is to be verified by action. But the key normative term in this definition is "efficacious." It is, in other words, another way of speaking about that prudent wisdom which knows how things work, how things get done in the world, and what it takes to be effective. Many in the clergy need prompting in this direction, but I will not focus on this point at this time for the simple reason that I do not think that "praxis" is what the church needs most. I fear that the appeal to "praxis" begs several questions: What is the basis of the initiating action? How do we know what actions will provoke the kind of reflection that does not become merely utilitarian or "technical," or even Machiavellian?

It is possible to answer such questions by saying "the gospel." But that is

---

3. Orlando Costas, "A Vision for the Future," unpublished manuscript presented at the American Baptist Seminary of the West, September 1986, p. 13.

just the point: "praxis" requires a prior theory of the meanings, the purposes, and the principles that ought to guide actions and the kinds of reflection that, when prompted by action, guide action in valid directions. Further reflection is itself an action, and the questions we confront today have to do with what actions and what reflections are worth doing. By what standards, to what end, under what principles? We must have, in other words, standards by which to know whether there are any guidelines by which we can give substance to "efficaciousness," or else we end up with a mere actionism.

Still further, it is a serious question as to what people mean by "the gospel." It may be that what we want to put into practice is faith, hope, and love. But, as I have already argued, these stand today only on confessional grounds, often disconnected from the wider civilizational and intellectual contexts that we must today encounter with new depths. Not a few versions of what the gospel is are quite unbelievable. Further, we want to know whether that in which we have faith, that by which we hope, and that through which we order our love is valid, especially since much of the world does not believe that what we do in the churches on these points has any foundations.

I turn to the key terms "truth" and "justice" to suggest those standards by which we guide our faith, our hope, and our loves — indeed, by which we wisely shape our "praxis." A public theology takes these as touchstones of the logos of God from the foundations of creation. They are, therefore, the foundations for a warranted praxiology. No God and no claims about God, no confessions about God and no appeals to have faith, hope, or love in God, no actions for God or reflections to guide action are believable unless they are true and just.

These two criteria have a particular pertinence in our world for reasons that Costas suggests. Two groups particularly need to know that there is a basis for Christian faith, hope, and love.[4] One group consists of those who have passed through the skepticism, suspicion, and doubt of the post-Enlightenment period. Many exposed to modern science, technology, sociology, psychology, anthropology, and philosophies have come to the conclusion that most of what "religion" talks about is a matter of personal preference, for which no public warrants can be given. Religion is thus relegated to private feelings, and has value primarily, as Robert Bellah has taught us, only insofar as it meets the needs of our therapeutic or managerial individualism.[5] Many,

---

4. Costas, "A Vision for the Future," p. 7.

5. Cf. Robert Bellah, *Habits of the Heart* (Berkeley: University of California Press, 1984).

if not most, of the leaders of intellectual, professional, and cultural life, and not the least, the media, have such a view. They are quite willing to have clergy cultivate the private virtues, massage people's feelings, and repeat a church confession, so long as no claims about their "truth" are made. Religious matters are "newsworthy" only when they are absurd (as Oral Roberts's claims seem to be) or when they are likely to have direct political fallout (as when the Christians, Jews, and Muslims shoot at one another in Lebanon). All claims about God or humanity or sin or grace or salvation are understood to be cultural opinions or psychologically variant perspectives that some people may choose to believe. As Timothy Jackson has demonstrated, however, this means that nothing can ever be taken as really, objectively, basically holy, right, or good — or, for that matter, "perverse," "heretical," "abominable," or "wrong."[6] Not only theology suffers, but also philosophy, jurisprudence, education, literature, and human rights everywhere.

I wonder, in this connection, how many clergy basically believe that what we are called to uphold to the world is indispensable to the salvation of the world; that societies collapse without a metaphysical vision that engages, deepens, broadens, and transforms its basic theoretic foundations; and that the gospel becomes most clear and compelling when it wrestles with, converts, and gives new coherence to that which is beyond itself. To put it in stronger terms, modern society has contracted a metaphysical disease. The somewhat deceptive, relative health of many institutions in modern civilization derives from the fact that many of them were formed in periods informed by a theologically rooted consciousness of God's truth and justice as it wrestled with the hard questions of civilizational formation. We are living on the capital of earlier public theologies. But that same relative health obscures the metaphysical emptiness of the present as well as the facts that no civilization has ever managed to exist without continued guidance from a credible metaphysical-moral vision, and that our society, deciding that one is either dispensable or impossible, has relegated all theological matters to the marginality of private opinion.

The people in our churches sense this, I believe; and that is why many "liberals" seek a "new spirituality" (which is not infrequently an old gnosticism), and why many "evangelicals" are tempted to fundamentalism (which is often a bibliolatry). Both seek a metaphysical vision that neither contem-

---

6. Timothy Jackson, "Ethics, Abominations, and Liberations," address to the Society of Christian Ethics, January 1987, pp. 6-7 and passim.

porary society nor confessional theology supplies. And if the people are not offered a public theology, nonsense or fanaticism will fill the vacuum.

The second group that needs to know that there is some foundation for Christian faith, hope, and love consists of those who have suffered dehumanization through slavery, colonialism, patriarchy, exploitation, or powerlessness. These seem to have much less of an "intellectual" or "metaphysical" problem than a "social" or "ethical" problem, for which justice is the only answer. It does little good to speak of faith, hope, and love with these folks, unless these virtues are connected to those public institutional transformations that make justice a possibility. Public theology, political theology, and liberation theology are agreed on this point.

But just at this point we face secondary problems. Our society has become unsure about what justice is, indeed of whether justice is at all. And many in the global community doubt that there are cross-cultural standards of justice — which means that people of one context cannot persuade others, from other contexts, of the righteousness of their protests against injustice, and that those outside a particular context can have nothing to offer those within that specific context.

Further, many of the analyses of the causes of injustice set forth on behalf of the dispossessed, the poor, and the oppressed today derive from modes of social analysis that, themselves, are very doubtful as to whether there is, or could be, anything like an objective standard of justice. The notion that there is, say some people, merely echoes of idealistic and intellectualistic approaches to reality, which were the artifacts of elites to control others and need to be overthrown. In the attempt to overthrow such "abstractions" they turn to "praxis" understandings of social reality with renewed vigor. But these seldom contain, as we have seen, any governing definitions of either justice or truth to give praxis a logos. The truth of the situations they encounter, they say, is contextual injustice, and cannot be understood by anyone who is not part of the acting-reflecting community, trying to be efficacious.[7] And at this point one sees a new, now secular post-Enlightenment confessionalism, rooted in contextual specificities, that does not, and cannot, claim that the core of what it is about is fundamentally just. The accounts of how cultures, communities, societies, and civilizations work in relation to basic theological and ethical norms, which derive from these analyses, do not convince anyone

---

7. Max L. Stackhouse, "Contextualization and Theological Education," *Theological Education* 23, no. 1 (Autumn 1986): 67-84.

not part of the enclave in the first place. And that is, in part, why "solidarity with the oppressed" has become a "preferential option."

It is not, I want to argue from the standpoint of a public theology, a preferential option. It is a matter of the truth and justice of God that is at stake. Claims about truth that are not linked with justice, and claims about justice that are not linked to truth, are not of God. And neither Christianity nor modern civilizations are served well in the long run by intellectuals who, because they do not believe in God, also doubt truth and justice, or by activists who believe in God but have no way of speaking about the truth and justice of God beyond the dynamics of their contextual confessions.

Perhaps it is now clear why I think that pastors today must not only continue to cultivate the virtues of Christian faith, hope, and love, with wisdom, in the contexts of our communities of worship, but also become, to do so in a convincing and genuine way, "public theologians" willing to take on the additional burdens of recovering and recasting the fundamental notions of truth and justice in the larger domain of public discourse. Our task becomes one that is constantly shuttling from the centers of Christian piety, tradition, and covenant to the periphery of apologetic encounter with the largest, most pervasive metaphysical-moral questions facing humanity.

We have some models in this regard. Reinhold Niebuhr's *Nature and Destiny of Man* remains a classic for our times. So do key works composed by pastors: I invite you to read again Martin Luther King's *Letter from a Birmingham Jail*, paying particular attention to the kinds of arguments he marshals to address the church and the public. Look also to the Roman Catholic Pastoral Letter on the nuclear problem. And note the irony that it is today the "learned clergy" among nonfundamentalist evangelicals and "Christian Unitarians" where questions of apologetics are most eagerly studied.[8]

And how can we who are not Niebuhrs or Kings or bishops or pastor-scholars begin to become public theologians? I think we have to begin with one area of study beyond our ordinary range of reading, thought, and reflection. It may be law, or medical ethics, or philosophy, or some dimension of the natural or social sciences. Or it may be one of the world's religions. And this we have to master, all the while inquiring as to how the deepest, broadest theological orientations we can find speak to, inform, transform, and integrate with the traces of truth and justice we find there. But more important,

---

8. See, for example, C. Stephen Evans, *Philosophy of Religion* (Downers Grove, IL: InterVarsity, 1985), and James Luther Adams, *The Prophethood of All Believers*, ed. G. K. Beach (Boston: Beacon, 1986).

Constructing a Global Public Theology

we have to ask what it is that theology has to say that would and could be persuasive to those who think, live, and work in this way — indeed whether we have anything important to say to that arena of discourse. I suspect that we will find the classic theological doctrines — such as Creation, Fall, Salvation, Trinity, and Sacrament — can and do connect with what we discover and provide resources to the field we have chosen that are not otherwise present. And once we have begun to see how to make the connections in one field, we will see analogues to others. Then we need to preach and teach on these matters, equipping the people to become theologians of God's truth and agents of God's justice in the worlds in which they live, empowered by a faith, hope, and love that have foundations.

I am well aware that this proposal would demand, in the long run, also the reform of theological education, the redefinition of the nature and character of the message we have to deliver, and the reorganization of what pastors read and do daily. It also demands that we look deeper into the traces of God's justice and truth that may be residually present in jurisprudence, economic theory, and behavior and in academic, artistic, and technological life; but I see no alternative if not only souls but also civilizations are to be saved.

PART FOUR

Looking Back, Looking Forward

Conclusion: The Lasting Significance of Max Stackhouse

Max's footprints are visible in many places; with an unusual level of energy, enthusiasm, and the gift of sociability, he has worked indefatigably for God's kingdom in several distinctive capacities. Serving as the Executive Secretary of the Society of Christian Ethics for many years, he helped the Society grow professionally and institutionally; he has been deeply involved in ecumenism from local and national to international levels; he has mentored and counseled numerous students (including the editors of the present volume), pastors, lay leaders, and professionals. Through his tireless engagements with other scholars, both religious and secular, Max has helped Christians understand what is at stake in contemporary social life, and how God is related to our current events and civilizational achievements. As a Methodist-turned-Reformed Christian scholar, he has helped to make Reformed theology and ethics a viable and attractive option today to the extent that it capably competes with other prominent paradigms of Christian public theology, most notably the Roman Catholic natural law ethics. His legacy will continue for a long time, not only through his published works but also through his students and his friends. This concluding essay examines, among his many achievements, Max's contribution as a theological ethicist, focusing on his legacy in three major areas: public theology, ethics of social institutions, and globalization.

Public Theology

Max Stackhouse is one of the best-known public theologians, one whose reputation reaches beyond the border of the U.S. Although the term "public

Looking Back, Looking Forward

theology" is not Max's own invention, he is now respected as a major authority in public theology by virtue of his prolific writings, ecumenical engagements, and professional activities. Max has made an enormous contribution in popularizing the discourses of public theology beyond a narrow Reformed scholarly circle into a wide ecumenical and international setting. Also, thanks to his work, any serious discussion of globalization cannot ignore the role of religion and public theology. There are few public theologians who can compete with Max in terms of his broad scholarly scope and the diverse topics of his research: human rights, business ethics, globalization, technology, theological education, covenant, military industrial complex, urban ethos, stewardship, ethical methodology, and so on. Such exceptionally productive scholarly works have been made possible by virtue of his multidisciplinary competence in theology, ethics, law, economics, political theories, and world religions.

To understand Max's contribution to public theology, we first need to briefly examine what his understanding of public theology is, and why he feels so passionate about it. As the practice of the prophetic and the kingly offices of Jesus Christ, public theology is a genre of theology that mediates the church and the public realm. Relying on God's word revealed through creation and Jesus Christ, it speaks to not only individual believers and churches, but also to social institutions, nations, and the global community for the promotion of their moral health and the common good of humanity. As an organic integration of theology, ethics, and social theories, public theology carries two major functions: critique and reconstruction. A public theologian analyzes and assesses individual issues in the context of an operating theology and a dominating ethos of society, and explores plausible moral directives for the issues in accordance with the criteria of the right, the good, and the fitting. Max is deeply aware that although Christian theology and witness in history could take many different forms, not all of them are faithful, competent, and capacious enough to engage with the pressing issues and challenges of a society.

In constructing public theology, Max draws upon several theological convictions and sources. He believes that Christian theological ethics is unapologetically "public" in nature. His public theology is first and foremost grounded in the doctrine of the triune God — creator, redeemer, and consummator. As the creator, God is in a sense the most public person in the universe. God touches every aspect of life; God works in history and communicates God's will to humanity in various ways. All moral claims and human activities are, therefore, ultimately subjected to God's judgment. In other words, public theology is grounded in the very public nature of God and God's governance (the reign of God).

With creation as the horizon of ethics, all human activities, religious or nonreligious, personal or institutional, are the subject matters of Christian theological reflection and ethical analysis. God has a stake in the holiness of social institutions, the justice of a society, and the sanctity of every creature. Likewise, theology, as a *logos* of *theos,* is a rational enterprise. It is intended for public proclamation and subjected to mutual scrutiny. Therefore, Christian theology cannot be fideistic or sectarian.

Max's understanding of God as public person led him to approach Christian doctrines from a vantage point of public theology. As the articulation of the nature and action of this public God, Christian doctrines have public ramifications. That is, doctrines are not an esoteric belief system for believers alone; they offer profound ethical insights and wisdom in organizing and guiding all human life. For example, while eschatology has to do with the common human *telos,* ecclesiology offers a model of human association; whereas the doctrine of the Trinity indicates a model of social pluralism, covenant is a mechanism of social bonding and self-organizing under the guidance of divine grace.

Viewed from this perspective, the church cannot evade the public nature and claim of God's reign. It is called to serve the common good in its most comprehensive sense; the church is God's public square where all human beings, Jew and gentile, male and female, are invited to work for the well-being of God's creation *(oikonomos).* Deserting its public responsibility will inevitably lead the church to lose its identity and sense of mission. Christian indifference to public ministry is ultimately detrimental to its kerygmatic ministry, for the church loses its spiritual and moral authority over people: its proclamation of the gospel loses credibility. The underdevelopment of public theological competence compromises the church's ethical discernment; churches often cannot tell who are adversaries or allies of the gospel, and they are often taken advantage of by politicians to support their partisan political agenda or a political ideology.

In articulating public theology, Max has consistently argued for a religious dimension of public life. For Max, religion is a ubiquitous and resilient aspect of human life — the powerful source of personal and social identity. Human life cannot be understood without grasping the religious dimension. Religion affects not only what and how we think and behave as individuals but also what kind of culture and social institutions we create in the long run. In short, religion constitutes the most comprehensive meaning system and cultural matrix of a society, one that traverses every aspect of human existence, giving distinctive shape to the development of institutions and a social system.[1] Therefore, religion is a major variable to be factored into any plausible social analysis and public policy formation.

While emphasizing a religious dimension of human existence, however, Max goes a step further by upholding a public theological and ethical standard of adjudication. He asserts that moral claims of religious groups can be tested and redeemed by the criteria of the first principles of the right, the good, and the fitting. Religious groups should be held accountable to their moral beliefs and actions. They need to explain why they believe what they believe and practice. Religious dialogue does not mean flattening of gods. However, not every religious social expression and moral teaching is laudable. He notes: "Only some religio-cultural traditions have prompted humans to develop certain of their potentialities into specifically transeconomic, transpolitical, transfamiliar, transcultural, and transreligious spheres of authority that become defining for social life."[2] In a pluralistic society where tolerance is the crown of the virtues, Max's position may sound intolerant, perhaps even imperialistic. However, a global society cannot ultimately avoid the hard question of adjudication among conflicting moral claims and even clashing worldviews. Given the enormous power of religion, assessment and adjudication are critical for the healthy expression and practices of religions. Honesty before truth and a willingness to concede to better arguments should be the basis of tolerance. Otherwise, the increasingly interdependent world will bring forth more conflicts and confusion.

Through the emphasis on honesty before truth, public redemption of moral claims, and a religious ground of human existence, Max's public theology makes several significant contributions to the church and public life today:

1. Public theology poses a profound challenge for the church's ministry today. Many conservative and evangelical churches today are suffering from a major social credibility problem despite their relative numerical success and political ascendance since the mid-1980s. After several presidential elections and foreign policy blunders (notably the Iraq War), the picture is clear:

---

1. Max Stackhouse, ed., *Religion and the Powers of the Common Life*, vol. 1 of *God and Globalization* (Harrisburg, PA: Trinity Press International, 2000), p. 50. Max is unique in seeing major world religions, like Christianity, Islam, Hinduism, Confucianism, and Buddhism as distinctive civilization-shaping forces.

2. Max Stackhouse, ed., *The Spirit and the Modern Authorities*, vol. 2 of *God and Globalization* (Harrisburg, PA: Trinity Press International, 2001), p. 1.

many churches do not know how to publicly engage today; a bad or flawed theology and ethics misguide them; more often than not, passion outruns intellect. This underdevelopment of public theology is taking a toll, alienating many intellectuals and young people. At the same time, many churches choose to stay out of politics completely, by avoiding challenging, complex, or controversial social issues and focusing instead on individual needs and personal comfort. They virtually segregate their faith and public witnesses. Lay Christians rarely learn how to connect their faith with their professional and institutional life. In the face of the daunting challenges of our society, they withdraw from the public out of fear or a sense of ineptitude. Hence, it is a pressing question whether American Christianity can defend itself intellectually and normatively in the public when globalization and information technology increase the opportunities for public exposure and interaction. In response to this challenging situation, Max's public theology is very relevant in equipping many Christians for their public engagements by providing a plausible theological and ethical framework and directives.

2. Public theology is useful in overcoming the growing dichotomy of the secular and the religious, evidenced by violent responses to the release of the video "Innocence of Muslims" in many Muslim societies, and increasingly hostile or intolerant attitudes of secularists toward religious beliefs and practices. Secularists and religionists mutually suspect or disdain each other because secularists do not recognize the religious root of modern civilization, while religionists do not know how to communicate their beliefs in the public realm. Increasingly, the possibility for communication between the two groups is rare; their perspectives are reified, as they insist on living in their own bubbles without dialogues.

With its emphasis on the public nature of truth on the one hand, and the indispensability of a religious dimension in human existence on the other, public theology could mediate the religious and the secular. Max challenges secular modernist claims on neutrality and the separation of fact and value. He argues that every philosophy or social theory carries in it certain explicit or implicit theological or metaphysical assumptions on human nature, society, and the ultimate reality. Max also corrects the biased assertion of seculars that all religions are particularistic, removed from public truth and morality, and are thus to be treated as private matters. Ethical claims of religious groups can be tested publicly on the basis of the first principles of the right and the good. Max counters secular intellectuals' quick dismissal of religions and their enduring influences; they ignore the formative and binding power of religions over cultural practices and institutional decisions. He proved the flaw of the secular bias by showing how practices of different religions lead to different civilizational formations, how they affect institutional formations and moral decisions (e.g., human rights). Max was vindicated by the rise of religious radicalism, and the resilience and growth of religion among many societies today, which took many secularists by surprise. For Max, the best way to address radical religion is not to avoid it but harness it with good theology and ethics, which is exactly the task of public theology. Secular ethics alone cannot refurbish the public square because it cannot sustain itself solely on the basis of social constructionism of knowledge or functionalism of human interests; skepticism and relativism are unavoidable.

On the other hand, Max challenges religious communities to develop their own public theologies in conversation with secular philosophies and sciences. In fact, any formulation of public theology is required to integrate ethics, theology, and social theories and philosophies. Religion has much to learn from secular disciplines and other religions about ways to interpret and communicate their beliefs. Religion becomes vibrant through public theological engagement — reciprocal exchanges — with "intellectual and social possibilities."[3] Religious communities therefore need to be open-minded; instead of harboring an attitude of suspicion or rejection, they should be conversing with philosophies and sciences as common inquirers of truth. Such dialogues are extremely helpful in understanding complex social phenomena such as urbanization, industrialization, and globalization, which is indispensable for their effective ministry today.

In summary, the current crisis proves that both fundamentalist/conservative Christians and secular liberals lack a capacious moral framework to address an increasingly complex public life. Max's public theology offers a constructive path to overcome the impasse between religion and the public realm. Through his public theology, Max offers a plausible alternative to the overpoliticized (or individualistic) religion and reified secularism today. His public theology is a plausible alternative to a truncated view of the public by either religious fundamentalists or secularists. Bridging the religious and the secular, it helps to revitalize our public sphere, which now faces major challenges in the ascendance of moral relativism, political withdrawal, and the assertion of utilitarian individualism and collective egoism. Public theology is a viable moral option to people who are overwhelmed by the expanding complexity of modern life and the demise of civic values, to people who increasingly find that secular skepticism and relativism cannot stand against

3. Cf. Stackhouse, ed., *The Spirit and the Modern Authorities*, p. 3.

the structural evils of institutional injustices, just as religious fundamentalism cannot adequately address the complexity of modern institutional life.

Vocation and Morality of Social Institutions

Max's public theology is distinctive in systematically addressing multiple, highly differentiated and complex institutions and spheres of society. More than any of his contemporary Christian scholars, Max deeply understood the theological meaning and significance of institutions and spheres. Max developed one of the most sophisticated forms of ethics of associations. Citing his own phrase, his public theology is the study of the *logos* of *socius* of *polis*.[4] Inspired by the idea of covenant, Max sees humans, among other characteristics, as institutional, associational beings who build and lead their life in the nest of diverse, complex organizations. A modern social system is made of diverse institutions with respective authorities and boundaries of autonomy. A modern civilization means, among other achievements, development of the complex institutions now sweeping the world.[5] Modern humans cannot live without institutions. Therefore a discussion of social justice today cannot be complete without the study of complex institutions and their influences; those who do not understand the significance of social institutions are likely to misunderstand the very nature of social life. Individuals often feel powerless before giant institutions that exercise enormous power. As we have seen in the 2008 financial crisis in the U.S., injustices are committed more by institutions than by tyrants or despots. How to theologically and ethically equip and guide them is a major challenge we now face. Unfortunately, today many Christians refuse to take institutions as the prime subject of ethical reflection. They have a very low view of institutions, often accompanied by an underdeveloped theological sociology. Their ethics are mostly individualistic, ecclesiastical, or utopian — all underestimating the power of social institu-

---

4. Refining and expanding the social pluralism of Abraham Kuyper, Johannes Althusius, and others, Max distinguishes three types of institutions, principalities and authorities, and regencies. He does not understand a society as a static entity, but rather as a dynamic process responding to ongoing technological and cultural changes, which is helpful in understanding the rise, development, and constellation of institutions in a global society.

5. Globalization is in a sense the expansion of modern forms of institutions and their influences (e.g., global media and popular culture, and corporations) to every corner of the world, and simultaneously the rise of new institutions and agencies (e.g., the multinational corporations, regional political and economic bodies, and NGOs) on a transnational level.

tions in shaping and affecting human life. Consequently not many leaders are properly equipped to teach their followers how to engage with modern social institutions.

Max's contribution in this area is unparalleled. His public theology of institutions is resourceful in revitalizing the inner spirit and impulse of social institutions in harmony with each other, to charge and instill professionals working in these institutions with a renewed sense of calling and responsibility. Max points out that historically Protestant Christianity, inspired by the idea of covenant, helped give rise to professional distinctiveness to each institution by assuring the autonomy of each institution from a tyranny of the state or the pope. Today these institutions are increasingly free from the moral and spiritual underpinnings that had made their autonomy and growth possible. Detached from this tradition, the institutions, some now transnational, could be corrupted and abusive as they are driven by their narrow interest and competition, forgetting about their own distinctive vocations and boundaries. Max is deeply concerned because he sees that the legacy and contribution of modern institutions will fade away when cut from their deep spiritual energy and moral roots provided through Christianity. Detached from their religious roots, social institutions are losing their moral compass and vision; they ignore their roots, are morally and spiritually empty, and focus solely on utilitarian values and achievements. Institutions can "neither repair what is broken nor improve what promises to get better."[6]

Max reminds us that engaging with these powerful institutions is indispensable to Christian ethics. He believes that not only individuals but also institutions need to hear the gospel in order to be released from their own indulgences and self-aggrandizement. Each institution needs a theologically informed moral vision and guidance. It must be reminded of its distinctive vocation (a mandate) from God, which is indeed the source of its authority and autonomy. None is free from God's sovereign rule; thus none is self-sufficient; cooperation and mutual checks and balances among institutions are necessary.

Globalization

Max's seasoned skills of public theology shine through his study of globalization. His four-volume work, *God and Globalization*, is the culmination of

6. Stackhouse, ed., *The Spirit and the Modern Authorities*, p. 30.

Conclusion

his work of public theology. One sees his lifelong study of Christian theology, ethics, social theories, institutional analysis, and world religions converge in this series in order to take on such a nebulous and complex phenomenon as globalization. One must add that his personal gifts of networking, long-nurtured friendship, and commitment to ecumenism played a no less significant role in mobilizing twenty high-caliber scholars with diverse traditions to the common task.

Max claims that globalization is an unprecedented social phenomenon in terms of its artificial nature and the scope of its radical impact. He sees globalization is an epoch-making structural transformation with the potential rise of a new civilization; it blurs traditional national and tribal boundaries, and unsettles institutional power structures and distributions, throwing people into both excitement and confusion. Globalization produces unparalleled high risks as well as new opportunities for humanity and the planet. That is, although communication and other technological inventions increase manufactured risks for humanity, it also could increase the possibility of peace and cooperation among humanity beyond narrow nationalism and tribalism through the rise of a new public space, such as global civil society. Max asks how we can come up with a new theological ethics (or public theology) that matches the scale of this new emerging civilization, and his collaborative work, *God and Globalization,* is such an attempt to conceive our theology and ethics in ways commensurate with the scale of globalization.

Max emphasizes that globalization should go hand in hand with the strengthening of global governance. Indicating the expanded common life and the rise of new social patterns and institutional life, globalization requires matching vision, norms, values, and governing structure on a global scale and form. In Max's view, public theology is indispensable for the construction of new global governance. Public theology offers a moral-spiritual frame of reference for the coordination and adjudication of competing interests and conflicting claims. Public theology helps to develop an inclusive form of global governance that integrates various global spheres and their institutions under the shared sense of the right and the good.

Although one may not agree with every aspect of Max's view of globalization and his claims, Max deserves credit for being boldly different: while many theories of globalization are simply critiques or even reactions to globalization, Max never loses the broad normative dimension of globalization and its concrete guidance for those working in institutions. Max should be praised for addressing the many sides of globalization by rejecting any form of reductionism. Institutional arrangements and governance that are just cannot be achieved by mono-ethical categories of peace, liberation, justice, or by one sector, such as economics, politics, jurisprudence, or religion. Unlike many mono-dimensional or mono-causal theories of globalization, Max's approach focuses on the complexity of multiple institutions and diverse social spheres, reigning religions, and worldviews. Using pluralistic sociology and multidisciplinary studies, he engages in a multilevel institutional analysis that connects the micro-, meso-, and macro-levels, together with normative study of various sectors of a rising global civilization. Max's approach is helpful in identifying what religious cultural forces arise and work, how they interact with each other, and what institutional and cultural constellations and movements they create. As such, his perspective offers a viable alternative to competing visions of globalization such as technocracy, economic fundamentalism, religious fundamentalism, narrow communitarianism, and secular cosmopolitanism.

Max reminds us that the quest for liberation ultimately cannot be accomplished apart from the ordering of a new society after liberation, for example how to deal with technological and institutional dimensions. This social ordering requires in-depth knowledge of institutional functions, patterns, dynamics, and their mutual relationships. As globalization becomes an irreversible reality, we have come to a point of thinking and accepting the world in its entirety — in complex but interlinked relationships of part and whole, local and global, particular and universal. Any ethics that does not take into account this rising global institutional reality will turn out to be incomplete in its analysis and prescription, and therefore eventually incompetent. Given the irreversible nature of globalization, Max's contention makes sense; a solution to the abuse and injustice of economic globalization is not local communalism or religious fundamentalism, but the construction of complex but dynamic global governance through the just arrangement of global institutions in their checks and balances and the invigoration of global civil society. Such a task requires the macro social imagination and ethics that a competent public theology provides.

Conclusion

Throughout his career, Max engaged with many sides of religious and public life. He has made a great contribution in making Christian theology relevant to contemporary life, plausible to public minds, and instructive to churches and their members. In the wake of this rising new civilization pregnant with many threats and promises, Max clarifies the confusion around the nature of the public good and the organization of our common life lived in complex institutions and emerging global spheres. Max offers an ethical framework that enables us to consider human moral reality in various nexuses and levels of institutions, not as isolated fragments. Max's public theology offers guidance on how people of different race, nationality, religion, class, and gender could engage in the rising global civil society by learning, correcting, and collaborating with each other for a shared life in a global polis.

As our social life becomes more fragmented, and thus desperately in need of spiritual and moral renewal, Max's question about what Christian theology and ethics have to offer for the common life, especially the ordering and refashioning of our social life, will remain a central question for the church in many years to come. He challenges whether churches are willing to live up to their confession in the first article of the Apostles' Creed: "I believe in God, the Father Almighty, the Maker of heaven and earth."

Max will find many enthusiastic and willing audiences among the churches in newly industrializing nations where social life is lived in increasingly complex and differentiated institutions, and also among many churches awakening from the shadow of persecution, marginality, and poverty. Otherworldly, sectarian, individualistic Christianity is not effective to equip such highly motivated and dedicated Christians who seek a theological framework that will energize not only their hearts but also enlighten their minds as they work as leaders of political parties, corporations, colleges, think tanks, NGOs, mass media, and so on. Max's public theology provides them with a theological and ethical framework to guide their own professional lives for the advance of the Kingdom, which makes a viable theological alternative to a pietism that does away with dialogue, to a sectarianism that gives up social responsibility, to an evangelicalism that promotes fideism and personal piety, to a liberationism that fails to offer a plausible alternative, and to a postmodernism that self-defeatingly lacks any objective moral criteria. These perspectives, despite their partial truth, are insufficient to help Christians live faithfully in a complex and highly differentiated world.

Max's public theology is helpful in charting and navigating the treacherous waters of globalization with wisdom, knowledge, and the conviction that the world is still under God's sovereign providence and mercy. Max's public theology challenges us to awaken from moral slumber and jump free from the grip of fear by reminding us that the modern institutions (constitutionalism, human rights, democracy, institutional pluralism) are the fruits of Christian experimentation. His public theology challenges us to have the courage to boldly proclaim the gospel to the powers, principalities, and spirits of the age with renewed confidence and knowledge. The cost of failing to heed his call is too high, shadowed by the risks and possibilities lying behind our deepening economic, ecological, and cultural integration.

A Response in Appreciation

Every collection of essays is more like a seminar or a symposium than a lecture or a treatise. It inevitably involves several perspectives, some alive and present, others deceased but influential still by way of echoes of previous reflections, or some just emerging out of new learnings, proven old insights, or proposed syntheses. Each essay brings to the conversation arguments, convictions, evidence, and clues as to the engagements and commitments of the author. It is hoped that the particular offerings of this volume will shed light on the central topic under discussion. Each contribution is more like a section of an unfinished symphony than a recital; thus there are debatable materials, sometimes clashing encounters, hopefully some memorable moments, and sadly some forgettable phrases.

This collection of essays differs from the more conventional collections because it is a contemporary selection of essays, reports, reviews, analyses, apologetic and polemical statements written mostly by the same person on a diversity of topics in the course of an attempt to form a more comprehensive picture of the dynamics in the current world situation. As I look back on these chapters in this collection, I begin to think of them as stepping stones from my doctoral dissertation (1965) to *Ethics and the Urban Ethos* (1973), *Public Theology and Political Economy* (1991), *Creeds, Society, and Human Rights* (1996), to the *God and Globalization* four volumes (2000-2007).

This selection of essays written for particular occasions, for clergy, seminarians, theological laity, and others interested in Christian thought in relation to the common life has a special meaning for me because it is edited by three younger scholars who are already recognized as notable contributors to faith-based social ethics in their own right. They have taken the trouble to digest not only my larger writings but the stack of fugitive articles that were hidden away in archives or library files, and they decided to pursue the project because they thought it might be of value to others. They were supported in their efforts by Jon Pott and other staff of Eerdmans Publishing Company. The essays they chose were developed over some four decades prior to my retirement, made necessary by health problems. The writings were encouraged by several other institutions such as the Center for Theological Inquiry led by Wallace Alston and later William Storrar, the *Andover-Newton Theological Review*, *The Christian Century*, the China Academic Consortium founded by Martha Chan, and a host of academic and ecclesiastical institutions and publications. During that period I tried to sort out the key elements and implications of a Christian worldview and a normative vision that could address a rapidly changing globe. I felt an urge throughout this endeavor to work in a collaborative fashion with some senior mentors, stimulating colleagues, gifted students, and sympathetic ecumenical leaders whom I encountered in travels for the mission board of my church. Some scholars who were on parallel tracks baptized this concern by inventing the term "Public Theology," which gave focus to pioneering work being done in several locations. This collection awakened parts of my memory about presuppositions that had to be clarified and integrated with other elements in this growing field of social ethics as shaped by an apologetic theology.

I must admit that part of my motivation was to critique or question some teachings that had become influential in contemporary theology, ethics, and philosophy. The reader of this book will find that I think they are highly inadequate in one or more of the necessary ingredients of a compelling theory. I could mention, for example, advocates' dedication to and honoring of the sacred scriptures and doctrinal teachings of the classical tradition; in fact, I thought it was necessary to have a systematic statement of the central meanings of Christian doctrine, but it seemed to me that they held it too close to their hearts and defended its purity in the face of contributions by other possible channels of thought. Thus in the kind of belief they protected, there appeared to be a fundamentalism or dogmatism that denigrated the inner action of the fruits of faith and the holiness that can be found in the depths of covenantal bonding and articulated by some forms of social theory, philosophy, and comparative religions.

I was drawn to those predecessors and contemporaries who studied the mutual impact of nonreligious fields on the study of theology, and the impact of theology on secular life, especially the formation of civilizations. I became convinced that the structure and dynamics of social history were comprised by doctrine, functional demand, and normative activation. Thus I began to explore the possibility that piety predisposes polity and polity predisposes policy, and reshapes piety. This disallows the possibility of holding to an isolated theological posture, social theory; it allows active engagement in reforming the world. This cycle of influence is a chief ingredient in forming civil society.

Where the impulse to work in this direction came from I do not know, but I have often been thankful that it was mediated to me by my parents and the institutions they supported. For example, during my early youth, our family often hosted missionaries who were on "deputation leave" and traveled from church to church raising support for their mission work and reporting on the missionary movement and its effects around the world (I remember learning about developments in Japan, China, Korea, and India). We children could stay up late after their evening presentations, listening to talk about encounters with peoples of other traditions and lands and how the fabric of their lives was shaped by their inherited religions and reshaped by their exposure to Christianity as they sought justice, compassion, improved living standards, and cultural enrichment. This often issued in concrete programs and policies: a quest for human rights, access to education especially for girls, organizations such as the YMCA for recently urbanized young men, building of clinics, hospitals, and orphanages, and training centers for industrial workers who were beginning to trade life in the fields and villages for life in factories in the cities.

In my graduate studies and early teaching years, I felt driven to seek an understanding of how the spiritual architecture and the material factors interacted to generate the great civilizations of history and define the moral imperatives that were to guide us in forming, informing, reforming, and transforming the enduring societies. Among the greatest changes at both the material and spiritual levels is what we call modernization. It led to fragmentation of societies and patterns of life in some respects and to consolidation and homogenization in other respects. My wife Jean and I came to the conclusion that one cannot understand cultural matters without accounting for the spiritual power that is exercised in artistic creativity. We had become convinced that one could not even understand the arts unless one took account of the religious foundations. Therefore we established the Berkshire Institute for Theology and the Arts, where, with others, we explored these dynamics. Along with this our sense of mission was broadened by opportunities to travel, live, teach, and learn in several regions of the world.

Many have become aware that when we experience another culture in some depth we also begin to access our home culture in new ways, including the patterns of our own family structures and with other peoples in our home culture. For me that meant involvement in the movement led by Martin Luther King Jr., which eventually brought me also to the conflicts over race in South Africa. All of these exposures intensified my perceptions of how cultures and subcultures are shaped by such social interactions. Reading the essays gathered together by Scott Paeth, Hak Joon Lee, and Hal Breitenberg triggered a question: Could the inner linkages of affective, intellectual, and spiritual lives lead people to help construct a new mental map that points us to the emerging global society, and beyond that, toward the heavenly city promised in several of the world religions?

Doubtless some readers will find difficulties in the matters about which I wrote in attempts to inspire widespread effects in a renewed cosmopolitan civilization. If they find something to be lacking in one respect or another, I invite them to refine, revise, and improve our thinking about these issues and join present-day conversations with traditions that generally are pointed in other directions.

I am aware of some incomplete gaps in my overall task. While I have written on the importance of keeping the distinction and implications clear about the difference between "nature" and "creation," the confusion in many people's minds has caused debates about global warming and other environmental crises. This entails problems in contemporary basic attitudes toward the biophysical universe. This issue must appear on the list of priorities of all theologians, philosophers, and ethicists as well as those advocates of recycling, reducing the carbon footprint, and altering personal consumption and habits. A second area that needs more concentrated attention is the encounter of the world religions. Should Christians develop a theology of Islam, Buddhism, etc., and should we invite each of the other religions to do the same for Christianity? Third, should the advocates of a public theology attempt to build communities of faith around the leaders of the major institutions of the globalizing world? The increasing number of excellent centers for the study of Ethics and the Professions gives us hope.

In each of these areas, I believe the following question is critical: Is our contemporary faith able to bring about a new reformation that can approximate, with the help of God, a just, peaceful, bountiful, and loving global society? I believe that it is possible, and pray that my faith is not in vain.

MAX STACK-
HOUSE
August 31, 2013

Max Stackhouse: A Bibliography

BOOKS AUTHORED BY STACKHOUSE

"Eschatology and Ethical Method: A Structural Analysis of Contemporary Christian Social Ethics in America with Primary Reference to Walter Rauschenbusch and Reinhold Niebuhr." Ph.D. diss., Harvard University, 1965.

The Ethics of Necropolis: An Essay on the Military-Industrial Complex and the Quest for a Just Peace. Boston: Beacon Press, 1971.

Ethics and the Urban Ethos: An Essay in Social Theory and Theological Reconstruction. Boston: Beacon Press, 1972.

Creeds, Society, and Human Rights: A Study in Three Cultures. Grand Rapids: Eerdmans, 1984; reissued, Nashville: Parthenon Press, 1996.

Public Theology and Political Economy: Christian Stewardship in Modern Society. Grand Rapids: Eerdmans, 1987; reissued, Lanham, MD: University Press of America, 1991; Korean edition, Yung & Geun, translators, Logos Press, 1991; Japanese edition, T. Yamamoto et al., translators, Seigakuin University Press, 2004.

Apologia: Contextualization, Globalization, and Mission in Theological Education. Grand Rapids: Eerdmans, 1988.

Covenant and Commitments: Faith, Family, and Economic Life. Louisville: Westminster John Knox, 1997.

Globalization and Grace: A Christian Public Theology for a Global Future. Foreword by Justo González. God and Globalization: Theological Ethics and the Spheres of Life, vol. 4. New York and London: Continuum, 2007.

BOOKS CO-AUTHORED OR EDITED BY STACKHOUSE

The Righteousness of the Kingdom. Walter Rauschenbusch. Edited and introduced by Max L. Stackhouse. Nashville: Abingdon Press, 1968; reissued with a new introduction, pp. i-xxix, and revised bibliography, Texts and Studies in the Social Gospel, vol. 2. Lewiston, NY: Edwin Mellen Press, 1999.

The Death of Dialogue and Beyond: Jewish-Christian Relations after the Near East Crisis.

Edited by Sanford Seltzer and Max L. Stackhouse. New York: Friendship Press, 1969.

On Being Human Religiously: Selected Essays in Religion and Society. James Luther Adams. Edited and introduced by Max L. Stackhouse. Boston: Beacon Press, 1976; revised edition, 1986.

Globalization in Theological Education: An Evaluative Report. Max L. Stackhouse and Charles West, with Stephen Healey, S. Mark Heim, Robert Pazmiño, Barbara Anne Radtke, and David Shannon. Pew Charitable Trusts, 1993.

On Moral Business: Classical and Contemporary Resources for Ethics in Economic Life. Edited by Max L. Stackhouse, Dennis P. McCann, and Shirley J. Roels, with Preston N. Williams. Introduction by Max L. Stackhouse, pp. 10-34. Grand Rapids: Eerdmans, 1995.

Christian Social Ethics in a Global Era. Edited by Max L. Stackhouse, Peter L. Berger, Dennis P. McCann, and M. Douglas Meeks. Abingdon Press Studies in Christian Ethics and Economic Life, vol. 1. Nashville: Abingdon Press, 1995. "Preface," "Chapter 1: Christian Social Ethics in a Global Era: Reforming Protestant Views," and "Conclusion: Joining the Discussion" by Stackhouse, pp. 7-9; 11-73; 127-30.

Environmental Ethics and Christian Humanism. Thomas Sieger Derr with James A. Nash and Richard John, general editor Max L. Stackhouse. Preface and Introduction by Stackhouse. Abingdon Press Studies in Christian Ethics and Economic Life, vol. 2. Nashville: Abingdon Press, 1996.

The Business Corporation and Productive Justice. David A. Krueger with Donald W. Shriver Jr. and Laura L. Nash, general editor Max L. Stackhouse. Preface and Introduction by Stackhouse. Abingdon Press Studies in Christian Ethics and Economic Life, vol. 3. Nashville: Abingdon Press, 1997.

Organization Man, Organization Woman: Calling, Leadership, and Culture. Shirley J. Roels with Barbara Hilkert Andolsen and Paul F. Camenisch, general editor Max L. Stackhouse. Preface and Introduction by Stackhouse. Abingdon Press Studies in Christian Ethics and Economic Life, vol. 4. Nashville: Abingdon Press, 1997.

God and Globalization, vol. 1: *Religion and the Powers of the Common Life.* Edited by Max L. Stackhouse with Peter J. Paris. Introduction by Max L. Stackhouse, pp. 1-52. Harrisburg, PA: Trinity Press International, 2000.

A Dialogical Approach to the Value of Modernity. Essays by Max L. Stackhouse, edited in English by V. Landgraf, translated into Chinese and coordinated with essays by Bao Limin, general editor. Shanghai, PRC: Scholars Press, 2000.

The Local Church in a Global Era: Reflections for a New Century. Edited by Max L. Stackhouse, Tim Dearborn, and Scott Paeth. Grand Rapids: Eerdmans, 2000. "An Introduction" by Stackhouse, pp. 1-15.

God and Globalization, vol. 2: *The Spirit and the Modern Authorities.* Edited by Max L. Stackhouse with Don S. Browning. Introduction by Max L. Stackhouse, pp. 1-36. Harrisburg, PA: Trinity Press International, 2001.

God and Globalization, vol. 3: *Christ and the Dominions of Civilization.* Edited by Max L. Stackhouse, with Diane B. Obenchain. Introduction by Max L. Stackhouse, pp. 1-57. Harrisburg, PA: Trinity Press International, 2002.

Max Stackhouse: A Bibliography

Essays on Ethics, Economics and Education. Translated into Korean and edited by My-Kyun Sin. Seoul: The Pastor's Press, 2005.

News of Boundless Riches: Interrogating, Comparing, and Reconstructing Mission in a Global Era. 2 vols. Edited and introduced by Max L. Stackhouse and Lalsangkima Pachuau. Delhi: Indian Society for Promoting Christian Knowledge (ISPCK), 2007.

ENTRIES IN DICTIONARIES, ENCYCLOPEDIAS, HANDBOOKS, ETC.

"Aggression," "Church," "Cursing/Swearing," "Ecclesiology and Ethics," "Institutions/Institutionalization," "Sect," and "Urbanization." In *The Westminster Dictionary of Christian Ethics,* edited by James F. Childress and John Macquarrie, pp. 16-17; 90-91; 142; 171-75; 304-5; 566-67; 638-39. Philadelphia: Westminster, 1986.

"Christian Social Movements," "Missions: Missionary Activity," and "Politics and Religion." In *The Encyclopedia of Religion,* edited by Mircea Eliade, vol. 3, pp. 446-52; vol. 9, pp. 563-70; vol. 11, pp. 408-23. New York: Macmillan, 1987.

"Gustafson, James" and "Ramsey, Paul." In *The Dictionary of Historical Theology,* edited by Trevor A. Hart, pp. 237-38; 453-54. Grand Rapids: Eerdmans, 2000.

"Business, Economics and Christian Ethics." In *The Cambridge Companion to Christian Ethics,* edited by Robin Gill, pp. 228-42. Cambridge: Cambridge University Press, 2001. Revised in collaboration with David W. Miller and published in the 2nd ed., pp. 239-56, 2012.

"Economic Ethics." Co-authored by David W. Miller. In *The Encyclopedia of Christianity,* vol. 2, edited by Erwin Fahlbusch et al., pp. 12-23. Grand Rapids: Eerdmans, 2001.

"Church and State," "Homosexuality," and "Theology, Public." In *Dictionary of the Ecumenical Movement,* edited by Nicholas Lossky et al. 2nd ed., pp. 186-90; 541-43; 1131-33. Geneva: WCC Publications, 2002.

"Political Theology," "Politics," and "Public Theology." In *The Encyclopedia of Christianity,* vol. 4, edited by Erwin Fahlbusch et al., translated by Geoffrey W. Bromiley, pp. 257-58; 258-62; 443-47. Grand Rapids and Leiden: Eerdmans and Brill, 2005.

"Economics." In *The Blackwell Companion to Religious Ethics,* edited by William Schweiker, pp. 451-58. Malden, MA: Blackwell, 2005.

"Vocation." In *The Oxford Handbook of Theological Ethics,* edited by Gilbert Meilaender and William Werpehowski, pp. 189-204. Oxford and New York: Oxford University Press, 2005.

"Troeltsch, Ernst." Co-authored by Friedrich Wilhelm Graf. In *The Encyclopedia of Christianity,* vol. 5, edited by Erwin Fahlbusch et al., translated by Geoffrey W. Bromiley, pp. 551-53. Grand Rapids and Leiden: Eerdmans and Brill, 2008.

"Ethics and Eschatology." In *Oxford Handbook of Eschatology,* edited by Jerry L. Walls, pp. 548-62. Oxford and New York: Oxford University Press, 2008.

"Civil Society." In *Cambridge Dictionary of Christian Theology,* 2011.

"Business Ethics," "Consumerism," "Covenant," "Democracy," "Dirty Hands," "Genocide," "Globalization," "Humanitarianism," "Public Theology and Ethics," "Rights," and "Taxation." In *Dictionary of Scripture and Ethics,* edited by Jacqueline E. Lapsley, Rebekah Miles, and Allen Verhey, pp. 110-13; 172-74; 182-83;

212-13; 230-31; 326-27; 327-29; 382-83; 646-49; 687-89; 763. Grand Rapids: Baker Academic, 2011.

ESSAYS IN BOOKS

"James Luther Adams: A Biographical and Intellectual Sketch." In *Voluntary Associations: A Study of Groups in Free Societies*, edited by D. B. Robertson, pp. 333-57, 432-34. Richmond, VA: John Knox Press, 1966.

"Today's City: Threat or Promise?" In *The Secular City Debate*, edited by Daniel Callahan, pp. 26-37. New York and London: Macmillan and Collier-Macmillan, 1966.

"Protestant Echoes of the Constantinian Era." In *Religion and Public Education*, edited by Theodore R. Sizer, pp. 287-315. Boston: Houghton Mifflin, 1967.

"Toward a Theology for the New Social Gospel." In *New Theology No. 4*, edited by Martin E. Marty and Dean G. Peerman, pp. 220-42. New York and London: Macmillan Company and Collier-Macmillan, 1967.

"Christianity and the New Exodus in East Europe." In *The Religious Situation: 1968*, edited by Donald R. Cutler, pp. 887-917. Boston: Beacon Press, 1968.

"The Continuing Importance of Walter Rauschenbusch" (introduction to *The Righteousness of the Kingdom* by Walter Rauschenbusch), edited by Max L. Stackhouse, pp. 13-59. Nashville: Abingdon Press, 1968.

"Abortion and Animation." Co-authored with others. In *Abortion in a Changing World*. Conference Proceedings, edited by Robert E. Hall, vol. 2, pp. 3-18. New York and London: Columbia University Press, 1970.

"Religion, Technology, and Urbanity." In *The Citizen and the City: Communications for a Humane Urban Community*, pp. 1-8. Atlanta: The Institute for Theological Encounter with Science and Technology (ITEST), 1974.

"Behind and Beyond the Boston School Crisis." In *Desegregation in Boston*, edited by R. Dewey. Boston: Christians for Urban Justice, 1975.

"Commentary [on Daniel Bell's Dilemmas of Managerial Legitimacy]." In *Proceedings of the First National Conference on Business Ethics*, edited by W. Michael Hoffman, pp. 24-29. Waltham, MA: Bentley College, 1977.

"Social Ethics: Some Basic Elements East and West." In *A Vision for Man: Essays on Faith, Theology and Society*, edited by Samuel Amirtham, pp. 326-38. Madras: The Christian Literature Society, 1978.

"A View of Christian Ethics." In *The Life of Choice: Some Liberal Religious Perspectives on Morality*, edited by Clark Kucheman, pp. 126-38. Boston: Beacon Press, 1978.

"The Perils of Process: A Response to Sturm." In *Process Philosophy and Social Thought*, edited by John B. Cobb Jr. and W. Widick Schroeder, pp. 103-12. Chicago: Center for the Scientific Study of Religion, 1981.

"Traditions in Dialogue: An Interpretive Report on the Roman Catholic-Reformed Bilaterals." In *Ethics and the Search for Christian Unity: Two Statements by the Roman Catholic/Presbyterian-Reformed Consultation*, edited by Ernest L. Unterkoefler and Andrew Harsanyi, pp. 1-11. Washington, DC: Publications Office, United States Catholic Conference, 1981.

"A Protestant Perspective on the Woodstock Human Rights Project." In *Human Rights in the Americas: The Struggle for Consensus,* edited by Alfred Hennelly and John Langan, pp. 142-58. Washington, DC: Georgetown University Press, 1982.

"Jesus and Economics: A Century of Reflection." In *The Bible in American Law, Politics, and Political Rhetoric,* edited by James Turner Johnson, pp. 107-51. Philadelphia and Chico, CA: Fortress Press and Scholars Press, 1985.

"Militarization and the Human Rights Situation in Asia: Implications for Missions Today." In *Human Rights and the Global Mission of the Church,* edited and with an introduction by Arthur Dyck and a foreword by Lorine M. Getz, pp. 83-89. Boston Theological Institute Annual Series, vol. 1. Cambridge, MA: Boston Theological Institute, 1985.

"Public Theology, Human Rights and Missions." In *Human Rights and the Global Mission of the Church,* edited and with an introduction by Arthur Dyck and a foreword by Lorine M. Getz, pp. 13-21. Boston Theological Institute Annual Series, vol. 1. Cambridge, MA: Boston Theological Institute, 1985.

"Religious Freedom and Human Rights." In *Our Freedoms: Rights and Responsibilities,* ed. W. Lawson Taitte, introduction by Andrew R. Cecil. Austin: University of Texas Press, 1985.

"Toward a Stewardship Ethics." In *Teaching and Preaching Stewardship: An Anthology,* edited by Nordan C. Murphy, pp. 87-111. Library of Christian Stewardship. New York: Commission on Stewardship, National Council of the Churches of Christ in the U.S.A., 1985.

"Democracy and the World's Religions." In *The Best of This World,* edited by Michael A. Scully, pp. 312-24. Lanham, MD: University Press of America, 1986.

"The Church as a Paradigm for Voluntary Associations." In *Honoring JLA on His 85th Birthday,* edited by Judy Deutsch, pp. 3-4. N.p.: James Luther Adams Foundation [1987].

"Piety, Polity, and Policy." In *Religious Beliefs, Human Rights, and the Moral Foundation of Western Democracy,* edited by Carl H. Esbeck, pp. 13-26. University of Missouri-Columbia [1987].

"Contextualization, Contextuality, and Contextualism." In *One Faith, Many Cultures: Inculturation, Indigenization, and Contextualization.* Foreword by Lorine M. Getz, edited by Ruy O. Costa, pp. 3-13. Boston Theological Institute Annual Series, vol. 2. Maryknoll, NY: Orbis, 1988.

"The Pastor as Public Theologian." In *The Pastor as Theologian,* edited by Earl E. Shelp and Ronald H. Sunderland, pp. 106-29, 133. New York: Pilgrim Press, 1988.

"Protestantism and Poverty." In *The Preferential Option for the Poor,* edited by Richard John Neuhaus, pp. 1-34. Grand Rapids: Eerdmans, 1988.

"Human Rights and the Global Situation Today." In *Value Education Today: Explorations in Social Ethics,* edited by J. T. K. Daniel and Nirmal Selvamony, pp. 134-41. Tambaram and New Delhi: Madras Christian College and All-India Association for Christian Higher Education, 1990.

"Religion and the Social Space for Voluntary Institutions." In *Faith and Philanthropy in America: Exploring the Role of Religion in America's Voluntary Sector,* edited by

Max Stackhouse: A Bibliography

Robert Wuthnow, Virginia A. Hodgkinson, and associates, pp. 22-37. San Francisco and Oxford: Jossey-Bass, 1990.

"Religion, Rights, and the Constitution." In *An Unsettled Arena: Religion and the Bill of Rights*, edited by Ronald C. White Jr. and Albright G. Zimmerman, pp. 92-114. Grand Rapids: Eerdmans, 1990.

"Globalization and Theology in America Today." In *World Order and Religion*, edited by Wade Clark Roof, pp. 247-63. Albany: State University of New York Press, 1991.

"Peace in Church, Family, and State: A Reformed View." In *Baptism, Peace and the State in the Reformed and Mennonite Traditions*, edited by Ross T. Bender and Alan P. F. Sell, pp. 69-86. Waterloo, ON: Wilfrid Laurier University Press, 1991.

"The Trinity as Public Theology: Its Truth and Justice for Free-Church, Noncredal Communities." In *Faith to Creed: Ecumenical Perspectives on the Affirmation of the Apostolic Faith in the Fourth Century*, edited by S. Mark Heim, pp. 162-97. Grand Rapids: Eerdmans, 1991.

"Brunner's Christianity and Civilization Revisited: Its Significance After the Collapse of Marxism." In *Theologie und Ökonomie: Symposium zum 100. Geburtstag von Emil Brunner*, edited by Hans Ruh, pp. 163-86. Zürich: Theologischer Verlag, 1992.

"The Christian Spirit in Contemporary Civilization: Its Significance After the Collapse of Marxism." In *Christianity for Tomorrow*, edited by Charles L. Holland, pp. 101-20. Fort Worth, TX: Biblical Studies Association, 1992.

"Liberalism Revisited: From Social Gospel to Public Theology [with Responses]." In *Being Christian Today: An American Conversation*, edited by Richard John Neuhaus and George Weigel, pp. 33-58. Washington, DC: Ethics and Public Policy Center, 1992.

"Religion, Society and the Independent Sector: Key Elements of a General Theory." In *Religion, the Independent Sector, and American Culture*, edited by Conrad Cherry and Rowland A. Sherrill, pp. 11-30. American Academy of Religion Studies in Religion. Atlanta: Scholars Press, 1992.

"An 'Evangelical' Impetus, a 'Catholic' Vision." In *A New World Order: John Paul II and Human Freedom*, edited by George Weigel, pp. 159-64. Washington, DC: Ethics and Public Policy Center, 1992.

"Public Theology and the Future of Democratic Society." In *The Church's Public Role: Retrospect and Prospect*, edited by Dieter T. Hessel, pp. 63-83. Grand Rapids: Eerdmans, 1993.

"Protestantism and the Problem of Senseless Violence." In *Religious Responses to Violence*. Albany: New York State Religious Leaders Conference, February 1994.

"Reflections: Secular Ministrations in Personal Development Programs — A Theological Perspective." In *A Fatal Embrace? Assessing Holistic Trends in Human Resources Programs*, edited by Frank W. Heuberger and Laura L. Nash, pp. 243-51. New Brunswick, CT, and London: Transaction Publishers, 1994.

"Spirituality and the Corporation." In *From Christ to the World: Introductory Readings in Christian Ethics*, edited by Wayne G. Boulton, Thomas D. Kennedy, and Allen Verhey, pp. 303-10. Grand Rapids: Eerdmans, 1994. Redacted from *Public Theology and Political Economy*.

Max Stackhouse: A Bibliography

"Conclusion: Joining the Discussion." In *Christian Social Ethics in a Global Era*, edited by Max L. Stackhouse et al., pp. 127-30. Abingdon Press Studies in Christian Ethics and Economic Life, vol. 1. Nashville: Abingdon Press, 1995.

"An Introduction to a Memoir." In *Not Without Dust and Heat*, by James Luther Adams, pp. ix-xiii. Chicago: Exploration Press, 1995.

"Introduction: Foundations and Purposes." In *On Moral Business: Classical and Contemporary Resources for Ethics in Economic Life*, edited by Max L. Stackhouse et al., pp. 10-34. Grand Rapids: Eerdmans, 1995.

"Preface." In *Christian Social Ethics in a Global Era*, edited by Max L. Stackhouse et al., pp. 7-9. Abingdon Press Studies in Christian Ethics and Economic Life, vol. 1. Nashville: Abingdon Press, 1995.

"Social Theory and Christian Public Morality for the Common Life." In *Christianity and Civil Society: Theological Education for Public Life*, edited by Rodney L. Petersen, pp. 26-41. Boston Theological Institute Series, vol. 4. Maryknoll, NY: Orbis, 1995.

"Spirituality and the Corporation." In *On Moral Business: Classical and Contemporary Resources for Ethics in Economic Life*, edited by Max L. Stackhouse et al., pp. 501-7. Grand Rapids: Eerdmans, 1995. From *Public Theology and Political Economy*, ch. 7, pp. 113-36.

"The Ten Commandments: Economic Implications." In *On Moral Business: Classical and Contemporary Resources for Ethics in Economic Life*, edited by Max L. Stackhouse et al., pp. 59-62. Grand Rapids: Eerdmans, 1995.

"Theology and the Economic Life of Society in a Global Era: On Mars, Eros, the Muses, Mammon, and Christ." In *Policy Reform and Moral Grounding*, edited by T. William Boxx and Gary M. Quinlivan, pp. 47-68. Latrobe, PA: Saint Vincent College, [1995].

"Beneath and Beyond the State: Social, Global, and Religious Changes That Shape Welfare Reform." In *Welfare in America: Christian Perspectives on a Policy in Crisis*, edited by Stanley W. Carlson-Thies and James W. Skillen, pp. 20-48. Grand Rapids: Eerdmans, 1996.

"The Heterosexual Norm." In *Homosexuality and Christian Community*, edited by Choon-Leong Seow, pp. 133-43. Louisville: Westminster John Knox, 1996.

"New Ethical Issue [Letter to the Editor]." In *The Downsizing of America*, p. 249. N.p.: Times Books, Random House, 1996.

"A Protestant Response [to Kenneth L. Grasso]." In *Caesar's Coin Revisited: Christians and the Limits of Government*, edited by Michael Cromartie, pp. 115-25. Grand Rapids: Eerdmans, 1996.

"Public Theology and Christological Politics." Response to Mark Noll. In *Adding Cross to Crown: The Political Significance of Christ's Passion*, edited by Mark A. Noll and Luis E. Lugo, pp. 61-77. Grand Rapids: Baker, 1996.

"Religion and Human Rights: A Theological Apologetic." Co-authored with Stephen E. Healey. In *Religious Human Rights in Global Perspective: Religious Perspectives*, edited by John Witte Jr. and Johan D. van der Vyver, pp. 485-516. The Hague: Martinus Nijhoff, 1996.

"Reflections on Remembered Dialogues." In *Kamp Må der Til: Engagementets Bryding*

Mellem Åbenhed Og Tradition, edited by Niels H. Brønnum et al., pp. 137-42. Hadsten, Denmark: Mimer Forlaget, 1997.

"Christianity and the Prospects for a New Global Order." In *International Society: Diverse Ethical Perspectives,* edited by David R. Mapel and Terry Nardin, pp. 201-14. Princeton: Princeton University Press, 1998. Reprinted in *Christian Political Ethics,* edited by John Aloysius Coleman, pp. 155-69. Princeton: Princeton University Press, 2008.

"Corporations, Faith, and Society in a Global Economy." In *Socially Responsible Investing: Theological Reflections and the Moral Context,* edited by Dana Burch and Tim Smith, pp. 90-92. New York: Interfaith Center on Corporate Responsibility, 1998.

"The Prophetic Stand of the Ecumenical Churches on Homosexuality." In *Sexual Orientation and Human Rights in American Religious Discourse,* edited by Saul M. Olyan and Martha C. Nussbaum, pp. 119-33. New York and Oxford: Oxford University Press, 1998.

"Broken Covenants: A Threat to Society?" In *Judgment Day at the White House: A Critical Declaration Exploring Moral Issues and the Political Use and Abuse of Religion,* edited by Gabriel Fackre, pp. 18-27. Grand Rapids: Eerdmans, 1999.

"Covenantal Justice in a Global Era." In *Struggling to Hope: A Tribute to the Rev. Dr. Eka Darmaputera (Bergumul Dalam Pengharapan: Buku Penghargaan Untuk Pdt. Dr. Eka Darmaputera),* edited by F. Suleeman, A. A. Sutama, and A. Rajendra, pp. 419-35. Jakarta: PT Bpk Gunung Mulia, 1999.

"Deciding for God: The Right to Convert in Protestant Perspectives." Co-authored with Deirdre King Hainsworth. In *Sharing the Book: Religious Perspectives on the Rights and Wrongs of Mission,* edited by John Witte Jr. and Richard C. Martin, pp. 201-30. Maryknoll, NY: Orbis, 1999.

"Human Rights and Public Theology: The Basic Validation of Human Rights." In *Religion and Human Rights: Competing Claims?* edited by Carrie Gustafson and Peter Juviler, pp. 12-30. Armonk, NY, and London: M. E. Sharpe, 1999.

Introduction. In *The Righteousness of the Kingdom,* edited by Max L. Stackhouse, pp. i-xxix. Texts and Studies in the Social Gospel, vol. 2. Lewiston, Queenston, Lampeter: Edwin Mellen, 1999.

"Preface." In *Perspectives on the Social Gospel: Papers from the Inaugural Social Gospel Conference at Colgate Rochester Divinity School,* edited by Christopher H. Evans, pp. xi-xiii. Texts and Studies in the Social Gospel, vol. 3. Lewiston, Queenston, Lampeter: Edwin Mellen, 1999.

"The Will of God and the Way Things Are or Issues I Have Debated with Frederick Herzog About the Relationship Between the Contextual and the Universal Dimensions of Christian Theology." In *Theology and Corporate Conscience: Essays in Honor of Frederick Herzog,* edited by Douglas M. Meeks, Jürgen Moltmann, and Frederick R. Trost, pp. 330-41. Minneapolis: Kirk House, 1999.

Introduction to *God and Globalization,* vol. 1: *Religion and the Powers of the Common Life.* Edited by Max L. Stackhouse with Peter J. Paris, pp. 1-52. Harrisburg, PA: Trinity Press International, 2000.

"An Introduction." In *The Local Church in a Global Era: Reflections for a New Century,* edited by Max L. Stackhouse, Tim Dearborn, and Scott Paeth, pp. 1-15. Grand Rapids: Eerdmans, 2000.

"Preface." In *Religion, Pluralism, and Public Life: Abraham Kuyper's Legacy for the Twenty-First Century,* edited by Luis E. Lugo, pp. xi-xviii. Grand Rapids and Cambridge: Eerdmans, 2000.

"Remarks on Globalisation [sic]." In *Dialogue on Globalisation* [sic], edited by I. John Mohan Razu and P. Moses Paul Peter, pp. 13-29. Bangalore: The Student Christian Movement of India, 2000. Excerpted as "Remarks on Globalization." In *In Essentials Unity: Reflections on the Nature and Purpose of the Church: In Honor of Frederick R. Trost,* edited by M. Douglas Meeks and Robert D. Mutton, pp. 502-8. Minneapolis: Kirk House, 2001.

"A Response to Alan Wolfe." In *What's God Got to Do with the American Experiment?* edited by E. J. Dionne Jr. and John J. DiIulio Jr., pp. 96-97. Washington, DC: Brookings Institution, 2000.

"The Fifth Social Gospel and the Global Mission of the Church." In *The Social Gospel Today,* edited by Christopher H. Evans, pp. 146-59. Louisville: Westminster John Knox, 2001.

Foreword to *Economics as Religion: From Samuelson to Chicago and Beyond,* by Robert H. Nelson, pp. ix-xiv. University Park: Pennsylvania State University Press, 2001.

Introduction to *God and Globalization,* vol. 2: *The Spirit and the Modern Authorities.* Edited by Max L. Stackhouse with Don S. Browning, pp. 1-36. Harrisburg, PA: Trinity Press International, 2001.

"After Terror's Shock." In *You Gave the Weary Your Hand: Bearing Witness to the Light through the Shadows of September 11, 2001,* edited by Frederick R. Trost. N.p.: UCC-EKU Working Group, 2001.

"Christ and Other Faiths in the World." In *Story Lines: Chapters on Thought, Word, and Deed,* edited by Skye Fackre Gibson, pp. 113-19. Grand Rapids: Eerdmans, 2002.

"Christianity, Civil Society, and the State: A Protestant Response." In *Civil Society and Government,* edited by Nancy L. Rosenblum and Robert C. Post, pp. 255-64. Princeton and Oxford: Princeton University Press, 2002. Reprinted in *Christian Political Ethics,* edited by John Aloysius Coleman, pp. 54-63. Princeton: Princeton University Press, 2008.

"Familial, Social, and Professional Integrity in Relationship to Business." In *Marriage, Health, and the Professions: If Marriage Is Good for You, What Does This Mean for Law, Medicine, Ministry, Therapy, and Business?* edited by John Wall et al., pp. 233-53. Grand Rapids: Eerdmans, 2002.

Foreword to *Whose Kids Are They Anyway? Religion and Morality in America's Public Schools,* by Raymond R. Roberts, pp. ii-viii. Cleveland: Pilgrim Press, 2002.

Introduction to *God and Globalization,* vol. 3: *Christ and the Dominions of Civilization.* Edited by Max L. Stackhouse and Diane B. Obenchain, pp. 1-57. Harrisburg, PA: Trinity Press International, 2002.

"Religion and Ethnicity: A Public Theological Overview in a Global Era." In *Faith and Ethnicity: Studies in Reformed Theology,* edited by Eddy A. J. G. van der Borght,

Dirk van Keulen, and Martien E. Brinkman, pp. 179-97. Studies in Reformed Theology, vol. 7. Zoetermeer, The Netherlands: Meinema, 2002.

"Theologies of War: Comparative Perspectives." In *Strike Terror No More: Theology, Ethics, and the New War*, edited by Jon L. Berquist, pp. 200-11. N.p.: Chalice Press, 2002.

"Capitalism, Civil Society, Religion, and the Poor: A Bibliographic Essay." Co-authored with Lawrence M. Stratton. In *Wealth, Poverty, and Human Destiny*, edited by Doug Bandow and David L. Schindler, pp. 431-63, 515-20. Wilmington, DE: ISI Books, 2003. First published as a booklet, Wilmington, DE: Intercollegiate Studies Institute, 2002.

"Public Theology and Political Economy in a Global Era." In *Public Theology for the 21st Century: Essays in Honour of Duncan B. Forrester*, edited by William Storrar and Andrew R. Morton, pp. 179-94. London and New York: T. & T. Clark, 2004.

"The Mainline Protestant Tradition in the Twentieth Century: Positive Lessons and Cautionary Tales." Co-authored with Raymond R. Roberts. In *Toward an Evangelical Public Policy: Political Strategies for the Health of the Nation*, edited by Ronald J. Sider and Diane Knippers, pp. 77-100. Grand Rapids: Baker, 2005.

"The Offices of Christ: Some Historical, Theological and Ethical Implications." In *The God of All Grace*, edited by Joseph George, pp. 202-16. Bangalore: Asian Trading Corporation and United Theological College, 2005. Revised as "The Offices of Christ from Early Church Through the Reformers." In *Who Do You Say That I Am? Christology and Identity in the United Church of Christ*, edited by Scott R. Paeth, pp. 25-41. Cleveland: United Church Press, 2006.

"Christian Ethics, Practical Theology and Public Theology in a Global Era." In *Reconsidering the Boundaries Between Theological Disciplines*, edited by Michael Welker and Friedrich Schweitzer, pp. 99-111. Münster: LIT Verlag, 2005.

"The Common Good, Our Common Goods, and the Uncommon Good in a Globalizing Era." In *In Search of the Common Good*, edited by Dennis P. McCann and Patrick D. Miller, pp. 279-300. New York and London: T. & T. Clark, 2005.

"Covenantal Marriage: Protestant Views and Contemporary Life." In *Covenant and Marriage in Comparative Perspective*, edited by John Witte Jr. and Eliza Ellison, pp. 153-81. Grand Rapids and Cambridge: Eerdmans, 2005.

"Why Human Rights Needs God: A Christian Perspective." In *Does Human Rights Need God?* edited by Elizabeth M. Bucar and Barbra Barnett, pp. 25-40. Grand Rapids and Cambridge: Eerdmans, 2005.

"Globalization and Christian Ethics." In *The Globalization of Ethics: Religious and Secular Perspectives*, edited by William M. Sullivan and Will Kymlicka, pp. 53-74. Cambridge: Cambridge University Press, 2007.

"The Sources of Human Rights Ideas: A Christian Perspective." In *Christianity and Human Rights: Influences and Issues*, edited by Frances S. Adeney and Arvind Sharma, pp. 41-54. Albany: State University of New York Press, 2007.

"Faith and Globalization." In *Prospects and Ambiguities of Globalization: Critical Assessments at a Time of Growing Turmoil*, edited by James W. Skillen, pp. 41-53. Lanham, MD: Lexington Books, 2009.

"Civil Society, Religion, and the Ethical Shape of Polity." In *A World for All? Global Civil Society in Political Theory and Trinitarian Theology*, edited by William F. Storrar, Peter J. Casarella, and Paul Louis Metzger, pp. 59-74. Grand Rapids and Cambridge: Eerdmans, 2011.

ARTICLES IN JOURNALS

"Troeltsch's Categories of Historical Analysis," *Journal for the Scientific Study of Religion* 1, no. 2 (Spring 1962): 223-25.

"Group Responsibility [Critique of Carnell's Social Ethics]," Letter to the editor, *The Christian Century* 80, no. 40 (October 2, 1963): 1219.

"The Ethics of Selma," *Commonweal* 82, no. 3 (April 9, 1965): 75-77.

"Today's City: Threat or Promise?" *The Christian Century* 82, no. 50 (December 15, 1965): 1537-41.

"A Guide to the Ploys of Some Catholics," *The Christian Century* 83, no. 9 (March 2, 1966): 275-76.

"Technical Data and Ethical Norms: Some Theoretical Considerations," *Journal for the Scientific Study of Religion* 5, no. 2 (Spring 1966): 191-203.

"Toward a Theology for the New Social Gospel," *The Andover Newton Quarterly* 6, no. 4 (March 1966): 3-20.

"Editorial Comment," *The Andover Newton Quarterly* 7, no. 3 (January 1967): 97-101.

"Christianity in New Formation: Reflections of a White Christian on the Death of Dr. Martin Luther King, Jr.," *The Andover Newton Quarterly* 9, no. 2 (November 1968): 95-111.

"A New, *New Testament*?" *The Archbishop* (December 1968): 5-9.

"The Formation of a Prophet: Reflections on the Early Sermons of Walter Rauschenbusch," *The Andover Newton Quarterly* 9, no. 3 (January 1969): 137-59.

"Reparations: A Call to Repentance," *Renewal* 9, no. 7 (September-October 1969): 4-12.

"Reparations: A Call to Repentance?" *The Lutheran Quarterly* 21, no. 4 (November 1969): 358-80.

"The Military-Industrial Complex: On the Critics of the Critics," *Christianity and Crisis* 30, no. 7 (April 27, 1970): 91 [Reply to J. W. Kuhn].

"Reparations: A Call to Repentance," *Colloquy* 3, no. 2 (February 1970): 18, 20-25.

"Whatever Happened to Reparations: Social and Theological Reflections One Year After," *Andover Newton Quarterly* 11, no. 4 (November 1970): 61-71.

"Countering the Military-Industrial Complex," *Christianity and Crisis* 31, no. 2 (February 22, 1971): 14-22.

"Salvation in a New Context," *Journal of Current Social Issues* 9, no. 6 (Autumn 1971): 11-13.

"Understanding the Pentagon," *Worldview* 14, no. 7-8 (July-August 1971): 14-16.

"Modern Man and Religious Simplicity," *The Hanoverian* (Hanover College) 4, no. 3 (November 1972): 14-18.

"The City as Possibility," *Journal of Current Social Issues* 11, no. 1 (Winter 1972-73): 18-23.

"Ethics: Social and Christian," *The Andover Newton Quarterly* 13, no. 3 (January 1973): 173-91.

"The Hindu Ethic and the Ethos of Development: Some Western Views," *Religion and Society* (Bangalore, India) 20, no. 4 (December 1973): 5-33. Revised as "The Hindu Ethic and Development: Western Views." In *On Moral Business: Classical and Contemporary Resources for Ethics in Economic Life,* edited by Max L. Stackhouse et al., pp. 375-82. Grand Rapids: Eerdmans, 1995.

"Military Professionalization and Values," *Military Review* 53 (November 1973): 3-20.

"Toward Economic Democracy," *Colloquy* 6, no. 8 (October 1973): 28-31.

"A Theology of Stewardship," *The New Pulpit Digest* 54, no. 410 (November-December 1974): 45-47.

"Toward a Stewardship Ethics," *The Andover Newton Quarterly* 14, no. 4 (March 1974): 245-66.

"Toward a Stewardship Ethics," *Theology Digest* 22, no. 3 (Autumn 1974): 226-31.

"On the Boundary of Psychology and Theology," *Andover Newton Quarterly* 15, no. 3 (January 1975): 196-207.

"Technology and the 'Supranatural,'" *Zygon* 10, no. 1 (March 1975): 59-85.

"Voluntary Associations and Social Change," *New Conversations* 1 (Spring/Summer 1975): 14-23.

"The Most Important Questions," *Inside* [Evangelical Committee for Urban Ministries in Boston] 6, no. 3, 4, 5 (June/August/October 1975): 113-17.

"The Background of the Boston Affirmations," *Andover Newton Quarterly* 16, no. 4 (March 1976): 237-38. Reprinted as "The Boston Affirmations: A Background Statement," *Journal of Current Social Issues* 13, no. 1 (Winter 1976): 58-62.

"The Location of the Holy," *The Journal of Religious Ethics* 4, no. 1 (Spring 1976): 63-104.

"Peace, Civilization and Culture," *Comprendre* 41-42 (1976): 151-68.

"Business and Ethics," *The Hastings Center Report* 7, no. 6 (December 1977): 10-12.

"Ethics and Holiness," *The Foundation* 82, no. 13 (Fall 1977-78): 4-10.

"Two Studies in World Holiness," *The Foundation* 82, no. 13 (Fall 1977-78): 11-18.

"Gesellschaftstheorie und Sozialethik," *Zeitschrift für Evangelische Ethik* 22 (October 1978): 275-95.

"A Perspective on the American Social Context," *Lutheran World Federation Bulletin* (1978): 20.

"Reaffirmations of Foundations for an Ecumenical Ethic," *Journal of Ecumenical Studies* 15, no. 4 (Fall 1978): 662-83. Reprinted in *Andover Newton Quarterly* 19, no. 4 (March 1979): 193-207.

"The Religious Basis of Cultural Activity," *Soundings* 61, no. 1 (Spring 1978): 7-22.

"Religious Ethics," *The Council on the Study of Religion* 9, no. 5 (December 1978): 128-31.

"Ethics and Law: Some Reflections," *The Cumberland Lawyer* 14 (Summer 1979): 6-7, 12.

"Energy, Covenant and Sacrament (Thanksgiving Meditation)," *The Christian Century* 97, no. 37 (November 19, 1980): 1119-20.

"Theological and Ethical Considerations for Business Decision-Making," *New Catholic World* 223, no. 1338 (November/December 1980): 253-59.

"The Church and Political Life: A Loss of Confidence," *The Christian Century* 98, no. 24 (July 29–August 5, 1981): 766-69.

"General Synod 13 — What's It All About?" *CONNtact* 18, no. 5 (May-June 1981): 8.

"The Religious Situation in the German Democratic Republic," *Occasional Papers on Religion in Eastern Europe* 1, no. 1 (February 1981): 1-8.

"Some Intellectual and Social Roots of Modern Human Rights Ideas," *Journal for the Scientific Study of Religion* 20, no. 4 (December 1981): 301-9.

"Christ and Culture in the South Seas," *The Christian Century* 99, no. 32 (October 20, 1982): 1052-56.

"The Covenanting Controversy in Britain," *The Christian Century* 99, no. 8 (March 10, 1982): 274-75.

"Coventry's Rx for Ethnic Conflict," *The Christian Century* 99, no. 10 (March 24, 1982): 339-40.

"Democracy and the World's Religions," *This World* 1 (Winter/Spring 1982): 108-20.

"The Philippine Tinderbox (Part I)," *The Christian Century* 99, no. 16 (May 5, 1982): 538-42.

"The Philippine Tinderbox (Part II)," *The Christian Century* 99, no. 21 (June 9-16, 1982): 697-701.

"Poland and the Peace Movement," *The Christian Century* 99, no. 12 (April 7, 1982): 411-14.

"A Puritan's Pilgrimage: Beyond the Iron Cage," *Union Seminary Quarterly Review* 37, no. 3 (1982): 205-16.

"Response to K. C. Abraham," *Bangalore Theological Forum* 14, no. 3 (September-December 1982): 232-36.

"Theology, the Church and Human Rights," *Bangalore Theological Forum* 14, no. 3 (September-December 1982): 191-210.

"Communion: Between Judas and Peter — A Meditation," *Masihi Savak* (India) (October 1982): 17ff.

"The World Religions and Political Democracy: Some Comparative Reflections," *Religion and Society* (Bangalore, India) 29, no. 4 (December 1982): 19-49.

"Ethics and Technology: Some Reflections," *United Theological College/Bangalore Magazine* (1982-83).

"An Ecumenical Perspective on Neoevangelical Politics," *The Journal of Law and Religion* 1, no. 1 (Summer 1983): 203-14.

"Faiths and Politics in South East Asia," *This World* 4 (Winter 1983): 20-48.

"Indian Theologians Prepare for Vancouver," *The Christian Century* 100, no. 10 (April 6, 1983): 316-17.

"Justification, Covenant, and Society: A UCC Perspective," *EKU-UCC Newsletter* 4, no. 1 (June 1983): 1-8.

"Moscow's Church Peace Movement," *The Christian Century* 100, no. 19 (June 8-15, 1983): 584-86.

"Public Theology, Corporate Responsibility and Military Contracting," *ICCR [Interfaith Center on Corporate Responsibility] Brief* 12, no. 11 (1983): 3A-3D.

"An Ecumenist's Plea for a Public Theology," *This World* 8 (Spring/Summer 1984): 47-79.

"Theology, History, and Human Rights," *Soundings* 67, no. 2 (Summer 1984): 191-208.

"The Free-Church Tradition and Social Ministry," *The Christian Century* 102, no. 34 (November 6, 1985): 995-97.

"Fundamentalism Around the World," *The Christian Century* 102, no. 26 (August 28-September 4, 1985): 769-71.

"Human Rights and Religious Freedom in the Philippines," *The Reformed Journal* 35, no. 4 (April 1985): 9-14. Also published as "Religious Freedom and Human Rights: A 'Public Theological' Perspective," In *Our Freedoms: Rights and Responsibilities*, edited by W. Lawson Taitte and with an introduction by Andrew R. Cecil, pp. 69-114. Austin: University of Texas Press, 1985.

"Preface [and Collaborative Editor]," *Bangalore Theological Forum* 17, no. 1 (January-March 1985): no page numbers.

"Missions: A Cross-Cultural Perspective," *TWIST* 4, no. 1 and 2 (July 1986): 21ff.

"Contextualization and Theological Education," *Theological Education* 23, no. 1 (Autumn 1986): 67-84.

"Obedience to Christ and Engaged in the World," *Prism* 1, no. 2 (Fall 1986): 4-16.

"Theology and Human Rights," *Perkins Journal* 39, no. 4 (October 1986): 11-18.

"Torture, Terrorism, and Theology: The Need for a Universal Ethic," *The Christian Century* 103, no. 29 (October 8, 1986): 861-63.

"Christian Social Ethics as a Vocation," *The A.M.E. Zion Quarterly Review* 99, no. 1 (April 1987): 9-18.

"Christian Social Ethics as a Vocation." In *The Annual of the Society of Christian Ethics*, edited by D. M. Yeager, pp. 3-16. Washington, DC: Georgetown University Press, 1987 [Presidential Address].

"Protestantism and Poverty," *This World* 17 (Spring 1987): 18-42.

"Response [to Jeffrey Gros]," *Ecumenical Trends* 16, no. 7 (July/August 1987): 127-28.

"Some Perils of Confessional Theology in Modern Politics," *Katallagete* 10, no. 1-3 (Fall 1987): 66-69.

"Some Sense of Calling in an Ecumenical Seminary," *Religion & Intellectual Life* 4, no. 3 (Spring 1987): 47-58.

"Standing Thoughts on Sitting Down," *The Judson Bulletin* 6, no. 2 (1987): 9-14.

"Tensions Beset Church of South India," *The Christian Century* 104, no. 25 (September 9-16, 1987): 743-44.

"UUs: Wonderful! and Wrong?" *The Unitarian Universalist Christian* 42, no. 4 (Winter 1987): 47-49.

"What Then Shall We Do? On Using Scripture in Economic Ethics," *Interpretation* 41, no. 4 (October 1987): 382-97. Reprinted in *On Moral Business: Classical and Contemporary Resources for Ethics in Economic Life*, edited by Max L. Stackhouse et al., pp. 109-13. Grand Rapids: Eerdmans, 1995.

"On Theological Ethics [Rejoinder to McClendon]," *Journal of the American Academy of Religion* 56, no. 3 (Fall 1988): 555-56.

"Public Theology and Community," *Religion & Intellectual Life* 6, no. 1 (Fall 1988): 99-111.

"Religion, Rights, and the Constitution," *This World* 21 (Spring 1988): 102-17.

"Teaching Values in South India: An Experiment in Education," *The Christian Century* 105, no. 3 (January 27, 1988): 82-85.

"Capitalism and Technology in Global Perspective: A Dispute," *The Christian Century* 106, no. 22 (July 19-26, 1989): 691-93.

"Rauschenbusch Today: The Legacy of a Loving Prophet," *The Christian Century* 106, no. 3 (January 25, 1989): 75-78.

"Solidarity with 'A Word of Solidarity,'" *Occasional Papers on Religion in Eastern Europe* 9, no. 4 (July 1989): 47-50.

"The Theological Challenge of Globalization," *The Christian Century* 106, no. 15 (May 3, 1989): 468-71.

"Thirty-Eight Theses on Christian Social Ethics and Sexuality with Particular Reference to Issues Posed by Gay and Lesbian Advocates in Church-Related Institutions," *This World* 25 (Spring 1989): 119-25.

"Grace and Covenant: Reformation Themes for the UCC Today," *New Conversations* (Winter 1989-90): 19-25.

"Implications Here of the Transformations There," *Occasional Papers on Religion in Eastern Europe* 10, no. 2 (March 1990): 41-44.

"Now That the Revolution Is Over," *The Reformed Journal* 40, no. 7 (September 1990): 16-20.

"The Sociology of Religion and the Theology of Society," *Social Compass: International Review of Sociology of Religion* 37, no. 3 (September 1990): 315-29.

"What Tillich Meant to Me," *The Christian Century* 107, no. 4 (January 31, 1990): 99-102. Reprinted in *Papers from the Annual Meeting of the North American Paul Tillich Society*, edited by Robert P. Scharlemann (September 1990): 13-16.

"A Postcommunist Manifesto: Public Theology after the Collapse of Socialism," co-authored with Dennis P. McCann, *The Christian Century* 108, no. 2 (January 16, 1991): 1, 44-47. Reprinted in *From Christ to the World: Introductory Readings in Christian Ethics*, edited by Wayne G. Boulton, Thomas D. Kennedy, and Allen Verhey, pp. 484-88. Grand Rapids: Eerdmans, 1994, and in *On Moral Business: Classical and Contemporary Resources for Ethics in Economic Life*, edited by Max L. Stackhouse et al., pp. 949-54. Grand Rapids: Eerdmans, 1995.

"Max Stackhouse and Dennis McCann Reply [to "Responses to a 'Postcommunist Manifesto'"]," co-authored with Dennis P. McCann, *The Christian Century* 108, no. 3 (January 23, 1991): 83-85.

"The Faculty as Mentor and Model," *Theological Education* 28, no. 1 (Autumn 1991): 63-70.

"Forum: The Decline of Mainline Religion in American Culture," with William R. Hutchison, Catherine L. Albanese, and William McKinney, *Religion and American Culture* 1, no. 2 (Summer 1991): 131-53, esp. 142-49.

"From the Social Gospel to Public Theology: A Liberal Protestant Perspective," *Lutheran Forum* 25, no. 4 (Advent 1991): 15-20.

"Godly Cooking? Theological Ethics and Technological Society," *First Things* 13 (May 1991): 22-29.

"John Paul on Ethics and the 'New Capitalism,'" *The Christian Century* 108, no. 18 (May 29-June 5, 1991): 581-83.

"Letter to the Editor [Response to Wielenga]," *Occasional Papers on Religion in Eastern Europe* 11, no. 2 (March 1991): 43-44.

"Proper 26: Theological Reflections," *Lectionary Homiletics* 2, no. 12 (November 1991): 4-5, 12, 16, 28.

"Renewing Our Public Vision," *New World Outlook* 51, no. 5 (May-June 1991): 39-41.

"Some World-Affirming and World-Denying Impulses in Our Ethical Traditions," *Andover Newton Review* 2, no. 1 (1991): 1-15.

"Many Pearls, Few Threads," *The Christian Century* 109, no. 5 (February 5-12, 1992): 149-53.

"Divisions and Consensus: An 'Ecumenical Perspective,'" *The Stewardship Journal* 2, no. 3/4 (Summer/Fall 1992): 56-60.

"Alasdair MacIntyre: An Overview and Evaluation," *Religious Studies Review* 18, no. 3 (July 1992): 203-8.

"White Candles vs. Red Flags: Religion and the Fall of the Berlin Wall," *Occasional Papers on Religion in Eastern Europe* 12, no. 5 (October 1992): 1-18. Reprinted *EKU-UCC Newsletter* 11, no. 1 (September 1993): 2-25.

"The Future of Human Rights: Multiculturalism in Vienna," *The Christian Century* 110, no. 20 (June 30-July 7, 1993): 660-62.

"The Moral Roots of the Corporation," *Theology and Public Policy* 5, no. 1 (Summer 1993): 29-39.

"Pietists and Contextualists: The Indian Situation," *The Christian Century* 110, no. 2 (January 20, 1993): 56-58.

"Ethical Vision and Musical Imagination," *Theological Education* 31, no. 1 (Autumn 1994): 149-63.

"On Christian Ethics, a Shattered Teapot, and the Postmodern: An Interview," with Mark Taylor, edited by Todd Shy and Dwight Davidson, *Testament* (Fall 1994): 4-9.

"Introduction [to a Psalmic Poem (by Peggy Shriver) and Sermon on the Psalms (by Fred R. Anderson)]," *Arts* 7, no. 1 (1994): 4.

"The Global Future and the Future of Globalization," *The Christian Century* 111, no. 4 (February 2-9, 1994): 109-18.

"The Homosexual Movement: A Response by the Ramsey Colloquium," co-author, *First Things* 41 (March 1994): 15-20.

"Responsible Society," *One World* 199 (October 1994): 16-17.

"'A Charismatic Sage': James Luther Adams, 1901-1994," *Harvard Divinity Bulletin* 24, no. 2 (1995): 4-5. Excerpted in "James Luther Adams: A Memorial Address," *The Journal of Law and Religion* 12, no. 1 (1995-96): 3-7. Reprinted as "James Luther Adams: A Memorial Address," *Faith and Freedom* 48, part 1, no. 140 (Spring and Summer 1995): 3-6 and "Adams, James Luther, 1901-1994," *Unitarian Universalist Christian* 49, no. 1-2 (Spring and Summer 1994): 104-7.

"Microenterprise Revolution," *The Christian Century* 112, no. 20 (June 21-28, 1995): 629-31.

"The Vocation of Christian Ethics Today," *The Princeton Seminary Bulletin* 16, no. 3 (November 1995): 284-312.

"The Moral Meanings of Covenant." In *The Annual of the Society of Christian Ethics*, edited by Harlan Beckley, pp. 249-64. Washington, DC: Georgetown University Press, 1996.

Max Stackhouse: A Bibliography

"Business as Usual?" co-authored with Dennis P. McCann, *The Christian Century* 113, no. 20 (June 19-26, 1996): 668-69.

"Tradition and Revelation: Changing to Preserve the Truth," *The Christian Century* 113, no. 32 (November 6, 1996): 1061-62.

"Humanism After Tillich," *First Things* 72 (April 1997): 24-28.

"In the Company of Hauerwas," *Journal for Christian Theological Research* 2 (1997). http://www2.luthersem.edu/ctrf/JCTR/Vol02/Stackhouse.htm.

"Living the Tensions: Christians and Divorce," *The Christian Century* 114, no. 22 (July 30–August 6, 1997): 685-86.

"Proper 9: Theological Themes," *Lectionary Homiletics* 8, no. 8 (July 1997): 4, 12, 19, 27.

"Public Theology and Ethical Judgment," *Theology Today* 54, no. 2 (July 1997): 165-79. Published in Chinese translation in *East and West: Religious Ethics: Proceedings of the Third Symposium of Sino-American Philosophy and Religious Studies,* edited by Zhang Zhegang and Mel Stewart, pp. 132-47. Beijing: University of Beijing, 1998.

"Theo-Cons and Neo-Cons on Theology and Law," *The Christian Century* 114, no. 24 (August 27-September 3, 1997): 758-61.

"Tillich and Liberalism: Max Stackhouse Replies [to D. K. Weber]," *First Things* 75 (August-September 1997): 7-8.

"For the Record [response to review of *Covenant and Commitments*]," *First Things* 78 (December 1997): 6.

"Assessing an Assessment: A Response to Ronald M. Green's Review of the *Journal of Religious Ethics*," *Journal of Religious Ethics* 25, no. 3 (25th Anniversary Supplement 1998): 275-79.

"On Human Rights: The Universal Declaration of Human Rights Fifty Years Later: A Statement of the Ramsey Colloquium," *First Things* 82 (April 1998): 18-22.

"Homosexuality, Marriage, and the Church: A Conversation," with David Heim, Luke Timothy Johnson, and David McCarthy Matzko, *The Christian Century* 115, no. 19 (July 1-8, 1998): 644-50.

"The Intellectual Crisis of a Good Idea," *The Journal of Religious Ethics* 26, no. 2 (Fall 1998): 263-68.

"Globalization, Faith, and Theological Education," *Theological Education* 35, no. 2 (Spring 1999): 67-77.

"If Globalization Is True, What Shall We Do? Toward a Theology of Ministry," *Theological Education* 35, no. 2 (Spring 1999): 155-65.

"On Sin, Fall & Evil," *The Living Pulpit* 8, no. 4 (October-December 1999): 13.

"Your Body Is a Temple: Confusions About Love, Sexuality, and Morality Today," *Catalyst* 25, no. 2 (February 1999): 1-3.

"Reflections on 'Universal Absolutes,'" *The Journal of Law and Religion* 14, no. 1 (1999-2000): 97-112.

"Music in Theology and Ethics," *inSpire* [Princeton Theological Seminary] 5, no. 1 (Summer/Fall 2000): 18. Available online: http://www.ptsem.edu/Publications/inspire2/5.1/feature_1/art7.htm

"Covenant in a Global Era: A Tribute to the Contribution of Daniel Elazar." In *The An-*

nual of the Society of Christian Ethics, edited by John Kelsey and Sumner B. Twiss, vol. 20, pp. 133-40. Washington, DC: Georgetown University Press, 2000.

"A Premature Postmodern," *First Things* 106 (October 2000): 19-22.

"Public Theology and Civil Society in a Globalizing Era," *Bangalore Theological Forum* 32, no. 1 (June 2000): 46-72.

"Publics, Apologetics, and Ethics: An Interview with Max L. Stackhouse." Interview by Ken Chase, March 16, 2001. http://www.wheaton.edu/CACE/CACE-Print-Resources/~/media/Files/Centers-and-Institutes/CACE/articles/publicsapologeticsethics.pdf

"Is God in Globalization?" *Discernment* [Wheaton College] 8, no. 2/3 (Summer/Fall 2001): 2-4.

"The New Moral Context of Economic Life," *Quarterly Review* 21, no. 3 (Fall 2001): 239-53.

"Global Theology," *The Christian Century* 119, no. 19 (September 11-24, 2002): 9 [Stackhouse's contribution to "What's Changed? Reflections on September 11," 8-11].

"The Moral Roots of the Common Life in a Global Era," *The Expository Times* 113, no. 5 (February 2002): 157-61. Revised and reprinted in *Loving God with Our Minds: The Pastor as Theologian: Essays in Honor of Wallace M. Alston,* edited by Michael Welker and Cynthia A. Jarvis, pp. 50-61. Grand Rapids: Eerdmans, 2004.

"Theologies of War: Comparative Perspectives," *The Princeton Seminary Bulletin* 23, no. 1 (2002): 15-27.

"Art, Artists, Audiences: The Salt Must Not Lose Its Savor," *CSSE (Center for Spiritual and Ethical Education) Connections* 21, no. 6 (February 2002): 1-8.

"Imagination: An Interview," with Wong Siew Li (Kairos Research Center, Malaysia), *Understanding the Modern World* (August 2002): 18-24.

"Kuyper in de States" (An Interview with Clifford Anderson and Jonathan Zondag), *Woord & Dienst* (Amsterdam), issue 52 (June 7, 2003): 8-9.

"Edwards for Us," *The Christian Century* 120, no. 20 (October 4, 2003): 32-33.

"Spheres of Management: Social, Ethical, and Theological Reflections," *Theology Today* 60, no. 3 (October 2003): 370-83.

"Reflections on Consumerism in a Global Era," *Business & Professional Ethics Journal* 23, no. 4 (Winter 2004): 27-42.

"A Christian Perspective on Human Rights," *Society* 41, no. 2 (January/February 2004): 23-28. Republished as "Sources and Prospects for Human Rights Ideas: A Christian Perspective." In *The Idea of Human Rights: Traditions and Presence,* edited by Jindøich Halama, pp. 183-200. Prague: Charles University, 2003. Reprinted as "The Sources of Human Rights Ideas: A Christian Perspective." In *Religion and Human Rights: Conflict or Convergence,* edited by Adam B. Seligman (Hollis, NH: Hollis Publishing, 2004), 69-84.

"Outsourcing — Job Creation or Worker Exploitation?" with M. Douglas Meeks, *Vital Theology* 1, no. 4 (April 2004): 1, 6-8.

"Civil Religion, Political Theology and Public Theology: What's the Difference?" *Political Theology* 5, no. 3 (July 2004): 275-93. Translated and condensed as "What Is

Public Theology?" *Journal for the Study of Christian Culture* 11 (2004): 3-13 [special issue: Publics of Theology (People's University of China, Beijing)].

"Public Theology and Democracy's Future," *Society* 42, no. 3 (March/April 2005): 7-11. Revised and reprinted in *The Review of Faith and International Affairs* 7, no. 2 (March 2009): 49-54. Available online: http://www.fpri.org/fpriwire/1202.200410.stackhouse.publictheology.html

"On Being Reformed: An Interview with Max Stackhouse," *Perspectives: A Journal of Reformed Thought* 20, no. 8 (October 2005): 13-16.

"Theology in the Public Square: Kuyper's Contributions Highlighted in New PTS Center," *inSpire* [Princeton Theological Seminary] 10, no. 2 (2006): n.p. Available online: http://www.ptsem.edu/uploadedFiles/Seminary_Relations/Communications_and_Publications/Publications/inSpire/2006_Winter_Spring/feature5.pdf

"The Christian Ethic of Love: A Dialogical Response," *Journal of Religious Ethics* 35, no. 4 (2007): 700-11.

"Reflections on How and Why We Go Public," *International Journal of Public Theology* 1, no. 3-4 (2007): 421-30.

"A Tribute to CISRS at 50 [Christian Institute for the Study of Religion and Society]," *Religion and Society* (Bangalore, India) 52, no. 2 (June 2007): 25-32.

"Social Graces: Christianity and Globalization," *The Review of Faith and International Affairs* 5, no. 3 (Fall 2007): 41-49.

"Signs of Hope for the World of Business," *Comment*, October 12, 2007, http://www.cardus.ca/comment/article/923/signs-of-hope-for-the-world-of-business/

"Natural Law Theory and Its Relatives," *Liberty University Law Review* 2 (2008): 929-44.

"Responses to My IJPT Reviewers," *International Journal of Public Theology* 3 (2009): 265-72.

"Why Theology in International Affairs?" *The Review of Faith and International Affairs* 7, no. 1 (March 2009): 73-76.

"Framing the Global Ethos," *Theology Today* 66 (2010): 415-29.

"Global Engagement: How My Mind Has Changed," *The Christian Century* 128, no. 8 (April 19, 2011): 30-34.

REVIEW ESSAYS

"Beyond Situationalism." Review of *Theological Ethics*, by James Sellers, 1966, *Moral Law in Christian Social Ethics*, 1966, by Walter Muelder, and *Elements for a Social Ethic: Scientific and Ethical Perspectives on Social Process*, 1966, by Gibson Winter. *Andover Newton Quarterly* 7, no. 4 (March 1967): 200-204.

"Christological Implications for Ethics." Review of *Christ and the Moral Life*, by James M. Gustafson, 1968. *Interpretation* 23, no. 3 (July 1969): 333-37.

"Protestantism and the City: A Review Article." Review of *The Meaning of the City*, by Jacques Ellul, 1970, and *The Unheavenly City*, by Edward Banfield, 1970. *Andover Newton Quarterly* 11, no. 4 (March 1971): 211-16.

"Ethics as Human Creativity?" Review of *Liberating Creation: Foundations of Religious Social Ethics*, by Gibson Winter, 1981. *Religious Studies Review* 10, no. 4 (October 1984): 334-39.

"Michael Harrington's Socialism." Review of *Socialism: Past and Future*, by Michael Harrington, 1989. *First Things* 4 (June/July 1990): 53-55.

"Aesthetics and Theology." Review of *Religious Aesthetics: A Theological Study of Making and Meaning*, by Frank Burch Brown, 1992. *Cross Currents* 43, no. 1 (Spring 1993): 123-24.

"Messianic Economics." Review of *Reaching for Heaven on Earth: The Theological Meaning of Economics*, by Robert H. Nelson, 1991. *The Christian Century* 110, no. 11 (April 7, 1993): 376-77.

"Through Contextualism to a 'Providential Deism?'" Review of *Ethics from a Theocentric Perspective*, vol. 2: *Ethics and Theology*, by James M. Gustafson, 1984. *The Reformed Journal* 36, no. 1 (January 1993): 21-26.

"Can 'Sustainability' Be Sustained? A Review Essay of John B. Cobb Jr.'s *Sustainability*." *The Princeton Seminary Bulletin* 15, no. 2 (1994): 143-55.

"Liberalism Dispatched vs. Liberalism Engaged." Review of *Dispatches from the Front: Theological Engagement with the Secular*, by Stanley Hauerwas, 1994. *The Christian Century* 112, no. 29 (October 18, 1995): 962-67.

"Trusting Economics?" Review of *Trust: The Social Virtues and the Creation of Prosperity*, by Francis Fukuyama, 1995. *Theology Today* 53, no. 2 (July 1996): 220-24.

"Living in God's City." Review of *Augustine and the Limits of Politics*, by Jean Bethke Elshtain, 1995. *The Christian Century* 114, no. 14 (April 23-30, 1997): 421-24.

"Revisiting the Church in Socialism." Review of *The Church for Others: Protestant Theology in Communist East Germany*, by Gregory Baum, 1996, *The East German Church and the End of Communism: Essays on Religion, Democratization and Christian Social Ethics*, by John P. Burgess, 1997, and *Religion, Federalism, and the Struggle for Public Life: Cases from Germany, India and America*, by William J. Everett, 1997. *The Christian Century* 115, no. 25 (September 23-30, 1998): 864-71.

"Kingdom Coming." Review of *The Kingdom Is Always but Coming: A Life of Walter Rauschenbusch*, by Christopher H. Evans, 2004. *The Christian Century* 122, no. 10 (May 17, 2005): 54-56.

"For Fairer Trade: Justice and the Global Market." Review of *Making Globalization Work*, by Joseph E. Stiglitz, 2006. *The Christian Century* 124, no. 16 (August 7, 2007): 28-31.

BOOK REVIEWS

Review of *Hope in Action*, by Hans J. Margull, 1962. *Harvard Divinity Bulletin* 27, no. 2 (January 1963): 25-26.

Review of *Christianity and the Social Crisis*, by Walter Rauschenbusch, 1964. *Harvard Divinity Bulletin* 29, no. 2 (January 1965): 51-53.

Review of *Christians in a Technological Era*, by Hugh C. White Jr., ed., 1964. *The Review of Religious Research* 9, no. 1 (Fall 1967): 56-58.

Review of *Witness to a Generation: Significant Writings from Christianity and Crisis (1941-1966)*, by Wayne H. Cowan, ed., 1966. *Journal of Ecumenical Studies* 5, no. 2 (Spring 1968): 416-17.

Review of *Guaranteed Annual Income: The Moral Issues,* by Philip Wogaman, 1968. *Religion in Life* 38, no. 1 (Spring 1969): 158-59.
Review of *Washington Gladden: Prophet of the Social Gospel,* by Jacob H. Dorn, 1967. *Journal of Presbyterian History* 48, no. 1 (Spring 1970): 87-88.
Review of *What Is Ethics All About?,* by Herbert McCabe, 1969. *Encounter* 31, no. 4 (Autumn 1970): 412-13.
Review of *Public Ethics,* by James Sellers, 1970. *Religion in Life* 39, no. 3 (Autumn 1970): 462-64.
Review of *The Church as Moral Decision Maker,* by James M. Gustafson, 1970. *Encounter* 32, no. 3 (Summer 1971): 248-50.
Review of *Can Ethics Be Christian?* by James M. Gustafson, 1975. *Religion in Life* 44, no. 4 (Winter 1975): 503-4.
Review of *Spindles and Spires: A Re-Study of Religion and Social Change in Gastonia,* by John R. Earle, Dean D. Knudsen, and Donald W. Shriver Jr., 1976. *Union Seminary Quarterly Review* 32, no. 3 & 4 (Spring and Summer 1977): 180-83.
Review of *Protestant and Roman Catholic Ethics,* by James M. Gustafson, 1978. *Religion in Life* 47, no. 4 (Winter 1978): 511-12.
Review of *Religious Reason: The Rational and Moral Basis of Religious Belief,* by Ronald M. Green, 1978. *Religious Studies Review* 6, no. 3 (July 1980): 177-82.
Review of *Ethics,* by Wolfhart Pannenberg, 1981. *Horizons* 10, no. 1 (Spring 1983): 184-85.
Review of *The Concept of Transcendence,* by Bishop Sabapathy Kulandran, 1981. *Religion and Society* (Bangalore, India) 30, no. 2 (June 1983): 75-81.
Review of *Dharma and Development: Religion as a Resource in the Sarvodaya Self-Help Movement,* by Joanna Macy, 1983. *Religious Studies Review* 10, no. 1 (January 1984): 59.
Review of *The Church,* by Wolfhart Pannenberg, 1983. *Horizons* 11, no. 1 (Spring 1984): 186-87.
Review of *Christian Faith and Public Choices: The Social Ethics of Barth, Brunner, and Bonhoeffer,* by Robin W. Lovin, 1984. *The Christian Century* 101, no. 24 (August 1-8, 1984): 748-50.
Review of *Walter Rauschenbusch: Selected Writings,* by Winthrop S. Hudson, 1984. *Theology Today* 42, no. 4 (January 1986): 561.
Review of *Cosmogony and Ethical Order: New Studies in Comparative Ethics,* by Robin W. Lovin and Frank E. Reynolds, eds., 1985. *Journal for the Scientific Study of Religion* 25, no. 4 (December 1986): 517-18.
Review of *Theology for a Nuclear Age,* by Gordon D. Kaufman, 1985. *Theology Today* 43, no. 4 (January 1987): 573-74.
Review of *Human Rights: Fact or Fancy,* by Henry B. Veatch, 1985; *A History and Theory of Informed Consent,* by Ruth R. Faden, Tom L. Beauchamp, and Nancy M. P. King, 1986; and *Human Rights in East Asia: A Cultural Perspective,* by James C. Hsiung, ed., 1985. *America* 156 (February 7, 1987): 109-11.
Review of *The Spirit of Revolt: Anarchism and the Cult of Authority,* by Richard K. Fenn, 1986. *The Christian Century* 104, no. 27 (September 30, 1987): 831-32.

Max Stackhouse: A Bibliography

Review of *Ethics: Systematic Theology*, vol. 1, by James W. McClendon Jr., 1986. *Journal of the American Academy of Religion* 55, no. 3 (Fall 1987): 615-17.

Review of *Ethics, Volume One: Basic Elements and Methodology in an Ethical Theology*, by Trutz Rendtorff, 1986. *Horizons* 15, no. 1 (Spring 1988): 190-91.

Review of *Religion and the Western Mind*, by Ninian Smart, 1987. *Review of Religious Research* 30, no. 1 (September 1988): 102-3.

Review of *The Prophethood of All Believers*, by James Luther Adams, ed. George K. Beach, 1986. *Critical Review of Books in Religion* (1988): 402-4.

Review of *Perplexity in the Moral Life: Philosophical and Theological Considerations*, by Edmund N. Santurri, 1987. *Theology Today* 45, no. 4 (January 1989): 474-78.

Review of *The Human Rights Movement: Western Values and Theological Perspectives*, by Warren Lee Holleman, 1987. *The Journal of Religion* 69, no. 3 (July 1989): 436-37.

Review of *Hindu Ethics: Purity, Abortion, and Euthanasia*, by Harold G. Coward, Julius J. Lipner, and Katherine K. Young, 1989. *Journal of Ecumenical Studies* 26, no. 4 (Fall 1989): 747-48.

Review of *Christ Without Absolutes: A Study of the Christology of Ernst Troeltsch*, by Sarah Coakley, 1988. *Theological Studies* 50, no. 4 (December 1989): 803-5.

Review of *Community and Alienation: Essays on Process Thought and Public Life*, by Douglas Sturm, 1988. *The Journal of Religion* 70, no. 1 (January 1990): 125-26.

Review of *Theology, Politics and Peace*, by Theodore Runyon, ed., 1989. *Andover Newton Review* 1, no. 1 (Spring 1990): 41-42.

Review of *The Structure of Love*, by Alan Soble, 1990. *The Christian Century* 108, no. 6 (February 20, 1991): 203-4.

Review of *The Divine Good: Modern Moral Theory and the Necessity of God*, by Franklin I. Gamwell, 1990. *The Christian Century* 108, no. 24 (August 21-28, 1991): 783-84.

Review of *The Protestant Work Ethic: The Psychology of Work-Related Beliefs and Behavior*, by Adrian Furnham, 1990. *Journal for the Scientific Study of Religion* 30, no. 3 (September 1991): 342-43.

Review of *Professional Ethics in Context: Institutions, Images and Empathy*, by Eric Mount Jr., 1990. *Journal of Church and State* 34, no. 2 (Spring 1992): 398-99.

Review of *A Christian Perspective on Political Thought*, by Stephen Charles Mott, 1993. *The Journal of Religion* 75, no. 1 (January 1995): 148-49.

Review of *Future Imperfect: The Mixed Blessings of Technology in America*, by Howard P. Segal, 1994. *The Christian Century* 112, no. 4 (February 1-8, 1995): 128-30.

Review of *Heterosexism: An Ethical Challenge*, by Patricia Beattie Jung and Ralph F. Smith, 1993, and *Against Nature? Types of Moral Argumentation Regarding Homosexuality*, by Pim Pronk, 1993. *The Princeton Seminary Bulletin* 16, no. 3 (1995): 372-75.

Review of *History, Religion, and American Democracy*, by Ronald M. Green, ed., 1993. *Journal of Church and State* 37, no. 4 (Autumn 1995): 899.

Review of *Paul Ramsey's Political Ethics*, by David Attwood, 1992, and *Tragedy, Tradition, Transformation: The Ethics of Paul Ramsey*, by D. Stephen Long, 1993. *Theology Today* 52, no. 3 (October 1995): 435-36.

Review of *Reinhold Niebuhr and Christian Realism*, by Robin W. Lovin, 1995. *The Journal of Religion* 77, no. 2 (April 1997): 325-26.

Review of *Sovereignty at the Crossroads? Morality & International Politics in the Post–Cold War Era*, by Luis E. Lugo, ed., 1996. *Religious Studies Review* 23, no. 3 (July 1997): 277.

Review of *Moral Action and Christian Ethics*, by Jean Porter, 1995. *Ethics* 108, no. 1 (October 1997): 242-43.

Review of *The Word Made Strange: Theology, Language, Culture*, by John Milbank, 1997. *The Journal of Religion* 78, no. 4 (October 1998): 640-41.

Review of *Marriage as a Covenant: Biblical Law and Ethics as Developed from Malachi*, by Gordon P. Hugenberger, 1998. *First Things* 96 (October 1999): 75.

Review of *Transnational Corporations as Agents of Dehumanization in Asia: An Ethical Critique of Development*, by I. John Mohan Razu, 1999. *Journal of Tribal Studies* 5, no. 1 (January-June 2001): 66-74.

Review of *Christianity, Art and Transformation: Theological Aesthetics in the Struggle for Justice*, by John W. de Gruchy, 2001. *Theology Today* 58, no. 3 (October 2001): 450-54.

Review of *Covenant and Civil Society: The Constitutional Matrix of Modern Democracy. Vol. 4, The Covenant Tradition in Politics*, by Daniel J. Elazar, 1998. *The Journal of Religion* 82, no. 1 (January 2002): 143-44.

Review of *Growing up Protestant: Parents, Children and Mainline Churches*, by Margaret Lamberts Bendroth, 2002. *Journal of Family Ministry* 17, no. 1 (Spring 2003): 92-93.

Review of *Joining Hands: Politics and Religion Together for Social Change*, by Roger S. Gottlieb, 2002. *Missiology* 32, no. 1 (January 2004): 100-101.

OTHER WORKS

Ministries to Military Personnel. Report of a United Church task force of which Max L. Stackhouse was a member. Philadelphia: United Church Press, 1973.

No Authority but from God, Religion Under Hitler, Liberalism and the Barmen Declaration in Nazi Germany, 1989. Twenty-six min. each, vol. 1-3 of The Adams Tapes. Narrated by Max L. Stackhouse.

Globalization, Public Theology, and New Means of Grace. Santa Clara, CA: Santa Clara University, Bannan Center for Jesuit Education, 2003. Available online: http://www.scu.edu/ic/publications/upload/scl-0301-stackhouse.pdf

"Responding to the Sermon on the Mount." Max L. Stackhouse, ed. *Bangalore Theological Forum* 17, no. 1 (January-March 1985): 1-97.

ONLINE ESSAYS

A Protestant View of Globalization (Part I). http://www.theglobalist.com/a-protestant-view-of-globalization-part-i/.

Globalization as a Massive Civilizational Shift (Part II). http://www.theglobalist.com/globalization-as-a-massive-civilizational-shift-part-ii/.

Max Stackhouse: A Bibliography

When Corporations Get Religion (Part III). http://www.theglobalist.com/when-corporations-get-religion-part-iii/.

Religion as a Globalizing Force (Part IV). http://www.theglobalist.com/religion-as-a-globalizing-force-part-iv/.

Max Weber: A Modern-Day Globalization Guru? (Part V). http://www.theglobalist.com/max-weber-a-modern-day-globalization-guru-part-v/.

Acknowledgments

The editors and publisher gratefully acknowledge permission to include the following:

"Toward a Theology for the New Social Gospel." *The Andover Newton Quarterly* 6, no. 4 (March 1966): 3-20.
"Rauschenbusch Today: The Legacy of a Loving Prophet." Copyright © 1989 by the *Christian Century*. Reprinted by permission from the January 25, 1989, issue of the *Christian Century*.
"Christianity in New Formation: Reflections of a White Christian on the Death of Dr. Martin Luther King, Jr." *The Andover Newton Quarterly* 9, no. 2 (November 1968): 95-111.
"What Tillich Meant to Me." Copyright © 1990 by the *Christian Century*. Reprinted by permission from the January 31, 1990, issue of the *Christian Century*.
"Alasdair MacIntyre: An Overview and Evaluation." *Religious Studies Review* 18, no. 3 (July 1992): 203-8. Reprinted by permission of John Wiley & Sons Ltd.
"A Premature Postmodern." *First Things* 106 (October 2000): 19-22.
"Edwards for Us." Copyright © 2003 by the *Christian Century*. Reprinted by permission from the October 4, 2003, issue of the *Christian Century*.
"Liberalism Dispatched vs. Liberalism Engaged." Review of *Dispatches from the Front: Theological Engagement with the Secular*, by Stanley Hauerwas, 1994. Copyright © 1995 by the *Christian Century*. Reprinted by permission from the October 18, 1995, issue of the *Christian Century*.
"The Tasks of Theological Ethics." Original version published as "Christian Ethics, Practical Theology and Public Theology in a Global Era." In *Reconsidering the Boundaries Between Theological Disciplines*, edited by Michael Welker and Friedrich Schweitzer, pp. 99-111. Münster: LIT Verlag, 2005.
"The Religious Basis of Cultural Activity." *Soundings* 61, no. 1 (Spring 1978): 7-22. Copyright © 1978 by The Pennsylvania State University Press. Reprinted by permission of The Pennsylvania State University Press.

Acknowledgments

"Public Theology and Ethical Judgment." *Theology Today* 54, no. 2 (July 1997): 165-79.

"Ethics: Social and Christian." *The Andover Newton Quarterly* 13, no. 3 (January 1973): 173-91.

"Reflections on 'Universal Absolutes.'" *The Journal of Law and Religion* 14, no. 1 (1999-2000): 97-112. Copyright © Center for the Study of Law and Religion at Emory University. Reprinted with the permission of Cambridge University Press.

"The Fifth Social Gospel and the Global Mission of the Church." In *The Social Gospel Today*, edited by Christopher H. Evans, pp. 146-59. Louisville: Westminster John Knox, 2001. Reprinted with permission of Westminster John Knox.

"Civil Religion, Political Theology and Public Theology: What's the Difference?" *Political Theology* 5, no. 3 (July 2004): 275-93.

"Covenantal Justice in a Global Era." In *Struggling to Hope: A Tribute to the Rev. Dr. Eka Darmaputera (Bergumul Dalam Pengharapan: Buku Penghargaan Untuk Pdt. Dr. Eka Darmaputera)*, edited by F. Suleeman, A. A. Sutama, and A. Rajendra, pp. 419-35. Jakarta: PT Bpk Gunung Mulia, 1999.

"A Postcommunist Manifesto: Public Theology after the Collapse of Socialism." Co-authored with Dennis P. McCann. Copyright © 1991 by the *Christian Century*. Reprinted by permission from the January 16, 1991, issue of the *Christian Century*.

"The Moral Roots of the Corporation." *Theology and Public Policy* 5, no. 1 (Summer 1993): 29-39.

"Spheres of Management: Social, Ethical, and Theological Reflections." *Theology Today* 60, no. 3 (October 2003): 370-83.

"Globalization, Faith, and Theological Education." *Theological Education* 35, no. 2 (Spring 1999): 67-77.

"A Christian Perspective on Human Rights." *Society* 41, no. 2 (January/February 2004): 23-28. Reprinted with kind permission of Springer Science & Business Media B.V.

"Living the Tensions: Christians and Divorce." Copyright © 1997 by the *Christian Century*. Reprinted by permission from the July 30–August 6, 1997, issue of the *Christian Century*.

"The Pastor as Public Theologian." In *The Pastor as Theologian*, edited by Earl E. Shelp and Ronald H. Sunderland, pp. 106-29, 133. New York: Pilgrim Press, 1988.

Index

Abolitionists, 34, 39
Abortion, 86, 134-35, 137, 324, 342
Abraham, 208-9
Abraham, K. C., xii, 333
Academia, x, 50, 83, 199, 267
"Act-deontology," 206
Adams, James Luther, xii, 24-25, 27, 49-52, 72, 74, 118n.4, 301n.8, 322, 324-25, 327, 336, 342-43
Aesthetics, 138, 340, 343
Althusius, Johannes, 67, 201, 235, 311n.4
Altizer, Thomas J. J., 7-8
Amnesty International, 161n.12
Anger, xxv, 23, 31-33
Annan, Kofi, 176
Anthropology, 7, 50, 109, 177, 183, 298
Antinomianism, 137, 259
Apostles' Creed, 315
A priori, 6-7, 11, 15, 19, 63; categories, 15, 63; religious, 11, 73, 76; truths, 130
Arendt, Hannah, 110
Aristotle, 57-59, 61-63, 74-75, 142, 192, 239, 260, 293
Association, 135, 144-46, 148, 200, 203, 212, 215, 223, 227, 230, 238, 243, 244, 279-81, 307, 311; spheres of, xxix; voluntary, 33, 148-49, 227, 234, 279, 324-25, 332
Augustine, Saint, xvn.2, 6, 57, 68, 74, 85, 87, 191, 293, 340
Authority, xiv-xv, 62, 65, 117, 122, 124, 127, 130, 134, 137, 144, 172, 191, 195-96, 203, 211, 222, 234, 240, 243, 264, 268, 274, 281, 292, 294, 306-8, 312, 342; and experience, xix, xxii; and reason, xix, xxii; and Scripture, xix, xxii, 97; social, 144, 274, 308, 312; and tradition, xix, xxii
Autonomy, 52, 79, 285, 311-12
Axiology, 147, 153

Baptism, 36, 189, 234, 274, 284, 326
Barmen Declaration, 71, 86, 193, 343
Barth, Karl, 8, 16-17, 48, 50, 65, 71, 86, 89, 109, 184n.23, 191, 193-94, 202, 264, 341
Being, 15, 51, 95, 108, 125, 188, 195, 236, 293
Bellah, Robert, 65, 68, 191, 298
Benedict, Saint, 63, 65
Benhabib, Seyla, 126n.8
Benne, Robert, 118n.5, 155n.4
Bentham, Jeremy, 62
Berger, Peter, 72, 107, 177n.14, 187n.1, 232n.3, 322
Bible, 23, 50, 80, 85-89, 169n.1, 190n.5, 213, 218, 224, 265, 275, 283-84, 290, 325; authority of, 97; uses of, 149. *See also* Authority: and Scripture; Scripture; Word, the
Bloch, Ernst, 71, 192
Bloom, Allan, 64, 66, 68, 123n.7

347

Index

Boff, Leonardo, 89
Bonhoeffer, Dietrich, 22, 63, 71, 86, 193, 202, 264, 341
Bretton Woods agreements, 273
Brown, Robert McAfee, 24
Browning, Don S., 95n.3, 155n.4, 322, 329
Brunner, Emil, 202, 293, 326, 341
Buddhism, 101, 129, 181, 183, 189, 224, 268, 308n.1, 320
Bultmann, Rudolf, 8, 63
Business, xiii, xv, xvii, xx-xxi, xxix-xxx, 88, 131, 179, 214, 217, 222-23, 226-28, 230, 233, 235-44, 249, 253-57, 267, 289, 306, 322-24, 327, 329, 332, 334-35, 337-39

Calvin, John, 36, 74, 77, 85, 120, 155n.6, 293
Calvinism, 15, 36, 76, 142, 180n.18, 188, 201n.18
Capitalism, 62, 64, 95, 110, 124, 159, 176, 182, 186-87, 195, 221-22, 224, 237, 249-52, 255-56, 330, 334-35
Categorical imperative, 53
Catholicism, 34-35, 37-39, 137, 164-65, 171n.4, 188, 190, 284
Character, 36, 65, 68, 82, 85, 87, 135, 214, 232, 257, 279; of God, 165, 205
China, People's Republic of, xiii, 45, 96, 129, 183, 186, 190, 196n.14, 200, 237, 245, 276, 296, 319, 339
Christ and culture, xxiv, 19, 50, 333
Christ and Culture (H. R. Niebuhr), 11n.11
Christianity, v, xii, xv, xvii, xxv, xxvii, 3-8, 11, 16, 23, 25, 28, 30, 34-35, 40, 44, 49, 60, 65-66, 69, 72-75, 83, 85, 100, 112, 117, 128, 149, 155, 168-69, 171, 181, 183-84, 189-91, 196, 201, 221-22, 224, 233-35, 244, 261-62, 268, 275, 281-82, 290, 296, 301, 308-9, 312, 315, 319-20, 323-24, 326-27, 329-31, 339-41, 343; essence of, 5-8, 10-11, 13-14
Christian realism, xvi, 24, 171-72, 194, 221, 255, 343
Christian sociology, 23
Church, ix-xi, xv, xviii-xxvi, xxviii, xxxi, 5, 11-12, 17-19, 22, 25-28, 30-32, 34-36, 38-43, 50, 52, 63, 71-72, 75-78, 82, 84-90, 94, 97, 118, 123, 133, 142, 148-50, 155, 167, 170-75, 182, 186-88, 191-97, 199, 201-2, 214-15, 218, 221, 226-27, 233-35, 240-44, 256-57, 262, 265, 270-71, 273, 280-84, 287-89, 293-99, 301, 303-9, 314-15, 318-19, 323, 325-30, 332-35, 337, 340-43
Church/sect typology, 76
Cicero, Marcus Tullius, 61, 67, 191
City, 208, 237-38, 270, 320, 324, 331, 339, 340
City of God, 87
Civilization, xiii, xv, 24, 27-28, 35, 48, 52, 64-65, 74, 87-88, 90, 93, 95, 97, 99, 102-8, 111-15, 118, 124, 132, 134, 137, 145, 166, 169, 173-78, 180-88, 198-99, 204, 215, 218, 222-23, 228, 230, 232, 238, 241, 244-45, 261, 263-64, 266, 268, 270, 272, 275, 281-82, 288-91, 295-96, 299-302, 308-14, 318-22, 326, 329, 332, 334
Civil religion, vi, xviii, xxviii, 186-91, 194-95, 203, 292, 339
Civil rights, xi, xii, xxv, 3, 29, 31, 72, 171, 173, 221, 238, 255, 274
Civil society, xvii, 75, 86, 94-95, 98, 102, 117, 132, 184, 191, 193, 196-97, 199-201, 203-4, 208, 213-17, 243-45, 247, 250-55, 257, 270, 276, 280-82, 313-15, 319, 323, 327, 329-30, 338, 343
Clash of civilizations, 245, 282
Clash of Civilizations and the Remaking of World Order, The (Huntington), 182, 188n.3
Clergy, 30, 41, 47, 196, 228, 232, 256-57, 270, 284, 293-95, 297, 299, 301, 317
Common good, xv-xvii, xxviii, 56, 67, 165-67, 175, 226, 231, 306-7, 330
Common grace, xixn.7, 41, 103n.11
Common life, xiii, xv, xix-xxii, xxx, 26, 77, 87-89, 93, 103-4, 111, 116-20, 134, 143, 157, 165-68, 173, 179-81, 185, 187-88, 196, 200, 208, 210-11, 214-15, 222, 233, 243, 253, 257, 263, 268-69, 277, 280, 288, 291, 294, 297, 308, 313, 315, 317, 322, 327-28, 338
Communio sanctorum, 287
Communitarianism, 72, 212, 314
Community, xv, xxxi, 3, 19, 31, 36, 40, 46, 56, 59, 62, 65, 69, 80, 86, 94, 103, 110, 116-17, 126, 135-37, 142-43, 147-53, 160, 168,

348

179, 183, 187, 195, 199, 203, 205, 208, 212, 214, 222, 227-29, 236, 238, 243, 265, 270, 276, 279, 284, 286, 291, 300, 306, 324, 327, 334, 342
Confessing Church (Germany), 86
Confessionalism, 295-96, 300
Confucius, 67, 112, 132
Consciousness, 14, 51, 108, 123-26, 128-30, 139, 179, 241-42, 261, 299; class, 223; collective, 191, 267; ecological, 272; ethnic, 239, 272; historical, 139, 223; human, 76, 165; national, 191; religious, 73; social, 45; time, 237
Constantinople, 89
Contextualism, contextualists, 325, 336, 340
Contextualist ethic, 138
Contextualist vs. principlist theology, xxiv, 8-11, 16
Contextualization, xx, xxiii, 300n.7, 321, 325, 334, 340
Corporation, 96, 110, 167, 175-76, 217, 225-28, 230-32, 235, 237, 240-41, 244, 246, 249-51, 253-57, 263, 289, 294-95, 311, 315, 326, 328, 330, 336, 343, 344; business, 226-27, 322; as covenantal community, 226-28; economic, 152, 230, 281; as *persona ficta*, 232; transnational/multinational, 96, 110, 174-75, 176n.13, 217, 231, 249, 253, 256, 294, 311n.5, 343
Cosmos, 21, 50, 93, 237
Costas, Orlando, 297-98
Coulange, Fustel de, 111
Covenant, xii, xiv, xix-xx, xxii-xxiii, xxviii, xxx, 17, 33, 39, 79, 81, 93, 103, 117, 131-32, 140, 143, 150-55, 163, 175, 184, 201, 204-18, 223, 226-28, 234, 243, 256-57, 264, 269-71, 277, 280, 285, 289-90, 301, 306-7, 311-12, 318, 321, 323, 328, 330, 332-35, 337, 338, 343
Cultural-linguistic traditions/ethos, 60, 84, 87, 126, 127
Culture, xii, xv, xvii, xxiv, xxvi, 5-6, 11, 15, 22, 30-31, 33, 36-37, 42-43, 50-51, 59, 61, 64, 76, 83-84, 86-87, 89, 94-95, 98-99, 103, 105, 107, 110, 115-16, 120, 124, 127, 129, 134, 145-46, 155, 158-60, 162, 166, 170, 174, 176-77, 180-83, 188, 195-96, 199, 202, 210, 215, 218, 227, 232-33, 235-39, 244, 260-63, 266-68, 272-76, 281-82, 285, 290, 293, 296, 300, 307, 319-22, 325, 332-33, 339, 343; American, 22, 72, 326, 335; bearers of, 104, 106-8, 110-15; capitalist, 159; complex, 131; human, 19, 161; indigenous, 251; liberal societies, xxvi; modern, 28, 43, 45; pluralist, 75; popular, 179, 311; secular, 53; socialist, 159; theology of, 133; traditional, 139; Western, 28, 72; world-comprehending, 162
"Culture Christianity," 3, 11

Dalai Lama, 181
Day, Dorothy, 25
Death of God, xxiv, 5-10, 13, 35
Deconstruction, 65-66, 126, 128
Dehumanization, 105, 176n.13, 279, 300, 343
Democracy, xi, xxiii, xxix, 16, 45-46, 54, 62, 64, 82-83, 88, 109, 117, 122-23, 132, 139, 162, 186, 190, 193, 198, 201, 215, 243-44, 257, 280, 292, 323, 325, 332-33, 339, 342-43; constitutional, 83, 96, 171, 173, 190, 199, 214, 230; and human rights, xxix, 127-28, 197, 221, 224, 315
Deontology, xx-xxi, xxvii, 61-62, 68, 206
Derrida, Jacques, 57, 65
Descartes, René, 130
Dialectic, 108-10, 114, 223
Dilthey, Edward, 75
Discernment, 46, 99, 101-3, 110, 139, 143, 195, 292, 307, 338
Discourse, xix, xxxi, 12-13, 119, 130, 156, 161, 163, 198, 224, 273, 292, 302, 306, 328; communities of, 292; human rights, xxx, 160, 271; international, 273; modes of, 161; moral, xxv, 9, 61, 66, 139-41; warranted, xix. *See also* Modes of moral discourse; Public discourse
Divorce, vi, xx, xxx, 80, 283-85, 337
Dostoyevsky, Fyodor, 140
Durkheim, Émile, 42, 64, 191, 203
Duty, *prima facie*, 136
Dworkin, Ronald, 156

Index

Ecclesiology, xxii-xxiii, 17-18, 20, 24, 76, 86, 151, 201, 215, 223, 227, 307, 323
Eco-feminism, 89
Ecology, 110, 248; industrial, 247; moral, 179; social, 179, 215, 265
Economics, xi, xiii, xxiv, 26, 29, 48, 76, 82-83, 101, 127, 162, 169, 174, 177, 181, 196, 222, 233, 241, 248, 256, 306, 314, 323, 325, 329, 340; capitalist, 34, 49, 105, 109, 159, 188, 232, 244, 245; communist, xiii, xvi, xxix, 49, 71, 82, 182, 340; market, 62, 88, 175, 246, 248, 251, 253, 257, 340; socialist, 19, 34, 47, 49, 64-65, 159, 170, 190, 217, 221, 223, 245
Economy, xvii, xxiii, xxix, 88, 94, 180, 213, 224, 231-32, 235, 238, 241, 244, 246, 249-53; global, xiii, 96, 188, 217, 248, 253, 328; political, xiii, xv, xvii, 26, 118, 155, 175, 222-23, 232, 241, 249, 257, 317, 321, 326-27, 330
Education, 161, 180, 192, 196-97, 203, 211, 214, 216-17, 222-23, 227, 230, 238, 244, 250, 253, 268, 289-90, 299, 319, 323-25, 331, 338, 343; theological, 259, 261, 263, 270, 300, 302, 306, 321-22, 327, 334-37
Edwards, Jonathan, xxvi, 78-81, 85, 120, 166n.19, 195, 293, 338
Elazar, Daniel, 132, 184, 201n.17, 338, 343
Emotivism, 48, 58
Encyclopedia, 66, 68
England, 122, 192, 215. See also Great Britain
Enlightenment, the, xxx, 54, 57-59, 66, 74, 77, 82-84, 99n.5, 100, 121, 123, 125, 127, 130-31, 178n.16, 182, 194, 240, 273, 295, 298, 300
Environment, 19, 225, 228-29, 239, 246, 255, 320, 322; business, xxix; cultural, 76, 182; ethical, 101; financial, 226; global, 181, 268; natural, 225, 246, 248; social, 163, 179
Epistemology, 54
Erasmus, Desiderius, 75
Eros, 50, 180n.18, 266-67, 327
Eschatology, 8, 36, 307, 321, 323
Ethicist, 9-10, 24, 96, 98, 136, 138, 140, 143-44, 147, 152, 179, 241, 320; theological, viii, x, xviii, xxi, 10, 97-98, 158, 166n.19, 198, 305
Ethics, xii, xv-xvi, xviii-xxi, xxvii, 6, 9, 14, 17, 27, 48, 53, 55-56, 59, 61, 63, 66-70, 74, 82-86, 94, 98, 102, 106, 116, 119, 126, 131, 133-53, 154-56, 158, 176-77, 182, 206, 214, 222, 229-30, 268, 287, 292, 295, 297, 301, 309-11, 314-15, 323, 332, 334; Christian, xi, xx-xxi, xxvi-xxvii, 36, 72, 75-76, 93-94, 97, 127, 189, 299, 305, 312, 322-23, 326-27, 330, 335-36; contextualist, xxiv, 8-10, 16, 138, 336; eudaimonistic, 62; philosophical, 141; principlist, 8-11, 16; religious, 73, 80, 176-77, 323, 332; social, xii, xxvi, 22, 118, 133-34, 141, 143, 147, 149-52, 169, 183, 198, 221, 224, 317-18, 320-22, 324-27, 331, 334-35; tasks of, 8, 100, 102, 151; theological, viii, x, xx-xxi, xxiii, xxvi, xxviii, xxxii, 3, 5, 8, 57, 62, 68, 90, 97-99, 100-103, 119, 138, 151, 174, 178, 179, 268, 306, 313, 321, 323, 334
Ethology, xx-xxi, xxvii, 61-62, 68, 98-99
Ethos, xi-xii, xvi, xx-xxiii, xxvi, 3, 16, 60, 63, 94, 98-99, 101-2, 131, 134-36, 141-44, 147-53, 169, 179, 195, 202, 223, 233, 236-37, 240-44, 255, 277, 306, 317, 321, 332, 339
Evangelicalism, 22, 25, 189, 315
Evers, Medger, 29
Existentialism, 36, 45, 49
Experience, xii, xviii-xix, xxii, xxx, 4-10, 13-19, 21, 23, 26, 37, 39-40, 44, 47-48, 52, 78, 82-83, 94, 97, 105-13, 116-17, 134-35, 139, 142, 146, 148, 152, 166, 168, 170, 176, 203, 208, 228, 240, 260, 266, 277-78, 287, 292, 294-95; moral, 9, 133, 137-38, 141, 151, 153; religious, 75, 194. See also Authority

Fackre, Gabriel, xii, 18, 328
Faith, xii-xiii, xv-xvi, xix, xxx-xxxi, 5, 7-8, 11, 14, 21-22, 24, 31, 35, 38, 40, 46-52, 65, 73-75, 78-80, 83-86, 88-90, 100, 103, 118-21, 125, 128, 131, 138, 149-51, 154-57, 162, 168-69, 173, 181, 184, 189, 191-97, 202-3, 210, 213-15, 221-24, 229, 241, 256-59, 262, 266, 269-70, 277, 279-81, 285-90, 293-302,

Index

306, 318, 320-21, 324-30, 333-39; leap of, 55; and reason, 52
Family, xi, xix, xxiv, xxx, 22-23, 37, 76, 80, 94, 105, 110, 135, 144-45, 152, 171, 180, 190, 196, 200, 214-15, 225-26, 230-35, 251, 264, 266, 287, 319, 321, 326
Fascism, 21, 34, 110, 170, 186, 202, 221
Feminism, feminist, 22, 80, 82, 89, 100n.7, 171, 296
Feudalism, 23, 174, 252
Feuerbach, Ludwig, 7, 42, 63, 65, 82, 107, 109, 203, 237
Fideism, 48, 168, 315
Fitting, the, xx, xxvii, 103, 138-40, 306, 308. *See also* Good, right, and fit
Formalism, 56, 62
Forms, Platonic, 56-57, 60-61, 63
Fox, Richard Wrightman, 24
Frankfurt School, 192
Free trade, 96
Freud, Sigmund, 42, 52, 62, 107, 109, 140, 291
Fundamentalism, 22, 47, 130, 193n.9, 202, 259, 299, 311, 314, 318, 334

Gandhi, Indira, 271
Gandhi, Mohandas, 30, 172, 180
German Democratic Republic (East Germany), xiii, 233n.4, 237, 271, 333, 340
Germany, 22-23, 71, 75, 77, 86, 122, 170, 188, 203, 340, 343
Gifford Lectures, 55, 58, 66, 68, 202
Gladden, Washington, xvi, 169, 183, 341
Globalization, x-xi, xiii, xvi-xvii, xx-xxi, xxiii, xxviii, xxix-xxx, 93, 95-96, 102-3, 162, 174-82, 185-90, 217, 248, 255, 259-69, 272, 305-17, 321-23, 326, 328-30, 335-44
God, x-xi, xiii-xiv, xvi-xvii, xix, xxi, xxiv, xxviii-xxx, 3-18, 22-32, 35-40, 43, 45-46, 50, 52, 57, 67-69, 73, 77-90, 93-97, 100, 103, 105-32, 135, 137, 141, 149, 151, 155, 157-65, 173-74, 178, 180, 182, 185, 190, 192, 195-98, 201-13, 216, 218, 222-29, 234, 236, 239, 242-43, 247-48, 256, 259, 261, 264-65, 268-70, 277, 279-80, 282-89, 292-302, 305-8, 312-17, 320-22, 328-30, 335, 338,

340-43; character of, 165, 205; city of, 87; death of, xxiv, 5-10, 13, 35; laws of, 165-66, 205, 207-8, 213; laws and purposes of, 93, 95, 248, 268. *See also* Jesus Christ; Trinity
Good, the, xx, xxvii, 56, 61, 79, 100, 137-38, 141, 165-66, 206-11, 213-16, 257, 309, 313
Good, right, and fit (or fitting), xx, xxvii, 136-42, 147-53, 306; first principles of, 308-9
Gospel, Gospels, 4, 17, 19, 22, 38, 43, 45, 63, 72, 76, 83, 171, 225, 241, 274, 297-98, 299, 307, 312, 316
Government, xv, xvii, xxi, xxviii, 87-88, 96, 117, 162, 169, 183, 200-201, 203-4, 214, 216, 222, 226-27, 233, 244, 249, 252-53, 262-63, 267, 271, 276, 289-90, 292
Gramsci, Antonio, 71, 192, 264
Great Britain, 39, 67, 186, 194, 333. *See also* England
Great Depression, the, 107, 169-70, 195
Grotius, Hugo, 67
Gustafson, James, 8-9, 72, 323, 339-41

Habermas, Jürgen, 155n.4, 156, 167n.22
Harnack, Adolf von, 7
Hauerwas, Stanley, xvi, xxvi, 65, 69, 72, 82-90, 127n.11, 189, 337, 340
Hegel, G. W. F., xi, 42, 58, 60, 62-64
Heidegger, Martin, 42, 48-50, 53-54, 65, 126n.9
Hermeneutics, 48, 127, 139; of suspicion, 58, 66
Himes, Kenneth, 88, 155n.4
Himes, Michael, 88, 155n.4
Hinduism, Hindus, 84, 95n.2, 101, 150, 163, 176n.12, 180-81, 183, 189, 202, 209-10, 224, 235, 261, 268, 271, 294, 308n.1, 332, 342
Hindutva, 186
Historicism, 25, 73-75
History, 4, 6 , 8, 10, 16, 18-19, 23, 31, 50, 67, 83, 107-10, 114, 119-20, 123-24, 131, 138, 144, 149-51, 162-64, 166n.20, 169, 175-76, 187, 204-6, 208-11, 213-14, 216, 223, 230-31, 234, 239, 261, 270, 273-74, 280,

351

Index

333, 342; of Christianity, 18, 76, 148, 169, 192, 255, 283, 287, 290; dialectic, 108-10; economic, 235; intellectual, 5, 7, 100, 110, 116, 121; Lord of, 4, 225, 265, 306; in MacIntyre's thought, 55-58; military, 48; problem of, 10, 13, 21; religious, 71, 204; salvation, 269-70; social, 71, 87, 94, 109, 166, 179n.17, 199, 201, 204-5, 237, 277, 282, 318; theological, 199, 268; theology of, 3, 13-18, 20, 139; theories of, 5, 108

Hitler, Adolf, 32, 50, 86, 131, 148, 202, 284, 343

Holland. *See* Netherlands, the

Hollenbach, David, xii, 198

Holy Roman Empire, 189, 244, 263

Holy Spirit, 25, 173, 229, 268

Homo religiosus, 293-94

Hope, 3, 7, 30, 39-40, 43, 46, 97, 138, 194, 208, 223, 238, 272, 286-90, 292-93, 295, 297-98, 300-302, 320, 339-40

Human condition, xvii, 98-99, 103, 132, 194, 223

Human Condition, The (Arendt), 110

Human Condition, The (Neville, ed.), 177n.14

Human dignity, xiv, xxx, 33

Humanism, 34-35, 37, 100, 105, 109, 123, 131, 169, 224, 322, 337

Humanitarian intervention, 96

Humanitarianism, 323

Hume, David, 55-56, 58

Hundred Years' War, 39

Hungarian uprising of 1956, 49

Huntington, Samuel, 182, 184n.23, 187n.1, 188n.3

Hypermodernism, hypermodernist, 54, 123-27, 129-30, 170

Idealism, xii, xvi-xvii, 14, 36, 48, 60, 106, 151, 157, 170, 260

Identity, 11, 21, 34, 45, 116, 135, 170, 217, 234, 251, 262, 276, 281, 289, 307; cultural, 188, 193; national, 188, 208-9, 212-13, 249; social, 135, 307

Idolatry, 17, 35-36, 188, 191, 195, 212, 266

Imago Dei, 85, 280, 286

India, xii-xiii, 95n.2, 96, 172, 176n.12, 181, 183, 186, 189, 215, 231n.2, 237n.9, 245, 271, 296, 319, 333-34, 336, 339-40

Individualism, 55, 124, 212, 232, 249, 251, 262, 279, 298, 310

Industrialization, 60, 149, 171n.4, 196, 310

Industries, 195, 228, 252-53; international, 245

Institutions, xiv-xv, xvii, xix, xxi-xxiii, xxviii, xxix, 4, 18, 26, 31, 33, 35-36, 39-40, 98-99, 101, 111, 117, 142-43, 146-48, 151-52, 166, 173, 175, 179, 184, 186, 195, 197, 202, 213, 217-18, 223, 230-31, 233, 240, 244, 255, 257, 261, 264-65, 267, 269, 273, 279-80, 289, 299, 308, 313-15, 318-20, 323, 342; church, 41, 318, 335; of civil society, 95, 197, 203, 216, 245, 247; of the common life, xxi, 180, 196, 208, 214, 268, 280; covenanted, 208; cultural, 148, 217, 226; economic, 146, 216, 227, 254, 262, 278; educational, 146, 217, 230; international, 202-3, 312; political, 135, 146, 152, 197, 253; religious, 202; social, xiii, 14, 64, 68, 120, 144, 152, 171, 180n.18, 192, 197, 200, 208, 214, 216, 231, 244, 250, 252, 258, 267, 281, 291, 305-7, 311-12; voluntary, 148-50, 152-53, 325

Intellectus, 47, 53

Internationalism, 176

Internationalization, 262

International Monetary Fund (IMF), 176n.13, 202, 251, 254, 261

Iraq, 96, 199, 245

Iraq War, 308

Islam, 95n.2, 120, 149, 181, 183, 186, 189, 202, 210, 224, 235, 239, 245, 268, 272, 276, 294, 308n.1, 320

James, William, 75, 82, 116

Jesus Christ, 7, 11, 16, 18, 20, 36, 57, 63, 83, 85, 88, 93-94, 117n.3, 157, 169n.1, 196n.14, 208-9, 229, 270, 283-85, 286, 306, 325

Jim Crow, 31

John Paul II, Pope, 89, 198, 326, 335

John the Baptist, 22

Judaism, 34-35, 37-39, 137, 149, 190, 209-10, 274-75, 282, 296, 321

Index

Judgment, ethical, xxvii, 61, 68, 116-32, 149, 156n.8, 178n.15, 337
Jung, Carl, 62
Jus gentium, 155, 203
Justice, xxiv-xxv, xxviii-xxix, xxxi, 13, 18, 28-31, 33, 35-36, 40, 43, 47, 49, 56, 60, 65, 68, 78, 82, 84, 95, 97, 106, 108-9, 117-20, 130, 136-37, 160, 162, 166, 170, 177-78, 185, 194-97, 200, 222, 236, 244, 253, 259, 264, 270-71, 273, 280, 291-93, 296, 300, 307, 314, 319, 322, 326, 328, 340, 343; covenantal, 204-18; economic, xiii, xviii, 38; God's, 302; and love, 30, 33, 45, 194, 222; social, xiii, xv-xvi, xxv, 23, 25, 221-22, 311; and truth, xixn.7, xxxi, 43, 46, 52, 68, 195, 197, 282, 291-302; universal, 73, 273
Justinian, 67
Justitia, 53
Justitia originalis, 85, 166n.19
Just war, 96, 137, 170

Kairos, 50
Kant, Immanuel, 42, 52-53, 55-56, 58-59, 62-63, 67, 85, 106, 130, 167n.22, 235
Kierkegaard, Søren, 65
King, Martin Luther, Jr., xi-xii, xxv, 22, 25, 28-46, 52, 72, 118n.4, 171-72, 196, 320, 331; assassination of, xxv, 29, 32, 46
Kingdom of God, 7n.5, 27, 36, 77, 137, 141, 151, 196, 207, 224
Kingdom of God in America, The (H. R. Niebuhr), 27
Koinonia, 36, 142
Korea, 96, 172, 183, 190, 296, 319
Kuhn, Thomas, 112
Kultur, 50
Küng, Hans, 53, 162n.13, 184
Kunst, 50
Kuyper, Abraham, xi, xiii, xv-xvi, 73, 118n.4, 120, 201, 264, 311n.4, 328, 338-39
Kyoto Accords, 96, 246

Laity, 42-43, 196, 284, 294, 317. *See also* Ministry: of the laity
Landes, David, 236-37
Language, 16, 29, 45, 59, 120, 157, 162, 210, 230, 256, 267, 275, 343; apocalyptic New Testament, 29; biblical, 81; death of God, 13; games, 157, 161; of human rights, xxx; metaphorical, 50; moral, 134, 136; "ought," 19; problem of, 49; systems, 6, 16-17; theological, 5, 195; and Tillich, 49-50
Lao-Tze, 114
Law: canon, 149, 230; of Christ, 9; common, 236; contract, 235; divine/holy, 210, 247, 270; of the Gospels, 45; international, 96, 157, 161, 163-64, 204, 253; moral, xxii, 52, 59, 67, 130-31, 156, 165-67, 206-9, 216, 243, 339; of Moses, 283; natural, xxiv, 9, 57-58, 103n.11, 155, 162, 164n.17, 166, 198, 264; religious, 181; Roman, 275; universal, 107, 206, 260
Legitimacy, 29, 102, 120, 281; crisis of, 291
Lenin, Vladimir, 49, 130
Leninist, 62, 99n.5
Leo XIII, Pope, 64, 73, 198, 264
"Letter from Birmingham City Jail" (King), 30, 301
Liberalism, xvi, xxn.7, xxvi, 25, 34, 54, 67, 82-90, 181, 326, 337, 340, 343
Locke, John, 58, 62, 67, 85, 130, 167n.22, 195, 235, 293
Logos, 11, 50, 84, 121, 163, 298, 300, 307, 311
Lonergan, Bernard, 293
Long, Edward, 72
Love, xxx, 9-10, 23, 29-32, 35-36, 40, 43-44, 46, 74, 78-81, 85, 87, 93, 105, 138, 141, 166, 180n.18, 194, 222, 227, 231, 274, 280, 285, 287-90, 293, 295, 297-98, 300-302, 337, 339, 342. *See also* Justice: and love
Lyotard, Jean-François, 126n.9

Machiavelli, Niccolo, 57, 123, 192
MacIntyre, Alasdair, xxv, 54-70, 99n.5, 123n.7, 155n.6, 336
Mahabarata, 89
Malcolm X, 44
Mammon, 26, 180, 224, 231-32, 242, 267, 327
Management, xxix-xxx, 33, 48, 228, 236, 242-58, 338
Mao Tsetung, 44-46

353

Index

Marcuse, Herbert, 44
Marcuse (MacIntyre), 62
Maritain, Jacques, 67, 197-98
Marriage, xxx, 23, 80, 88, 95, 182, 214, 238, 255, 265, 267, 278, 283-85, 329-30, 337, 343
Marty, Martin, xviiin.3, 116nn.1-2, 118n.4, 194-95, 324
Martyr, 22, 46, 71, 193
Marx, Karl, xi, 18, 42, 48, 50, 52-53, 58, 60, 62-64, 66, 73, 75, 107, 109, 112, 140, 192, 237, 243, 264, 291
Marxism, Marxist, 34, 49, 53-54, 62-64, 68, 71, 96, 149-50, 172, 174, 181, 186, 212-13, 221, 223, 271, 326
Matthews, Shailer, xvi
McCann, Dennis, xxi, xxix, 72, 118n.4, 198, 221, 230, 322, 330, 335, 337
Meaning and worth, 145-47
Medicine, 180, 217, 268, 289, 329
Melanchthon, Philipp, 75, 192
Mencius, 132
Metaphysical-moral: disease, 118; logic of universe, 95, philosophies, 97; questions, 301; vision, 223, 291, 293-94, 299
Metaphysics, 13, 35-36, 72
Method: of correlation, 52; in ethics, xxvii, xxxi, 306, 321, 342
Metz, J. B., 193, 290
Milbank, John, 72, 101n.9, 127n.11, 343
Mill, John Stuart, 55-56, 62
Ministry, xxxi, 21, 31, 94, 102, 224, 257, 268, 286-88, 293-94, 297, 307-8, 310, 329, 333, 337, 343; of the laity, 228, 270
Missio Dei, 265
Mission, xxii-xxiii, xxviii, 22, 83, 168-85, 208-9, 215, 218, 226, 269-70, 287, 307, 318-19, 321, 323, 325, 328-29, 334
Missionary, 26, 101-3, 169, 172-73, 183-84, 195, 230, 253, 261, 273, 319, 323
Modernism, 34, 124, 126, 181, 221, 259, 262
Modernity, 37-38, 55, 57, 63-66, 74-75, 83, 99n.5, 121-23, 125, 127-31, 167n.22, 169, 174, 188, 230, 235, 241, 261, 295
Modes of moral discourse, 61, 66
Moltmann, Jürgen, 193, 290, 328

Money, 32, 39, 41, 79, 180n.18, 227, 239-40, 256, 267, 285, 294
Montgomery, Alabama, 28, 172n.5
Moore, G. E., 55-56
Morality, xiii, 56-62, 99n.5, 100, 107, 109, 116, 119, 122-23, 125, 128, 130, 132, 151, 157-58, 161-62, 164, 182, 196n.14, 209, 216, 225, 275-76, 284, 311, 324, 327, 329, 337, 343; personal, xxviii, 165-66; public, xxiii, 182, 309; social, 154, 166n.20, 211; universal, xxx
Moral law, xxii, 52, 59, 130-31, 156, 167, 206-9, 216, 243, 339; first principles of, 207; universal, 67, 165, 166
Moses, 67, 140, 169, 208-9
Mouw, Richard J., 54, 69
Muhammad, 67
Münzer, Thomas, 36, 192
Murray, John Courtney, 67, 116, 198
Music, xvii, 81, 105, 126, 138, 144, 217, 261, 336, 338
Mythos, 50

Narrative, 27, 56, 89, 126, 157, 161, 275; and MacIntyre, 55-57, 60-61, 67-68; theology, 21, 82, 224, 244
National identity, 188, 208, 212-13, 249
Nationalism, 34, 96, 124, 160, 174, 176, 179, 212-13, 222, 239, 273, 313
Nation-states, xvii, 192, 216-17, 249, 263
Natural law. *See* Law, natural
Nazism, 173, 271
Neoliberal, 71
Neo-paganism, 53, 170, 173, 186, 202, 212, 224, 273
Neoplatonic, Neoplatonist, 51, 74, 293
Netherlands, the, xi, xiii, 48, 122, 188
Neuhaus, Richard John, xx, 123n.7, 171n.4, 325-26
New Deal, the, 25, 72, 169
Nicaea, 89
Niebuhr, H. Richard, 11, 14, 27, 72, 85
Niebuhr, Reinhold, xii, xvi, xviii, 16n.14, 24, 27, 52-53, 68, 70-71, 85-86, 100n.7, 116, 118n.4, 140, 166n.19, 171n.3, 172, 193-95, 202, 287, 293, 301, 321, 343

Index

Niebuhrians, Niebuhrianism, 48, 82, 172n.5
Nietzsche, Friedrich, 42, 48, 51-52, 54, 64-66, 73, 75, 99n.5, 107, 109, 126, 128, 162, 291
Nihilism, 57, 64, 126, 129
Nomos, 206
Non-Governmental Organizations (NGOs), 234, 244, 291, 311n.5, 315
Nonviolence, xii, 172
Norms, 64, 93, 95, 98-102, 112, 135, 167, 179, 194, 233, 274, 276, 300, 313, 331
North Korea, 189
Novak, Michael, 24, 72

Occam, William of, 57
O'Donovan, Oliver, 68, 70, 193
Ogletree, Thomas, 77
Oikoumene, 260
Old Testament, 67, 111, 142
Ontology, 110, 138
Optimism, 63, 68, 166, 170, 223, 260, 274
Organization, organizations, 39-41, 43, 98, 112, 187n.1, 197, 230-31, 233-34, 243, 322; transnational, 216-17
Otto, Rudolf, 48
"Ought," 15, 19, 99, 116, 131, 134-38, 140-43, 151-52, 155-56, 163, 279

Pacifism, xii, 82, 170-71, 172n.5, 296
Pagan, 118, 121, 238, 294
Panikkar, Raimundo, 293
Pannenberg, Wolfhart, 89, 341
Parks, Rosa, 28
Parliament of World Religions, 182, 261
Parsons, Talcott, xii, 52-53
Pastor, xxx-xxxi, 12, 21, 42, 47, 86, 88-89, 102, 183, 193, 225, 228, 256, 270, 286-302
Patriarchy, 95, 226, 300
Pax Romana, 244
Peace, 18, 28, 35, 46, 106, 108-9, 170, 198, 226, 244, 261, 273, 313-14
Pentecostalism, 183, 196, 256
Perry, Michael, xxvii, 154-67, 279
Pessimism, 63-64, 248, 260
Philosophy, 5, 7, 12, 40, 48, 51-52, 54, 57, 65, 83, 99, 101, 107, 118-19, 121-26, 131, 139, 148-49, 187, 194, 209, 281, 293-94, 299, 301, 309, 318, 324; British, 5; Christian social, 38, 52, 75-76; Eastern, 30; German, 50; Greek, 50, 275; Hegelian, 63; Marxist, 62; modern, 294; moral, 55-56, 59-60, 62, 66, 68, 141; Neoplatonic, 74; political, 123, 154; postmodern, 82, 128; of religion, 47, 120, 301n.8; social, 44; Western, 128
Phronesis, 56
Pietas, 47, 53
Pietism, 22, 25, 44, 115, 138, 189, 315
Piety, xi, 22, 30, 36-37, 42, 84, 112, 121, 138, 168, 180, 190, 193n.9, 222, 231, 289, 295, 301, 315, 319, 325
Plantinga, Alvin, 53
Plato, 35, 56-58, 61, 63, 67, 100, 106, 126, 142, 260
Pluralism, x, xvii, xxx, 54-55, 73, 76-77, 161, 163, 184, 198-99, 210, 271-72, 277, 280, 294, 307, 328; institutional, 315; moral, 294; religious, xxiii, 184; social, xiv, xvi, 307, 311n.4
Polis, 57, 110, 117n.3, 311, 315
Political theology, xxviii, 26, 71, 186-203, 290-91, 300, 323, 339
Politics, 23, 26, 43, 47-48, 50, 76, 82, 86, 95n.2, 104-5, 117, 122-23, 133, 142, 147, 154, 156, 175, 177, 180-81, 188n.3, 192, 197, 200-201, 215, 222, 227, 231, 249, 289-90, 292, 294, 309, 314, 323, 327, 333-34, 340, 342-43
Postmodernism, postmodernity, xviii, 54, 65, 73-75, 87, 124-26, 128, 162, 181, 241, 259, 315
Poverty, xii, 3, 63, 119, 187n.1, 223, 234, 235n.6, 238, 246, 251-52, 255, 284, 315, 325, 330, 334
Power, xxvii, 17-18, 23, 36, 40, 43, 45-46, 76, 79, 81, 85-86, 96, 99n.5, 102-5, 107-8, 114, 118, 120, 123-24, 126, 138-39, 148-49, 154, 172, 175-76, 180n.18, 192, 196, 200, 202-3, 234, 243, 253, 264-70, 292, 294-96, 311, 319; ethical/moral, 4, 9; levels of, 144, 146; patterns of, 144-45; of persuasion, 296; of religion, 237, 308-9; and sex, 234-35; ultimate, 43, 151-52, 186. *See also* Worth and power

355

Index

Powers and principalities, xiii, xvi, xxx, 29, 72, 93, 103, 197, 316
Practice, social, 36, 58-59, 67, 98, 209
Pragmatism, 65
Praxis, 26, 297-98, 300
"Preferential option," 222, 301, 325
Principlist, 8-11
Principlist-contextualist debate, 10, 16
Professions, professionals, xxiii, 86, 88, 94, 97, 115, 180, 228, 257, 268, 296, 305, 312, 320, 329
Property, 192, 235-37
Protestantism, 21-23, 25, 34-39, 44-45, 54, 72, 74, 76, 112, 165, 190, 284, 290, 325-26, 334, 339
Prudentia, 56
Psychology, 50, 75, 82, 236, 298, 332, 342; of religion, 133
Public discourse, xixn.5, xxxnn.7-8, xxvi, 103, 110, 116-17, 120, 122, 128, 154, 174, 182, 197-98, 290, 296, 301
Publics, xxvii, 117-18
Public theologian, xi, xviiin.3, xxii, xxxi, 286-302
Public theology, viii-x, xiii-xv, xxiv, xxv, xxviii, xxix, 27, 52, 82, 97, 99-100, 116-32, 155, 156n.8, 174, 178-79, 182-84, 186-203, 218, 221-29, 255-56, 289-92, 297-98, 300-301, 305-15, 318, 320-21, 323, 325-28, 330, 333-35, 337-39, 343; definitions of, xvn.2; global, xvii, xxxi, 228-29; methodology, xxii-xxiii, xxvi-xxvii; Stackhouse's, viii, ix-x, xiv-xv, xviii-xxiii, xxv, xxvii
Public world, 288-90, 295
Pufendorf, Samuel von, 67
Puritans, xii, 57, 75, 78-80, 166n.19, 169, 190, 196

Racism, 21, 30-32, 34, 36, 95, 109-10, 140, 151, 160, 171, 182, 199, 221-22, 239, 265, 272
Radical orthodoxy, 72
Ramsey, Paul, 9n.8, 10, 72, 86, 118n.4, 166n.19, 323, 343
Rationalism, 47, 58, 259, 295
Rauschenbusch, Walter, xi, xvi, xviiin.4, xxiv, xxviii, 3-4, 20, 21-27, 39, 52, 86, 118n.4, 169, 170n.2, 172-73, 180nn.18-19, 183, 195, 321, 324, 331, 335, 340-41
Reason, xv, xix, xxii, 9, 38, 42, 47-48, 50-52, 58, 65, 74, 85, 94, 97, 123, 125, 129, 151, 154, 166, 171, 198, 211, 213, 243, 262, 280, 293, 295, 341. *See also* Authority
Regencies, 251-52, 311n.4
Relativism, 48
Religion: psychology of, 133; sociology of, xxv-xxvi, 11, 73, 133, 335
Renaissance, 83, 100, 112, 120, 125, 194
Responsibility, 21, 36, 83, 97, 104, 108, 112, 115, 139-40, 147, 157, 169, 178, 195-96, 201, 212, 217, 228, 236, 238-39, 249, 254, 256, 265, 267, 269, 277, 285, 307, 312, 315, 331, 333
Resurrection city, 29
Revelation, xv, 13, 21, 28-30, 48, 57, 119, 122, 166, 187, 194, 210, 292, 337; general, xix, 85
Revolution, 7, 25, 29, 37-38, 44-46, 127, 172, 213, 254, 280, 335-36; French, 123, 186, 191, 193, 197, 230, 243, 264; Industrial, 59, 107, 169, 174, 230; Russian, 107; scientific, 112
Right, the, 79, 100, 141, 206-16, 313. *See also* Good, right, and fit
Right and wrong, first principles of, 167, 206, 208, 277
Righteousness, 10, 15, 26, 29-30, 33, 35, 41, 43, 77, 87, 97, 100, 142, 152, 177-78, 185, 207-8, 215, 270, 300, 321, 324, 328; first principles of, 209
Ritschl, Albrecht, 19
Romanticism, 53, 73, 295
Rorty, Richard, 65, 156
Ross, Andrew, 127n.10
Rousseau, Jean-Jacques, 191, 203, 264
"Rule-teleology," 206

Sartre, Jean-Paul, 42, 48-50, 107
Schmitt, Carl, 71, 192
Science, 48, 55, 61, 64, 66, 76, 83, 101, 112, 119, 120-22, 125-30, 180n.18, 187, 223, 244, 262, 264, 267, 272, 298, 310; theology as, 295, 297

Index

Scientism, 48
Scripture, xixn.5, xxii, 25-26, 42, 50, 94, 97, 110, 133, 149, 283, 287, 290, 318, 334. *See also* Bible; Word, the
Sectarianism, xvii, 259, 315
Secularization, 39, 59-60, 123, 183, 262, 293-94
Segregation, 67
Sex, 44, 80, 231, 234-35, 272
Sexism, 21, 110, 140, 151, 182, 222, 239, 265, 272
Sin, xiv, xxii, 31, 85, 100, 165, 170-72, 194-97, 207, 224, 227, 280-81, 299, 337
Situationalism, situationalist, 53, 339
Slavery, 29, 67, 208, 278, 300
Social gospel, xii, xvi, xviiin.4, xx, xxiii, xxiv-xxv, xxvii, 3-20, 22, 24-27, 30, 34, 38-39, 72, 168-85, 195-96, 221, 255, 321, 324, 326, 328-29, 331, 335, 341
Socialism, xiii, xvi, 32, 48-49, 109, 117, 124, 159, 179, 186, 195, 200, 221-23, 225, 237, 245, 335, 340; Christian, 77
Socialismus, 50
Social life, xv, xxix, 49, 54-55, 60, 119, 121, 124, 181, 201-2, 206-7, 209, 245, 258, 267, 291, 305, 308, 311, 315
Social science, 66, 94, 97, 120, 133, 140, 149, 266, 301
Society, sectors/spheres of, xiv, xxi, xxii, 98, 144, 147-48, 218, 264, 311
Sociology, 11, 23, 25-26, 48, 50, 60, 183, 298, 311, 314, 335. *See also* Christian sociology; Religion: sociology of
Sovereignty, 123, 157, 216, 231, 235, 263, 276, 279, 281, 343; of God, xxx, 27, 202, 229, 265; sphere, xv, 175, 201, 264-65
Spinoza, Baruch, 58, 192
Spirit, 11, 17, 31, 34, 42-43, 181, 223, 232, 266-67, 286, 296, 312, 326
Stalin, Josef, 49, 148, 202, 243
Stalinism, 21, 192
State, xv, 26, 76, 170, 200, 214-17, 231, 233-35, 243, 291, 312, 326-27, 329
Stoics, Stoic thought, 57, 74-75, 117n.3, 155, 260, 293
Stone, Ronald, 71

Stout, Jeffrey, 54, 70
Strauss, Leo, 72, 123n.7
Subsidiarity, 73, 175, 198
Symbols, 14, 33, 39-40, 43, 45, 53, 105-6, 111-15, 150-53, 189, 191, 267, 270

Technology, xxiii, xxix, 53-54, 83, 101n.8, 145, 180, 187n.1, 223-24, 226, 228, 237, 248, 257, 262, 268, 272, 279, 298, 306, 309, 324, 332-34, 342
Teleology, xx-xxi, xxvii, 59, 61-62, 68, 103, 138, 141, 163-65, 167, 206, 208, 210
Telos, 55, 58, 68, 206, 307
Ten Commandments, 67, 137, 278, 327
Terrorism, 31, 266, 274, 334
Theology: black, 172; Catholic, xii, 197, 199; contextualist, xxiv; Dalit, 172; liberation, xi, xxv, 25, 71, 172, 196n.14, 300; Minjung, 172; narrative, 21, 82; natural, 55, 191; political, xxviii, 26, 71, 186-203, 290-93, 300, 323, 339; practical, 93-94, 97, 102, 330; principlist, xxiv; process, 82; Protestant, 123, 198, 340; radical, 26; systematic, 3, 20, 187, 189, 342. *See also* Public theology
Theonomy (in Tillich), 52
Theoria, 104, 114-15
Theos, 84, 121, 307
Thirty Years' War, 39
Thomas Aquinas, Saint, 6, 57, 59, 61, 63-64, 66-68, 74, 85, 106, 120, 192, 239, 293
Tillich, Paul, 337
Tillichians, 51, 53, 82
Time, 4, 17, 94, 110, 114, 164, 209, 236-37; of revelation, 28-30
Tocqueville, Alexis de, 191
Toffler, Alvin, 109
Torah, 67
Touchstones of authority/of theology, xix, xxii, 94
Tracy, David, 53, 72, 116, 118n.4, 155, 198-99
Tradition, traditions, xixn.5, xxii, 29-30, 56, 59-61, 65-68, 73-77, 83, 87, 94-95, 117n.3, 121-23, 133, 151, 161, 195, 198, 269, 275, 283, 287, 289, 318, 324, 330, 333, 336-37; bib-

357

Index

lical, 194, 212, 281, 284; Catholic, xii, 35, 76-77, 116, 154, 170, 171n.4, 180, 241, 284; Christian, xxiii, xxvi, 86, 187, 193, 268; Jewish, 209; Judeo-Christian, 30, 149-53, 273; philosophical, xi, 130; Protestant, 241, 284, 330; religious, 29-30, 84, 121, 130, 149, 184, 199, 209-10, 266, 282, 308; theological, xiv, xxvi, xxiv, xxvii-xxviii, 12, 25, 150, 156, 160n.11, 169, 189, 195, 197, 199, 244. *See also* Authority
Traditionalism, 54, 66, 122-25, 186
Trinity, xxii, 88-89, 151, 302, 307, 326
Troeltsch, Ernst, xi, xxv, 7, 25, 35, 51-52, 71-77, 85, 118n.4, 193, 199, 264, 323, 331, 342
Tutu, Archbishop Desmond, 85

Unbedingt, das, 50
Unconditioned, the, 50-51
Unions, 148, 195, 226, 230, 243
United Nations, 67, 131, 189, 199, 202, 204, 273; documents of, xxx, 72, 155, 166n.19, 182, 198, 202-3, 271, 278, 337
United States of America, xxv, 22, 96, 98n.4, 169-70, 175, 179n.17, 186, 189-90, 215, 243
Universalism, 163
University, 45, 75, 84, 94, 133, 148, 259
Urbanization, xxiii, 60, 149, 272, 310, 323
Usury, 239
Utilitarian(ism), 62, 68, 222, 297, 310, 312

Values, xxi, 4, 16, 36-37, 45, 52, 59-60, 67, 73, 98-102, 104-5, 110-13, 115, 135, 147, 171, 179, 187n.1, 188, 190, 194, 196n.14, 203, 212, 233, 235, 244-45, 254, 272, 275-77, 289, 295, 310, 312-13
Van Huyssteen, J. Wentzel, 101n.9, 125n.8
Veritas, 53
Vietnam War, 30, 53, 84, 221
Violence, 30-32, 38, 80, 86, 106, 128, 173, 182, 235, 266, 273, 284, 289, 326

Virtue, virtues, xv, xxi, 40, 55-57, 61, 63, 67, 82, 85, 87, 90, 97-99, 110, 122, 157, 166, 191, 209, 244, 267, 288, 296, 299-301, 308, 340
Voluntary associations, 148

Walzer, Michael, 264
Wealth, 213, 225, 230, 234-35, 249-51, 254, 330
Weber, Max, 25, 52, 73, 85, 140, 237-38, 264, 344
Weigel, George, xxn.7, 171n.4, 326
Weimar Republic, 71
Weinberg, Stephen, 127n.10
Wesley, John, 36, 85, 120
Westphalia, Peace of, 188, 192, 263
Whitehead, Alfred North, 25, 42, 48, 85, 293
Whose Justice? Which Rationality? (MacIntyre), 55, 58-61, 64-65, 99n.5, 155n.6
Williams, George H., 14n.13, 52
Winter, Gibson, 72, 339-40
Witte, John, 128n.13, 155, 161n.11, 162n.13, 327-28, 330
Wittgenstein, Ludwig, 42, 48
Wolterstorff, Nicholas, 53
Word, the, 6, 8, 14, 21, 40-41, 198, 343
World Bank, 176n.13, 202, 251, 254, 261
World Missionary Conference, 261, 273
World religions, 132, 180-85, 215, 235, 260, 268, 272, 306, 308n.1, 313, 320, 333
World Trade Organization (WTO), 251-52, 254
World War I, 71, 107, 169-70, 183
World War II, xi, xxx, 71-72, 107, 171, 179, 190, 192-94, 204, 266
Worth and power, 40, 113, 143, 151-53. *See also* Power

Yoder, John Howard, xvi, 72

Žižek, Slavoj, xxiv